I REFUSE TO DIE

MY JOURNEY FOR FREEDOM

KOIGI WA WAMWERE

SEVEN STORIES PRESS
New York | London | Melbourne | Toronto

Extended quotations from *Facing Mount Kenya* by Jomo Kenyatta (Vintage) used by permission of the publisher.

Seven Stories Press
140 Watts Street
New York, NY 10013
www.sevenstories.com

In Canada:
Hushion House, 36 Northline Road, Toronto, Ontario M4B 3E2

In the U.K.:
Turnaround Publisher Services Ltd., Unit 3, Olympia Trading Estate, Coburg Road, Wood Green, London N22 6TZ

In Australia:
Palgrave Macmillan, 627 Chapel Street, South Yarra, VIC 3141

Library of Congress Cataloging-in-Publication Data
Koigi wa Wamwere.
    I Refuse to Die: My Journey for Freedom
    ISBN 1-58322-521-8 (Cloth); 1-58322-615-X (pbk)
1. Koigi wa Wamwere. 2. Human rights workers—Kenya—Biography. 3. Kenya—Politics and government—1963–1978. 4. Kenya—Politics and government—1978–   1. Title.
PQ7079.2.R55 C8413
863'.64—dc21

                                                    00-032936

9 8 7 6 5 4 3 2 1

College professors may order examination copies of Seven Stories Press titles for a free six-month trial period. To order, visit www.sevenstories.com/textbook, or fax on school letterhead to (212) 226-1411.

Book design by Cindy LaBreacht

Printed in the U.S.A.

C O N T E N T S

ACKNOWLEDGMENTS

A ll those living and dead, mentioned and unmentioned, without whom neither my life nor my story would have been: Ancestors, Grandparents, Mother, Father, brothers, sisters, in-laws, relatives, friends, Kenyans, the world, even enemies. *I Refuse To Die* is as much their story as it is mine.

All those who told me I had a story, encouraged me to tell it and never to despair. I hope what they read is what they expected. If it falls short, the fault is all mine.

My wife and our children for the company and attention that I denied them when writing this book. Without their sacrifice, this book would have been impossible. In reading the story, may they reap as much as they sowed.

All those in Kenya who risked much to help my family and me survive in days of imprisonment, detention and flight. Without their sacrifice, effort and camaraderie, this story would never have stuck together as it does now.

Norwegian government and friends like Einar Lunde, Anders Breidlid, Ian Bryceson, Yacoub Cisse, Amani Buntu, Andreas Skartveit and William Nygaard. The book is partly a fruit of their generosity, friendship and solidarity.

Bruce Friedman for reading and correcting my earlier drafts. Our dream that some day, we might sit in a cinema, eating popcorn and watch *I Refuse To Die* on the screen was the fuel that kept my writing motor running.

My friends in America like Neil Getnick, Micere Mugo, Jonathan W. Cuneo, Michael Koplinka Loehr, Andre Balazs, and Ravi S. Bhalla for connecting my story with its destiny.

Kerry Kennedy Cuomo and Nan Richardson for their introduction and for putting me in touch with Publisher Dan Simon and Seven Stories Press whose good judgment and embrace finally gave my story a voice and wings.

Last but not least, my editor Jill Schoolman for her expert midwifery in the delivery of this book.

KERRY KENNEDY CUOMO
AND NAN RICHARDSON

Koigi wa Wamwere is one of Africa's bravest men, a powerful defender of
human rights and Kenya's best-known political prisoner. His personal and
probing story, which unfolds in many layers and through many voices in the pages
that follow, is extraordinary by any measure, and his passionate response to the events
of his life—his attitude of tolerance and justice and his ability to transmute experience into literature in the form of plays, poems, novels and this marvelous book
you hold in your hands now—catapults him into the level of greatness on the
world stage.

I Refuse to Die is a graphic and passionate account, a powerful mix of story-
telling and penetrating dissection of the underlying forces at work in Kenya,
including the ethnic tensions underlying the country's complex political system,
President Daniel arap Moi's misdeeds and the West's maladroit interventions. You
cannot read this book without pain; you cannot finish it without a sense of joy. It
shows a knowledge so thorough, a passion so scalding, a morality so vigorous that
we come away from it feeling energized to do something. While we may understand through narrative, we remember through poetry and song. The power of
this story is in its texture and voice, a voice filled with spirit and physicality. We
feel the reality as much as see it; because the reality is wooed and not dictated, our
understanding is significantly greater.

That understanding is the legacy Wamwere wishes to leave us with: the
knowledge and wisdom that will bring forth change at last not just in Kenya, or
Africa, but in developing countries everywhere in the world, and for people
experiencing the loss of fundamental liberties in every country on this globe.

But you must understand some things about Koigi wa Wamwere to fully
appreciate the difficulty of the road he has walked, the choice it represented for him.
He is a man blessed with gifts: intelligence, initiative and, as his remarkable story
narrates, the gift of choice. There were many moments when he could have walked
away, far away, to gentler waters of life. Instead he chose again and again to thrust
himself into the tumult, the moral battle, because of his convictions and dreams.
He has risked his home, his own life and psychic equilibrium, as well as the safety
of his family and friends.

Born to a poor family in a forest community, Wamwere excelled in school and was eventually awarded a scholarship to study at Cornell University, where his studies were interrupted in 1973. Rather than staying in the United States, he courageously returned to Kenya to work for democratic reform, running for Parliament in 1974, until his criticism of the Kenyan president and his government led to his arrest in 1975. He was held for three years—with no charges, no judge and no jury.

Released in late 1978, Wamwere again ran for Parliament—and this time he won. He served a poor rural district for the next three years; then he was held in prison without charges until 1984. In 1986, he sought exile in Norway. But while he was on a visit to Uganda in 1990, Kenya's security forces crossed the international border, kidnapped Wamwere and detained him for yet another three years. In an interview he did for *Speak Truth to Power,* he described this ordeal: "I was put in the basement police cells and woke up in a sea of water. I was naked and had been sitting in it all night. I stayed in that water for about one month." Again he fled into exile. And again he returned to Kenya, where this time he was arrested on trumped-up charges that carried the death penalty.

Wamwere received a show trial and was sentenced in 1995 to four years in prison and six lashes with a cane. Even President Moi, dictator of Kenya, tried to stop Wamwere's outspoken speech. Wamwere describes a meeting with the president in which he told Wamwere he should stop asking for better land distribution and for repeal of detention. Moi said to him, "Let sleeping dogs lie or you will be the one to lie." But the threat, while taken seriously, was still ignored. In spite of efforts by the police to force Wamwere to falsely confess, he resisted, commenting, "Life is a permanent struggle between good and evil. In this struggle there isn't room for neutrality. I couldn't possibly see myself crossing the floor to the other side. I could never be at peace with myself. I would rather die." Wamwere was released on December 13, 1996, to seek a treatment abroad for a heart condition after domestic and international pressure was put on the government.

Wamwere's attitude of uncompromising resilience, of energy, determination and principle in the face of oppression, has been his rock and shield. But he has infused his whole life with grace rather than with bitterness for the time stolen from him and the tortures inflicted on him. He has chosen to celebrate what can and should be in the political and social life of his country, and to dedicate his every breath to the fulfillment of his dreams and the dreams of others.

His commitment is owed much by everyone who cares not just about the future of East Africa but about the truth. Koigi wa Wamwere has emerged from his ordeal, at the midpoint in his path of life, with a wisdom and a sense of peace almost beyond imagination. May you take some of that wisdom with you and learn from this man—he is one of those spirits who walk among us and show us all the way.

INTRODUCTION

I wrote *I Refuse to Die* out of frustration with the level of ignorance about the state of Africa and the true nature of the Kenyan government as a dictatorship and product of colonialism and the Cold War.

I conceived the book to tell my story as an African native: our village life, struggles, laughter, cries, joys, tears, hopes and frustrations, as opposed to the often-told, glamorized, filmed, heard-and-seen story of a white settler in Africa, his safaris and obsession with wildlife.

Written without regret, *I Refuse to Die* is the painful narration of the victims of African misrule, not the loud boast of an African dictator, general, businessman or prosperous professional. It is a book for those who value freedom more than power.

Through the story of one, *I Refuse to Die* tells the odyssey of voiceless millions who suffer and endure horrible terror in Kenya and around Africa under Western-supported dictatorships. Told through the unsophisticated eyes of an African village youth rather than the pen of a university academic, my story is as honest as possible, a reckoning with the truth of fascist arrogance and the cruelty of British colonialism and the great African betrayal.

I Refuse to Die is a story of suffering. But it is also a story of strength—how Africa has remained alive and moving under the incredible weight of imperialist plunder, the slave trade, colonialism and postcolonial dictatorship. A weaker spirit would have collapsed and died many centuries ago. I hope this book will demonstrate to those who still have their freedom, human rights and democracy to guard against their erosion because once inside the jaws of human crocodiles, wrenching them back leaves many injured, mauled and cast into the wilderness of exile.

I Refuse to Die shows how the West, in its fight against communism, sacrificed and continues to betray democracy in Africa. Now we doubt whether those who betray democracy—abroad and at home—are themselves democrats.

I wrote my autobiography to explain my fight to my children and to let them know why they are growing up in exile, without all the things that they would like to have.

I wrote *I Refuse to Die* to tell how I escaped death in the den of lions for thirteen years. Stalked by death from conception, in both pain and pleasure, we live rather than just survive for as long as we do because we refuse to die. It is our refusal to die that gives us the will to live. When there is no refusal, there is no will. We let go and die.

As you read *I Refuse to Die*, you might think of the pain of resisting death, without remembering the joy of birth and reception of new life. Do not. Though the sword of danger has drawn blood by cutting me here and there while I did battle with it, whenever I have knocked down or chased away the dragon, I have experienced rebirths that have, by far, outweighed my pains and given me joy greater than what I felt when I was first born.

Our world is a reservoir of life whose volume increases the more we draw from it and the cleaner we keep it, by our adding into it the purifiers of freedom and justice and removing from it the pollutants of poverty, disease and oppression. The more life there is in the pool, the more there is for each one of us to share. To refuse to die is therefore not just to draw from the reservoir of life, whose level is dangerously low and inaccessible to millions in many countries, but to maximize it by adding freedom and justice to it, taking out the poverty, disease, oppression and exploitation that poison and drain it, and fighting for the right of all to drink from it.

I refuse to die, to not just survive but to live fully, for others' and my own sake. There is a human osmosis that makes my misery dilute the life of others and their unhappiness diminishes mine. When others are happy, I, too, am happy. When I am miserable, I see the light in the faces of others go out. There is a balance of shared life between us. We are freer and happier when the world is out of chains and in celebration. We live less when others are hungry and more when everyone is in song. We refuse to die by fighting the oppression of one another.

Of course, we all die and *I Refuse to Die* does not mean I will live forever. But by living right, we can chose to live for the infinity of human life—through our spirit, good works and whatever we do to perpetuate life. Despite our inevitable end, we have a choice whether to die or not to die. I will tell you how I made my own choice—not to die.

In the end, I wrote *I Refuse to Die* with the hope that, when you finish reading it, you too will refuse to die. After all, if you are living in the depths of our ever-expanding hell or in the periphery of our tiny and ever-shrinking heaven or are simply a good human being, you really have no choice. You must refuse to die.

Koigi wa Wamwere
May, 2002

I am my father's son. My father's father was called Kuria wa Wamwere. He had three wives: Mwihaki, Wairimu and Wangu. All of them were my grandmothers, their sons were my young and older fathers, their daughters were my aunts and their children were my brothers and sisters. With Mwihaki, my grandfather had six children: Wamwere (my father), Wairimu, Njeri, Mungai, Njoroge and Mwibiri.

My maternal grandfather was called Mung'ura wa Kiarie (Kariuki). He had six wives—Gacui, Mumbi, Njeri, Wambuthia, Wanjiru and Kagiri (Njeri).

With Kagiri, he had three children—Kariuki, Wangari and Wangu (my mother).

My parents, Wamwere and Wangu, had nine children—Koigi (mc), Kuria, Mwihaki, Njeri, Kariuki (Kiarie), Wairimu, Mungai, Njoroge and Wambui.

My father-in-law was called Ragui Karanja. With Waithira Mucene, he had ten children—Karanja, Waboro, Wairimu, Wangari, Wanjiku, Mucene, Kimwaki, Nduta (Gatuu), Wambui and Nduta (my wife).

I, Koigi wa Wamwere, and Nduta have three children—Wamwere, Ragui and Kuria.

PEOPLES OF THE PLAINS AND MOUNTAINS

Maasai | Ogiek (Ndorobo) | Taita-Taveta | Kamba
GEMA (Gikuyu, Embu and Meru) | Tharaka | Mbeere

PEOPLES OF THE HIGHLANDS

Gusii | Kuria | The Kalenjin | Ilchamus (Njemps) | Kipsigis | Nandi
Sabaot (Bok, Bongomek, Koney, Sebei) | Tugen | Marakwet | Keiyo

PEOPLES OF THE LAKES

Luo | Luhya (Abaluhya) | Suba | Iteso

PEOPLES OF THE DESERT

Turkana | Gabbra | Sambur | Pokot | Dassanich | El-Molo | Rendille

PEOPLES OF THE SAND AND SEA

Boran | Somali | Pokomo | Bajun | Swahili | Shirazi
Mijikenda—Giriama, Digo, Duruma, Chonyi, Jibana, Ribe, Kaambe, Rabai
Burji | Orma | Boni | Waliangula | Dahalo | Segeju

CHAPTER I

C H I L D H O O D   1 9 4 9 – 5 8

My Other Self

Among our people, life does not start at birth. When I asked my mother who I was before I was born, she told me:

You were my father. That is why I called you him.

Before him, did I live?

Yes, you did.

Have I always lived and shall I not die?

People do not die, she said, we only move from one form of life to another and from one world to another. Life does not begin at birth and it does not end with death. Both birth and death are mere handmaids of life. Birth opens the door into this life and death opens the door into the next life. Though we have not been blessed with the desire to die, death is the beginning of a new life.

But, Mum, how can I be my grandfather when he is still alive? How can he live in himself and me at the same time? Mustn't he die first for me to be him?

Not necessarily, she said. When I named you after him, his spirit moved into you. Because a spirit can live in many people at the same time, my father's spirit is in him, in me, in all my brothers and sisters and also in you and his other namesakes.

So my spirit existed before it moved into me? I asked.

Yes, long before I conceived you. The naming was a mere confirmation, my mother said.

Tell me more about my other self, I asked my mum.

Your other self was an orphan who lost his parents early and was therefore brought up by relatives who were none too generous. You were born in 1880, fourteen years before the birth of Kenya Colony. When you were a child you worked hard and were underfed. After children of the home had been given enough food, you were always asked to scrape the pot for what you could find. For doing this, they called you *Mung'ura*, the Pot Scraper. But as the Gikuyu proverb goes, *Being starved does not always stop success*. Starvation spurred you to great success.

Without land, you were among the first Africans in Kenya to take refuge and seek wealth in the colonial trade that was taking place in Nairobi, then a British outpost. With early Indian traders centered in Nairobi, you specialized in buying and taking foods to Nairobi and buying clothes, salt, soap, beads and sugar from Indian merchants in Nairobi to resell them in rural markets. With little competition, you were soon a rich man who forbade any grandchild to be called a Pot Scraper like you. Instead you said all your namesakes should be called *Koigi*, or a spokesperson, a strange name to choose since you were never one.

As a rich man you did not see wealth as an end in itself but as a means of helping poor people. To help the poor, you married women from poor families and used your generous dowries to uplift their standards of living.

As a father you taught us, your children, to live, love and share as brothers and sisters. And just as you strove to love us equally, you expected every mother to love all your children equally. Having suffered discrimination in your childhood, you used to say your home had no children of the stomach and others of the back. We were all equal.

You never bragged about your wealth. But when your sister, our aunt, died, you took her four children as your own and asked your fourth wife to breastfeed the youngest.

You were not good only to people of your family. You opened the doors of your stores to the poor every Monday and Thursday when those who had no money could get food, clothes and tobacco for free.

But, Mother, how could grandfather give food, clothes and tobacco free to the poor and not go bankrupt?

First, because the poor were not so many and people with food never cheated to get free food, clothes, sugar or tobacco. People then were a lot more honest and self-respecting than they are today. And getting free things was considered almost shameful. Further, your grandfather also asked other African merchants to be generous to the needy and that way shared the burden with others.

Like so many other ordinary Kenyans who fought for freedom, you did not have a public reputation as a freedom fighter but during the war for independence, you provided fighters in the forest with necessities like food, clothing and medicine. Yes, in your other self, you were a rich man. However, your greater wealth was not in money but your spirit of generosity.

As you grew older, you were afraid that when you died, your wives and children might fight over your wealth. So you wrote a will that divided your wealth among your sons equally. Nor did you forget the poor in your will. Your will gave all clothes in one of your big stores to the poor and strictly instructed that none of those clothes should go to any of your relatives. In turn people called your home area *Kairi ka Mung'ura* (Kairi, home of Mungura) in your honor.

Is my urge for justice the spirit of my grandfather? I asked my mother.

Yes, she told me, it is your old and real self. If ever it flickers out, you too shall die.

Conceived in Rebellion

Wangu, my mother, was born in 1928. She grew to be a youthful beauty of average height. She liked to talk, laugh and always wore a broad smile. She believed that it is harder to survive problems without humor. After all, people said, even when someone's house is burning, one may keep warm beside the fire, *ona ikihia mwene ni otaga*. Like other girls of her time, she wore a traditional dress, earrings and bangles on her arms. Although her father or *guka* (my grandfather) had many wives, she was raised as a *mukristu*, a Christian. In her family, Christianity coexisted with the African tradition that allowed polygamy, as long as the man could take good care of all his wives and children. Mother wanted to be a *mathia*, a nun, at the age of twelve. In those days, however, educating a girl child was considered a waste of both money and time. A woman had value only as a mother and for household jobs. As a result, Mum could not join a convent to follow her dream. Though Christian, her family did not want her to become a nun and even prohibited her from thinking about it. We can be Christian, they said, without having to give our daughter to white people.

In defiance of her parents' wishes, Mum thought about it constantly. At that time, it was impossible for her to imagine any other life. Consequently, she had dreams that were so strong that they scared her. Some called them hallucinations of a sick mind, but to her they were visions. Mother once told me:

I never liked telling my dreams or discussing them with anyone but I could not keep them to myself any longer. One night I dreamt that I was in two different worlds. In one, I was tormented, tortured and ordered to do things against my will. Though my only wish was to become a nun, *ngoma*, or evil spirits, forbade me. For my defiance, they started to torment me physically. I was seriously attacked at night. My left eye was stabbed and flesh was left hanging down my cheekbone. The following morning, the news spread to everyone in my neighborhood and many people came to see me. When I told them that spirits had stabbed me, nobody believed me. Instead they accused me of shielding the man who had stabbed me. *Athuri a kiama,* the elders, questioned me about it though they believed that a person with whom I had quarreled must have stabbed me. After accusing me of protecting the person who had stabbed me, they ordered that I should not be taken to the hospital. Now I lived in a world of confusion and agony when what I needed most was medical attention and spiritual strength.

I felt besieged by the devil himself and the story reached the priest and the nun of our church. They came to our home and negotiated with my parents and the elders to rush me to the hospital. The elders gave up—I was taken and admitted to Kiambu district hospital.

But my mysterious encounters with spirits did not end there. In bed, the wound was once again stabbed and the bandages thrown away. Early in the morning when the nurses came to see how I was doing, they found a completely exposed wound without bandages. They thought that I had fallen from bed. Though I knew I would not be believed, I told them what had happened. The wound was once more treated and bandaged. Thereafter, there was no more interference and the wound healed. I was discharged from the hospital, but I was not free from the spirits. The same night I was discharged, the spirits appeared again. I became so scared, but they assured me that they would not hurt me physically again. Instead, I was to suffer psychologically for the next three years and for fifteen years during old age.

I always try my best to forget dreams, but however hard I try, I cannot forget how I suffered for three years before I got married. It was such a tough time. A certain tycoon came into my life and insisted that I marry him as his second wife. He also promised to pay my father a heavy *ruracio,* dowry. My protective spirits never said yes and in a vision I was shown a different man who would be my husband. But it was not a woman's business to say who her husband would be and I was afraid that the elders might force me to marry the tycoon. Fortunately, my father wanted his children to choose their own partners in marriage. He agreed that I should pick my own man.

The tycoon never thought that anyone would dare say no to his wishes. When I completely refused to be married to him, he became enraged and took the case to the elders. He wanted them to force me to marry him. The council of elders was very annoyed that I dared say no to such a rich man and accused my father of encouraging me to rebel against men and tradition. Father was taken to Gatundu court. In the meantime, I was considered an outcast and ostracized. I was treated with a hatred that was completely unbearable. Yet I had only said no to a person of money and wealth and had not committed any crime. Even my family could not protect me now. They, too, were required to ostracize me and they did. And though social isolation was unbearably painful, I chose to be an outcast rather than marry that tycoon as a second wife.

Fortunately, the tougher things got, the stronger I became. In 1947, I ran away from home. I traveled as far as I could. I got hungry. I got thirsty. I became tired and scared. But I never looked back. I walked in the day and hid and slept in the forest at night. When I asked for help, men only offered to make me another one of their wives and the babysitter of their children. I refused and continued to run. One day I was hired to work and traveled on the food I was given as pay for the next two days. To this day, I don't understand why wild animals did not kill me. But they say *wa Ngai uraragio ni magoto,* the fire of God is preserved with the bark of the banana tree.

At last, I arrived at a home where people were kind enough to take me in, feed me and give me a place to sleep. One day, the young men of this home kidnapped me and took me to be married to their elder brother. The moment I saw him, I knew this was the man who would be my husband and the father of my children. His name was Wamwere wa Kuria, your father.

Your father then was living at Menengai Crater, employed by the Forest Department of the colonial government. He was much older, but I cared nothing about age. I felt confident that here was the man for me. But at first I had no peace. His relatives and those who knew him well thought I was just trying to cheat him and reported me to the police as a potential criminal. They did this to protect him. Even then your father was a very polite, kind man who liked people very much. He had wonderful laughter and *utana,* generosity. His ringing laugher radiated the joy of life and affected everyone around him. Later, of course, problems would mount, dim the light of life and joy and dry up the fountain of his laughter. Long before he became a father, colonial tyranny had made life impossible and killed the better part of him. Just as nothing could make me marry the tycoon whom I was running from, nothing would stop me from marrying your father. Loudly I prayed to God: Please, God let nothing separate me from this man. You are my witness that I love him. People heard my prayer and left us alone.

For the first two years I lived with your father, my parents thought I was dead. And instead of feeling sad, the tycoon who wanted to marry me saw my disappearance as a chance to make money. He sued my father to return him the dowry he had not paid. My father said, Return my daughter and I will return your dowry. If you do not have my daughter, I do not have your dowry. Everywhere, rumor said I was dead. Some even claimed to have seen my skull and skeleton.

By sheer coincidence, I met a certain woman from my home area. It was 1949, two years since I had left home. We did not talk, but she knew we came from the same place. When the woman returned home she heard of the well-known case between my father and the tycoon and stories of my disappearance and death. She wondered whether I was not the woman she had seen in the Rift Valley. With their hopes rekindled, relatives came to check whether I was their lost one. When they saw me, we all cried for joy. They, because I was not dead and I, because of their love for me. Your father made *njohi,* beer, and slaughtered a goat and we all ate and drank to celebrate the reunion of life and love. Then they returned home to give the good news to my parents.

Later, your father and I visited home. A dowry was negotiated and paid. We got my parents' blessing and our marriage was accepted by all, including the tycoon and his elders. When we returned to the Rift Valley, we settled down to the business of living, taking care of your father's brothers and relatives and lending God a hand in the never-ending business of creating life. Created in God's image, we knew we were gods too, though enslaved by colonialism and bearing the twin duties of creating and liberating life from servitude. In doing this, I benefited a lot from both the spirit and the education of my father.

As Mother told me all this, and I responded that she did not sound like a very good Christian, she became philosophical: You see, my son, African Christians cannot be exactly like European Christians. We must have and keep our cultural differences. For instance, I saw nothing wrong with the polygamy of my father. I believe in *irua,* circumcision for men and women, and I have my own ideas about God and who we are. When God created us, he transferred his divinity and made us gods like him. But our divinity increases in our unity with one another. As individuals, our divinity is very limited. Therefore, we create very little. Our divinity grows when we unite with others. As fathers and mothers, we are gods, but only in unity with one another. As husband and wife, we create life. When we unite with others, we become even greater gods. We create life and knowledge, we build machines, save life and push death back in our lives. In life, our destiny is to create and save lives, to become greater gods and to come as close as we can to our Creator, whose divinity is also enhanced by the unity of all his separate selves.

So, my mother met my father in the Rift Valley, a region that adjoins Central Province, their home region to the east. How did Pap end up there?

My father was born at his father's home near today's Kiambu town in 1911. The first step in his journey from the Central Province to the Rift Valley was laid out long before he was born. It was because of the Berlin Colonial Conference in 1885, a meeting of European colonial powers, that the land that was later called Kenya was put under the sphere of British imperial influence. The British laid claim to Kenya for no other reason than the fact that their explorers were among the first Europeans to come there and had the military might to enforce their greed against both Africans and fellow white colonialists.

Father took the next step on his forced journey to the Rift Valley in 1895 when Kenya was turned into a British Protectorate. His third step was taken in 1915, when the Crown Lands Ordinance declared all land in Kenya to be officially "crown" land that the government could lease to white settlers for 999 years.

The African area that was hit first and hardest by European alienation was the southern part of the Kiambu District, where the Governor of the Protectorate, obsessed by the idea of settlement, allowed the incoming Europeans to claim any Gikuyu land, occupied or not. As a result, some 60,000 acres of southern Kiambu containing some 11,000 Gikuyu passed into European hands. The administration told the settlers to pay the displaced Africans two rupees for each cultivated acre and two rupees for each hut, but only two-thirds of them were ever paid. The bitterness of survivors is immortalized by John Spencer in his book *The Kenya African Union:* "A European came to our home one day with Chief Kinyanjui. He had been told that he was free to settle on our land…we were given seven days to quit. Seven days later the European returned on a horse and told us to remove all our belongings from our huts. He then burnt them down to the ground."[1]

My grandfather Kuria was driven from his father's land and the huts of his three wives were torched when my father was only four years old. Grandfather and his family were then forced to live together with other Africans in a small area that was set aside for them called the African Reserve. Here, they had no land where they could farm or graze their animals. He was required to pay a head tax and a hut tax that could only be rendered in British money to be earned solely by working for the colonial government as a laborer, policeman or soldier or for white settlers as a farmhand.

It was therefore the colonial theft of African land, the search for space and land to graze his animals, and the search for work to earn tax money, that forced my grandfather to move to Kijabe in the Rift Valley. Simultaneously, this happened to millions of his contemporaries in the whole of Kenya and Africa.

By the time Winston Churchill visited Kenya Colony in 1922, Father was eleven years old and already employed by the Forest Department of the colonial government as a *mboi,* or kitchen boy. If father had ever had any hope of returning to his grandfather's stolen land in Kiambu, I knew it was brutally shattered by Churchill when I saw the documentary called *End of Empire* and heard what Churchill shamelessly told the white colonial settlers in Kenya: "This land is yours, the settlers', in perpetuity. Not only for you, but also for your children and grandchildren."

These words guaranteed that Mother would meet Father at the Menengai Crater in the Rift Valley and not at Kiambu in the Central Province. These words also ensured that not only every white man and his children would be masters and landowners in Kenya, but that, just as my father and mother were colonial slaves, I, too, would be conceived and born a slave of the white man.

Similarly, these words clarify that my parents and other Gikuyu people did not march into the Rift Valley as robber barons, as some people claim today, but were driven there as impoverished and wandering slaves looking for a place to settle and for money to pay British-imposed taxes. Churchill's words also sowed the first seeds of the Mau Mau rebellion and revolution that white people planted in the hearts and minds of the Kenyan people. As Churchill arrogantly gave Kenya to the white settlers, Kenyan Africans asserted their God-given right to the same land in several songs. In one such song, our people said they were given Kenya by no less an authority than their God himself:

Gikuyu was taken by *Mwene Nyaga* (God)
On top of Mount Kenya
And asked, do you see all this land?
I give it to you and all your descendants.

In another song, our people said that in Kenya, contrary to what Churchill thought, white people had no right to own land or live as masters.

As African people challenged Churchill's right to give away their country, they wondered what right the British had to take the land that *Ngai* had given them. To Africans, the answer was obvious. They believed that, while Churchill's guns might be more powerful than their spears, the British were not greater or more powerful than *Ngai*, their God. One day, they would challenge this theft of their country and the colonial slavery that followed.

Ukombo, utumwa, or slavery, is not meant to be endured by any human being, but to be rebelled against. When my father and mother conceived me, most Gikuyu and other Kenyans were in a state of rebellion against colonial slavery. And conceived as a slave, my rebellion against servitude and oppression must have started in the womb.

Yes, I said my parents were rebels against the colonialism of white people and the oppression of negative African traditions. They were also rebels against the Western moral decadence that the British brought to Kenya.

Father used to tell me that at the time of my conception and birth, tobacco and the national newspaper, *Muiguithania (The Unifier),* needed no sellers. In the streets they sold themselves because Africans had declared war against cheating and theft. Rebellion against colonialism also called upon Africans to rebel against colonial values and abuse of everything African—color, rights, names, customs, religion, polygamy, circumcision and so forth. Among African people, the strong were not allowed to steal from the weak, leaders to steal from the people or people to steal from one another. Also forbidden were the worship of money, sale of sex, disloyalty for money, aping European mannerisms, "Christianity" that taught African people self-hate and colonial education for African enslavement. So I was conceived not just in an atmosphere that rebelled against evil, but in one that rejected corruption and sought and revered the highest possible morality in African society.

When my father got work, he was happy to be the keeper of his father, mothers, brothers and sisters. Where he got work, they too got land to cultivate and graze their animals in the endless, unused tracts the colonial government and settlers owned everywhere. This tolerable state of affairs went on until the late 1930s when Kifagio Laws permitted the colonial government and settlers to confiscate African animals. In 1945, Africans working in government forests and settler farms were not allowed to keep cattle, cultivate more than two acres or keep more than fifteen animals. Now it was no longer possible for father's parents, brothers and sisters to live with him. They were forbidden and ordered back to Kiambu, where they had no land once more.

Birth in Tears

December 18, 1949 was a Sunday, but Mother was not to go to church that day. And though Mum was completely heavy with me, she was not on leave from work. Maternity leave was not for African women. Father woke at 5:00 A.M. and asked Mum, Will you still go for this forced coffee picking today? Wouldn't it be better for you to rest?

Mum shrugged her shoulders and looked up with an expression that seemed to ask, Is it I who refuses to stay home? Instead of answering, Pap went on with his monologue: The baby might come today. It is already late.

Then mother asked, What can I do? Tthey won't give me permission to stay at home, will they?

Let me see whether they will, he said.

Father rushed to the village gate where the lorries from European coffee plantations came to collect forced laborers. When he saw the *nyapara,* the overseer, Pap asked, Can my wife rest today from coffee picking? She is very heavy and is expecting.

No, said the overseer, *bwana,* the boss, says everyone must pick coffee today. The harvesting is already late.

Father was mad with anger: Is this not a Sunday when everybody should be resting and going to church? You won't even let a heavy woman rest? What kind of Christians are you?

Well, the overseer said, Christianity says that if your one sheep falls in a pit on the Sabbath, you must lift it out. The master's coffee is in a pit and it must be pulled out on the Sabbath.

Father fumed: Which is the more important to pull out on the Sabbath, your master's coffee or my child and its mother?

Either your wife picks coffee or *utaona cha mtema kuni,* you shall suffer dire consequences.

Pap walked back home in defeat and shame. Without permission, mother shouldered her basket and sacks and left home to pick coffee. By 8:30 A.M. she was already at the coffee plantation. In the meantime, I could not wait to get out. In my mother's womb, I had a hearty appetite and ate a lot. Equally, Mother was generous and easily let food come to me. Most important, her hilarious laughter was an expression of inner peace and happiness that she passed on to me in abundance, making me a very contented and peaceful child. Under the circumstances, I was very big by the time I reached nine months.

Being a working rural African woman, mother fed me on the same foods she ate—Irish potatoes, green peas, maize, a little meat after a long time and maize meal porridge. Not great food, but enough to give me more than average size.

Although many times before mother had taken me to the coffee plantations, that day, which was sunny and dry with a blue sky, I did not like the pushing and shoving in the overcrowded lorry. Moreover, that morning Mum had only taken a cup of *turungi,* black tea, for breakfast. I was therefore hungry, angry, as anxious as mother was—and kicking. Little did I know that my kicking was opening the door of this life for me.

Not feeling too well, Mother did not want to show it. She felt a twinge of sadness but did not want to dwell on it. She knew that other people, like those of Olenguruone (a place near our home), were being evicted from their homes by the British and were suffering worse problems than hers. Instead of brooding over her own problems, she was irresistibly drawn to sad Olenguruone songs that she hummed in hushed tones for fear of notice by African overseers, who if they heard them, would report to the white owner of the coffee plantation, with dire consequences. Maybe it was being at work when her condition was so critical that swelled her anger against the British, who were jailing Africans at Olenguruone and burning their homes.

> There was great wailing in Olenguruone
> Even as we collected together our belongings
> The enemy had scattered about.
> The enemy was telling us:
> Hurry up, quick.
> Are you forgetting you are criminals?

Other women sang the chorus in equally hushed tones:

> We will greatly rejoice
> The day Kenyan people
> Get back their land.

Mother continued:

> We are being oppressed all over this land.
> Even our homes have been destroyed.
> And our bodies have been exploited.
> But do not be afraid.
> We are heading for a great victory.

> The British came from Europe
> In order to oppress our people.
> Since then they have continued oppressing us.
> Ngai, when will they go back to Europe?

By now she was already sobbing and tears streamed down her face:

> The children of Olenguruone saw for themselves
> Their goats and cows being taken away.
> The Catholic priest too was a witness
> To the destruction of everything in Olenguruone.
> Forests as well as hopes of the people.
>
> From earthen cells people were taken
> To offices to be finger-printed.
> They refused to be branded criminals
> So some were taken to detention at Yatta,
> Others to prison in Nakuru
> Because they asked for land.

She continued to sing and sob for Kenya, herself, imprisoned Kenyans and their suffering children:

> There was great wailing all over Olenguruone
> Of tiny suckling babies
> Bitten by bitter cold.
> As the cold rain poured
> Babies cried to one another...
>
> Teacher Koirugo was arrested.
> He told colonial soldiers,
> I will not abandon my pupils
> As if they are orphan children.
> If you like it so
> Find me at the school
> And take us to prison too—"

Ooooih! ooooih!—Mum said with obvious pain. Please, somebody help, she begged through clenched teeth. Without warning, labor had struck and struck viciously. It was I kicking hard to be freed. I saw no reason to stay inside any longer, when everything outside was burning.

Let me ooout, *reke nyumeee,* I shouted from inside.

More women gathered around mother. They put her in the shade of a coffee tree, took out their shawls to hurriedly construct a roof and a wall around the coffee tree, thereby making a small room into which I would be born. Because I was big, delivery was not easy. As Mother pushed and pushed, the other women laughed, enjoying the joy of birth, but Mum would not be placated and continued to cry—not out of pain, but from a mixture of happiness for herself and sadness for Kenya. She pushed and pushed. Then—ooh!—I came out. At exactly 9 A.M.

When I came out, the women asked, What do we call this one who is born in tears and is too impatient to be born at home: *Kihiko,* the impatient one, *Kahuaini,* born in the coffee plantation, or *Wamaithori,* born in tears? Who is this boy who has come? they asked.

Mother now laughed and said, He is Koigi.

The women rang out five ululations, *ithano cia kahii,* to welcome me into the world. When they finished, one woman said, Welcome Koigi. Our struggle needs all the men it can get. May you grow to be a brave freedom fighter.

I was then given to Mum. Lovingly she held and cuddled me, as one woman rushed to fetch water from the open drum that held water for coffee pickers—water made warm by the African sun and brown by the light brown dust of Bahati coffee farms. When the water came in a pail, Mother drank some and then washed me. In the meantime, two other women dug a hole with sticks, into which they buried the placenta and the remains of the umbilical cord. When they finished doing so, one of them whispered into my ear, "Koigi, *thigira,* or the placenta and remains of your umbilical cord, that we have buried here are the roots that bind you to this land and link the land to you. One day you must reclaim what is yours by right from the white man who today owns it by might. I don't know what I said to this, but I heard.

As Mother rested in the shade, the overseer arrived to inquire about what was going on. He was told my mother had delivered. Without shame, he peered into the makeshift room and congratulated Mother. He then gave the other women a hostile look and ordered them back to their coffee picking. Without anyone to take Mother home, she ate some green maize for lunch and suckled me until evening, when she was paid less than five cents for the one tin of coffee berries she had picked. At 5:30 P.M. we all boarded the lorry and were driven home. We arrived just as night was settling in.

Two women accompanied Mum to help her with cooking. When we reached home, we found Father waiting, with a big grin on his face. He seemed certain that I had come. As soon as we were inside, he took me in his arms, close to his chest. For blessings, he spat upon me and said, "He has big, beautiful eyes." Then he gave me back to Mother. Pap rushed to the shop to buy sugar, tins of cocoa and bread. As the women were cooking, Father made a huge fire and called two of his friends. He singled out his biggest *ndurume,* ram, and slaughtered it. Some of its meat was roasted for Mother and others. The rest was boiled in order to make, with herbs, a special, delicious soup. Together with porridge and brown peas, this preparation helped Mother to recover fast and make enough milk for me.

A Child of All

Even before I spoke, the first thing that I learnt from my parents and other people in our village was love. To my parents, I was their greatest gift from God and love to me was their only way of thanking God. But the first reason my parents loved me was not because I was God's gift to them but because I was an extension of their own lives and they would continue to live through me after their own deaths. Loving me was not like loving somebody else. It was self-love and more. In a setting where death was an ever-present threat to life, people beat their own death by having children who would live to perpetuate their own lives.

And as a son I was endowed with greater love than if I had been a girl because, through me and my sons and grandsons, my father's family name would continue to live and hopefully never die.

But I was not just the son of my parents, I was also an additional member of my clan and my larger community and for this I was also loved. In our community, a child was always an asset to be loved by everybody and never a liability. In our village, children were loved by all. Those who did not love children were considered so different and dangerous that they were called witches.

Above all, my parents simply loved me because I was a beautiful being, an object of love that deserved to be loved in my own right. To our people, children deserve human love before flowers, pets, cars, money and all other things. This is why it was never heard that a child could ever be sold for money.

In my childhood, however, I don't remember hearing anyone calling me *darling, sweet-love, honey* and whatever else that one hears today. Instead love for me was expressed through body language that speaks louder than words and is incapable of lying—hugs, stretched arms, lifts, smiles, tears, care and concern for me. Whenever my mother fed me, I felt her love. Whenever she struggled to heal my cold, I felt her love. Whenever my mother took me in her arms and pressed me close to her, I felt greatly loved. Whenever mum saw me hurt and shed tears, I felt so much love that it hurt. Similarly, when my father picked some ripe berries in the forest and brought them home to me, I felt his love. When Pap took me to the village hotel, where he cooked sometimes and treated me to a cup of tea and *andazi*, a Kenyan doughnut, I felt his love. When he took me and sat me on his lap, I felt greatly loved. Today, I still remember that whenever my father escorted me to school and had to leave, when we waved each other good-bye, I felt so loved and loved him so much that I was simply overwhelmed with tears. Whenever a neigh-

hor took me into her hut because my mother was still in the garden and it was raining and cold outside, I felt greatly loved. Yet in the expression of all this love, I never
heard the word "love", just as I never heard the word uttered between Mother and
Father or between other adults.

To justify brutalization and colonization of Africans, some European people
argue that Africans of yesteryear were brutal and knew no love because they had
no extravagant use of the African words for love. Such people could not be further
from the truth. Many times, those who enjoy expressing their love openly and
publicly, feel much less than those who only express their love in private and
mainly in body language. Sometimes love is like a piece of ice for a thirsty person.
The more you expose it to sun, the sooner it goes and the more you keep it covered, the longer it lasts and the more you thirst for it.

But love only survives in reciprocity. As a small child, I instinctively loved
back each time my parents or others loved me. I instinctively smiled back each
time I was smiled at. Nevertheless, as a child, there are many acts of love that I could
not return. For instance, I could not feed when I was fed. I could not take care of
my parents when sick in return for their care and I could not escort my father to
school the same way he had for me.

Where I could not reciprocate, love was a debt to those who loved me. When
my parents fed me as a child, I was expected to feed them in old age when they were
too weak to feed themselves. When my parents looked after me as a sick child, I was
expected to do the same for them later. As a child, my parents stayed with me not
because they expected that I would stay with them when old, but out of love. Similarly, when I stay with my parents in old age, strictly speaking, I am not doing so
because they stayed with me as a child, but because I love them as they loved and still
love me and I cannot neglect the welfare of those I love. A debt of love is truly not
like any other. It is returned in love, not because it must be repaid.

Though I was expected to love back in the future whenever I could not
love back immediately, as a child, I could and was expected to love back those
who loved me by showing them as much respect as possible. For my parents, I
showed them respect by doing what they asked; never using bad or disrespectful language against them; behaving well when they were around and never
calling them by their names. Though my mother is called Wangu, I was not
allowed to address her (or my father) by name. I could only call Mother *maitu*
or *mami* and Father, *baba*. I once addressed my mother as Wangu instead of
Mum. She looked at me with disbelief, but she did not smack me. I did not call
her by her name again.

Just as love did not come to me from my parents alone, I was not expected to
love them alone. So I was expected to address all men and women who were parents as "Mother and Father of so-and-so" and never by their names. Equally I

could only address my grandmother and grandfather as *cucu* and *guka,* respectively, never by their names.

As for Father's brothers, they were all fathers too—young fathers, if they were younger than Father, old fathers, if they were older. Father's wives were young mothers, if they were younger than Mother, and old mothers if they were older. As for mother's brothers, they were all my uncles. Mother's and Father's sisters were my aunts.

All these titles of respect belonged to all those who were older than me. In Gikuyu society, all children are expected to respect all those who are older, even if there are no specific titles for them. All young men and women who were circumcised and initiated into adulthood were given a lot of respect by young boys and girls that were not. In large part, it was this respect plus the privilege of sexual love that made young boys and girls crave circumcision. In the Gikuyu society, all respect was given according to age groups with the oldest receiving the greatest measure. But respect, like love, can only survive in reciprocity. So as children respected adults, adults, too, had to honor them. The more respect an adult received from a child, the more one had to give back. Accordingly, it was disrespectful for adults to fight or exchange insults before children and it was equally wrong for adults to take off their clothes or make love where children were. It was also in return of greater love and respect that those whom we called young and old fathers and mothers treated us exactly like their children.

But of all the people the children loved and respected, none gave back more love and respect than grandfathers and grandmothers. Among the Gikuyu, grandmothers and grandfathers love and spoil their grandchildren so much that one of our proverbs says that one who is brought up by his grandmother is incorrigible. In fact, grandparents love and protect their grandchildren to such an extent that they grant all the demands grandchildren make and will not permit parents to smack or correct grandchildren when they are present. If I was beaten when my grandmother or grandfather was present, they took that beating as an insult to them. So grandchildren and especially those who are named after grandparents could never be disciplined when their namesakes were present.

In our village we lived like a family. We respected all adults as we respected our parents. No adult would leave a child out in the rain if the parent was not home or find a sick child alone and not take him home. The moral duty on all adults did not end with giving food, shelter or taking home a sick child. It was also considered an act of love for any adult to punish any child who was rude or was found doing something wrong. If any adult found me doing something wrong, I ran not to be smacked. My flight was, however, a momentary reprieve because the adult would report me and my parents would punish for the offense just as if they had caught me doing it themselves.

I particularly remember one man whom we called *Nuhu Matu* (Noah of Ears). He drove an old Bedford lorry for his Asian employer. Every time Noah of Ears came home to visit his family, he had to drive the lorry over a steep hill just before he entered the village. On the hill, the lorry moved very slowly. All naughty children would chase the vehicle, cling to some part of its rear door and have the lorry carry them from there. It was a risky thing to do in case the brakes of the old lorry failed and the lorry had to reverse in high speed. But who cared about danger? As soon as the lorry was over the hill, having seen us from the rear mirror, Noah of Ears would suddenly stop the lorry, get out of the vehicle and come after us. If he caught any one of us, Noah of Ears would start biting our ears so hard that sometimes he would leave them bleeding. Our parents knew about our mischief of riding this lorry and approved when Noah of Ears bit our ears for it. Instead of sympathizing with us, when we returned home with bitten ears, our parents just gave us more punishment.

The fact that parents were allowed to punish children other than their own also meant that they had to treat all children with total equality when it came to conflicts between them. Many times when I went away from home and fought with other children I got beaten, but I could not run home for protection. If I ran home crying and pleading to Mum—Help me, Kamau wants to kill me—she would just chase me away. Go away all of you, she would say, I want to hear nothing of your fights. And if I went home crying and saw Mum coming towards me while saying, Come here, I would simply take off because I knew she wanted to beat me for getting involved in fights with other children. In children's fights, parents agreed never to take sides; they treated us as equally guilty and punishable and individually responsible for what we suffered. Instead of Father and Mother going to quarrel with other parents whose child bested me, they beat me and other parents did the same with their children. I thought my parents were very unreasonable and unwilling to help.

Only once did Mother blame an older girl for beating me. The girl was a neighbor and our huts were adjacent to each other. So we more or less shared the same compound to play in. This Sunday morning, I had gone to visit this girl's younger brother. She did something and her mother was beating her outside their hut, where we were playing by ourselves. As she was being beaten, her brother and I were competing to see who could jump on a tree stump longest. At the moment of her punishment, it happened to be my turn to jump on the stump. Seeing me jumping up and down on the tree stump, this girl thought that I was enjoying and celebrating the beating she was getting. In fact, I was so engrossed in our competition that I hardly noticed. Unaware of my disinterest, when she was let go, she came for me straight away with a hard cabbage stem. Like one gone crazy, she knocked me down and hit me so hard on the right side of my face between the ear and the eye that she punctured one of the tiny veins, which drew a jet of blood from it. Since my face and shirt were drenched in blood, Mum and her mother ran after this girl together but she disappeared beyond reach. That was the only time I saw my mother really angry at some other child.

Learning to Say No

I don't quite remember but mustering speech must have been as great an excitement for me as learning to walk. Learning to call Mother *mami*, Father *baba*, grandmother *cucu* was a great thing. As was calling *irio* food when I was hungry. Then I learnt how to ask a small question like *wi mwega*, How are you?, and get a small reply like *ndi mwega*, I am fine or *ii*, yes. There were other important words that Mother taught me like *onga*, suckle, and *ria*, eat. Because I was a very big child, I learnt to speak before I learnt to walk.

Even after learning to speak, the body language of crying and laughing remained my main form of expression. To emphasize my needs and feelings, I learnt to use both speech and body language. So when I was hungry, I would say *irio* and cry at the same time.

Among the many words that I was taught, there was one that was central to what was going on then—and now. *Aca. Hapana.* No. Before learning to speak, I cried to say no and Mother shook her head to say no to me. "No" is not an expression that I was taught to say in words only. I was also taught to say the same word in actions. As my parents were teaching me to say no, they and other Kenyans were saying no to British colonialism by fighting and rebelling against it. In all the four languages I have learnt to speak, some well and some not so well, I have probably learnt thousands and thousands of words. Yet no other word has had a more profound impact on my life than the word "no."

In teaching me to say no, none of my parents ever sat me in a session of learning how to say no or what to say no to. When to say no and what to say no to were dropped to me imperceptibly all through my childhood, the way one drops grains to a bird sure it will pick up what it is hungry for, if not today, tomorrow, until all the grains are eaten up. One day Mum would say, Son, if you see anyone who wants to hurt you, say no to him. Or, When I leave you with your sisters and brothers, protect them. Say no to anyone who wants to hurt them.

Another day Mum might say to me, When you feel like taking food from your young brothers and sisters, say no to yourself. When you feel like doing something that might hurt someone else, say no. When you feel fear going to draw water from the center of the village at night, say no. When you feel lazy in the garden, say no to yourself. When you feel like wanting to despair because your schoolwork is difficult, say no to it. Always say no to what hurts you from within yourself or from someone else. To live, you must always say no to death in whatever form it might approach you. And never fear to say no to those who are stronger than you. Today we are saying no to the British although they are stronger than us. Finally they will heed our cry.

These are the grains with which my parents fed and strengthened my spirit. This is why I have been saying no to oppression, injustice, racism and inequality and yes to freedom, justice and equality of man all my life.

Living with Rats

When I look back at my life in the colonial village, I cannot believe that I survived its harshness. Yet as a child, I don't remember thinking about how difficult life was. I just lived it as if there was no other. Until I came across rich white people on the settler farms. That suddenly reminded me how poor and miserable our existence was. When I was born, African life was just tolerable. But as the conflict between African people and white settlers grew, African life grew more and more unbearable.

Before the white man came, a typical Gikuyu homestead used to have several huts. There would be the main house where the mother and daughters lived. The father would have his own quarters called *thingira* where he ate, spent his evenings and slept with the small sons. Bigger, circumcised but unmarried sons would have their own *thingira,* where they would eat, sleep and receive their own friends. Outside the huts, there would be an enclosure for animals called *kiugu* and an *ikumbi,* or food store.

This structure of our homes was created and maintained to preserve hygiene, to avoid overcrowding in one single hut and to increase respectability between parents and children, mothers and sons, fathers and daughters and brothers and sisters by reducing familiarity between them. The Gikuyu people believed that though staying together is a source of compassion, staying too close can be a source of undue temptations and quarrels, *muikaranio ni guo muharano.* Perhaps it was to induce disputes and destruction of African families that colonial authorities went out of their way to crush the traditional African homestead.

Now, we lived in a forest where there was plenty of timber and stone but only white officers of the Forest Department had good stone and timber houses. Later, the most loyal and elevated African servants like teachers, welfare officers and forest rangers had timber and stone houses built for them, though not as good as those of white forest officers. The racism of colonialism forbade black and white to be at par.

As forest workers at the bottom of the ladder, where almost all African workers were, my parents were allowed to build only one hut to live in and one food store for maize and potatoes but not with stone, good timber and corrugated iron sheets. The living hut had an earthen floor. The walls were built with slabs of outer timber and thatched with long grass. The huts were the size of our living room today. Yet the center of the hut was the living room, the fireplace and the kitchen. The same hut had a corner that was an open bedroom for my father. There was also an enclosed corner that was a bedroom for Mum and the smallest child and an inner storage area for cooked food called *kibaca.* The round hut also had a corner that was a bedroom for the boys, a corner for the bedroom of my sisters and a *gicegu,* a pen for one or two animals that were being fattened. When we went to sleep, the sheep were let in to sleep in the living room while our hens huddled around the fireplace for warmth. We were not permitted to keep more than ten sheep, and goats were not permitted at all—they were accused of destroying young saplings. The forest was an ocean of grass, but no forest worker was allowed to keep a cow. When we woke up in the morning or went out in the dark at night to help ourselves, we would stumble against the sheep and into their dung, which littered the center of the hut.

The hut for the forest worker had no heater. It was kept warm by a fire and by our damp warmth and that of our animals. When we went to bed, the fire was not put out. It was buried in ashes to preserve it and prevent it from burning anything. To dry the firewood, a rack called an *itara* was built at the ceiling level of the house. The rack was always pitch-black with thick soot. Stalactites of soot that hung from the bottom of it sometimes broke and fell into cooking food and denied us a meal every now and then. On account of high altitude, the forest where we lived was a very cold place. We had therefore to make fires in the hut both for cooking and for keeping ourselves warm. In the rainy season, which ran from March to September, wet firewood made poor fires that half filled the hut with thick smoke that made our eyes red, painful and teary all the time.

Without money for paraffin, we also made fires for light. When learning to read and write, we all crouched before these fires with ashes spread out before us as writing slates. We could not afford to buy exercise books or writing slates. When the fires were particularly smoky, we would bend over the ashes writing while our faces ran with sweat, our eyes with tears and our noses with thin mucus. Still we soldiered on.

Father was paid wages of one dollar a month. The only clothes he could afford for my mother were a couple of second- or third-hand dresses, a shirt and a pair of shorts for himself and *gacuka,* a sheet of white cloth for me, which I put over my back and half covered my front with. Later I was bought a pair of shorts and one shirt for school and the same to wear at home. Though it got very cold in the months of May, June and July, we never had pullovers, umbrellas and coats to shield us from cold and rain and no clothes to change into when we were beaten by the heavy rains and returned home drenched to the bone. Many times I saw Pap wear a blanket because he had no clothes to change into. When Mum came home and had no other dress to change into, she would stay in the same wet dress until it dried.

Only the white men, women and children were allowed to wear shoes. So Father and Mother never wore shoes and we children never wore anything on our feet. We all walked barefoot but eventually, we were allowed to wear *nginyira,* open sandals made from rubber tires.

Our school uniform didn't include a jacket, a woolen pullover or shoes. In fact anyone who wore a pair of shoes to school was beaten up by teachers. And it is not just the pair of shorts that were short, the school shirt was also short-sleeve. In the extreme cold of July, we therefore shivered and gnashed our teeth in unheated classrooms while the soles of our feet were cracked wide-open by the cold dew that covered the grass every morning.

At home we had only rags for blankets. The walls of our hut had wide and long openings between the slabs of timber through which wind blew in cold and water into the hut. In the months of heavy rain, the floor reeked of water that we let out of the house in tiny rivulets, while the grass roof leaked with drops of rain that we caught in *thuburia,* cooking pots, and *irai,* washing basins, before it made tiny puddles on the earthen floor. We were glad that rain brought us food. It also brought us cold, wetness, perpetual cold, influenza and pneumonia that killed sick babies who could not get medicine. Often, when it rained at night and the roof leaked, we would wake in great annoyance and shift our beds to avoid getting drenched.

The food we ate bespoke our poverty. In the dry season, we ate *githeri,* boiled, hard grains of maize flavored with salt. For a change, maize was ground into flour and cooked into a hard cake called *ugali. Ugali* is eaten with *mboga,* a mixture of green vegetables and meat. In the forest, meat was rare and in the dry season, we had no greens. We ate our *ugali* with saline water. When things were not so bad, we ate *githeri,* treated with beans. I liked neither *ugali* nor *githeri.*

We had better food in the rainy season when we had potatoes, cabbages, carrots and plenty of other green vegetables. I really looked forward to late April and early May, when there would be new potatoes that tasted as sweet as soft green maize. Despite the wetness and cold, the rainy seasons were the best time of the year because we had plenty to eat. Then, potatoes, green maize, green vegetables or peas were pounded together to make *mukimo,* the favorite food of my childhood.

While we were growing up, milk was out of the question, as were tea and coffee. Instead, we drank *ucuru,* porridge without sugar. To make it palatable, porridge was treated with salt or bicarbonate of soda that corroded our teeth and made them brown. Without a dentist, toothpaste or plastic toothbrushes, we cleaned our teeth with charcoal and toothpicks. This was before I discovered *muti wa thi-*

gara, the root of a creeper that was a great brush with a wonderful smell which gave *mukimo* an incredible taste.

Every day in the coffee-picking season, Mum picked coffee. Without money however, she could not drink it. Without coffee, Mother suffered headaches. Completely desperate, she roasted sugar in a spoon and dipped it into boiled water to make it brown. She drank this as her coffee. There were times when Mother could not make her coffee. That was when rats had stolen her steel spoon and hidden it in their underground homes. It was not just my mother's spoon that rats stole and hid. They stole other spoons, needles, buttons and whatever coins they could find and hid them in their bunkers. Unfortunately, whenever rats stole money, it was we kids who got beaten for stealing it. We were beaten for disappeared money until the rats' bunkers and their loot were discovered. When needles and spoons were borrowed, Mum had to buy others to replace them. The rats were many both in our hut and in our store for maize and potatoes. They ate our maize and contaminated it with dung. Without other food, we ate the same dirty food they had contaminated.

During the day when no one was at home, rats made our house their racecourse until someone came back—then they would all go scurrying to their bunkers again. Sometimes they were so daring that they raced across the hut in our presence and you could see their tiny, shiny eyes watching us from where they were hiding. At night, rats literally took over the hut. When the fire was put out and we were all in bed, all the rats came out of their bunkers to look for food and play. They ate, chased one another in the hut, fell down from the roof, jumped onto our beds to eat the soles of our feet while talking and laughing among themselves. Bite the sole of that one, one would say. The other would bite and I would move my bitten sole. Stupid, not so hard, the one biting would be warned by another. Blow some breath where you bite or he will get up and spoil everything for us. Yes, the one biting would say and continue nibbling at my foot. And don't waste all your time with such an old, hardened sole. Go for the young, soft one. It is easier to bite. When we woke up in the morning, we would find layers of skin peeled off from our soles and know that rats had been feasting on us at night. Sometimes hens would wake us up in the night fighting rats that were getting too close.

To kill rats, we brought in a cat. But a cat in the hut was not always welcome because at the few times we had little meat and milk, at night the cat would open the cupboard, steal, eat and drink both the meat and the milk. You should have seen the anger in our eyes when we woke and found our precious meat and milk gone. Everyone wanted to kill the cat, but it would run away.

I hated rats more than I did the cat and wanted to kill them all the time. Not just because they ate our soles and food but also because they carried fleas in their fur, making it impossible for us to get rid of them. During the dry season, fleas were so many in our hut that one could see them jumping around on the earthen floor. From the floor, they would jump into our clothes and into bed, where they hid in the folds of our clothes and tattered blankets. When hungry, they would come from hiding, bite, suck blood and hide again as soon as one moved. The bite of the flea is painful and unbearable. They were particularly vicious at night. They allowed us no sleep, biting our legs, back, neck, shoulders, stomach, ribs, buttocks, eyelids and even lips. Yet the war with fleas was unwinnable because at night they were impossible to catch and kill. They particularly liked to burrow themselves between toes, in the cracked heels of our feet and in the nails of our fingers. If they dug in early in our sleep, by morning, they would be completely burrowed. They would then proceed to lay eggs and become jiggers that would burst open into tiny fleas. Because a place with jiggers is very itchy, at night we would put our feet up and scratch our heels against the rough walls of the hut. We would scratch jigger-infested places with our nails and stones. Finally, we would take thorns and needles, open up the skin to remove the jiggers and kill them. The opened-up places would look like tiny, ugly, sore craters. To keep the sores clean our antiseptic was the bitter pulp of *ndongu,* a poisonous apple. Squeezing it into the sore was excruciatingly painful. Jiggers gave us the feet of frogmen and exposed us to ridicule and shame. But my worst experience with fleas was yet to come.

One day while asleep, I heard fluttering in my ear. I turned my ear down in order to remove it. Instead of dropping off my ear, the flea went farther and farther inside, where it settled in some groove. The canal seemed too, too hot for the flea because as soon as it was there it started jumping up and down and in all other directions in search of some way out. By now I was already up and crying to Mum and Pap to help me remove the flea that was no longer a tiny insect but some monster that felt bigger than an elephant. As the flea jumped up and down inside my ear, I too cried and jumped hysterically with the whole world seeming to collapse upon me. Pap tried to suck the flea out of my ear by pressing a wet arm upon the ear like a suction pump but it did not draw the flea out. Liquid chicken fat was put into the ear in the belief that the flea might float or slide out of the ear. It did not work either. Finally at their wits' end, my parents had to rush me to the dispensary and wake up the sleeping medical orderly. With all the fleas in the village, the medical orderly seemed quite familiar with the problem. He took a syringe from his cupboard, filled it with water and powerfully pumped the water into the ear and drove the flea out. I felt more relieved than I had ever been before. My father too was relieved. He told the medical orderly that my experience had reminded him of the Swahili proverb *chura huua tembo,* a frog can kill an elephant.

Without getting any respite from rats and fleas, we were also plagued by bedbugs and lice. Bedbugs hid in the cracks of our beds and emerged from there to bite us at night. Lice bred in our hair and the folds of our clothes and blankets. We spent weekends boiling water to kill bedbugs and exposed our clothes to the tropical sun to kill them.

This then was our world and I can't say that I was very happy with it. When my moods were low, I would ask Mum:

Why do we live in a hut like this and not in a nice house like the ones white people live in?

Because the white man that is boss of the forest likes us to live in a hut like this.

Can't we refuse, Mum?

No, we cannot, she would say.

And why can't we eat bread, Mum? I would ask some other day.

We have no money, Son.

And why can't we eat *chapati*, meat and rice and drink tea with milk and sugar everyday? Eating bread, *chapati*, meat and rice is much better than eating *githeri* or *ugali* and drinking tea with milk and sugar is much better than drinking porridge with salt and bicarbonate of soda.

True, my mother would agree, but we have no money.

But, Mum, Why do you not have money? I would pursue to her great annoyance.

Because the white man does not like us to have more money, she would explain with exasperation.

Why does he not like us to have money? My mother would then explain without knowing for sure whether I understood or not:

When we lived on our own, we were *andu*, human beings. Since we started living with the whites, *nyakeru*, they are the *andu*, human beings, and we are their beasts of burden, *nyamu*, and slaves, *ngombo*. As their animals and slaves, they have decided our needs are less and don't require money. If they could, they would put us in sheep's pens, *ciugu*, and give us leaves to eat. To them the whiter you are the more money you should have and the better food you should eat. This is why we are the poorest and don't eat the meat and bread that white people eat, the *chapatis* that Indians eat or the rice that Arabs and Somali people eat.

But you could slaughter a sheep and a chicken for us or give us an egg more often, Mum?

I would like to, but if we eat our sheep, chickens and eggs, we cannot sell them and get money for your school fees and school uniforms, she answered. You see, the food we eat is not good but you can survive on it. Without education, you will never leave this goddamn place, you will probably not survive in this world or ever eat the good food that you lack and miss today. This is why we must sacrifice everything for your education. We must sacrifice everything to make sure that you are not stuck in this place as we are.

Many times I heard men and women in our village ask one another, Shall we ever pull ourselves out of here?

Backbreaking Work

To forest workers and their families, working in the forest was exactly like working in hell and their ultimate dream was to one day get out of there with their families. But looking at their condition realistically, they knew they had almost no chance of getting out. The best they could hope for was to get their children out of there through education, which they always talked of as a lifeline that only parents could weave for their children. There was nothing too precious to sacrifice for the education of the children. But if parents were ready to sacrifice their own lives for their children, they wanted them to sacrifice something for their education too. So life in the forest was not just one of the worst possible deprivations, it was also a life of hope that at least the children could use the ladder of deprivations and sacrifice to climb out of the colonial hell.

In the rainy season our world was like one big, cold hole with a roof of dark clouds from which heavy rain poured and poured until the ground became one big marsh and our roads turned into quagmires of mud and rivers of thick brown rainwater. When thousands and thousands of bare feet trod upon our wet earthen roads every minute of every day, the earthen roads were no longer roads but troughs of kneaded mud. Walking in these furrows was difficult and caked our feet with so much mud that we seemed to walk in plasters of mud that cracked when the sun struck and left the skin of our feet cracked and bleeding. Forever we were cold and wet. Without raincoats or warm clothes, we shivered and gnashed our teeth. Many times in the cold months of May, June, July and August, we walked to the gardens in thin rain, worked the whole day, ate cold and wet food and returned home in the same drizzle. When we played at home and went to and from school, it was in the same drizzle. In the afternoons, the cold drizzle would turn into a storm of hailstones that painfully pelted our unprotected heads.

In our forest village, children worked more than they played and sometimes just as hard as our parents did. When I was a toddler, my mother carried me to the garden to pluck the white farmer's coffee every day. Then she dug a small depression where I sat when she worked. There, I would play, giggle and eat soil alone. When I was too big for Mum to carry me to the garden and there was no one to look after me at home, my mother then arranged for me to go to the grazing fields with other children and look after our animals. When my brother came and he was too big to be carried to the gardens by Mother, it became my job to stay at home with him, feed him and in the meantime learn to draw water with a small gallon pail. By the time I went to school, I was an accomplished babysitter. In addition, I could draw water, feed my brother and sister, put our wet clothes into the sun and back into the house—generally look after the home when Father was at work and Mother was in the garden. Like all children, when we left school at noon I would have preferred to stay at home and play. But I could not do this. Instead I went to the nearby garden in the afternoon and worked there—planting, weeding and harvesting—until four. On the way home, I cut and carried a big bundle of fresh leaves for our animals.

When I came home, I had to draw water, cook, and, if my parents returned home very late at night from the far-off gardens, feed my brothers and sisters and put them to bed. Doing this work was, of course, not a pleasure and pleased me only when I saw my parents happy with what I had done.

If the work we did made our life a torment, the labor my parents did was the greater agony that created our own hell. Except on Sundays and for a few hours in the night, we were never with our parents. They were always at work. Father woke at four in the morning to go to work every day without breakfast, whether it was raining or not. By dawn he would be a long way from home, working. In the rainy season, his main work was carrying heavy boxes with seedlings on his back, digging holes, planting these young trees and covering them with soil. The planting of young trees was always done with rain pouring nonstop to ensure the trees did not dry out. But in rain, the boxes were very heavy and the planting was backbreaking. As forest workers did this work, they had no boots to protect their feet or raincoats to shield them from rain.

When Father was not planting, he was working in the tree nursery, filling boxes with topsoil, planting seedlings and feeding them with water which he had to carry in buckets all day long. Father's back was broken early by this repetitive and laborious work that he could only alternate with the equally difficult labor of pruning branches from growing trees in order to create space between rows and rows of trees. To prune trees, forest workers had no ladders and had to climb up the slippery tree trunks using their bare feet while they carried saws. They would climb up and down one tree and then move to another from before dawn to half past three in the afternoon, only resting during the brief half-hour lunch break at about one o'clock. Of all the work that my father did, pruning trees was the most dangerous. When accidents happened, no compensation was ever paid. And when injured workers were too crippled to work, they were simply sacked.

After three-thirty, my father did not come home to rest. He went to fell and burn trees, uproot stumps and clear bushes in the two-acre plots that he was given every two years in which to plant crops like potatoes, maize and beans. After two years, the plot was planted with young trees from which we had to clear weeds for another two years. Clearing huge chunks of original forests to be replanted with trees from Europe and cleaning weeds from young trees was the unpaid labor that my mother did from morning till evening. It was also the unpaid work my father did from three-thirty in the afternoon to nine at night and the unpaid work that all of us children did when we cleaned weeds from our food crops. It was the unpaid work that we could not say no to if we wanted to eat enough.

The final miserably paying work Father did for the Forest Department was putting out fires. To do this work, Father could be summoned any time of the night and be away from home for any number of days or even weeks. Forest workers were given no protective equipment and suffered many burns when putting out fires.

Altogether, Father put in more than thirty years of donkey work in the development of Bahati, Dundori, Kinari, Menengai and Elburgon forests and there is no corner of these woods whose soil has not absorbed his sweat, blood and tears.

Our donkey did not work as hard as Mum did. She and my father cut down the trees, cleared and burned the bushes and uprooted tree stumps before making holes into which she planted potatoes, maize, peas and cabbages in all our gardens. When the crops came up, she cleaned the weeds from them and from the young growing trees. Every day Mother would harvest a big basketful of potatoes, maize, beans and peas that she brought home on her back. Beneath the big basketful, sometimes Mother would carry a big bundle of firewood and either my young sister or brother, on her stomach suspended from a cloth pouch like a kangaroo. Before we were big enough, Mum would also draw water and cook all the food. Mother seemed tired all the time. In the garden, I often saw her lie down on a sisal bag and sleep for about an hour before getting up and continuing to work. By the time she got home, she would be so fatigued that she would sleep on her wooden stool while the food cooked. Many times she cooked but did not eat because she was so exhausted.

Queen UUU

As I grew bigger, my father was worried that doing too much domestic work like cooking, cleaning utensils, drawing water and peeling potatoes might make his sons effeminate. To stop this, my father ordered that my brother and I could only do work that was meant for men.

Among African communities, the division of labor between men and women is quite strict. For instance in my village, men were the only ones who were hired to work for the government. I never saw a single woman employed as a manual laborer with the Forest Department. The only job I saw women employed to do was teach.

Unemployable by the government, the only work that women could do was cook and work in the gardens and in the white man's coffee and pyrethrum plantations. At home, it was a woman's job to take care of everything. In other words, my father worked outside the home and my mother worked both outside and inside the home.

But it is not that men never cooked at all. My father was in fact an excellent cook but he only cooked for the white man. At home, he only cooked special dishes—like stuffed chicken—on special occasions like Christmas. But slaughtering animals, roasting, cooking and sharing meat was the absolute preserve of my father. My mother could only slaughter, cook and share chickens. While it was Mum who made tea, it was my father who cooked and treated soup with herbs and also shared it out. Similarly, it was my father's work to prepare and share out traditional beer, *muratina*. My father could not make tea and my mother could not prepare beer.

In keeping with this division of labor, it was my father's duty to look after the animals, take them out to graze and cut leaves for them. It was also his duty to fatten the rams that were fed inside the pen. It was his job to dig the foundation of all our huts and build their walls and erect their roofs. Once the structures were ready, my mother took over and plastered the walls with kneaded mud and thatched the roof with grass. The only work I remember my Mother and Father doing without a hint of whose job it was, was weeding, planting and harvesting.

Subsequently my father gave my mother instructions that I was no longer to draw water. If he found me drawing water, he poured it out. He instructed that I was no longer to peel potatoes or cook. If he found me peeling potatoes or cooking food, he immediately stopped me. In the meantime, I was to help my father fetch leaves for our rams. He also taught me how to prepare traditional beer. He gave me as much practice as he could in slaughtering a sheep into parts for roasting, boiling and so forth. I was also taught to pick the right herbs for soup and how to beat the soup with a *kibiri,* a stick fitted at one end with a vertebral bone, until it was a most palatable mix.

While my mother had no objection to my knowing how to do the men's work, she thought the arrangement completely unworkable and impractical given our special circumstances. Because I was big enough, she insisted that I should help in drawing water, peeling potatoes, cooking food for my brothers and sisters and washing utensils when both my mother and my father were late coming home from the garden. She argued that it was not anybody's fault that I had not been born a girl or that she had to work so late. She did not agree that cooking or working in the home would make me effeminate when doing the same work for the white man had not made my father so. She thought it unfair that I should sit at home doing nothing after school merely because I am a boy and wait for her to do all the work when she came home late in the night. After all, she argued, learning to do all work in the home would stand me in good stead when I started to live alone later in life. But my father was obstinate and many times threatened to fight over the issue. For him, it was a matter of honor and he could not afford to lose face among other men. I did not even have a choice in the matter.

Finally my mother left and temporarily went to live in the home and seek the help of our uncle (our young father) who tried to intervene. Later my mother sought the help of her parents. My father went to her parents' home to try to bring her back. But my mother could not come back without a proper resolution of the dispute. Finally my father was convinced that the difficult and particularly oppressive circumstances under which we lived did not permit the kind of training he intended for his sons. It was agreed that since my sisters were small, I had to do the work they would have done had they been bigger. In the changing times, my father was also convinced that sons and daughters were equal, and sons were not children of the stomach and daughters children of the back. When Mother and Father returned home, my father was a changed man who took his daughters and sons as equals and no longer objected to our doing any kind of work. But after conceding the equality of his sons and daughters, did my father also concede equality between him and Mum? No, he did not. He continued to take himself as the head of the home and my mother did not even challenge my father's leadership of our family. There can be no family without a man at the head, she said.

In Gikuyu country, at times prejudice against women runs so deep that one old man told me that women are an enemy tribe whom men must always guard against. This man told me that once women ruled the Gikuyu society, and their queen was called UUU. The man also told me that Gikuyu women derived their leadership of the men from the fact that the founding father and mother of the Gikuyu people, Gikuyu and Mumbi, only had nine daughters and no sons. When the nine daughters of Gikuyu and Mumbi got young men—offered from God— to marry them, they did not surrender the leadership of the Gikuyu society to their husbands. Instead the nine daughters became the foundation and heads of the nine Gikuyu clans that make up the Gikuyu community to this day.

With the clans of the community headed by women, families were led by women, children and properties were owned by women and the whole community was ruled by a queen. In this community, the old man told me that men were just slaves and breeders who owned nothing and were treated very badly. Then came the era of Queen UUU and women became so brutal in their rule that men conspired to overthrow them by making them all pregnant. When they were all pregnant, men everywhere attacked and overthrew the government of Queen UUU. As men attacked women, women everywhere called out "UUU," asking her to send help. To this day, women still cry out "UUU" when they are under attack.

His story illustrated to me how deeply men feel threatened by the power of women and how hard they are determined to fight to keep women down. When this man talked about women, he gave me no impression that he was talking about his mother, the mother of his children, his sisters, his aunts, his daughters and fellow human beings to whom he owed his love, because they, too, had given him much love.

Hirizi

To be quite honest, when the question of gender inequality was being fought over, I was on my father's side because I wanted to do less work. It is only now that I see how unfair it was to my mother. But the way the question was resolved, I had more work to do and felt more deprived. But, however deprived, there were two things that both my mother and my father strictly forbade my brothers and sisters and me to do. Never steal and never beg.

In our village there was an open market every Sunday when people sold and bought all kinds of foodstuffs from our forest and outlying areas—maize, potatoes, bananas, salt, cabbages, arrowroots, sugarcanes and many other things. Although the market was not far from home, we often got very hungry when we were there.

One day I was walking home from the market when I felt very hungry. In front of me, was a man eating sugarcane and dropping the remains of the chewed sugarcane as he went along. As I followed him, I picked these remains and chewed them a second time for whatever little juice they could still yield. As I did this, someone saw me and reported me to my father.

When I got home my father was very angry. Right away he asked me: Who bought you the sugarcane that you have been chewing on your way home?

Nobody, Pap, I answered.

But I see that you have eaten some sugarcane, he said while looking around for something with which to beat me. Have you forgotten that I told you never to beg or steal?

No, Pap, I said.

Grabbing me with his big arm he said, Picking and chewing sugarcane remains is worse than either stealing or begging. Would you have died before you got home? Why do you shame us so?

I was thoroughly thrashed, taken to the market and bought a long sugarcane that I had to eat until it was finished.

Both my father and my mother did not believe that lack alone could turn us into thieves or beggars. They believed one can be poor, upright and dignified. But if they hated picking sugarcane remains, they hated begging even more, as I would soon learn. And our parents forbade us to beg by using either words or eyes.

One day I had again gone to the shopping center that we called *mung'etho,* where the Sunday market used to be. There some friends and I saw a white man for the first time and drawn by curiosity approached to see him better—his white skin, his long nose, his lack of color on the skin, his horselike hair and his different clothes. While all the grownups seemed scared, wary and afraid to get close to the white man, we were not, just curious. To the consternation of black men who stood around unable to stop us, we fearlessly got as close as we could to the white man, stopping just short of touching him. The white man was drinking a soda and seeing us looking up at him thought we were begging him to give us the soda he was drinking. He gave us the one he was drinking and bought another one. Unconscious of any implications, my friends and I took the soda and drunk it. Word soon reached home that other boys and I had begged a soda from the white man. When I arrived home, I found my father waiting for me. As soon as I was home, Pap shut the door behind me and asked me why I had begged a soda from the white man. I told him the truth that though I had drunk the soda, I had not looked at the white man for his soda but only wanted to see how he looked more closely. My explanation was not convincing, and I got my due beating.

Afterward, Pap said he wanted me to take him to the forest to harvest honey from one of his hives. I loved honey and accepted my father's offer with alacrity though I could tell that he was trying to make up to me somewhat. My father took with him his honey bag, a matchbox and a transparent plastic bag punctured with holes. When we arrived at the place where the hive was, a reasonable distance from the tree that carried the hive, my father lit a fire. With the fire he lit a very smoky torch, asked me to stay where I was and not to move; he took his honey bag, put his head into the punctured plastic bag and left. Half an hour later, he returned with his honey bag full of honey and put it down. He then moved to a nearby tree and removed a big piece of bark. When he came back, he sat down and put some honey on the piece of tree bark and welcomed me to a feast of honey.

As we ate honey, my father told me that his first European employer loved to go to the Kenyan coast with him as his cook:

Once there, he would get on a big boat and sail out into the big waters, *baharini.* Other times he would cross the ocean to Unguja, Zanzibar. In the middle of the big sea, I saw no land, and I always thought we were lost. The white man would then take a small round object that Swahili people called a *dira,* compass. The *dira* had four arrows that pointed to the north, south, east and west. Whenever the white man looked at his *dira,* it told him where we were and how to get back to the dry land. It was an oracle. When the white man died, he passed the *dira* to his son, who never went to the sea like his father.

Like the white man and his son, I too want to give you something that I would like you to always keep. It is a *hirizi,* or talisman, that I bought from a Chinese merchant on one of our journeys to Unguja. As you can see, it is a very expensive piece of wood. The Chinese told me it is for protection, luck and direction in our journey here on earth. But it has no arrows like the white man's compass.

On it was drawn the picture of a happy smiling human face. I asked Pap what the face meant and he told me humanity, *umundu:*

This *hirizi* will always remind you that you are a human being. When you look at it, you will always find your way around the world. It will be your compass. You may think you need no reminder that you are a human being but many times we forget, as white colonialists have, and lose our values and behave beastly with one another. The face on this *hirizi* is not yours. It is a face you see in everyone. It will remind you that you share humanity with others. Whenever you look at it, remember that your humanity is like a small stream, it adds to and draws from the ocean of collective humanity. The beauty of humanity is that it is bountiful. To it, we give in drops. From it, we receive in bucketfuls. And don't forget its smile. It makes all the difference. I want you to always wear this *hirizi* as my employer carried his compass. Never put it down. In humanity, you can never lose your way. Take it as my gift to you. If it helps you, pass it on to your children.

Before I wore it, I asked, Pap, I hear a *hirizi* protects people against death; will it protect me from dying too? Yes, it will protect you from spiritual and moral death but not against the physical death that we all die every minute we live. That death is part of life. When you live, you die.

You cannot be protected against it. But since we die by living, we should not fear death any more than we do life. You cannot avoid death when its time has come, so, don't even think about it. Just live. The only evil this *hirizi* will protect you from is the spiritual and moral rot that kills us by making us less human.

Thank you, Pap. I wore the *hirizi* around my neck and we returned home. It is funny, but whenever I looked at the *hirizi,* I felt better and happier. Then one day, its string broke and I lost it. I came home and told Pap that I had lost it.

Where did you lose it?

I don't know, Pap. We went looking for it but never found it.

What do you feel now? he asked me.

Bad, I said.

Then don't lose your humanity. Without it, you will always feel bad.

I don't know where my father went but one day he brought me another talisman, with the same human face on it. When he gave it to me, he said, Don't lose this again. You cannot do without it. In life, you shall need a smiling face to get by. Wear it both on your neck and in your heart. If lost, never forget it.

Hares and Foxes

One day I went to my father and asked, Pap, Why does the white forest officer always look down when somebody looks at him?

Have you been looking at him again? Did I not tell you not to look at grownup people in the face? It is bad manners.

I was not looking him in the face, I said, it is just that I saw that every time somebody looked at him, he always looked down or the other way.

Have you not heard that when you want to kill a monkey, you do not look him in the face?

Why, Pap?

If you look at him in the face you will not have the strength to kill him. You hunt monkeys. Have you not been overwhelmed with compassion, trying to kill them?

Yes, I have, they look like human beings.

To kill human beings, you suppress your compassion by looking the other way, Father concluded.

In the village people compared and talked of other people and even themselves in animal terms. Some people—black and white—were called hawks, others leopards, some hares, while stupid and lazy ones were called *ngombe*, cattle, and *kondoo*, sheep. When we asked for anything that our parents could only give us with great sacrifice, Pap liked to say they were mother warthogs, and we were puppy warthogs.

Why? I would ask.

Do you know what a warthog does when its puppies are hungry? Father would ask back.

It gives them milk.

When the milk is not enough?

I don't know, Pap.

It runs very fast and rams itself hard against a huge oak tree, shaking it violently to bring down the acorns. The mother warthog then collapses and sometimes dies from the collision, but the puppies eat the acorns and live on.

After this I would quickly withdraw my difficult requests to my parents.

Another time Pap told me that the colonial settlers were *ndia nyama*, meat-eating animals, and Africans were *ndia nyeki*, grass-eating animals. At school each morning, our headmaster would roar like a lion and ask, When the lion roars, who dares to play with him? Of course, none of us poor pupils would.

Pap, however, told me that the British were the real lions. They came to Kenya as such:

Once upon a time, there was a heavy thunderstorm in a forest where an African man had built a little hut for his family. While the family warmed themselves by the fire, a lion came knocking at the door.

My good man, will you please let me put my head inside your door and shelter it from the torrential rain?

The man said yes. My dear white lion, my hut is very small, but there is room for your head and my family. Please let your head inside gently.

You have done me a good deed, said the lion in gratitude. One day I shall return your kindness. What followed was far from kind. As soon as the lion put his head inside, he snarled, bared his teeth and claws and flung the man, his wife and a few children out in the rain. He then lay down comfortably while making himself a meal of the rest of the man's children. To add insult to injury the white lion told the African man, Since God has been very generous and given you many children, you can return the favor, and give me some of them. I will rear, Christianize and deliver them to heaven for you.

I asked Pap whether the man had any chance of ever saving himself from the lion, given its formidable strength and ferocity. He said he had: Nothing that treads on earth cannot be trapped, *ng'enda thi ndiagaga mutegi*. I did not pursue the issue, yet it was not clear how man could trap a lion. One day, I came home from hunting carrying a bundle of meat wrapped in leaves.

What did you catch today? Pap asked.

A small hare.

You should not kill hares. They might save the African man from the lion.

How, Pap? I asked.

Here is the story of Miss Doe. It might answer your question:

One day, Mr. Hare was walking about in the woods. Suddenly he appeared where Miss Doe was arguing with Mr. Leopard. But Miss Doe was not arguing in freedom; she was pleading for her life under the paws of Mr. Leopard whom she accused of treachery. When Miss Doe saw Mr. Hare she called out and asked him to stop and listen to her case. When Mr. Hare stopped, Miss Doe was quick to explain her case to him: "Mr. Hare, listen. I just saved Mr. Leopard. He was caught up in this trap here. I was passing by when he pleaded with me to save him. No sooner was he safe than he pounced upon me. Instead of thanking me, he now wants to eat me up. Is this fair?"

"Mr. Leopard, is what Miss Doe here says true?" Mr. Hare asked.

"Yes, it is true," Mr. Leopard said.

"Why then do you want to eat your friend Miss Doe, if it is true that she saved you?"

"Because I am so hungry. If I don't eat her I am going to die."

"Then I don't believe Miss Doe saved you. Mighty animals like you are not in the habit of being saved by weaker animals like does and hares," Mr. Hare insisted.

"Well, it is true that I was saved by Miss Doe."

"How? This trap looks too small for you. Can you return in it for me to see how you were saved?"

"Yes." And Mr. Leopard walked into the trap again.

Once Mr. Leopard was back in the trap, Mr. Hare asked Miss Doe, "Did you find him in the trap exactly like that?"

"Yes," she said.

"Do you want to save him from the trap a second time?" asked Mr. Hare.

"No," Miss Doe said most emphatically.

"Come then, let us go our way. Never take out of a trap one who is himself a trap, else you end up in the belly of the trap yourself," Mr. Hare advised her.

"But you cannot leave me in the trap!" protested Mr. Leopard. "You must free me before you go. I only returned into the trap for demonstration. How can you take my freedom and life away from me again? I was already free when you came."

"True," said Mr. Hare, "but you deserve neither freedom nor salvation. Who will save you when your gratitude is to eat up whoever saves you? If you die, it is because the ungrateful deserve to die when their intention is to thank their saviors with death. Good-bye and good luck."

After the story, Pap added, here the leopard was trapped with intelligence. If intelligence does not work, force does. Meat-eaters do not have a monopoly on violence.

Lions are the most powerful animals on earth. How can any other animal beat them? Son, Father said, the eater can also be eaten. He told me another story:

One day, Mrs. Leopard stole an entire antelope from Mrs. Fox, thereby causing her young ones to starve to death. For this, Mrs. Fox swore to avenge herself against Mrs. Leopard. Once her young ones were dead, Mrs. Fox swallowed her pride and went to Mrs. Leopard to ask for work. "For a little meat, can I take care of your cubs when you are gone to hunt?"

"Sure," replied Mrs. Leopard without shame. "I was just looking for someone like you, when you showed up! But to work for me, you must be a very kind animal to my cubs. I require you to be this because they cry a lot when I am not around. If you do your job well, you can be sure that what I get, we will eat together." And off she went to hunt, leaving her cubs behind with Mrs. Fox.

Moments later, Mrs. Fox went into Mrs. Leopard's lair and found all her ten cubs sleeping. Immediately, she grabbed one and ate it. When Mrs. Leopard was back, she asked Mrs. Fox to bring the cubs to her for suckling. Mrs. Fox took eight cubs to be suckled once, but the ninth one twice for suckling. Through this deception, Mrs. Leopard thought she had suckled all her ten cubs. Grateful, she gave a piece of meat to Mrs. Fox.

The following day when Mrs. Leopard went to hunt, Mrs. Fox ate another of her cubs. When Mrs. Leopard returned and asked for her cubs, she was brought six, whom she suckled once, and two, whom she suckled twice. Grateful, she gave a big piece of meat to Mrs. Fox again.

On the third day, when Mrs. Leopard was again gone to hunt, Mrs. Fox ate the third cub. When Mrs. Leopard was back, she was given four cubs to suckle once, and three cubs to suckle twice. Grateful once more, she gave Mrs. Fox a bigger chunk of meat to eat.

Even as the pieces of meat she was getting from Mrs. Leopard were getting bigger and bigger every day, finally Mrs. Fox ate all of Mrs. Leopard's cubs. When Mrs. Leopard asked where her cubs were, Mrs. Fox replied sarcastically, "You ate up all your cubs and then ask me to bring them to you?" and ran away.

Mrs. Leopard was furious. She ran after Mrs. Fox. Just before Mrs. Fox was caught, she said to Mrs. Leopard while pointing to a place that had many bees teeming and buzzing around it. "Your cubs are in that hole over which all those bees are hovering. The buzzing is from your cubs. They are in a school in there. Listen carefully and you will hear them singing."

As Mrs. Leopard was listening, Mr. Baboon came along and asked her what she was doing. She said she was listening to her cubs sing. Mr. Baboon said he would like to see Mrs. Leopard's cubs.

To let Mr. Baboon see her cubs, Mrs. Leopard started digging into the hole where the bees had their hive. Angry and furious at this unwarranted attack on their hive, the bees came out and savagely attacked Mrs. Leopard. She ran away but was chased by the bees into a nearby river where Mrs. Leopard immersed herself. Whenever she tried to put her head out of water, bees would be there to sting her back into the water until she finally drowned. That is how the weak, the oppressed and the seemingly powerless can overcome the strong.

A Childhood Nightmare

In our village, there were good reasons to consider fear taboo. Living on the edge of a forest and having to travel to the gardens and back home through thick and dark woodland, we always came into contact with wild animals. The most feared was *ngari,* the leopard.

Leopards are extremely fast, shy and efficient killers that keep hidden in the forest. They have a reputation for attacking only when hungry or threatened. Because they stay out of sight and do not attack unless necessary, leopards sometimes hide in bushes or high up in trees with thick branches near forest paths, from where they like to watch people who walk nearby. I particularly remember one spot near a village called Kandurumu, where I could not pass late in the evening without my hair standing on end, because a leopard always hid nearby. Not infrequently, I felt so frozen with fear that I did not know whether I should run or stand still.

Once in the middle of the night, this leopard escorted my father and me to the Kandurumu village by walking beside us in the bush from where it appeared until we entered the village. A well fed leopard was never known to eat people. But when we heard it, my hair stood on end and I grabbed by father's arm. Calmly he asked me not to fear and we walked on. As we walked, the leopard would playfully put its long tail on our path to test whether we had the impertinence to step on it. I have always wondered whether the leopard laughed at our cowardice when we did not step on its tail out of fear. After we passed it, the leopard would continue to walk beside us making a cracking noise as it stepped on dry leaves and broke dry twigs. Two or three times, it put its tail on our path and each time we avoided the tail as we would leprosy. Finally, we entered the village gate and our escort returned to the forest. By the time we reached home, I was frozen with the fear of our uninvited escort.

I did not encounter leopards only when I went into the forest. Since we lived on the edge of the forest, oftentimes leopards came to our home to steal sheep. They would wait until the entire village was asleep and silent. They would then approach huts like our own, which were on the edge of the forest, jump over the high fence that enclosed the village, take one sheep and jump with it back over the fence, escaping into the forest. Knowing how dangerous leopards were, Pap would shout threateningly and beat *sufurias,* cooking pots, together to scare the beast, but would not challenge it alone. The following morning we would follow the tracks, which usually led us to the tree where the leopard had hoisted the sheep to drink its blood, eat its inner organs and abandon the rest. Because of its reputation for cat-like cleanliness, eating an animal that leopards had ravished was not considered unclean. When we found our dead sheep, we would bring it down, take it home, slaughter it properly and eat it. Often we had leopards to thank for the rare occasions when we ate meat.

One day, a leopard was spotted at the place called Kangari—the place of leopards. When told, an adventurous young white forest officer decided to kill it. He drove to the spot, armed with a gun and surrounded by African forest guards who carried spears and machetes.All the people gathered to watch the spectacle. By now the leopard was forewarned by the presence of the people who gathered at the foot of the wooded cluster. It became particularly alert when the forest officer and his entourage of armed guards approached its tree. As the officer positioned himself to shoot, the leopard took cover among the branches with the thickest foliage. While the officer repositioned himself where he could best see the animal, the leopard leaped and landed squarely, knocking him to the ground. He was an agile man who quickly grabbed its forefeet and started wrestling with it, while enduring vicious cuts from the claws of its hind feet. They rolled and rolled over each other so fast that for some time the guards with spears dared not stab, for fear of striking the officer. The leopard then gained the upper hand and pinned its prey. While the animal's hind feet immobilized the man, he managed to keep a firm grip on its forelegs, which he held away from himself, together with its head and sharp teeth. The leopard tried to rip his face and neck. But the failure of the man's strength proved to be his salvation. With the leopard's whole body now exposed, it was easy for the guards to approach and spear the animal to death. As the village cheered, the forest officer, who was now unconscious, was put into a Land Rover and taken to the hospital while the leopard's carcass was deposited at the forest office. After recovery, people called the forest officer *Kangari*. His image, bleeding with the snarling leopard held up over his chest and head, never left my consciousness.

For many years thereafter, every time I had a nightmare, it was of a leopard running to catch me against the slippery, steep slope of a red sandy hill where we played, over which I could never climb. A friend would be kneeling at the top, extending his hand out to me. I would frantically try to get over the hill, while all the time sliding backward on the sand. As the leopard got closer and closer to catching me, I would surprisingly yell out, not to my friend, but to my mother, "Maaaaaaaaaaaami, save me." I would suddenly awaken, panting and sweating with fright, only to discover how lucky I was. It was a bad dream. Mum would hold me close and reassure me, "Don't cry, Son, you are safe. It was only a dream." I would fall asleep again in her arms.

Eking Out a Happiness

In my childhood, the forest was not just a source of leopards, fears and nightmares. It was also a source of freedom and many of my childhood pleasures. As I said earlier, I hated going to the forest to cut leaves for our sheep, but I loved going to the forest to hunt for all kinds of small animals like rabbits, antelopes and dik-diks, duikers, hares, sunis, wild pigs and tree hyraxes. And while I loved to go hunting for meat with grownups, I loved more going to hunt animals with my friends and our dogs. Nothing gave me more pleasure than going to hunt in the afternoons and on weekends. Chasing animals at breakneck speeds with our dogs and finally catching our prey gave us real pleasure. After catching our prey, if it was a dik-dik or a suni, we would immediately slaughter it, take out its *ini* or liver and eat it while it was still warm. In the evenings, we would wrap up our meat and take it to one of the homes of the bigger boys. Later in the night, we would all gather in the hut of the leading boy, who would be the son of one of the head *nyapara*, overseers. In his hut, we would not be interfered with, and we would roast our meat and eat it.

In one such a hut, the leader boy had built a second floor for his bed and a staircase to ascend there. The meat would be roasted in the fire below according to his instructions and divided as he ordered. Usually he would take all the best parts, order his friends to take their share and then ask the rest of us to fight for the remaining parts. For greater fun, he would order the fire to be put out when we scrambled for the meat that was still in the fire. I remember once, when we fought over this meat, the brother of the big boy was pushed into the fire and got no meat. When he cried, his brother ordered that all of us return the meat we had taken and hit us each with a thick stick on our open arms. Fearing to lose what I had managed to get, I put it in the pocket of my shirt and then hid it in the sand when they started searching our pockets. Later I took it from the sand, wiped it off and ate it.

Though hunting animals was a joyous activity for us, our parents hated it because it made us bad boys. I would avoid going to the garden to go and hunt. I would avoid going to Sunday school to go and hunt. If I could, I would also avoid going to school to go hunt. I would even abandon looking after my young brothers and sisters to go hunt. But our friend Kung'u was prepared to do even worse to create time to hunt. One day we found him looking after his baby brother while his mother weeded in the garden. We told him we were going to hunt and asked him to come with us. He told us he was looking after his baby-brother but we could wait for him if we went ahead a little into the forest. We did. Shortly afterwards we heard the baby-brother screaming as if he was drowning and Kung'u's mother cursing Kung'u like hell. Kung'u came where we were in great speed while looking over his shoulders. We asked him what had happened. He told us that he had tried to suffocate his baby-brother to death but the little brat alerted the mother by screaming. We asked him why he could not have quietly stolen himself from the garden, but he said that he did not think of it. We then went hunting. Before we had gone very far, I was myself caught in the leg and thrown into the air by a trap that was meant for a big antelope. Fortunately the trap was made with a sisal rope instead of a wire string, otherwise my leg would have been broken in two.

As our hunting companions, we loved our dogs immensely. And there was hardly a home with a boy without a dog. To show our appreciation, when a dog killed an animal, we gave it the hind leg of that animal and its owner, the biggest share of the meat. Boys were so close to their dogs that they went with them everywhere.

One of my friends was named Gichohi wa Mwari. He had a dog called Tommi. One day when we were hunting, a wild pig cut open the stomach of this dog. Gichohi looked at Tommi and cried. Less experienced with dogs, I gave Tommi up for dead but Gichohi did not. He stripped the bark of a tree and made a thread from its fibers, quickly fashioned a wooden needle and then sewed together the torn stomach. He carried Tommi home on his back while we carried the meat. At home Gichohi took such great care of Tommi that he recovered fully and went back to hunting as before.

Gichohi was not the only boy whom I saw cry for his dog. Another boy's dog was shot dead by colonial administrative police who threw him into a ditch. The boy who owned the dog sat by the ditch and cried for his dog until the colonial police apologized to him and begged him to leave.

Although dogs did not stay in the huts with people, they were considered part of the family. There was therefore real sadness when a family dog was ill. Many a time, I saw mother nursing our ailing dog with almost the same care she gave us— giving him the food we ate, covering him with a blanket and taking him to a veterinary doctor. When monkeys and apes were eating maize in the gardens, it was our dogs that chased them away while we slept. When we stayed in our garden shelters, *ithunu,* that shielded us from cold and rain, it was the dogs that barked at the thieving monkeys. They also guarded our homes against thieves.

Those were our dogs. Others' dogs were not so useful. When we went to the farms of white people we not only met people who said they were different from us, we also met dogs that were completely different from our dogs. They were much bigger than our dogs. They were better fed and were a lot fiercer than our dogs, just as the Swahili proverb says: The dog of a fierce hunter is also fierce. In fact, white settlers' dogs were not only better fed than our dogs, they were also better fed than us Africans. But the thing that frightened us most about these dogs was that while we hunted animals with our dogs, white settlers hunted black people with theirs. Anytime I saw a white colonialist with a dog, I saw two enemies against whom I could not defend myself.

Because I could not defend myself against the white settlers' dogs, each time I saw a white settler with one, I made straight for the bush. When the white man walked about with his dogs around his farm, he carried a gun. When he and the dogs met a black person, he would stop him and sadistically enjoy the fear in his eyes. And sometimes the white man would go even further and set his dogs on the passerby and enjoy the fight and screams of his victim. And woe to the African who would dare to fight back against the white settler's dog, because he would stand accused, be tried, and executed on the spot.

For Pap, all creatures deserved our kindness. He could not stomach anyone who was cruel to our dogs and donkeys. Once during a busy harvest season, I was asked to escort our donkey home while it was loaded with two sacks of potatoes. Because we needed to return to the garden for another trip, I tried to hurry the donkey. Overloaded, however, it could go no faster. Foolishly, I cut its behind with a small machete that I had, thinking that cutting it might make it move faster. It did not. Instead the blood attracted some tsetse flies to the donkey, bit it and made the donkey stop in order to chase away the attacking flies with its tail. To hide my crime, I smeared the wound with wet mud. When we returned to the garden, Father discovered my mischief, which I tried to deny. He smacked me with a warning never to do it again: What has this donkey done to you? It did not kick you or insult you, why did you cut it? Can't you see that hurting this donkey is the same as hurting yourself? Where would we be without it? Can your mother or you or I take home all the potatoes that this donkey takes home everyday? Never, never again hurt him.

When we were not in the forest to hunt for animals, we were there to gather all kinds of wild fruit; the most popular was a fruit called *ngoe*. The fruit is a green berry but changes into blue when it is ripe. *Ngoes* have a lot of sweet juice and are very nice to eat. Again, our parents hated our going to the forest to gather fruit because it made us disobedient. It was also a dangerous activity; many of us did not see this until it was too late.

Ngugi's mother cursed her son when we went to ask her to go and fetch her son from the forest where he had fallen from a very high tree: Uuuuuu, don't tell me about it. Let him die where he is but don't come and tell me about it when you did not tell me that you were going there. How many times must we forbid you little devils going to climb those high trees? Let him break his legs if he will. Ngugi could not walk and we could not touch him because he screamed like hell.

At about three in the afternoon, we had gone to the forest to gather and eat fruit. I suffer from the fear of heights and never climbed any tree to collect the best fruit. I contented myself with eating those that had fallen. That afternoon all those boys who could climb had gone up a tree that had big and fully ripe berries. We had a very good time until Ngugi got on a tree that hosted a hive of bees and disturbed them. As they started to fly about, other boys climbed down the tree very fast, but Ngugi stayed on a branch using one arm to cover his head with his shirt and the other arm to hold on to the branch he sat on. One boy made the mistake of throwing a stone at the hive. That drove the bees mad. They came buzzing all over Ngugi, whom they mistook for the attacker. As they flew about, some stung his exposed back, forcing him to lower his shirt and cover his back. When he lowered the shirt, he uncovered his head and the bees went for it. In the process of playing this hide-and-seek game, one bee saw the exposed hand that was holding the branch and quickly stung it, forcing Ngugi to release his grip. That made him fall down the tree, hitting the ground with a heavy thud. He shrieked with pain and began to groan. Instinctively, his young brother also screamed in fear and shared his pain. We knew something was terribly wrong because he would not let anyone touch him. It was then that we rushed home to call his mother.

When we returned to the spot where Ngugi was lying, his mother was still cursing and wishing him the worst. But when she tried to turn and carry him, his broken bones cracked as the pieces fell apart. The same mother who had—in fear, I guess—wished that Ngugi could break his legs as a lesson, now screamed hysterically: "Uuui, Uuui. Please God, don't take my Ngugi from me. Uuui, Uuuui." She carried Ngugi home. We trooped behind until they reached their house. Later Ngugi was taken to the hospital where his broken legs were plastered.

Despite the tragic fall of Ngugi, we never stopped going to the forest to look for fruit. I guess this was because our bodies needed them. In our godforsaken forest village, it was not just fruit and meat that our bodies needed and lacked. Our spirits needed pleasure, but it was almost nowhere available legitimately. So we got it legitimately where we could and illegitimately where we could not.

It is funny that although our parents and everyone else taught us that sex was evil and forbidden by both tradition and Christianity, as early as I can remember, whenever we took our sheep to graze alone without grownups, one thing boys and girls always did was play father and mother with one another. Usually the bigger boys and girls would start the game and then bring us into it to seal our mouths against disclosure. Once I had tasted the game, it did not merely silence me. It also made me look forward to taking our animals to graze. I guess the mistake of tradition and Christianity was to forbid one kind of play for the boys and girls without substituting another.

There was even one girl who was bigger and so active at playing mother that boys would stand in a queue to play father with her in turns. Standing next to her, one of her cousins kept track of time while all the boys got lost in their pleasure. This illegitimate escapade did not last long. It stopped as soon as we quit taking our animals to graze and joined school. Once in school, my other sources of pleasure were sliding on grassy slopes with very smooth timber sliders and rolling down hills on handmade carts with four wheels and a string for a steering wheel. We engaged in these activities during the dry season when the ground and the grass were dry and slick. During the rainy season when the ground was wet and slippery with mud, we put our heels in grooves of rainwater and slid down the slopes with great speed.

My last childhood pleasure came from watching both traditional and European dances that old people took part in. To make heavy work light, young women and young men used to work in gangs moving from one garden to another. While working, they sang and laughed, often lifting and dropping their hoes to the rhythm of the song. In the evening, the person for whom they had been working would prepare a lot of tea and food for the women and traditional beer for the men. All the tea and the beer would then be drunk as the men and women sang and danced traditional songs and dances. Of course, these songs and dances were not for children like us but only for men and women who were circumcised. But they were beautiful to watch and listen to, and small boys especially would suffer great inconveniences like cold just trying to watch.

As we grew bigger, we bought small mouth organs that we played in our own dances, which were only rarely graced with the presence of girls. For lack of girls and guitars, our dances never seemed as good as others, and we only resorted to them because we could not go to the others.

Ujima

One who eats alone dies alone, *muria wiki akuaga wiki,* so says a Gikuyu proverb. One who refuses to cooperate with others is a witch, *mkataa kikoa ni mchawi,* says a Swahili proverb.

Today I live in a European neighborhood where I don't say hello to my next-door neighbor. Similarly, in Nairobi, African elite neighbors never say hello to one another and live in houses that are enclosed behind high walls with spiked iron gates that are guarded by fierce dogs, *mbwa kali.*

Before this intrusion by Western civilization, Gikuyu tradition decreed that society could not survive without socialization. It made people different from animals. People did not talk only to friends or those they knew. When one met a visitor, the greeting took a long time and sometimes ended in the visitor's being invited home. Among the Gikuyu, greeting meant full identification. One person would ask, How are you?

I am fine and you?

I am fine.

My name is Njoroge wa Kamau, what is yours?

My name is Koigi wa Wamwere. I come from Githunguri Kia Wairera, from the clan of Wambui and house of Kuria. At home, everyone is fine. I am on my way to visit my brother Kuria wa Wamwere who lives at Engoshura...

By the time the greeting was over, the visitor would have identified himself as a man of peace and sometimes a relative. In that case, he would not be allowed to travel but would be invited to share a meal and to stay for the night. Even today the inclination to converse is still alive among our people. But it has suffered serious inroads from European culture, which discourages openness with strangers.

In our village, not greeting another person was unthinkable. People said, Greetings are not sold, they are free, *ngeithi itiendagio.* Not smiling at another person was unforgivable, so much so that people used to say, the tooth smiles at a spear, *igego rithekagia itimu,* meaning that even an enemy is smiled at. Among our people, walking in the same direction with another person and not talking was considered rude. Even today, common people do not travel in a bus without talking. People did not do all this merely in order to pay homage to some old customs, but because talking, greeting and smiling were the natural things to do. One needed absolutely no reason to talk, greet or smile at another.

For instance, despite oppression, hard work and things we could not change, people did things together, not because our ancestors had lived communally or ruled that people should live cooperatively. They did so because living and working in such a way made their burdens lighter and often gave them real happiness. By living and working together, people made difficult things easy. In our village, people believed living means sharing, working, talking, visiting, eating, celebrating, creating, suffering and mourning together.

Accordingly, our neighbors were people we visited without appointment, who took us in when our parents were not home, and with whom we shared food, sugar and salt. We always responded to each other's calls for help. How could people have neighbors they did not talk to or call upon when in need? When neighbors could not talk or visit with one another, it was time to move on. When our neighbors had visitors, our parents always went to greet them and took tea and food to them.

Under colonialism, except on very special occasions, Father hardly ever slaughtered any of our few sheep. When he did, it was unthinkable to slaughter without inviting our neighbors and friends from the farthest corner of our village. My parents could never buy or brew beer to drink alone. It was always shared with friends and neighbors. Nor could a passerby be denied food and drink if he came into our home at mealtime.

Our family gardens, *migunda,* were about ten miles away from home. There was no greater torture than walking there, working and coming home alone. The torture was transformed into joy the moment I had the company of friends. Travel to these far-off gardens became pleasurable by racing other boys. Fortunately, since fathers and mothers wanted to talk in freedom, they never asked us boys to walk with them. This gave us freedom to run and say what we wanted in these long journeys.

But it was not just going to the gardens that was made light by company. Women and girls went to fetch firewood and water in the forest together. Work in the gardens was done together by groups of men and women, young and old. I never looked forward to work except when we had group work, *ngwatio* in Gikuyu, or *ujima* in Swahili. Then, work became a festival where people worked with song, laughter, rhythm and great speed. At night, these workers would gather in the hut of the beneficiary of the day's work to eat, drink, dance, laugh and while the night away. If you saw us, you never would have guessed that we were a colonized people.

People did not come together only to work, drink, eat and make merry. They were never too busy to visit a sick neighbor, feed his children, fetch water, firewood and food or cook for him. They did these things with the same happy heart with which they helped one another and did their own work. When death visited, neighbors turned up every night for several days to cry and mourn with the bereaved until the dead was buried. This sharing of loss, pain, tears and sorrow is what made not just the burden of death but colonial oppression bearable. People called the struggle a heavy log they had to carry across the river together.

In the village, we had no TV, cinemas or radio for our entertainment. We had to entertain one another. As small boys we participated in simple games. We held running competitions where winners, losers, staggerers and the fallen entertained one another equally. These unpaid competitions were so much fun that their mere anticipation gave us joy. Other times, we chased butterflies or made beetles fly like kites from strings.

Parents had weekend beer parties, where they entertained themselves with dances. Children were never allowed at these parties. Though colonialism was in the process of killing African culture, it allowed two agricultural show days a year when workers entertained one another with traditional dances that did not subvert the colonial order.

Colonialism banned all traditional songs that subverted it and tried to replace African traditional songs and dances with European ones in schools. African dances were slowly killed and replaced with church choirs and other dry and uninteresting physical exercises in boys' schools and with Irish traditional dances in Catholic girls' schools. Up to this day, I am amazed at the arrogance of the white colonialists who had no shame calling our traditional dances primitive and replacing them with their own traditional dances that were no better.

African traditional dances and songs evoke great emotions and are performed in praise of many things. Many a night I saw Father—when drunk—sadly sing for his dead mother, Mwihaki, until tears ran down his face. Each time I saw him singing in such depression, I would walk over to him, and he would hold me and then sing until both of us slept. Mother would then help Father to bed and take me to sleep.

Because of their frank language and subject matter, traditional songs were sung and danced in age groups. People would wear different, colorful, elaborate costumes. I still remember how small boys and girls held hands from under our feet and jumped along singing:

> The clan of partridge
> Take your child
> To go and drink water
> In the spring.

We played hide-and-seek singing:

> My little bird
> Hide quickly.
> If you are caught
> You are not mine.

When we got bigger, we dressed in cloth imitations of the animal skin dresses that children wore before the white man came. Our heads were shaven clean, shined with castor oil or animal fat and we donned hats made from white-and-black colobus skins or gray skins of vervet monkeys. We painted our faces with dots and lines of red and white ochre, wore skin belts, carried wooden swords and fastened closed-up tins that were half-filled with noise making gravel around our ankles. We would then move forwards, backwards and from side to side, stamping our feet to the ground while making other elaborate movements with our sword-carrying hands. We moved our heads and waists; danced and sang until our faces streamed with sweat:

> I was nearly swept away
> By rivers Marewa and Irati
> In pursuit of Njeri.

As we grew older, circumcision songs taught us sex education, introduced us to the secrets of manhood and womanhood and inspired us with great courage:

> What shall I now be called, *hahi huui*?
> I will be called a bee, a thief of honey.
>
> They say they are not old enough *hahi huui*
> But they are spitting teeth with spittle!
>
> I will make a fist, *hahi huui*
> When I unmake it, I am a full man.

Circumcision songs attracted me the most, I guess, because they were songs about sex, a taboo except during the initiation ceremony, *irua*, when the freedom of song was unlimited. Then I could even walk up to a grownup beautiful girl and say how much I wished to sleep with her. And though this could not happen, it was exciting to be able to ask without censure or punishment. Traditional songs were also sung to warn against greed:

> You the slave of the stomach
> You have sold your child
> To fill your belly!
>
> Elephants you went to salt licks
> You may die and perish
> You left your children with hyenas
> May you die and perish

When your child cries it is silenced:
You!
When the other cries, it is taunted:
Have a mouthful of dung,
And sleep!

Old men's traditional dances were called *muthunguuci, njukia* and *mucung'wa* and old women sang and danced *nduumo* and *gitiiro.* When colonialists forbade these dances, older folk were like old birds without feathers and young people who danced European dances resembled de-feathered birds that wore ill-fitting feathers of other birds.

In our culture, songs did not just entertain. They allowed people to pose riddles, narrate history, pass information, discuss politics and seduce with beautiful poetry of complicated metaphors that were fun to follow and decipher:

Woman:
You came unshaved
And made the skin the shaving blade.
Man:
I don't ask to sleep there
Only enter and get out.
W:
I heard people talking about you
Saying your sword has grown rusty in the sheath.
M:
I will seduce and take her
To give them a good cause to gossip.
W:
These guns you see
Some have no bullets.
M:
Bullets they have
But they shoot without noise.
W:
Don't make me that man
That dances with eyes on his wife.
M:
I fell from a bed
In the house of an unfaithful wife.

W:
It is not that you fell
It is the bed that collapsed.
M:
I seduced a woman
It was like opening up an virgin forest.
W:
I did not know you are a whip
That is why the queen complains.
M:
I was circumcised among sugar cane
That is why I am full of sweet juice.
W:
When you dance, watch,
The seducer's wife is also seduced.
M:
We only need two shake-ups
To get a Njeri* we can send.
W:
A squirrel seduced me
I could not follow him into the hole.
M:
If you are seduced by a man of age accept
A goat's head is never thin.
W:
Now that it is dark
Let the leopard that wants to scratch, proceed.

Christmas

In the midst of colonial gloom there was one day, Christmas, when light was lit in our lives neither in celebration of God's kingdom on earth, nor in celebration of humanity but in celebration of colonial presence in Kenya. Though we celebrated Christ's birthday on Christmas, celebrating birthdays was not part of our tradition. Yes, life was celebrated joyously each time someone was born but thereafter, there were no subsequent birthday celebrations of the same person. To us, once born, one did not waste time looking back on the day one was born. Instead, one lived on, looking forward and celebrating other achievements in one's life like initiation and graduating into other important stages of one's life.

* an infant girl

While we did not have our own birthdays to celebrate, each year on December 25, we stopped everything to celebrate the birth of Jesus Christ. Jesus Christ was portrayed to us as a white man and his divinity as proof of European superiority and African inferiority. But all this came later.

In my childhood, Christmas was the greatest day of our lives. And it looked special because often it fell on a dry, clear, blue-sky and warm day. Nobody worked that day and preparations for it began days before. Two days in advance, every family could be seen buying sugar and wheat flour to make pancakes, or *chapatis*. Most homes would also have traditional beer, *muratina*, made. On the eve of Christmas, almost every home would send a girl or boy to buy a bottle or two of skimmed milk from a neighboring European farm with which to make tea. The *wazungus* (Europeans) did not permit us to buy or drink whole milk even on Christmas day. Whole milk, cream, butter and cheese were not for *natives*. They were exclusively for *wazungus*. Even without butter, there would be a lot of tea and coffee in every home. However hard times were before or after, on Christmas day everything was heavenly.

On Christmas Day, all children would be up early for our dirty and rough feet to be scrubbed clean, for our heads to be shaved clean and shined with animal fat and to be dressed in ironed khaki shirts and shorts. But the first thing I woke up to do was to help Mother draw water and Pap slaughter a sheep for that day's meat. On that day, there was no home that did not kill an animal and nobody who did not eat meat. As Pap and I slaughtered, roasted the meat and put some aside for cooking, Mother would be cooking *chapatis* and frying meat, cabbages, potatoes and peas to prepare *gitoero*, a tasty stew. There was sweet scent of meat and fried *chapatis* everywhere in the air on Christmas day. With plenty of meaty bones around, even vultures seemed to celebrate Christmas. Only the sheep thought Christmas was a horrible day.

After we had finished slaughtering and washing, Mother would serve us a breakfast of tea with milk together with slices of bread or scones. We might even drink sodas on that day if we were lucky. Eating this breakfast once a year, it tasted absolutely fabulous. After dressing up, we all except Pap would go to church, which was boring except for the Latin hymns and beautifully dressed girls. In the church we were told nothing about the evils of colonialism and imperialism, the hypocrisy of a colonial Christianity that supported colonialism in its enslavement of us and said absolutely nothing of Christ as a savior of colonial subjects. The Jesus we were celebrating was a Jesus who supported colonialism, colonial religion and colonial culture and thought very little about us. Bored with all this, I could not wait to return home in the company of my friends for lunch.

One particular Christmas, I remember my friends Kamau and Musa and I went to our house and ate and drank tea. We then moved to Kamau's home where we ate and drank tea. From Kamau's home we moved to Musa's home. And though we tried not to eat too much at each home, our stomachs were stuffed full when we finished eating at Musa's home. From Musa's home we visited the home of a girl whom I loved very much. There we were each given a plateful of the same food. We pleaded that our stomachs were full but it was insisted that we must eat. We tried to eat as slowly as we could to create extra space for the food that we had before us. Then I felt the urge to go for a short call. When I was gone, my two friends played a trick on me. They put some of their food in my plate. When I returned I thought my food had become more but I was not sure and was too shy to ask. So I continued to eat until I finished the food. By then I was like a python that had swallowed a whole goat. I could hardly move. After a short while we said good-bye and left. Outside there was a small gate to climb over. When I tried, food that was now full in my food pipe just poured out. It was my first lesson in the wisdom of the Gikuyu proverb that sweetness consumes, *murio niwiriagira.*

Looking back on the happiness of Christmas that had just passed, it felt like a dream that had been too good to be true, like a deception almost. Waking up to the reality of our daily misery and the drabness of our village life and knowing how long I had to wait before the next Christmas, I wanted to forget this fleeting happiness with the same speed that people forget unreal dreams.

African Civilization

As a child I did not understand much about colonial racism, but whenever I saw a white man he carried a gun for killing. Whenever I saw a white man, he wore shoes and socks and made us walk barefoot or wear tire sandals. Whenever I saw a white man, he owned land and we had none. Whenever I saw a white man, he lived in a big house and we in poor huts.

When Father worked as a cook, he addressed the white man as master, *bwana mkubwa,* and his wife as madam, *memsahib.* He addressed white boys as young master, *bwana mdogo,* and white girls as young madam, *memsahib mdogo.* The use of these titles for the white man meant he was our master and we were his slaves. But when the white man and his family called Father, *boy* and Mother, *girl,* to them, my parents were slaves and something less—children who would never be adults. To the white master, Father was always less, and to the white madam, Mother was less. Father and Mother were not even equal with the young master and madam. They were less. Accordingly, white children were absolved from respecting African adults and encouraged to treat them like dirt.

For me, the treatment of my parents as slaves and children put me in a quandary. To begin with, as the child of a slave, I knew I too was destined to be a slave and this thought frustrated my ambitions beyond belief. As a child, I wanted to be like the white children whom I saw—not to be white but to have everything that they had—shoes, trousers, nice jackets, nice shirts, a tie, long socks, a small bicycle. I wanted to go to a nice school. As a grownup, I wanted to have everything the white man had and Father did not have—a nice house, land, a car, nice clothes, nice food, a good job, full rights, dignity, security and respect. This to me was what freedom meant. I wanted to be an adult who could marry and have children. But how could I be any of these when Father remained a boy? If Father was called a boy, it meant I would also remain a boy all my life. How would I ever become a man and a father?

But adulthood and freedom were not the only things that the white man denied Father and Mother. They were also denied humanity. Often, I heard the white man call Father and Mother bloody *nugu*, ape, and bloody *kima*, monkey. The white man was denying them humanity and calling them animals that he claimed God created to serve him. This idea squared with what we were told in the church—that when God created heaven and earth, he created all other beings for the use of human beings. Black people were not human beings according to this line of thought. Clearly, colonial denial of black humanity was meant to justify the exploitation of black people. As a child of course, I did not understand this logic. I only knew the humiliation of my parents being called boy, girl and bloody monkeys. It hurt me without my even knowing all its other implications.

We were also called primitive, uncivilized, or *shenzi*. To the arrogant mind of the British imperialist, there was only one civilization and that was European and colonizing. Because we stood outside European culture, colonialists claimed we had no civilization. But we had our own civilization that to us was more advanced than the European one because it gave us land, food, freedom, identity, spiritual peace and happiness. To the extent that our civilization met all our needs, we were not primitive. Europeans considered themselves more advanced because they could conquer, kill and rob more efficiently. Black people could not possibly prefer a civilization that killed and colonized them to their own.

More incomprehensible logic was to come. Having judged us as primitive, the white man proceeded to tell us, The reason I have killed and conquered you is not because I want to steal your land, minerals, timber and labor but because I want to civilize you (or turn you into what I am). In other words, I want to turn you into the one who kills you, transform you into your own enemy!

Frantz Fanon writes in *The Fact of Blackness in the Anatomy of Racism* that before the white man colonized Africa, many African nations, people and communities had their own civilizations whose men:

> ...knew how to build houses, govern empires, erect cities, cultivate fields, mine for metals, weave cotton, forge steel.

Their religion had its own beauty, based on mystical connections with the founder of the city. Their customs were pleasing, built on unity, kindness, respect for age.

No coercion, only mutual assistance, the joy of living, a free acceptance of discipline—Order—Earnestness—Poetry and Freedom.

From the untroubled private citizen to the almost fabulous leader, there was an unbroken chain of understanding and trust. No science? Indeed yes; but also, to protect them from fear, they possessed great myths in which the most subtle observation and the most daring imagination were balanced and blended. No art? They had their magnificent sculpture, in which human feeling erupted so unrestrained yet always followed the obsessive laws of rhythm in its organization of the major elements of a material called upon to capture, in order to redistribute, the most secret forces of the universe...

Monuments in the very heart of Africa? Schools? Hospitals? Not a single good burger of the twentieth century, no Durand, no Smith, no Brown even suspects that such things existed in Africa before the Europeans came....

But Schoelcher reminds us of their presence, discovered by Caille, Mollien, the Cander brothers. And, though he nowhere reminds us that when the Portuguese landed on the banks of the Congo in 1498, they found a rich and flourishing state there and that the courtiers of Ambas were dressed in robes of silk and brocade, at least he knows that Africa had brought itself up to a juridical concept of the state, and he is aware, living in the very flood of imperialism that European civilization, after all, is only one more civilization among many—and not the most merciful.[2]

And how did the colonizing white man mean to civilize us? By destroying African civilizations, imposing slavery on Africa and claiming the slave house to be superior to African culture. How did the white imperialist destroy African civilizations? By smashing their governmental and military organizations, uprooting their economies and killing their gods, cultures and religions.

Once African civilizations had been axed, African societies were collected from the ground and grafted to the tree of European civilization. Although never fully included, their blood, sweat and resources were welcomed. So the white man did not come to Africa to develop us or make us his equal. He came to rob us. He came to enslave us. He came to eat us up. Obsessed with the belief that it can prosper only by destroying other civilizations, European civilization came to Africa like a python, to thrive by swallowing up African civilizations, resources and people. Hence the Gikuyu lyric:

The clan of the white man
You came to Kenya
To be here
Forever persecuting us.

Grandma Speaks

In 1687, Father Cavazzi wrote of Africans, "These nations think themselves the foremost men in the world, and nothing will persuade them to the contrary…They imagine that Africa is not only the greatest part of the world, but also the happiest and most agreeable."[3] Nearly 300 years later, Guy Arnold in *Kenyatta and Politics of Kenya* would tell how, early in 1950s, a white settler in Kenya asked Fenner Brockway, a British MP, "How can you ask us to regard Africans as equals? Every African is dishonest, a liar and lazy. Their language has no words for love, gratitude and loyalty."[4]

Who can believe a lion that complains that a deer is dishonest, lazy and a liar because it is refusing to go down its throat? And how would a colonialist who did not learn African languages be an expert on them or on Africans or know that we call love *wendo* or *upendo,* gratitude *ngaatho* or *shukrani,* and loyalty, *wihokeku* or *uaminifu?*

One of my paternal grandmothers was an expert. She had lived both in the days before and after colonialism. When she talked to me of the days before colonialism, she painted a bright past of happiness. She completely disagreed when white people said they had come to save us from a hell of killing one another, perpetual hunger, poverty and godlessness and to take us to heaven:

Before the white man came, we all lived together, each family on its own land. Now our land is taken away and families live separated by the white farms they work in—parents from children, wives from husbands, and brothers and sisters from one another.

Before the white man came we had no masses of slaves and foreign people who owned everything in our country. I never suspected that I would in my lifetime see the servitude that I see now—white men owning everything and black people owning nothing. The white man has put us back to the times when Ngai had not given us this country, back to the times when we did not know what and who we were. How can we live and not own land on which to grow our food and build our houses?

Before the white man came, we went to bed happy, woke up rested and looked forward to a new day. Today we go to bed angry and wake up exhausted. We retire to worry, not to sleep. We wake up to curse the day ahead of us. We report to work at the first cockcrow, still staggering with sleep. No day brings us true laughter.

Before we knew colonialism, no one worked for another. We all woke up when we had slept enough. We worked at our own pace until we had sweated enough for the day. We returned home not to drop dead with fatigue but to continue life at home.

Before I saw the white man, work was a part of life, something we enjoyed. Now it is an enemy. In our freedom, everyone worked each according to one's ability. Boys and girls took animals to the fields. Men and women worked on the farms. Old men and women served as advisors, judges and religious leaders. Grandmothers and grandfathers looked after grandchildren. Even spirits of the dead were called upon to heal the sick. No one was useless and each person's work was considered invaluable for collective survival and happiness. Today, all of us who cannot work for the white man are considered trash.

In our society, only the sick and the elderly did not work but they were looked after with pleasure and compassion because in the end even they were not useless. Their function was to remind us of what all of us would be, to make us humble and better human beings. Service to them was service to us since all of us would get there some day.

Before we saw white people, happiness was the fuel that powered our lives. Not to die, we never allowed our lives to run out of joy. Every day we celebrated something—a birth, a marriage, an initiation of young men and women, a harvest or something. We sang and danced every day. Today we are allowed to be happy only on Christmas Day. Before the colonial tragedy befell us, we had no days that were better than others, no days to overwork and no days called Saturdays and Sundays when we could rest and worship. All days were equal. There were no days of drudgery and days of pleasure. Every day we worked. Every day we rested. Every day we sang. Every day we danced. Every day we worshipped. White people say they are more religious but six days a week, they worship money and only one day worship their God.

We did not rush through life. Every day children played. Every day men and women visited one another, ate, drank and talked together. We savored life.

Yes, every family lived on its own land but the families were held together in a society not by force but by friendship, shared blood, marriage, justice, everyday trade and a shared defense. This was our government.

Look at us today. We are prisoners in our own huts and in the white man's farm. We live enclosed like goats in pens. Before, we could go wherever we wanted in the entire breath and width of our land and nobody could stop us. We could sing and beat our drums at night and nobody could stop us.

Before the white man came, we never had prisons and no one was punished before guilt was established by everyone in the community and family members. In our free society, no one was ever killed for repulsing an attacking dog. And when people killed, life was not paid for with life but with animals and labor. If you killed and were found guilty, you paid for the life you took with animals and not with your life. If you and your clan could not pay the animals, you took the dead person's place in his family. We knew nothing of the injustice of an eye for an eye and a tooth for a tooth that commits the same sins it punishes other people for.

They say they came to save us from Arabs. But Arabs did not enslave us all on our own land. White people have enslaved every one of us—men, women and children—including their collaborators. They say they came to save us from hunger, but they have taken all our land away. Before, we suffered occasional hunger when there was drought. Today without land, all times are times of unending drought and hunger.

Grandson, when you grow up, you will also hear the white man say he came to save black people from killing one another. But when the Gikuyu raided the Ukabi or the Maasai, it was never to kill, enslave and take land. It was only to steal cattle. Today the white man does what no African did to another: Takes all cattle and land, enslaves everybody and kills for pleasure. Before he came, the abomination of young people taking up arms against their own people was unknown. Today the colonialist has turned sons against their own people and calls it government. If the white man came to save us from one another, in reality it is so that he may kill us.

Do not believe the white man when he says he came to save us from our own godlessness. From time immemorial we have always known our own God just as other people have known their own Gods. If other people call their God Jehovah, Allah or Jesus Christ, we call ours Ngai. Ngai gave us land, life, rain, good harvests and tranquility in the land. In turn we worshipped, thanked him with sacrifices and respected him no less than Europeans respect their own God:

> The name of Ngai of the Gikuyu
> Is truly holy and special.
> Ngai told Gikuyu
> It should never be
> Mentioned by people in vain.

White people say their God is greater than Ngai. To us, he is not. He may be stronger but he is not greater. He may have conquered Ngai in the struggle for control of our country. He may have given the white man the power to take our land and enslave us. For that, they say he is our God too, but he is not. Our only God is Ngai. The God who has conquered our Ngai and us cannot be our God. Under Ngai, we knew happiness. Under their God we know misery. They say Ngai was not God, only their God is God. But with Ngai, we never felt godless. With their God, we feel so because he does not take care of us. He minds white people only.

We cannot accept a God who disperses us throughout the land. While I can ask Ngai to help me against colonialists, I don't see how I could possibly ask the God of white people to help me against them.

Your Mum tells me our God, Ngai, and the God of white people are the same. If Ngai and their God are the same, why don't they worship Ngai? And why should I abandon Ngai for their God? Is Ngai not better? We called him *Mugai* (divider) because he gave to everybody—*nyakeru* (white people), *nyakairu* (black people), *arabu* (Arabs), *uhindi* (Indians). Instead of giving, their God takes away from us what Ngai gave us. Ngai made us free but their God makes us slaves.

This is why I now do not celebrate Christmas, Easter or any other Christian holiday. To celebrate Christmas or Easter is to celebrate our own submission. I do not see why I should celebrate the birth and death of Jesus Christ whose followers have brought us only death and destruction. They say Jesus died so that I may live. If I have to follow someone who died for me, that person is Waiyaki wa Hinga whom the white people killed at Kibwezi, fighting for our freedom. If Jesus Christ empowered white people to conquer black people then he died so that our blood may be shed, too.

Koigi, changing Gods is not like changing clothes. People should only change their God only if the new God will make them better people morally. And who will say the God of the white man has made us better morally? When we tell our young men and women to exercise sexual discipline, the white men claim our traditions are oppressive. Then they bring us abominable diseases like syphilis and gonorrhea and turn our young men and women into sex commodities that anyone may pay to abuse, infect with disease and use to make children that nobody wants. What kind of morality is it that tells men not to marry more than one wife and then gives them freedom to have irresponsible sex with those same women they refuse to marry? What kind of morality is this that allows men and women to see their own children roaming the streets like stray dogs and not feel hurt or concerned?

They say that their God makes us better. What better people are we, when in towns, young men and women drown themselves in an ocean of cheap beer that stupefies and turns them into drunk and dazzled birds that cannot fly in the face of danger. What superior morality is this that has turned whole African nations into slaves and beggars? To the God of white people, does morality only mean depravity?

Grandson, colonialism is another *mangu,* leprosy. It has more than enslaved us. By taking Ngai and our religion from us, it has made us spiritual orphans. Religiously homeless, the white men ask us to seek shelter under their God, in their own religion. But their God has his own chosen people, children of his stomach, as we say. Under their God, we shall be children of his back, the unloved ones.

These colonialists are merciless. They have made us political and economic slaves. They have made many of us religious orphans. Now they want to make us cultural orphans as well by taking Gikuyu and Mumbi from us. They say these were not our first parents. They say we, too, are descended from Adam and Eve, their first parents. If we came from Adam and Eve, how come we do not remember them or they us? They make us feel like imbeciles when they suggest that we forgot our real first parents and remembered others who are not. How could we have called Mumbi our creator if we had another mother, Eve? If we abandon Ngai, Gikuyu and Mumbi, we shall be a tree without roots. Now we are down. Soon, we shall also wither and die, Grandmother concluded.

Later, when I came to know that the first man came from East Africa, I wondered whether the possibility was not greater that Gikuyu and Mumbi had given birth to Adam and Eve and not the other way round.

Black Beauty

I knew the white man did not wish us well or want us to have equal accommodation inside his so-called superior civilization once I went to the home of a European settler who lived nearby to buy skimmed milk. I had already learnt some English at school and was dying to impress someone with it. You can therefore imagine how happy I was when I saw the old settler himself coming to the dairy where we stood in a queue to buy milk. Here was my moment to prove how much I had mastered the language of civilization. When he came close enough, I stepped forward and said to him: Good evening, sir. He did not answer or look at me. He just kept walking. Thinking he had not heard me, I followed him and said to him, Good evening, sir, a little more loudly. He still did not answer. He stood there and gave me a most menacing look. I was undaunted. To the consternation of everybody, I once again said to him: Good evening, sir. Bloody brat, the settler blurted out furiously and gave me a kick that would have hurled me into the air had it caught me squarely on my back. But I saw it coming and jumped over a hedge of flowers and ran for my life. This particular settler whom we called Gitirima, or one who walked with a stick, was also a member of our school board. Yet instead of being happy that I could speak English, he wanted to kill me for daring to speak the language of his civilization of which I was definitely not a part. From this day on, my curiosity for the white man turned into active fear.

As I sought to master the English language, Grandma continued to resist assimilation into the white civilization. She never wore the white man's clothes or names and continued to resist Christianity.

Before the white man came, the sense of beauty among our people was strictly our own and had two components—moral and physical. Today our white conquerors talk as if they are the inventors of morals. Before they came, our society knew all about good and evil, kindness and cruelty. Indeed we were as committed to friendship, sharing, fairness, justice and loyalty as they were committed to enmity, greed, inhumanity, injustice and treachery. To us, however, beauty is not just physical attraction. It also means to be good, kind, friendly, generous, just and loyal to your people, your friends, your spouse and your children. Of course, most beautiful is that person who is both inwardly and outwardly attractive. But one who is only inwardly beautiful is more beautiful than one who is only physically attractive.

The beautiful one is never eaten, *muthaka ndariagwo*, Grandma always told me. To us, moral beauty is greater than physical beauty because one can eat moral beauty but not physical beauty. Because you can choose to have or not to have it, moral beauty is also better because it is available to all, while not everyone is born physically beautiful.

Before they came, I never heard that black is ugly and white is beautiful, she said. All our beauty was black. In fact, I have yet to see a single beautiful colonist. Our white oppressors may be beautiful to one another, but never to us. To us, beauty and oppression are like oil and water. They do not blend.

Stupid colonialists even say that before they came, black people knew no beauty. But who said a pursuer of beauty does not cry, *mwendi uthaka ndacayaga?* Long before we saw the white man, we adorned both our bodies and our clothes—to transform ourselves into human butterflies and flowers. We pierced our earlobes, adorned our skins and wore all kinds of ornaments to enhance our beauty.

At this point, I remember telling my grandmother that I thought the white man's clothes looked more beautiful than the clothes she wore.

You are a fool boy, she admonished me; you have never seen Gikuyu beauty. What you see in us are Gikuyu slaves not Gikuyu beauties.

Crying, she then told me, Grandson, you are right. We don't look beautiful. How can we when we have no food to eat? How can we look beautiful when our faces and skins are so dry and we have no animal fat or castor oil to shine them? How can we look beautiful when we have no ornaments for our earlobes, for our hands and for our ankles? How can we look beautiful when we have no beautiful skin clothes to wear? I wish you had seen your grandfather and me when we were young and well-fed before our white enemies came; we were beautiful beings.

Yes, we were beautiful and we called ourselves beautiful names. It makes me weep today when I see beautiful young black men and women calling themselves white names whose meanings they don't know. To us, unlike the passbooks they make us carry around, a name is someone's real identification. When you are called Koigi wa Wamwere, it means you are a spokesman and also the son of Wamwere. But if you call yourself a *nyakeru's* (white man's) name, for all you know, you might be calling yourself a dog or a devil and also identifying yourself as a white man's slave. This is why I will never wear a white man's name just as I will never wear a white man's clothes. They are clothes that are worn by people who are afraid to show their limbs

and skins to the sun and other people. To me, they look tasteless and uncomfortable. If they say they are beautiful, why are they afraid to show their legs, their feet,
their hands, their heads and even their eyes? Clothes should make me more beautiful. I don't wear clothes to hide myself.

However opposed to colonialism *cucu* (Grandma) was, she did not underes-
timate it. Often she told me: *Muthoniwa* (the father of my son's wife, since I was
called after my maternal grandpa), this *ukoroni* (colonialism) that you see is a most
dangerous *itarara* (python). It has already swallowed up our lands—from coast to
our border with *mbaganda* (people of Uganda). Yet it is not content. It has swallowed up our sheep and cattle. Yet it is not content. It is now swallowing our
clothes and our names. Yet it will not be content. Since it came, this *itarara* has been
trying to swallow up our Ngai, our *mitugo* (customs) and our *ndini* (religion)
because people without their God, customs and religion are much easier to swallow than those who have their God, customs and religion. This *itarara* knows that
it is not safe when we are alive. Its final intention is to swallow us all. To survive,
we must keep our own God, customs, religion, names and clothes. Then we will
be too big to swallow.

Night Kindergarten

Where I grew up, colonialism did not permit kindergartens for black children. So
I did not go to a normal kindergarten. But in our village, there was a young man
called Kariuki wa Mwari, an older brother of my friend Gichohi wa Mwari. Of
course, Kariuki was not a young man to me. He was a big, educated and very special man. He had finished intermediate school and was with his parents in the village for some months while he looked for work. Because his father was a forest
worker, after Kariuki was eighteen, he could not stay with him in the forest without work. He had to look for work outside and get out. Now he stayed because he
was looking for work. Nobody wished to see him take up employment here and
end up a slave like his parents.

While he was in the village, Kariuki earned a little money teaching adults and
a few children how to read and write in a friend's hut, from eight to nine o'clock at
night three times a week. This was our only kindergarten. The teaching was meant
for our parents, but we children tagged along. I learnt to read and write in Gikuyu.
But that was all the written Gikuyu that I learnt because, living in the Rift Valley,
when I went to school, I was taught no more of it. Instead, I was taught Kiswahili
in the first two years and started learning English in the third year. By the fourth
year, English had become the language of instruction and Kiswahili relegated to a
mere subject. From fifth to the seventh year, if I spoke either Gikuyu or Kiswahili
in school, I was given a round piece of timber called monitor, for whose possession

I was punished at end of the day. Once it was given to me, I had to hold on to it until I passed it on to some other "offender."

In our kindergarten, we had no black slates to write on. We spread out ashes to write on in front of the fire. We got slates to write on later when we went to class one. For now, we had to bend over ashes and write with the heat of the fire beating our forehead worse than the noonday tropical sun. Yet when I look back on it, I can't even say that we endured it. It was fun and we enjoyed it.

Our kindergarten was held at night because that was the only time our parents could find for it. Their colonial employer did not even know that they were learning how to read and write at night. He would not have approved of it. Forest workers were not considered Africans whom colonialism needed to give some limited education to. Their work was strictly manual and learning was considered subversive.

Pap did not attend. Only one or two men did. The night school was mainly for women and today I marvel at why our mothers were more interested in learning than our fathers. Today, many people take their children to school with an eye on good jobs. But learning would not have earned our mothers better jobs with the colonial government and we had no newspapers in the village to read. Yet our mothers sacrificed rest after hard work in the *shamba* (fields) and cooking to learn how to read and write! Maybe they were attracted to learning by the desire to conquer something new or by a determination to muster the white man's magic, the secret behind his power. But why women and not men?

Mother and the other women did not sacrifice rest only for night school, but also to attend catechism. I even remember that there were fights at home because not only did Father not go to catechism, but he objected to Mum attending it. He thought it was a waste of time and an intrusion into his sacred territory by colonial enemy forces. But Mother persisted on both fronts; she learnt how to read and write and was baptized. Once baptized, literacy now allowed her to read stories about saints and martyrs, strengthening her conversion and resistance against any opposition to her new faith. Many a night, I remember Mother and the other women struggling to read about all kinds of saints who were said to have had strange powers. They took these saints' names during baptism. This, they hoped, would make them just as strong and take them to heaven.

In our night kindergarten, we were taught English songs that we sang without understanding a word of what we sang:

> Swing low, sweet chariot,
> Comin' for to carry me home!
>
> I looked over Jordan and what did I see!
> Comin' for to carry me home!

A band of angels comin' after me,
Comin' for to carry me home!

A Kiswahili proverb says that a child follows the nape of his mother. I did not only follow Mother to the night school, I also followed her to the wooden shack that we called the church to learn catechism. And there I learnt Latin songs that were just as incomprehensible to me as the English ones:

Gloria in excelsis Deo,
Et in terra pax hominibus bonae voluntatis
Laudamus te.
Adoramus te.
Glorificamus te…

Although these Latin and English songs made me feel very pious and part of the white man's world, I understood nothing. Why teach me English and Latin songs that I did not understand instead of Gikuyu songs that I could understand? My teachers were definitely in a hurry to make me a Christian. But did the white man's God know that I did not understand a word of what I sang for him? I believed he understood only English and Latin just as Ngai understood Gikuyu only. If Ngai and the Christian God were one, why could I not sing to him in Gikuyu? Why did the Christian God permit me to sing songs to him that meant nothing to me? He must have approved of my being turned into a parrot by colonial Christianity.

Later I discovered that our teacher of catechism did not understand Latin either. He taught us Latin songs that he did not understand, the way one parrot would teach another. The white priest said the Mass in Latin. By rote, during Mass, we were taught where to sit, where to stand, where to kneel down, when and what to sing and what to answer. What the priest said was nothing but noise to us. Disparagingly, white priests, *abia,* called our religion sorcery because they did not understand it. But for decades, the whole ritual of Mass in Latin was nothing to us but the white man's sorcery. It was incomprehensible. Most followed it because our worship was no more, many because whatever belonged to the white man was thought superior, and others because the victor is always right.

Despite my joy at the night kindergarten, we were still very poor. I was therefore not taught how to fathom time with a clock. (In fact, I saw my first clock when I went to class one.) Instead I was taught how to judge time with shadows and the sun. When shadows were short, I knew it was close to noon. When they were long, night was coming.

At night we relied on tree hyraxes to know when to sleep. Every night, tree hyraxes made piercing and far-reaching cries. When we heard them, we thought they had gone to sleep and were snoring. To us, it was time to sleep too. I even felt sleepy. Later I found out that when hyraxes cry, they are awake and foraging. They sleep in the day without snoring.

Hyraxes set our time to sleep and cocks set our waking time. I never heard the first time that cocks crowed, about 2 A.M. The second crow at 4 A.M. awakened Mum and Pap to go to work.

By this time, another cock that I was unfamiliar with, history, had also crowed to awaken our people to the darkest hour, just before the rebirth of our nation.

Storytelling

In our village lived a storyteller who was called Wambui. She was not the best of persons because she was a *mukari,* a very mean person, but she was a damn good storyteller.

Ordinarily, *arata,* or boys, who were friends, visited one another in the evenings, sharing meals as they moved from the home of one to the other. However, whenever we reached the home of the storyteller with one of her sons, we got no food. If the meal was already cooked, the storyteller's son was never given his food to share with us. Instead, he would get his when we were gone, to eat alone. When we found the food cooking, everyone who belonged to that home would scoop out his share from the cooking pot, put it in his palm and eat it from there, pretending to check whether the food was ready or not. Since it was unthinkable that a visitor could take from the cooking pot in someone else's house to taste whether it was ready, to our disappointment we never ate in the storyteller's home.

But the storyteller softened her meanness with entertainment. Each night after she had finished her work, Wambui would settle into telling us *ng'ano,* stories about everything. She had an inexhaustible mental library, but her best and most thrilling tales were about animals and *marimu,* ogres.

Once, the storyteller would begin, a young man called Maumau went to forge swords, hoes, small knives and spears with other young men. These were the iron instruments that people needed for cultivating their gardens, for defense and for slaughtering goats. Forging was done in a forest forge far from home, built right in the heart of the jungle.

When he went away, the young man left his wife, Kenyaa, pregnant and expected their baby soon. But forging took longer than expected and the woman's time to deliver came before he had returned. When she was in labor, *irimu rieru,* a white ogre came by and delivered her child. Afterward, the young woman told the ogre, "I am so weak that I cannot feed myself. Please help and give me food."

The white ogre settled in the home to help the new mother with cooking. He would fetch beans and bananas from the store, cook and pound them into *mukimo*, divide the food into two portions and give the smaller portion to the new mother, saying, "Kenyaa, here, take some food." But before she could take it, the ogre would put it into his mouth and say, "If you do not want the food, I eat." Later the ogre would also eat the bigger portion.

Another time and day, the ogre would fetch more food from the store, cook, mash and divide it into two portions, the bigger portion for him and the smaller portion for the new mother. He would then make as if to give the food to Kenyaa, but put it into his mouth before the young mother could take it. "If you do not want to eat," he would say, "I eat." He would later devour the rest of the meal and leave Kenyaa starved. And as the mother withered with hunger, so did her young child.

After eating, the ogre would take pound millet from the *ikumbi,* food store, and cook porridge. He would make as if to give Kenyaa some, but would drink it before the new mother could take any and declare, "If you do not want to drink, I drink." Later he would consume the remainder of the porridge alone and leave the new mother thirsty.

After some time, the white ogre took the biggest ram in the home and slaughtered it for the new mother. He roasted half the meat, telling Kenyaa that it was going to be a big feast for her. As soon as the meat was roasted, the ogre would cut a choice piece and ask Kenyaa to take it. Before she could, he would snatch it back. "If you do not want to eat, I eat." He would repeat this until all the roasted meat was finished. Thereafter, he boiled the rest of the meat and made an excellent soup with herbs. But he ate all the boiled meat and soup, as he had eaten the roasted meat and as he had drunk all the porridge. "New mother, kill your hunger with this piece of the ram heart." Before Kenyaa could take the piece of meat, the ogre would take it back saying, "If you do not like ram heart, I will eat it." The ogre would then fill a *kiihuri,* half a calabash, with soup and tell Kenyaa, "Quench your thirst with this soup." Before she could take the *kiihuri,* the ogre would take it back saying, "If you do not like soup, I will drink it."

Day by day, all the food in the store was eaten up, nearly all the rams in the pen and all the goats in the yard were eaten up. Now the new mother could not sleep in fear that soon it would be the turn of her child and herself to be eaten by the ogre. The mother had to scrape the pots before they were taken to the river for washing, and to survive she would steal some soup when the ogre was asleep.

Every day after eating, feeling satisfied and looking quite beautiful, the monster would go away to visit other white ogres who had also taken people's homes, to look for firewood or to compete in dances in villages where people did not know that he was an ogre. In those villages, he would make love to black women who were attracted to him and leave them to bear children, as other white ogres were doing with other black women. He would also kill the girls whom he could persuade to escort him into the forest, bring back their meat, cook it, eat it and throw away the bones.

When the ogre was away, the new mother would come out of the house and sit under the roof, to fret over when her husband would come back, while basking in the sun and watching some *tunyoni twa nja,* sparrows, collecting grains of millet in the compound. As she sat in front of the house, Kenyaa would look at the small birds and wonder: These little birds, if I send them to my husband, will they go? And can they fetch him before we are eaten?

Since she did not tell the birds her thoughts, they continued to peck whatever they could find in the compound in silence. Then one day she said, "Little sparrows, if I give you enough millet and send you away, will you go?" The birds said yes. Kenyaa went back into the house and brought out a lot of millet. When they had eaten, she told them, "My husband went to the east. He went *uturi* to forge and has been gone a long time. When he left, I was expectant. Now I have a baby and an ogre looks after me. After cooking, he gives me a little food, but before I can take it he says, 'New mother, if you do not like to eat, I will eat.' The ogre has taken over our home, has eaten all the food and has eaten nearly all the goats. Now, you go and tell my husband that I have a baby. Tell him that I am looked after by an ogre and that this fiend is about to eat both the child and me. Tell him I am as thin as a reed because I eat nothing."

The birds did not refuse. They flew to the forest forge far away, where Maumau and fellow young men were forging and said: *Cu, cu, cu, cu, cu,* from the top of trees. Disturbed, the young *aturi,* blacksmiths, frightened the birds away by throwing stones at them and asked one another, "Now, why did these birds come to ruin our ears?"

But the flock would not go far away. When stones were not being thrown at them, they came back and made the same sounds: *Cu, cu, cu, cu, cu.* One man among them then said, "Maybe these birds are trying to give us a message, let us listen to them." When they sat down to listen, one bird sang:

> Blacksmith that forges
> Cangarara i ca.
> Stop forging and hurry home
> Cangarara i ca.
> Your wife has given birth
> Cangarara i ca.
> Delivered by a white ogre
> Cangarara i ca.
> Your wife is fed like this

Cangarara i ca.
Nursing mother take this food
Cangarara i ca.
Before she eats it is taken back
Cangarara i ca.
White ogre has taken everything
Cangarara i ca.
Home, land and all animals
Cangarara i ca.
The blacksmith that forges
Cangarara i ca.
Hurry save your wife and child
Cangarara i ca.
The blacksmith that forges
Hurry save home, land and animals
Cangarara i ca.

"Did you hear that?" one man asked. "Which one of us left his wife heavy?"

"It is I," Maumau said. "When I left, my wife was pregnant."

The birds continued to sing the same song over and over until the men told Maumau, "Take what you have forged and go home. Perhaps the birds are singing a message from your wife."

Maumau did not sleep in the forest one more night. He took his sword, spear and everything he had fashioned and hurried home. *Ku, ku, ku, ku,* he walked all night until he arrived at a hill overlooking his home at noon the following day.

From the hill, Maumau saw that his homestead was not accessible to him. Heavily armed white and black ogres formed a ring round it and held his wife and child prisoner inside. He was so angry that he could not reach his home and rescue his wife and child that he was tempted to drive the spear through his stomach and end his own life and misery with it. But he controlled himself and rather than commit suicide, decided to go back to the forest and tell the young men what had happened.

After singing their message to Maumau, the small birds had returned to the new mother with the confirmation that they had already given him her message. Sure that her husband was on the way to rescue them, Kenyaa had struggled and taken down all the food and porridge from the rack where the white ogre had kept it. Hungry for many days, she had just finished eating and drinking when the ogre returned home carrying a big bundle of firewood. He dropped the bundle outside the house with a heavy sound, sighed with fatigue. "Huuu," he cursed, "May the new mother in this house drop with that sound."

Inside the house, Kenyaa said, "May you too drop with that sound!"

Surprised at the defiance he had never heard from Kenyaa, the ogre said, "The new mother is very brave. Have those who went to the forest forge come back?"

"Stop reminding me of the lost ones," the new mother replied. The ogre entered the house. But when he reached for the food, it was not there. So he asked, "Where is the food?"

Kenyaa replied, "I don't know."

When the ogre reached for the porridge, it was not there. Again he asked, "Where did the porridge go?" Kenyaa said, "I don't know. Ask the porridge where it went, not me."

"The new mother is very brave," said the ogre. "Have those who went to the forest forge come back?"

"Don't remind me of the lost ones," said Kenyaa.

Fuming with rage, the ogre then spread himself on the floor of the house and told the young woman, "You must tell me where the food is."

In reply she said, "How can I tell you where the food is when I don't know where it went? Ask the food where it is."

At that the ogre burst out, "Where were you when the food was eaten?"

Suspecting that something was afoot, the white ogre went out and asked his white friends and their black children to come and help defend what he now called his land, home, people, animals and property, although he had stolen it all from Maumau. They agreed and came to protect their fellow's stolen property.

As white and little black ogres continued to guard Maumau's homestead, the young man returned to the forest forge. The other men were surprised to see him back and looking so worried. "What happened?" they asked eagerly.

"There is trouble at home," he said. "I found my home completely surrounded by white and black ogres. My wife, child and animals are all held prisoners inside. I could not possibly fight an army of ogres. So I am back to ask you for help." While he said all this, tears streamed down the face of Maumau. As other men watched one of their own crying, they dropped all their business at hand, armed themselves with swords and spears and left the forest forge to go and liberate the home of their friend. An attack on one was an attack on them all.

On their way to Maumau's home, they gathered intelligence from other village sparrows that their own land and homes had been taken over by other white ogres and their families enslaved. Suddenly they were no longer on their way to liberate Maumau's Kenyaa. They too were Maumaus going to liberate their own Kenyaa from conquest and exploitation by white ogres and their black children. To fight effectively, they divided themselves into small units, which then went to attack ogres wherever they were.

Burning with curiosity, we asked the storyteller, Did they attack the ogres and did they win?

They attacked armed white ogres and their black children wherever they were.

Not satisfied with such a short answer, we asked for more: Did the Maumaus win the war?

Ask me this again about thirteen years from today and I will tell you the rest of the story.

We felt cheated. Because we wanted Maumaus to win the war against ogres so much, we were disappointed. Our storyteller only laughed. She was such a good narrator that all her stories sounded so real, so full of life, so thrilling and so frightening that afterward, we dared not leave her home at night—unless we were escorted—for fear of being caught and eaten by ogres. Some of the stories were a national prayer, though Wambui never told us so. And though our storyteller always talked of ogres as real, many people said that they never lived and that there was nothing real in the stories. Even when we asked her directly whether ogres were real, she always said they were.

Ogres are very real, she would say. Just keep your eyes open. They are white. They are black. And they come in all shapes and sizes—small, big, adults and even children. At that we would all ask, Am I an ogre? Ask your mother, was all she would tell us, laughing.

CHAPTER II

MAU MAU YEARS 1952–59

Oath of Unity

What I seem to remember well about these early Mau Mau years is a lot of talk about Jomo Kenyatta among older people, and other things that were talked about in whispers and kept silent about whenever children were close enough to hear.

As for Kenyatta, he was talked about as the man of courage, *njamba*, and a leader, *muthamaki*. Everybody said he was the only black man who had been to the land of the white man, the only man who did not fear the *mzungu*. But it was a song Grandmother taught me that shaped my childhood impression of Kenyatta:

> When Kenyatta was born by his father and mother
> He was born a leader.
> But his mother and mother did not know
> Only Ngai knew.
>
> When Jomo grew up
> And became an adult
> He started to think hard
> What the future of Kenya would be
> In the days to come.

Grownups said Kenyatta had talked to a big meeting of Kenyans where he had asked them not to think the white man was anything but human. He felt hunger, went to toilet and felt pain like us. The meeting had laughed hilariously when Kenyatta said that even the white queen blew her nose and had calls of nature like everybody else.

For seeking equality with him, the white man hated Kenyatta and tried to kill him many times. One story said that when Kenyatta was returning home from a meeting at Njoro, he had seen an antelope cross the road ahead of his car. Sure that it was an ill omen, he hitched a ride on a lorry that was loaded with charcoal and avoided white assassins who missed him when they stopped his car.

[83]

Another story claimed white people had tried to kill Kenyatta by bribing his wife to poison his food. When he came home and was served with sweet-smelling meat, he gave some to his guardian cat. When the cat refused, he too did not eat it.

Colonial settlers were accused not just of wanting to kill Kenyatta but of fearing him. They said Kenyatta had powerful and magnetic eyes that overwhelmed his enemies—white or black.

One day I asked Granny why other people were not called Kenyatta or Jomo.

Kenyatta, she told me, is his nickname for wearing *kinyatta*, a Maasai belt of beads. His other name, Jomo, means *itimu*, or sword. Before his nicknames, Kenyatta was called Johnstone Kamau Ngengi.

Kenyatta was a good speaker and inspired Kenyan people as no other leader had. He had lived in England and had a picture of white people as ordinary people instead of the picture that colonialists painted of themselves as supermen. Kenyatta also spent a lot of time trying to persuade European settlers to resolve the conflict between them and black people constitutionally and peacefully, but his efforts bore no fruit. Kenyatta's failure to talk change with white people had persuaded him to tell a large public rally that the tree of freedom did not live on water but was watered with blood. He asked people whether they wanted to eat the fruits of freedom, and they said yes. Then he asked them whether they were ready to water the tree of freedom with their blood, and they said yes.

If I hold the lion by the jaws, are you prepared to bear the claws of the beast? Kenyatta asked, and the crowd roared back, Ye-e-e-e-e-e-e-e-e-e-s!

When people came home from these meetings, these are the stories of Kenyatta they told everywhere. And while these stories gave people hope, courage and to many a readiness to die for freedom, they also introduced into the air a sense of foreboding, anxiety and danger. As Kenyatta told people to be ready to bleed, white people heard these things and tension between white and black rose. As Kenyatta talked war in public meetings, in villages, people continued to speak in whispers. I would later learn that they were discussing the oath in whispers.

The white man was in the country because he had fought and defeated the black man's *itungati*, freedom fighters. He had strong weapons and had many black people fighting for him. Since the white man had won his war with the black man and decided to live in the country by force, he had many times told the black man that he would never give him peace or let him live like a human being again. He wanted the black man to live like his beast of burden. Having refused to live like a slave, the black man had concluded that in Kenya, the white man was a visitor who had abused his host's hospitality and now was the time for him to leave. In reply, the white man had not only said that he would not leave, he had declared Kenya his own country. The black man had refused to accept this and had for a long time been preparing himself for a war with the white man.

When our people talked about our conflict with the white man, we talked of ourselves as black people, *andu airu,* not as Gikuyu people, *Agikuyu,* and in our definition of *andu airu,* we included all black people of Kenya. Today, Mau Mau war is analyzed by some as a Gikuyu war not just to drive out the white people, but also to dominate other Kenyans. But at a place called Kwa Ojwan'g there was a Luo man called Ojwan'g who ran a small hotel and shop where we bought sugar and popular cakes called *mandazis.* Among all the people, old man Ojwan'g was as popular as his *mandazis* and today, I don't remember my parents or other people talking of this man as an enemy or someone whom they wanted to dominate or enslave once black people were free.

Having decided to fight the white man, black people were now taking *muuma,* or the oath, that would give them the spiritual strength they needed to accept and make sacrifices and eventually endure great pain and death for the recovery of their land and freedom. And believing that an army without secrecy is defeated by one club, *ita ritari ndundu rihuragwo na njuguma imwe,* people took *muuma* to be bound to one another in the greatest possible secrecy that was necessary in their war against the white man.

As a child, I could not be let into the secrets of *muuma.* Today, I know that to take oaths, people were taken to secret places and taking *muuma* involved slaughtering a he-goat of one solid color, collecting its blood in a gourd bowl and cutting out the chest area of the goat. The goat's skin was then cut into one long piece, which was tied together to form a large ring. The oath administrator wore loose sheets of cloth and an oddly shaped hat and smeared himself with clay or red soil. The persons taking the oath each put on a large necklace of woven coach grass, and the administrator put the skin ring around them. At the entrance of a ceremonial arch of rushes, there were stalks of sugarcane flanked by arrowroots. Just in front of the arch was a trough filled with Gikuyu foods mixed together with soil and goat's blood. Those to take the oath were cut seven times and their blood was mixed with that of the goat in the bowl. After the oath administrator had surrounded the people with the skin ring, he asked each one to say what he was. The oath taker would answer, I am a Mugikuyu.

As each person answered, the oath administrator touched the forehead with a stick dipped in blood from the bowl, saying, You have been marked on your forehead that you have agreed to be united to other black people in pursuit of your country's freedom. After that, oath takers would bite the goat's chest meat, heart and lungs that had been dipped in blood and then walk through the arch seven times repeating the words:

If you ever disagree with your nation or sell it, may you die of this oath.

If a member of this Society ever calls on you in the night and you refuse to open your hut to him, may you die of this oath.

If you ever sell a black woman to a foreigner, may you die of this oath.

If you ever leave a member of this Society in trouble, may you die of this oath.

If you ever report a member of this Society to the white man's government, may you die of this oath.

This oath started with an assertion of identity because people's identity was endangered by a European cultural onslaught and also because people who did not know who they were could not fight for their freedom and independence. But what I have described above was not the standard oath among black people from other ethnic communities. Luo people, Maasai people and Luhya people took this same oath in a different form that was dictated by their particular culture.

Not long ago, I was visiting my Aunt Wanjiru with my brother and with great pleasure she told us how she had attended the famous Kenyatta meeting at Njoro and how she had afterwards taken *muuma*. As we talked she told her husband, You, too, took the oath afterwards though you never attended the meeting at Njoro. Do you know who arranged for you to take the oath? He said he did not know. It was 45 years later that my aunt told her husband that it was she who had arranged for him to take the oath. I could see the surprise in my uncle's face as our aunt could, of course, see the surprise in our faces that secrets of *muuma* could be kept for nearly half a century. To this day, I cannot say whether my father took *muuma*. I vaguely remember Mother at night carrying me into a crowded hut in Gwa Gacicio for oath taking, but a strong attack of nausea always stopped her from taking it. In any case, they always supported the struggle and I never saw them treated like traitors by anyone.

The Forest Department did not keep any cattle or sheep. But all around us there were settler farms that bred dairy cattle. Soon stories were coming from these farms that unknown people were cutting the leg tendons of cattle and slicing their stomachs open with swords and leaving them to die in great pain. Sometimes dogs and cats would be killed and hanged near the gates of whites' homes or left hanging upon fences of whites' farms. When you beat a chicken, you are after the owner of that chicken, *ukimpiga kuku wamtafuta mwenye kuku huyo,* so says a well-known Swahili proverb. When colonial settlers heard stories of these happenings, they must have known that young black men were spoiling for a fight with them.

Then we heard more ominous stories that prominent black collaborators were being killed in Central Province and Nairobi. People now knew the war was coming and coming soon. We saw more forest guards, *askari wa misitu,* posted to our forest. Then came news that a notorious senior chief Waruhiu had been shot dead on October 7, 1952 near Nairobi. All the older people knew the war was finally at hand. As a child, I could only tell that something was amiss from the fact that my parents and all the grownups in our village looked unhappy, too thoughtful, seemed to talk and visit one another less. Father drank more beer than before and Mother seemed easier to annoy.

Two Births

For a long time, Mother had been growing bigger and bigger in the stomach; but I did not know that my brother Kuria was on the way. Then in the middle of the night of October 20, 1952, I was awakened by some commotion in the house. I heard a child cry: Yaa, yaa, yaa. I heard one woman say, It is a boy, it is a boy, *ni kahii, ni kahii*. What is he called? someone asked. Mother said, "Kuria," in a voice that sounded both exhausted and happy. Immediately there rang out from all the women, *Ariririri, aririririri, aririririri, aririririri, aririririri,* five *ngemi*, or cheers, for the newly born boy. By now I was awake to see my brother. Mother asked me to go back to bed but I did not. I just sat there looking at my brother, who looked so small. I wondered whether he would ever walk and catch a butterfly.

What we did not know was that there was a lot of commotion, not just in our village but all over the country. As my brother was being born, the colonial police and army were out to arrest Kenyatta, Bildad Kaggia, Kung'u Karumba, Fred Kubai, Achieng Oneko, Paul Ngei and thousands of other Kenyans in order to stop the national struggle for land and freedom. But in arresting African leaders, British colonialism was also giving birth to the Kenya Land and Freedom Army (KFLA), or the Mau Mau army, that would fight the python of colonialism from within until it was forced to spit out the country and its people from its belly. But that would not be until 11 years later. Now was the time for the Mau Mau, as a midwife of history, to help the country give birth to freedom after a pregnancy of seven decades.

That night colonial forces were out patrolling everywhere. When my father stepped outside they immediately arrested him and took him to the most notorious screening and torture center in the area, Kwa Nyangweso. Without a radio, Pap did not know that the British had that night declared the Emergency that forbade all black people to be out at night unless they were collaborators. Well, Father was nabbed. When he did not show up after one hour, then a whole two days, Mother was absolutely terrified. She was convinced he was dead.

On the third day, he arose from the dead and appeared at the door like an apparition. He was in bad shape. He told Mother how he had been arrested by a group of black police led by white officers. They called him a Mau Mau, beat him senseless, threw him into a Land Rover and drove him around picking up any African men they found out at night. When the Land Rover was full, toward dawn, they were taken to Kwa Nyangweso torture camp where they found expert white and black torturers.

Father was very scared. He had heard that here, the white man bred giant red ants in enormous holes, which bit to death rebellious Africans tossed to them. Upon arrival, the men were all herded into an open compound and lined up. A hooded government informer, *gakunia,* was brought before them to identify those who had taken the Mau Mau oath. Those who were identified were put in their own hut. Father and other unidentified men were put into different huts.

Father was later led into another hut where he found white men with bloody clothes.

Are you a Mau Mau? they asked him.

No, I am not.

Have you taken the Mau Mau oath?

No, he said. At that, a white man who wore steel buckles on his knuckles hit Father in the mouth. Father felt his teeth break. When he rubbed his hand across his mouth, he saw blood on his hand. He spit out blood and two of his teeth to the floor. For spitting on the ground he was called *shenzi,* primitive, and boxed again by the same man. As if from a signal, other men kicked him all over and soon he passed out.

When Father came to, it was dawn the following morning. His clothes were all dusty since he had been rolling in pain all night on the dirty floor. His entire body ached. During the day, he was neither fed nor beaten. Another man was taken from their hut and when he was returned, he could only stumble with his feet wide open. Blood was running down his feet and his trousers were wet with urine and blood. A European officer had castrated him, first by crushing his testicles with a pair of pliers and then slicing them out of the scrotum.

In the afternoon, when Father thought the torture was over, a settler police reserve officer entered the cell, accompanied by some five black *watesi,* torturers. All of them carried *viboko,* rhino skin whips, and viciously started beating the men at random without asking any questions until, drenched in sweat, they stopped out of exhaustion. When they stopped, the white officer asked, *nani amekula kiapo,* who has taken the oath? And added, If you do not confess we will kill you here. None of you will leave this place alive unless you tell us you are Mau Mau. And if you think I am lying, get up and follow me you *nugu,* apes.

Those who could not get up on their own were helped onto their feet by the black torturers. They were lined up and led into an open area half the size of a soccer field. There they found another group of men crouching down together naked. From this group, about twenty police made a corridor between which one of the men was marched and put between two Land Rovers. He was then asked to stand with his legs and stretched arms apart. One leg and one arm were tied to one Land Rover while the other leg and arm were tied to the other. The two Land Rovers were then driven slowly in opposite directions. The man being torn apart made a deafening scream and then stopped. As the Land Rovers moved, the wire ropes with which the man's arms and legs were tied screeched. The legs and arms were then torn apart from the body, remaining with the Land Rovers, while the body fell on the ground in between. Father was petrified with terror. He retched but dared not throw up.

Wearing a sadistic grin on his face, the *mzungu* looked at them and asked, How many of you have taken the Mau Mau oath? Confess now or go and crouch there with those Mau Maus. Out of fear, three men put up their hands and said they had taken the Mau Mau oath. The *mzungu* officer shook his head knowingly and with his head ordered the black police to remove the confessors from Father's group. Brutally, the three men were separated from the others but they were not put together with the crouching men. Instead they were taken to another area where men and women were digging graves supervised by more police. Father's group was now led to a spot from where they could see those who were digging graves. When the graves were dug, the diggers were asked to stand before them. Behind them, *askaris* shot them into the graves. Other men and women were asked to bury them and start digging their own graves. Father was scared stiff. Still he asked himself, Why dig my own grave if they are going to kill me? If they ask me to dig my own grave, I will refuse. They will kill me, dig my grave and bury me. But his group was not taken to dig their own graves. They were returned to the cells at around six in the evening. For the first time, they were brought some nearly raw maize meal cake, *ugali*, and asked to eat their last meal. But you can still save yourself, they were told, if you agree to confess. Father did not understand the logic. How does one save oneself by confessing when those who confessed were made to dig their own graves into which they were later shot? He ate his last meal anyway and drifted into a light slumber.

In the morning, Father's group was led to another compound where black women were being tortured by having their nails pulled out with pliers, their long hair plucked out of the skull like feathers and glass bottles broken into their private parts with army boots. They screamed and screamed but no one heeded them. When their bodies could take no more pain, many of them fainted and were taken to another hut. From this compound, Father and five other men were taken to an office where a *mzungu* said he was releasing them to go and take another oath and exactly what they had witnessed would happen to them and their wives. Go and tell others what a nice activity taking *muuma* is.

They were taken to the gates and asked to go home but first to report to their white employers where they had been. Father walked straight to the office of the forest officer. When Father told him where he had been and what had happened to him, the white officer told him he was lucky:

Go home and keep out of trouble. If you want to work here and stay alive, keep Mau Mau and its *muuma* away from you.

Yes, master, *ndiyo bwana,* Father nodded and left.

When everybody saw Father without teeth and with bruises all over his face and heard what had happened to him they cried with both pain and joy. Most were surprised that Father had come from Kwa Nyangweso alive. But Mother was most pleased at her man's resurrection. From a tragedy, it turned into almost another birth. As she cried with the pain of tragedy, she also laughed at the joy of what seemed like the gift of two births.

Kenyatta's Arrest

The same night Father was arrested, the whole country was grieved by the arrest of Jomo Kenyatta, Bildad Kaggia, Paul Ngei, Fred Kubai, Kung'u Karumba, Ochieng Oneko and many others. Many years later, a school choir would capture the mood of the nation:

> It was on October 1952
> When all people heard
> Kenyatta was arrested.
> Kenyatta was not arrested alone
> But with other heroes of independence.
> Ooi, oi, oi
>
> Fathers, mothers and children
> All shed tears saying
> Ooi, Ooi, Ooi,
> Release Kenyatta and others.
>
> It was weeping all over Kenya.
> All people felt
> Great sadness.

After Kenyatta's arrest came his trial and sentencing on April 8, 1953. Kenyatta and the others on trial with him were sentenced to seven years' imprisonment and restriction to the Northern Province of Kenya for life for the so-called crime of managing the Mau Mau. After Kenyatta's sentence, European settlers told

Africans to give up their fight for freedom and independence because Kenyatta their leader would never return. Guy Arnold wrote: "Both the Governor, Sir Evelyn Baring, and the Colonial Secretary, Alan Lennox-Boyd, promised that Kenyatta and the others would never return to Gikuyu country. Their houses were destroyed and their land disposed of."[1]

Government planes flew above telling people to forget *uhuru* and Kenyatta because they would never see him again. Kenyatta's eldest son, Peter Muigai, was one of the announcers that Kenyatta would never return. Kenyatta's name was banned. It could be mentioned only at the risk of arrest and detention. After Kenyatta's disposition into the desert prison, many people walked around dazed, hopeless, feeling that their world had come to end and their slavery would never end.

War Starts

Colonialists were convinced that they had decapitated and killed the movement for independence by jailing Kenyatta. But Kenyatta was not the head of Mau Mau. He was the political leader. Unknown to the British, the war movement had other heads—Dedan Kimathi wa Waciuri, Mathenge wa Mirugi, General Kago and others—and so it lived on. These were the young leaders who led thousands of other Kenyan men and women who took to the forests of Mount Kenya and the Aberdare mountains where they waged a bitter war of independence for the next four years.

While Kenyatta had hopes that he might be able to persuade the British to give Kenya independence peacefully, his jailing and banishment for life left many Africans convinced that only fighting could end colonialism. When people heard Kimathi had gone to the forest to fight, they sang in fanatical support:

> When our Kimathi went up
> To the mountain alone
> He was given strength and courage
> To defeat the white people.
>
> We cry because we are black people
> And we are not white.
> Nor are we beneficiaries of their blessings
> Ngai is our leader.
> He said all the footsteps
> That I have taken
> You must take them too
> And drink from the same cups.

Do not let persecution make you afraid
Not even to be sent into detention camps
Nor to be robbed or to be killed
With Ngai in our leadership.

The support for Mau Mau was so strong that wives were known to ask what sort of men their husbands were if they had not already gone to the forest to fight. But as the monster of British colonialism spread terror everywhere, strains and arguments began to appear in every home among those who wanted to fight and those who wanted to be more cautious.

Mungai Joins the Mau Mau

The outbreak of the war found my young father (paternal uncle) Mungai without work and thirsty for freedom; he was drawn into the vortex of nationalism as one is caught in a whirlpool. When those who were recruiting Mau Mau fighters approached him, he jumped at their offer with alacrity. Fighting for land and freedom had become his religion and purpose of life.

But there were people—especially older people—who were awed by the might of British colonial forces and did not believe that the British could be fought out of Kenya. My grandfather, for example, was the only one in my father's family who had not taken the oath that bound people together against the British.

When Mungai was asked to take *muuma,* the fighter's oath, he felt honored to join the Kenya Land and Freedom Army. The KLFA never called itself Mau Mau and nobody seemed to know what the name meant in Gikuyu. Some people say it was an unintentional mispronunciation of the words *uma uma,* get out, get out, that the British police heard someone shout to people in a hut at the sight of them. But whether intentional or not, the word stuck, and later people said the six Mau Mau letters meant *Mzungu Aende Ulaya Mwafrika Apate Uhuru,* European Return to Europe so the African can Get his Independence.

Anyway, after taking the warrior's *mbatuni* oath, knowing that his father did not oppose independence as such, Mungai informed him that he intended to go and fight for freedom. He wanted his blessings. Instead Grandfather just scorned the idea.

You people are just fleas trying to fight an elephant. You will be crushed like lice, Grandfather told his son.

But white people die just like us and we are more. And, Father, have you never had a flea in your ear? When we get into the ears of these white people, will they not listen to us? Mungai asked rhetorically.

My son, do not be like the inexperienced young bull that approaches the cow from the head. The British are stronger than we are. They have guns, bombs, planes, big lorries and huge armies. Look at their strong stone houses and tell me who of us has the power to uproot them. Kenyatta is no more. Who else has power to drive *nyakeru*, white people, out? You people are daydreaming when you talk of defeating *nyakeru*. You better talk, not fight, Grandfather insisted.

Mungai responded, but Kenyatta has been talking and now he is in jail. Talking to these people is worse than talking to a banana tree. Only harm can come out of it. Now that they have jailed all our leaders, what should we do, Father? Surrender? Mungai asked in frustrated anger.

Grandfather then advised, Son, cool down and remember that as the Swahili people say, One who walks slowly does not knock his foot against a rock, *mwenda pole hajikwai*, and that reason breaks a taut bow, *kihooto kiunaga uta mugeete*. If you talk and reason with these people, you might win. If you resort to arms, you will only get killed.

But, Father, said Mungai, it is also our people who say that one who refuses to listen to reason will not refuse to listen to the club, *ndungirega kihooto norege njuguma*. After all, we are right and they are wrong. Father, if we want to be free, we cannot afford to be afraid. In the home of fear, poverty never ends, *guoya uturagia ukia mucii*.

Son, you argue well, but also remember: The one who is chased away with a club comes back, but the one who is chased away with reason does not come back, *muingatwo na njuguma niacookaga, no muingatwo na kihooto ndacookaga*. If we want to chase white people away from here, never to come back, let us use reason rather than clubs, which they have more of than we do. Son, in the world of yesterday, reason used to break a taut bow but in today's world, might is right.

That may be so, Father, but we cannot live as slaves in our own country. It is better to die fighting than surrender to the might of our enemies.

Tell me, Son, which do you want to be, a dead lion or a living dog?

Father, shall we live like dogs in our own country merely because we fear to die like lions? Now Mungai was almost talking to himself rather than arguing with his father.

Son, this is not a matter of clever arguments. It is a matter of life and death. As your father, I don't think you should play with fire like a moth. Do you know how much pain your death would give your mother and me? But maybe people are right: The ear that wants to die does not hear medicine, *sikio la kufa halisikii dawa*.

Grandfather did not convince the son. But Mungai wanted his father to understand and bless him. Then he would have gone to fight and, if need be, to his death cheerfully, knowing that his father was proud of him. Even without his father's blessings, Mungai would not go back. Secretly he joined the Mau Mau army and went to Aberdare forest to fight. When his father learnt of it, he shook with anger and fear—fear that when colonial authorities did not see Mungai around, they would think that he had gone to the forest with his blessings. The only way to avoid this association was to denounce both his son and the Mau Mau.

Mungai Is Killed

After two years of fighting, Mungai was shot in the leg. His comrades brought him home for shelter, food and medical treatment from his family. He was hidden in a grove at the base of several thick banana plants that grew together near Grandmother's hut. Knowing how angry he would be, Grandmother never informed Grandfather. Every day, Grandmother secretly fed her son, cleaned, treated and dressed his wounds, hoping he would heal soon enough to go back to the forest before his father or anyone else unsympathetic discovered his presence. However hard she fought against it, my grandmother's fear would not go. Instead, it grew from her knowledge of the proverb saying the cow with fear is the one that is slaughtered. But Mungai seemed undisturbed by any fear. His confidence had almost succeeded in dismissing her fear when disaster struck.

That night Grandpa had heard some movement near the banana plants. In the morning when it was light, Grandpa went to the garden to see whether he could see any footsteps where he had heard the movement at night. When he reached the grove, he saw what he did not expect to see. He saw his son lying in the grove, awake and looking at him. He was dressed in a blanket and beside him lay his rifle.

So it is you, Grandfather said, shaking his head.

Yes, Father, it is I, the son replied with half a smile. I did not mean to cause trouble, I got wounded, he added.

What are you doing here? There was menace in his voice. You left home without my permission. You cannot come back without it.

Father, I only came because I was wounded. Please, just give me a few days and I will be well enough to go away.

Let you stay? Grandfather asked. Do you want to have us all killed?

Let me then go away now, Mungai pleaded.

Crying, Grandmother also pleaded, where will he go in the day? Please let him stay until night.

Keep quiet, woman. You should have brought up your son better. He was brave enough to go into the forest. What is he afraid of now? Then he turned to his son.

Yes, your mother is right. I will not let you go back now. I must call the chief and his *askaris*. You will reap what you have sowed.

Please, Father, don't call the chief.

Grandfather did not answer. He was already on his way to tell the chief that his terrorist son was hiding at home wounded. Two grandmothers ran after him pleading with him not to betray his son. He refused to listen and would not stop. When it was clear that nothing would deter him, the grandmothers turned back to hide the son before the chief came. They knew they would be killed for hiding him but how can a mother just wait for someone to come and kill her son. Is not dying for a child also the duty of motherhood? But it was too late. The chief arrived with his *askaris*. When all the family members gathered outside Grandmother's hut saw the chief, they knew all was over for Mungai.

The chief came wearing a big grin on his face. For him, Mungai was a prime catch. His mind was racing: They say even a featherless bird might fly, *niyumbukaga i mbute,* but there is a good chance that I will get my cash reward for killing a Mau Mau terrorist, or immediately be promoted to senior chief. This is my day. As for the poor father of this terrorist, I will give him a bit of the money, just to thank him. After all, when you take a young one from the mother ape, you throw a pumpkin to her, *ona igitunywo mwana ni ikagirio mungu.*

Suddenly the chief jumped out of his trance when he realized he was smiling instead of looking dead serious. After all, he was dealing with a dangerous Mau Mau terrorist. And who could tell for sure? Maybe fellow terrorists were lurking in the bushes nearby. He had to finish doing what he had come here to do.

What is this *kimaramari,* terrorist, doing here? He asked sternly. Did you come to kill my people, you murderer and enemy of peace and government? Mungai did not answer. He saw no need to argue with an enemy he could not convince. He just looked at him.

Will you not answer me or don't you know I have power to do with you what I want?

Black slaves of white masters have no power of their own. You can only do what your white masters have asked you to do, Mungai replied calmly. Grandfather then said to him, Why do you answer the chief so? Can't you be polite to *munene,* the chief?

To what purpose? Mungai asked his father. Is this not what you wanted when you called him?

If you are brave, why are you hiding among bananas? Come out of hiding and surrender, you terrorist, the chief shouted.

I will come out but never surrender. I am a freedom fighter, not a terrorist. If I terrorize the British and their collaborators like you, it is because you are terrorists, too. Forgetting the danger Mungai was in, people around were almost beginning to enjoy the exchange. Then the chief shouted: Shut up! Who do you think you are to talk back to me?

I am a soldier of freedom. You are a soldier of foreign tyranny, Mungai said bravely. Drag him out of here, the chief ordered his *askaris.*

Mungai was then marched out of the grove and placed before the chief. The chief slapped him hard, spat on him while hissing at him like a snake.

Confess, you terrorist! Confess or I kill you! the chief thundered out.

I have nothing to confess and you may kill me if you want, replied Mungai.

Then say your last prayer, as we shall not even give you a last meal, said the chief, as he grabbed a spear from one of his *askaris.* The chief's action now set the grandmothers, older and younger mothers, aunts and other women wailing while beseeching the chief to spare their son and brother.

Please spare him, they said. He is your son, too. Please spare him and Ngai will also spare you.

This is not anybody's son. He is a terrorist, the chief said in answer to their prayer.

We beseech you upon the breasts that suckled you. Please spare him, the women insisted.

Let him confess then. Let him beg for mercy. Mercy is given only if it is asked for, the chief said now with a grin on his face.

I have nothing to confess and I don't need the white man's mercy. What mercy of your own can you give? Mungai asked the chief. And turning to his mothers and sisters he said, Mothers, do not give pleasure to this killer by crying or asking mercy for me. How can one who is already dead give life or mercy? A dead man can only give death. Convinced he was about to die, Mungai showed no fear of death at all. He reached the ground with his hand, scooped a handful of sacred soil and raised his hand saying, I am ready to die for land and freedom. I am ready to die so that Kenya may live. Long live *itungati,* our freedom fighters. Long live Kenya.

That was the final challenge, the final provocation. Immediately the chief's spear hit Mungai, followed by a hail of others. His blood splattered the clothes of his killers as he collapsed instantly and died with a ring of spears in his body. To exact maximum humiliation upon a freedom fighter, the black agents of colonialism dragged Mungai's bleeding body on the ground and deposited it at the chief's camp fully covered in dust. They all spat on it as if Mungai was their personal enemy. Mungai's head and arms were cut off, put in a basket and taken to the white district officer as irrefutable evidence of his death. The rest of his body was dumped into a hastily dug grave and covered with soil without any burial ceremony at all.

Meantime, at home, the crying and mourning continued for many days. It killed Grandmother soon after. In the forest, fellow freedom fighters bitterly mourned the death of Mungai for many days. They lost a comrade, and the country lost a great son. To immortalize him, they sang:

Wamwere, Wamwere, Wamwere,
You ask me not to betray you,
You ask me not to betray you
And leave our house, being set on fire.

After the death of his son, Grandfather lived in fear that freedom fighters might come and kill him. They never did, but fear never left him. It was a painful sentence.

No Rebirth

Another Mungai was born, my second brother. He was particularly close to me because I was the one who always carried him on my back when Mother had work to do. Maybe I loved him more because he was very quiet and did not cry much. He looked as if he were always observing, which made him seem older.

Then he caught *muthanduku,* yellow fever, together with other children in the village. This disease always attacked many children at once. For treatment, Mungai was washed with *muratina,* traditional beer. When beer did not cure, he was smeared with soil freshly dug up by a mole, *tiri wa huko,* which was considered medicinal. Despite this treatment that cured some other children, I woke up every day to see my little brother wither like a fallen leaf in the sun. I continued to hope he would get well but one night, he died. When we woke up, Mother was crying. Father was very sad. Grief was everywhere. When I realized my little brother was dead, I cried and called him to come back. He did not. As we cried, I heard Mother ask, What must we do to make you stay, Mungai? She was convinced that her Mungai, like other Mungais in the family, died because he refused to stay.

Because of his father's betrayal, my young father Mungai had died a very angry man. His spirit would not be propitiated, and he refused to stay every time his brother and sisters bore him. Afterwards, I heard people say that Mungai was determined never to return to his father's home or to his family. His brothers and sisters desired him back and never gave up. Disappointed many times, they did everything they could to appease his angry spirit. They slaughtered animals. They offered libations of *muratina* to him. They apologized for their father. For a long time, he would not be appeased. But when his father died, they must have talked and reconciled. Thereafter, he softened and agreed to stay. Unfortunately, my brother Mungai did not come back. By the time he agreed to stay, it was the turn of his brothers to come home and our parents did not get enough boys to give him a second chance. But he lives in our hearts.

Village Internment

Our village had about one hundred fifty workers and seven hundred people. It was round and had about 200 round, timber-built and grass-thatched huts. Most workers had a *nyumba nene*, a *thingira*, a men's hut, and an *ikumbi*. The three huts together belonged to a single fenced compound. Hut floors were earthen. Each compound also had a pen for animals. We had no electric lighting or heating and drew our water from the river until a single water tap was built in the village. There was always a long queue for water. The village was built in a forest from which we cut firewood, gathered grass for thatching and got timber for building the huts.

The headman, a colonial administrator, was the leader of home guards and the chief of the village. Other important people in the village were the overseers, *nyabaara.* The school, the church, the shop, the butchery, the ramshackle hotel and the dispensary were in the food center, Mung'etho, outside the village. Teachers, the village nurse, the agricultural officer, and the welfare officer lived at the center.

When the war was declared, settlers wanted the whole village closed down and all the workers and their families imprisoned in a concentration camp at Jack's farm near Nakuru town, Kwa Njeki. They wanted them screened for any connection with Mau Mau and removed from where they might give food and support to Mau Mau. When a few workers and their families were interned at Kwa Njeki for screening, life there was very difficult. They were given terrible food and interrogators and camp guards beat them brutally. Children did not go to school. They were kept dirty and thirsty. They were given little medical attention. There was no privacy for women or adults. Tortured until they confessed to false guilt, many were deported, detained and others killed.

As workers continued to be taken from the forest to the concentration camp, it dawned upon one white forest officer whom people called Kahara for his bald head, that loss of forest workers to the camp was making his work of developing the forest impossible. He wanted workers screened in the forest for any connection they were said to have with Mau Mau, and he said no to any more arrests and transfers of his workers to the camp. People in the forest hailed Kahara as *Muhonokia,* their savior. But he was not to be. As a clever forester and colonizer of Africans, he secured their labor and exclusion from Mau Mau by interning them in the village. And he expelled some workers from the forest.

Kahara increased the number of forest guards. The village was encircled with a high fence and a trench fifteen feet wide and deep whose floor was crisscrossed with sharp baboon spikes meant to kill instantly anyone who fell upon them. Armed personnel secured the fence and entry into the village against Mau Mau by keeping it guarded day and night. Finally, a high watchtower was built in the center of the village and manned round the clock by armed guards. So watched, forest workers could now work without any possibility of supporting the freedom fighters.

One morning, Kahara mobilized all forest workers, marshaled them into a two-mile-wide line and forced them to walk abreast of each other, combing the forest for Mau Mau, whom they never found, for twenty miles from Rugongo village to Dundori. Though long-starved for meat, when the workers surprised animals in their lairs they were not allowed to catch them. They were looking for Mau Mau, not animals.

Workers were very sad when Kahara left the forest. They showered him with gifts of sheep, chicken, pumpkins, potatoes and what little money they had. New workers wondered why. Older workers said, though he had put them into a forest of hyenas, he had rescued them from one of leopards. But he was not typical.

After him, came Kimutwe, the big head. He beat workers for pleasure. He organized women, even pregnant mothers, to dig holes for planting seedlings all day without pay. When mothers came home from forced labor, there was no food to cook. He forced workers to work harder and longer every day. He was everywhere, checking who was doing wrong where, as if the mission of his life and race was to enslave and terrorize the African.

Why Mau Mau Fought

For Africans, land meant more than food and a house. It was their permanent residence before, during and after life. To fight for land and freedom, Mau Mau were trying to secure their eternal existence. Refusing to understand this, the British had subjected them to great misrepresentation. They called them *itoi,* rebels, *imaramari,* terrorists, *washenzi,* primitive people, as well as atavistic, cannibalistic and beastly. In the minds of the British, Mungai and his comrades were not fighting for freedom. Africans knew of no freedom. They were fighting to return to a past of primitiveness, darkness, death and evil. The British accused Mungai and his comrades of foolishly sacrificing their lives for death.

Mungai went to the forest not to lose his own life, but to protect African life from being snuffed out by British colonialism. He went to the forest not because he loved going for days without food as a guerrilla, but because he wanted to recapture stolen lands and end hunger for himself and other Kenyans. Mungai preferred to die rather than live as a *njuna ndara,* one who licks the meat grills of white people.

Contrary to British propaganda, Mungai did not love the cold and rain of forest life. He went to the forest because the cold of colonial racism and the color bar was greater. He was willing to freeze in the jungle to end the cold and rain of racial discrimination, unemployment and the hunger of the perennially underfed African child.

Like other young men, Mungai was married and wanted to have a family but he did not want to be a father whom white people called *mboi,* a boy, and humiliated before his own children. He did not want to be a father and a husband who begged the white man for food for his family. He died for the security of his wife and children against colonial rape and assault. He went to the forest to fight for human rights of his people.

Mungai did not fight in the Second World War but he knew that Africans who fought in that war died not just for the freedom of Europe but Kenya, Africa and the world. After the war, Africans expected the British who had fought Adolf Hitler as an enemy of freedom, democracy and humanity to concede the same rights to them. Instead, Winston Churchill said he did not become prime minister "to preside over the liquidation of the British Empire" after the war. With these words, it was as if he had told Africans, If you want freedom, fight for it. Mungai went to the forest not for the love of war, but because he hated betrayal of freedom. The British had forced him into war.

Despite Churchill's betrayal, the Second World War had taught Africans two lessons: With guns, they could kill white people. If the German Hitler could be fought, so could the British Hitler. After the war, British soldiers had come to Kenya to be rewarded with land. African soldiers had returned home, not to be given land, but for the lucky ones to be hired as laborers of those who had fought with them in the same trenches in Europe and Burma. This was the injustice that had driven Mungai and the Mau Mau to the forests.

Divide and Rule

After learning why Mungai refused to stay and how he died, I missed him a lot and often asked him, Why did you agree to die when you could have begged for mercy and lived? Mungai would whisper into my soul, I would rather die on my feet than live on my knees. It was better to die than beg for mercy and surrender.

To him the solution to all our problems was quite simple: The British had to go. The British, however, saw the colonial question differently. They had not come to Kenya and Africa in order to leave as soon as they were unwanted or after they had built homes and settled. They had come to stay, to "civilize" the Dark Continent and have a good life. They had tasted the good life and would not give it up without a fight.

For the British, the solution to the Mau Mau rebellion was to beat Africans into submission and force acceptance of colonialism. Of course, the British feared to be hurt in the war just as the Kenyans did. They preferred African submission to war. But given the choice between giving up colonialism or fighting for it, they were ready to do battle. I doubt, though, that their aim was to kill off all the

Kenyans. Colonialism could not survive without them. For colonialists to have their wealth and comforts, they had to browbeat Kenyans into working for them. If Africans refused to work or were annihilated, colonialism would die too. It is only because Africans agreed to work for them that colonialism proved profitable. It would have made little sense for colonialists to kill off all Africans. The war was to force Africans to submit. But how could so few Europeans beat so many Africans into submission and slavery?

British colonialists had been into other parts of the world before they came to Kenya and were experienced in the art of making war against other people. In the course of their colonial adventures, they had learnt that for tiny foreign minorities to conquer and rule hostile native majorities, they had to divide them into antagonistic parts. This was the tactic of divide and rule.

As the Mau Mau war raged, I heard nothing about divide and rule. Many years later, I would be intrigued. In the forest, there was only one white man and his family, yet he ruled over thousands of African families. Everywhere I went, one white man owned land and ruled over hundreds and hundreds of African workers. In police stations, one white police inspector carried a pistol and ruled over tens of African police who carried bigger guns. Even in the army, there were more African soldiers fighting Mau Mau freedom fighters than white soldiers.

How could so few dispossess, rule over and wage war against so many? I asked one old man.

Son of Wamwere, he told me, I don't know how the white man works. I have never been to his school. But look at me. I am one man and have five wives. How do I rule over them? The white man ruled over us the same way. But you do not have five wives. Let me tell you how it is done.

To rule over five wives, the first thing society has helped me to do is own everything in my home. The land, animals, food, children and even the wives belong to me. I own them. I must give my wives food and everything else they need and want. And to give my wives a nice piece of meat, a beautiful dress or build them a nice hut, they must obey me completely. If they do not, society has allowed me to beat them. It is intolerable that a wife I had paid dowry for should disobey me. For providing for them, my wives must not only obey, they must also be grateful.

To remain the boss of my family, I split my wives. But how do I oppress women who are my wives? They give me love, wealth, every service, children and more happiness than I give to any of them. Instead of paying back in kind, I subvert their peace and friendship. They must not be good friends or they will unite against me. To prevent them making war against me, I pit them against one another. They are not entitled to the same happiness. I engender permanent rivalry among them by always having a *ngatha*, favorite wife, and those I love less. I flatter some, demonize others and keep them at each other's throats. The rivalry in the same compound ensures that no two wives can unite against me.

Though I oppress and beat them all, they are never able to unite and over-throw my rule. When I fight one, others do not help. When I attack all, they disperse. They have no collective defense. Indeed, when I fight the *ngatha,* others cheer and help me to put her down. As the lord of my home, my children follow me, do what I ask and take my name. They never join their mothers to fight me.

At my home, I have a different house for every wife. This is for their independence, but also to keep them isolated from one another. While no wife may live with another, I move in with all, inciting one against the other with malicious and false gossip. Kept to themselves, they are never able to discover the untruth of my lies and they keep on fighting.

What I do to my wives is what the white man did to us Africans. He dispossessed us, owned us and demanded obedience and conflict between us for us to have a home, a job, money, food and to stay out of prison. When a brother—in the army, police or government—was fed and paid by the white man to kill his brother, he did so to keep his family and himself alive.

Colonialists created a separate district or province for each ethnic community. And while Africans could not move in, out of, or between these ethnic regions without a passbook, *kipande,* or travel permission from a white man, the colonialist moved freely between them, gossiping and telling lies about communities to one another. Unable to meet, we could not expose the untruth of colonial gossip and lies and remained enemies, willing to follow the white man in any war he declared against any one African community. Passbooks kept us divided, subdivided, separated, ignorant and weak. These colonial lies, falsehoods, prejudices and stereotypes that were told, whispered and seemingly innocuously hinted to us are the genesis of our current ethnic hatred for one another that we call *ukabila,* ethnicity.

As our sons and daughters went to the forests to fight the white man, to make sure that other African communities did not join us in this war, the white man went to all other ethnic communities flattering them that they are better than us— the Gikuyu, Embu and Meru (GEMA). He called us cannibals and demonized us to them. He told them Mau Mau fighters were their enemies who intended to enslave them after driving the white man out of Kenya. This is why Gikuyu detainees sang:

> When we arrived in detention
> We were placed at the gates.
> Many Aduruma people came to look at us.
> They were very frightened
> Having been told we were cannibals.

Freedom fighters and Gikuyu people were also vilified as beasts with tails and hooves. Often the white man called us bloody *nugu mwenye mkia*, bloody apes with tails, and we said, *ndiyo bwana*, yes, master, because we dared not call him a liar.

So, convinced that white colonialists were their protectors against future domination by Gikuyu people, many ethnic communities considered it a pleasure and a privilege to join the colonial army and kill Mau Mau freedom fighters. In schools, markets, public meetings and churches, whites called Mau Mau freedom fighters enemies of peace. They accused them of starting the war and of refusing to surrender to end the war. People who hated warmongers were given spears and guns to hunt down and kill Gikuyu people as Mau Maus.

In our homes, Christianity was used as an instrument for dividing families and recruiting collaborators and soldiers for colonialism. Those who refused to join Christianity were branded enemies, rebels and children of the devil, and it was demanded of those who joined the white man's religion to defend Christ and the Queen by fighting against their own country, freedom, kith and kin.

Colonial education was introduced. Its possession gave you a better job and more money. To have it you had to denounce your culture, religion and independence. You had to become a puppet. They brought a colonial parliament that they called Legislative Council (Legico) and local councils. No Gikuyu person could vote, be nominated or be elected into these bodies unless he was loyal to colonialism and had denounced the Mau Mau.

Land was confiscated from Africans and returned only to those who denounced Mau Mau and supported colonialism. Colonialists fed people in drier areas with food they had stolen from areas with more rain, but only if they were willing to enlist as soldiers and kill freedom fighters.

Numerically, Africans were a majority and white settlers a minority. When we could not travel and combine the numbers of our ethnic communities, the white man transformed his weakness into strength. Divided, our people had no strength. They were like my five wives. I can rule them even if I am one.

Curfews and Searches

Mau Mau times were hard times and our imprisonment as a people was completed with the imposition of dusk to dawn curfews throughout the land (from 3 P.M. to 9 A.M.). Only Father got up earlier to go to work under armed guard. This curfew that especially forbid womenfolk to leave the village before nine o'clock in the morning made things very difficult because the gardens were far and everything that we used from firewood to water to food had to be collected far away from home.

Women had to be escorted by armed guards to the forests to cut firewood and bring it back home. They had also to be escorted to fetch water from the river.

For the remaining short hours, women were escorted to the gardens to plant, weed and collect food. Unattended for weeks and months, our gardens were overgrown with weeds that smothered crops. We scavenged from these overgrown fields. To and from the *shambas,* mothers were always hurried like slaves.

After fetching their own food, firewood and water, mothers were forced to take some of their firewood, water and food to the guards and cook it for them. While these forest wardens were policing us, our mothers were digging and weeding their gardens. On weekends, they came to our homes to drink free beer *muratina,* and eat free eggs and chickens. The most sadistic would compel forest workers to slaughter their fattest rams for them, roast and wrap up the meat, and take it to the guards' homes—without tasting a piece! Women raped by forest guards never dared complain about the crime.

On coming home from work and gardens, people were required to cook, eat, put out fires and go to bed by 8 P.M. But before they slept, every hut had to be searched for hidden Mau Mau and contraband like guns, bullets or subversive literature. We called these nightly inspections *mbirigiceni.*

Every night, there were several search teams in the village that were made up of home guards, forest guards and African police and led by white officers. All white officers wore camouflage uniforms, and it was difficult to know which branch of the colonial forces they came from except when the officer was the known forest officer, one of the nearby settlers whom we knew or Father Tui, the white Catholic priest who said Mass in our church.

Father Tui evoked particular interest when he came for searches because no one expected a priest to double up as a police or army officer, although many did. The same priest who looked so pious in his priestly robes at 3 P.M. during Mass would look so stern and hostile in his military camouflage at night. Often, like a naughty child, I tried to look him in the eye but without success. As chaperones of colonialism, white priests were so anxious to protect the regime that people in our village would not confess to them if they had taken the Mau Mau oath before converting to Christianity for fear of arrest.

Search teams were gangs of terror. Though they came in the name of looking for Mau Mau, they beat our fathers and us children, raped our mothers and sisters and stole our sheep with impunity. After every search, we were left trembling with fear. For saying they had seen no Mau Mau in the village, our fathers were beaten and taken to screening camps for more torture, deportation, detention and death. In the morning, the telltale signs of a night search were the ugly bruises on the faces, hands and feet of men and women.

One night a search team came to our house. After they looked into every nook and cranny for Mau Mau, Father was called outside. He was asked about rumors that freedom fighters had come to the village the night before to administer an oath, *muuma.* Father said he had not heard anything about the alleged visit by the freedom fighters or the *muuma.* Four African police, *askaris,* turned him around and held his hands behind his back while the white officer set upon him viciously with slaps, punches and kicks. One of the punches to his mouth knocked out three more of his teeth and Father collapsed. He was held up again and the merciless *mzungu* continued to punch and kick him. Father groaned with pain, tears involuntarily ran down his face but he did not scream. At one point, the *mzungu* let his hands go out of weariness. While he rested, an African policeman took over and beat Father even more mercilessly to convince his master that he was not soft with fellow Africans.

In the meantime, Mother was crying and pacing up and down the muddy floor of our tiny hut greatly pained and hissing with fury. Suddenly she grabbed the sharpened *panga,* machete, that Father went to work with and rushed outside. She told the perplexed search team, Let him alone. If any of you touches him again, I will cut him into pieces. The *askaris* let Father go and went away without a word. They thought her mad. And maybe she was temporarily. She was ready to kill and be killed.

Inside the hut, Father just dropped on the dirty floor, battered and exhausted with pain. Mother changed his clothes, cleaned his bloody face and his injuries with hot salt water and carefully laid him on his bed. Looking down on his face, I noticed that a growth on his left cheek was missing. A blow had torn it off! With that big gap in his mouth, this beating made Father look 20 years older.

Jamrih

Father was not the only victim of nightly police terror. An *askari* loved the wife of a local shop owner. Secretly he planted a bullet in a bag of rice in the shop and then reported the man as a suspect of trafficking in bullets and weapons to the Mau Mau. When the shop was searched and the bullet found in the bag of rice, the shopkeeper was arrested, kicked, boxed, clobbered and shot dead as a Mau Mau terrorist.

But the most memorable of these inspections was done in the day, at about 1 P.M. in the home of a Quaker (*mukurino*) woman called Jamrih. Against curfew rules, she used to sing all night and kept long hair under her headscarf—a tradition that colonial authorities hated. She sang Quaker songs that had been banned in the 1940s for likening colonial Kenya to the Egypt of the Pharaohs. Instructed to stop singing the banned songs, Jamrih claimed God ordered her to continue singing and sent evil spirits to torment her when she did not.

There was a heavy noonday downpour when we saw a white officer, the colonial headman and a team of police, home and forest guards, heading for Jamrih's home. Moments later, they came back, frog-marching and whipping Jamrih while she sang the forbidden songs at the top of her voice. Stop! they ordered her but she would not. Then they beat her, but the more they beat her the more she sang:

> When children of Israel
> Were in Egypt
> They were made to do
> Very hard labor
> Of making bricks
> And cutting grass.
> They cried to Jehovah
> To free them from slavery.

Jamrih wore white robes and a white headscarf and it was an unforgettable and tearful spectacle to see this white-robed African lady walking and singing in the rain while blows and whips from the ten men who surrounded her rained on her ceaselessly and mercilessly. The song itself drew tears from my eyes while her loud sobbing as she sang bravely made us all sob with her. In their desperation, the colonial forces started tearing off her garments and headscarf and cutting her long black hair, not with scissors, but with machetes, and throwing it into ponds of water. All the children in our side of the village came out of our homes in the rain and followed Jamrih and her tormentors to the headman's post, where she was roughly bundled into a waiting Land Rover. Moments later she was driven away to Kwa Nyangweso, the torture camp. But the brave, defiant and glorious figure she cut in the rain was truly a spectacle to behold!

Her courage was impressive. In her bravery and defiance, she symbolized the fighting Mau Mau freedom fighters, and in her persecution and suffering, she personalized the suffering Kenyan nation. In the context of her song, we knew Mau Mau was our Moses. Like the Egyptian charioteers, would the British colonial army, now in hot pursuit of Kenyan people, also perish in the Red Sea of Kenyan forests?

Meeting the Mau Mau

> Traitors at Kiria do not sleep
> Looking for freedom fighters
> To win three thousand shillings.

One day, Mother and I were rushing home from an area of gardens that was called Kigundu. It was about 3 P.M. and we were hurrying home to beat the curfew.

Although it was not too late, being the rainy season, the sky was overcast with heavy black clouds, every tree and bush was in heavy dark-green leaf and it looked quite dark already. To make it worse, the path we walked in and every single leaf overhanging our path was wet. As we were the only ones walking home, Mother walked at a quick pace, though she had on her back two large baskets of Irish potatoes and green maize combs; I walked closely behind her.

Midway, we came to a small valley through which ran a small river. As we came to the river, I felt afraid because the forest was thicker here and felt like the sort of place where leopards hide. Suddenly to my right, I saw some dark, thick smoke going up in the forest not far from where we were. Then I heard the shuffling of leaves from the same direction and I stopped in fear, clutching Mother's dress. As Mother stopped, a man of average height with thick, long dreadlocks and wearing a leopard skin over a heavy coat greeted Mother.

Mother of the nation, *nyina wa ruriri,* how are you?

I am fine, Mother said.

The man looked quite friendly but I was transfixed in a mixture of fear and amazement at his extraordinariness. Are you not afraid to be walking home this late? he asked Mum.

If you are not afraid, why should I be? she replied with half a smile. Just then another man appeared, eating roasted green maize from a maize comb. He broke some off and gave me a piece as he greeted me: How are you young man?

I am fine, I said.

What is your name? he asked.

Koigi.

Ah, it is a fine name. What then do you say to people?

I kept quiet. I did not know what to say.

I am called Njogu, Elephant. Can I sing you a short song? he asked me.

I was delighted.

> We agreed to carry this log together
> When we reached middle of the river
> Some ran away,
> Others sold their people.
>
> Again Mumbi will give birth.
> Gikuyu had a good issue.
> If Mumbi gets a boy
> We shall call him Freedom.
> If she gets a girl,
> We shall call her Land.

> We honor our leaders in Nyandarua forest,
> Deadan Kimathi and General Mathenge,
> General Kago and General Waruingi.

Do you like my song? he asked me. Before I could say yes, the other man asked, Njogu, what are you telling our young friend? Let them go home. It is late.

Mother pulled me to her and we nearly ran up the hill before us. I did not hear what the other man had told her but Mother seemed more afraid now than when she was talking to the Mau Mau. As we hurried up the hill, I was wondering about Mother's new state of obvious fear and why the man told me he was called Elephant. Although I knew the name Njogu, I thought his was a nickname. It reminded me of the Gikuyu proverb that an elephant's tusks are never too heavy for it, *njogu nderemagwo ni muguongo wayo*. Were hunger, cold, rain and insecurity in the forest the tusks that these elephants were carrying to make us free? I was on the verge of asking Mother when she told me: Koigi, what you saw, you never saw, and what you heard, you never heard.

Yes, Mum, I said.

Never mention this to anybody.

Yes, Mum. Forget this as you forgot how to suckle.

Yes, Mum, I promised. Now I understood why she was so afraid. To meet the Mau Mau and not tell the authorities could lead to her execution.

When we got to the gate of the village, it was already closed. We knocked. As the gatekeeper opened it, he asked, Why are you so late? The sun cheated me, Mother said. You are lucky to find me, he said. Someone else might say you were late meeting the Mau Mau. I won't be late again, Mother said, sweating. At home, Mother said nothing.

Six months later, the whole village—men, women and children—was summoned to a meeting at Mung'etho, the trading center, derisively called idlers' territory. Nobody knew what the purpose of the meeting was. When we arrived at the center, I saw the white forest officer and many other men wearing wet coats and hats and carrying guns. We were assembled in the middle of the center where the white forest officer's Land Rover was parked and heavily guarded. When all of us were there, the headman coughed to demand total silence. Then he said: This is not my day to say anything. *Bwana mkubwa*, the Big Master, is here and he wants to talk to us. *Karibu bwana*, you are welcome, sir.

When the forest officer stood to speak, he asked the African police to bring a table from the local hotel. He then asked the police to lay the table with four naked dead bodies that were brought from inside the Land Rover, decapitated and amputated. Nobody could tell anything about these dead men except that they were African. After the bodies were laid on the table, four heads with big and long dreadlocks, four pairs of cut arms were laid beside them. When I saw the heads with dreadlocks, I knew these were Mau Mau freedom fighters. My eyes swelled with tears and my stomach felt sick. But I dared not shed a tear.

When the white officer stood to speak, he said. Come forward, all of you. I want you to see well who is on the table. Here are the bodies of four dead Mau Mau terrorists. Pointing to the armed men around him, he said, My men here and I just came from a hunt in the forest. Every time we come for night inspections, you people deny there are Mau Mau terrorists in this forest. But I have always known that all of you are liars. Yesterday, a bird told me it had seen some cowardly Mau Maus hiding in my forest. As you know that the days of a thief are no more than forty, this morning we paid a surprise visit to my guests and ordered them to surrender. They hesitated and got what they went to the forest for. I am sure Kimathi and his dogs pretend that he went into the forest to get you—he turned to the headman and asked, What do they call it? The headman said, *Wiyathi*. Yes, freedom. Now you see what Kimathi and all Mau Maus will harvest—death. Look well at these men. If any of you see any of them in our forest and keep quiet, you will harvest the same thing. At this point, sweat ran down my armpits. I thought the white man would next talk about Mother and me but he did not. I felt calmer as he talked on. But if you see them and report them to either the headman or me, they will reap what they deserve and for each of their heads the good government of Her Majesty the Queen of England will give you fifty shillings. As for these men, I will feed their dirty bodies to the dogs and pass on their heads and arms to the government as evidence of the excellent work that my men here have done.

Last thing. Again, take a good look at these dead terrorists and ask yourselves who has been feeding and hiding them. I am a good man and will forgive you this time. But next time a Mau Mau is caught in this forest, for each Mau Mau captured, I will pick by lot from among you either a man, a woman or a child to kill. Listen again. This will be one forest in Kenya without a single Mau Mau in it and I will make sure it is. Help me make it so or you will go down to your grave before I do.

After this tirade, we were put in a long line and forced to go round the table with the four dead human scarecrows. I felt like I was paying my last respects to them. When I looked at the severed heads, I saw Njogu, the freedom fighter who had shared his maize with me. I felt bad and sad and wondered, Now that the Elephant is dead, who will now carry his tusks and fight for us? I looked at Mother and she pinched my hand. It meant, not a word, *hau kunyu*.

Kimathi's Capture

After the mist, the hailstorm, says a Gikuyu proverb. We were still mourning the dead Mau Mau when we heard that Field Marshal Dedan Kimathi, the leader of

Mau Mau freedom fighters, was ambushed and captured by British armed forces on October 20, 1956. Everywhere military and police planes dropped leaflets carrying the information and a picture of Kimathi on a stretcher and in handcuffs surrounded by his white captors. He looked greater than our enemies—or was it all in my eyes? Though in enemy hands, people still hoped that Kimathi would live and eventually win. They said generals are only captured, never killed.

Kimathi's capture had an electrifying dual effect on the whole country. The African nation was plunged into sadness and near despair. White colonialists and their African collaborators were plunged into a mood of victory and an orgy of celebrations and happiness. White settlers drove about drinking beer and insulting Africans. One of them told us, You have lost, you monkeys. Your savior is in our hands to do what we want with. Long live the Queen! We said nothing. Though Kimathi's capture was our bondage, we did not believe everything was over yet. A defeathered bird can fly, *niumbukaga imbute,* says the proverb.

Without newspapers or radio, our village was in the dark about Kimathi's trial and conviction. Four months after his arrest, people got their worst news since the beginning of their rebellion. On February 19, 1957, Kimathi was hanged and buried in Kamiti prison, where his remains lie unhonored with a state burial to this day. Though stunned by the blow, people would not let their hope for freedom die with Kimathi. Desperate people hope desperately.

The most stubborn of our people believed that the justice of their cause was indestructible and immortal. The British military had beaten the Mau Mau freedom fighters, but they could not destroy the African spirit, need and determination to be free and independent. The spirit of freedom can never be extinguished from the human soul. In captivity, in defeat, it burns forever. Momentarily, the buoyancy of that spirit had been dimmed but not killed.

The belief that all was not lost was strengthened in our people by a physical happening that played into their religious superstition. The day Kimathi was hanged, it rained heavily. Tropical downpours were common in our place but many chose to believe that the heavy rain on the day Kimathi died, like that on the day Jesus Christ died, portended a resurrection of Kimathi and the Mau Mau.

When Kimathi died, nobody thought that the cause of African independence would rise from his ashes like a phoenix. But by the time Kimathi was captured and killed, Mau Mau was slowly killing the British confidence and will to fight for and maintain direct colonial rule in Kenya and Africa. Later, when Harold Macmillan, a British foreign minister, traveled to Africa and talked about a wind of change that was blowing across the continent, toppling colonial regimes and paving the way for African independence, however tarnished and compromised, he was announcing Kimathi's and the Mau Mau's victory. But for now, it was colonial business as usual.

God Save the Queen

I still remember a bright, sunny January morning in 1957. I was clothed in a pair of new khaki shorts and a khaki shirt that Father had ironed for me. I was thoroughly washed but wore no shoes, no sweater and no jacket. For the occasion, my hair was also thoroughly combed. It was Mother who escorted me to school. Hanging down by my side, I had my new schoolbag with an exercise book, a pencil and an eraser. I went to school with many of my village playmates but there we were joined by lots of other girls and boys from the surrounding villages.

The school was an instrument of colonial rule. Though by now people fully recognized the need for Western education, Africans objected to the way it was delivered to dull the minds of their children. To circumvent this, they started their own schools that were later shut down and banned. At that point, only colonial schools remained. Still Rahab, our Sunday school teacher, inspired us to join the school:

> Young man you spend all your time at home
> Wearing a sheet of cloth.
> When your cows are no more
> What will you eat?

My parents took me to school because they, like Rahab, realized that without land and cattle to give me, education was the only thing that could help me survive life in a colonial setting. African parents always dream of leaving their children an inheritance but colonial exploitation made my parents so poor that the only thing they could give me as an inheritance was education. They knew that in a colonial economy, I could not survive without a better job than the ones they had, a better job that I could not get without an education.

To my parents, education was not just an inheritance. It was the key that would let me out of the hell we lived in, the bridge to a better life they never had. As a bonus, they must also have hoped that my education might be their lifeline out of hell. As Africans who understood that they were victims of colonialism, my parents must also have hoped that the education of their children might one day come in handy as a weapon for getting freedom and independence. By taking me to school, my parents were therefore also equipping me with a sword for fighting colonialism.

That was my parents' view of education. Colonial authorities thought otherwise.

To them, school was a kiln to mould African children into perfect colonial servants. In the school, it was criminal for a teacher to give black children thoughts or aspirations of freedom. But did our parents know this? Yes, they did. As employ-ces of the colonial government, none of our teachers were ever critical of the colonial order. Still, parents had a stubborn belief that like Samson in the Bible, their children might be able to harvest honey from the carcass of a dead animal.

In our village, teachers were the vanguard of colonial forces, at the first level of colonial conquest and administration. They were the first colonial authorities we called masters. Their first responsibility was to introduce our young minds to the supremacy of the British people and colonial discipline. Like at any colonial military outpost, every morning the first thing we did was clean up the school. After that we were assembled into a parade where we were inspected for cleanliness like soldiers. We were punished for any transgressions of discipline. The headmaster read orders to us. We stood at attention, raised the Union Jack and sang "God Save the Queen":

> God save our gracious Queen!
> Long live our noble Queen!
> God save the Queen!
> Send her victorious,
> Happy and glorious,
> Long to reign over us,
> God save the Queen.
> O Lord our God arise,
> Scatter her enemies,
> And make them fall;
> Confound their politics,
> Frustrate their knavish tricks,
> On Thee our hopes we fix,
> God save us all

Every morning, we sang and prayed for our own damnation. How could the British be so arrogant? They came to our country. They beguiled us into letting them in as our guests. They made war on us. They conquered us. They stole our land and livestock. They enslaved us. When Mau Mau took up arms to reclaim our land, dignity and freedom, they made another war on us. After all this and more, they lined us up and asked us to call their queen gracious and noble. As if that were not enough, they ordered us to ask their God to save their Queen and scatter us! Indeed, he who is weak has no rights, *mnyonge hana haki.*

Did we believe in what we sang, that the British queen should scatter Mau Mau freedom fighters, make them fall, confound their politics of liberation and frustrate their efforts to make us free? What gall! They made their God our God; their queen our queen; their wishes our wishes; and their prayers our prayers, at our own expense. We did not give a hoot, but singing their national prayer over and over again might have made the words seep into the minds of some, making us colonial parrots. Colonialists must have known this. Many times they called educated Africans, bloody *kasukus,* or parrots.

In class we were taught English and European history, geography, mathematics and other subjects, not in order to make us knowledgeable but to give us skills that made us fit to deliver colonial services as police, *karanis,* milk clerks, or *waalimu,* clerks in government offices and teachers. The education in a colonial school was meant to make Africans best in service and poorest in ownership. Hence the colonial order put Europeans at number one for their so-called ability and integrity; the Muslim and the Indian at number two for their thrift and industry; the Arab at number three for their so-called tolerance and experience; the Somali at number four because they were Muslim albeit not Asian. Kenyan Africans were put last for their adaptability to colonialism.

The African school was built of mud or slabs of timber, had no lighting and gave a slave's education. But the white school I saw on my way to town was beautifully built, lit with electricity, had a swimming pool and beautiful playing fields. White children ate there, wore shoes, socks, sweaters and jackets and received a master's education.

Violence Without End

Throughout my first five years at school, I don't remember a day that I was not beaten. Our palms were beaten with twigs cut from the bush and canes imported from Singapore and the backs of our hands with rulers. We were beaten with belts and plastic pipes made firm with sticks inside. Often we were slapped and kicked. One teacher threw machetes at pupils whenever he got hysterical. My ultimate humiliation was having my naked buttocks caned in full view of schoolgirls. The worst perpetrator of school violence was Headmaster Zacharia. In his former school, he beat pupils so brutally that they ran into the forest to hide from school. He was a sadist who laughed hilariously when he punished us for wearing unwashed uniforms by kneading them into the mud with his feet.

I was not given just one beating a day. I was beaten so many times that one day I had to wear a piece of antelope skin inside my shorts to protect my skin from the vicious canes. But one morning I was unlucky. I decided to wear brand-new shorts inside my old pair. Mother had just bought me these shorts after I was sent home for lack of a decent uniform. To my great consternation, as another boy called Gathii was being beaten the headmaster discovered that he was wearing a piece of animal skin under his shorts. He was undressed and the piece of leather removed. He was then caned on his bare buttocks. Seeing this, I was sure my new shorts would also be discovered. Before I was reached, I feigned stomach trouble and asked for permission to visit the toilet. With permission granted, I did not go there. I went to the bush, hid my new shorts in a tree and returned to the parade feeling safe. Luckily, I was not beaten but when I went to collect my shorts after classes, they were gone. I went home scared to death. Where would I say my shorts were? The following day Mother asked me to wear my new shorts. I pretended to look for them but could not, of course, find them. When Mum looked for them, she was no luckier. Everybody wondered who could have taken them. Mum and Pap concluded some thief must have stolen them but I suggested that rats might have taken and hidden them as they did spoons. For a long time, I regretted that I had taken the new shorts to school. Worse, that I had not worn them and hidden the old ones instead. But nobody starts with wisdom.

In class four, a fierce competition for the big girls developed between bigger boys and male teachers. One morning it got out of hand. After the parade, many of us were called out and ordered to sit alone on the soccer field. Teachers then sat around the pitch, each with a bundle of canes. Each of us was called before each teacher for interrogation. When I reached my first interrogator, I was given very painful strokes and asked, Koigi, you are accused of saying that Madam Njoki sleeps with the headmaster. Did you say this or not?

I did not, I said.

Between you and us, who is lying?

When I said, I am not lying, sir, I was given more strokes and sent to another teacher. He received me with more strokes and more questions: Did you say that Master Andrew is a friend of Anastacia in your class?

I did not, sir, I said. More severe strokes and off I was sent to a third teacher who thoroughly whipped me and sent me to the fourth teacher. I was sent to all seven teachers, getting more strokes at each stop. By the end of the morning, I had been given more than thirty strokes. There was no lunch for us that day. Only the teachers ate.

Between 3 and 4 P.M. all the interrogating teachers gathered in one classroom into which all of us were called one by one. A teacher stood behind seven tables. When I was called in, I was put on all the seven tables and given severe strokes at each. After the last table, I collapsed on my way out and vomited with pain. One teacher yelled at me: Get out of there double quick or catch hell. I barely dragged myself out of there and got away. All over my body I had bruised, purplish stripes like a black zebra.

Before this bizarre saga was over, Njoroge, one of the bigger boys, was called in and butts of *kiraiku*, hand-wrapped cigarettes, were found in his pocket. For this, the seven teachers descended on him with canes and kicks and Njoroge screamed like hell. His brother, Kabata, came to his rescue and hurled machetes at teachers like missiles. Some teachers ran to their houses and others locked themselves in the classroom as the whole assembly of pupils rioted. We wanted to beat up the teachers but each time we advanced, they retreated in fear and later went home. That day school was a battlefield. When we returned the following day, tempers had cooled but teachers still looked at us not as their pupils but as real enemies. Though neither teachers nor pupils could be in the school without the other, later that week a list of boys to be expelled was put on the notice board. They left and we stayed to await another explosion.

The lesson was clear. Teachers and all authorities were right all the time and to be obeyed without question. To guarantee the production of "educated" African robots, disobedience in colonial schools would be countered with unalloyed violence and expulsions, however unreasonable.

Playing Truant

Whenever I saw a white man, I flinched as a man who has been bitten by a snake does whenever he sees a rope. As for my teachers, I feared them so much that whenever I saw one coming, if I could, I hid in the bush. This violence did not inspire me to work harder or make me more obedient. It made me fear and hate school. For about three years, I was almost the last in my end of term exams. Then, slowly, I graduated from doing poorly to playing truant.

It started in class two. When I left home, instead of going to school, I joined my friend Johana to go to the forest and play the same game colonialists played with us. We captured different live insects, put them together and made them yield pleasure for us. If we could, we would have made them dance or fight to entertain us. Now, we caught as many of them as we could and one by one pierced them with sharp thorns, to see which one would last longest. Unsatisfied, we would play with danger by going to school, crouching along the veranda and peeping into our class to see what was going on. One time one of the lady teachers caught a glimpse of us. When she came to look, we were gone. Had we been caught, we would have received a beating like no other.

After school, we would walk out of the bushes and join the others to go home as if we too were coming from school. One day, in Father's presence, my brother Kuria Munene wondered aloud why he had not seen me in school for some days. I said I went to school every day. Father was skeptical and asked Kuria to check my books. When they were looked at, it was clear I had missed school for a whole week! As Pap eyed me in disbelief, I dashed out like a deer. I walked about the village in the dark; it was cold, I was afraid and I turned back, sat leaning on our hut, sleeping and snoring until Pap came out and caught me in my sleep. Not that night, but the following morning, I was sent to school with a beating that rescued my entire school career.

Pyramid of Violence

When one animal is pushed, says a Gikuyu proverb, it pushes another, *yaikio iik-agia ingi*. Our village was a pyramid of violence with those at the top lording it over those directly below them, violence that gathered moment and intensity as it flowed downwards. The white forest officer stood at the top of it like a god holding a stick of colonial authority. Below him stood African forest rangers carrying long whips. Further below came *wanyapara*, overseers, and soldiers, *askaris* who beat workers with even longer whips.

The source of this violence, however, lay outside the village. It started thousands of miles away with the white queen in England. Like a river, it grew as it was taken over by the white governor in Nairobi; the white provincial commissioner (PC) in Nakuru, the provincial capital; the white district commissioners (DCs) in Nakuru, district headquarters; and the white divisional officers (DOs) at Bahati. From there, the baton was passed on to the black chiefs, village headmen and home guards. When this powerful stream of violence reached Father, it knocked him down with its brutality.

Unlike fire that purifies gold, violence does not purify its victims. It makes them violent. Father was a victim of some form of violence every day of his colonial life. If it was not physical assault, it was exploitation, humiliation or verbal abuse. This brutality put him under great stress, and he came home in a terrible mood every day. Many times I saw Father slap Mother or hit her with burning firewood merely because food was not ready or merely because Mother had asked a question. Every time I saw Father rub burning firewood against a firestone, I knew he was about to hit Mother with it. This burning firewood would land on Mother's body, head, hair or hand and flying sparks would scatter and force us children to scurry for cover under the bed, while Mother ran out into the dark. She would stay out in the cold and sometimes rain and come back when Father was already asleep. With Mum gone, we slept without food. These were sad days, and many times I cried for Mother. When she was under attack, it was painful to hear Mum screaming for help when all we could do was plead with Father to leave her alone. Please, Pap, don't beat Mother. Sometimes he listened, other times he just pushed us aside.

The violence Father endured at work seemed to drive him in two directions. It made him edgy towards Mother, and it made him drink excessively whenever he could on payday at the end of the month. Every such time, he bought beer for himself and the other men. He was very generous even with children, for whom he bought sweets and gave pennies. On such days, I would be on my way to the shop and meet him followed by a long line of village children like the Pied Piper. If he had any more pennies left, he would give them to us to buy sweets. He would go home empty-handed and sing sad songs for his mother all night until he finally collapsed with exhaustion and slept. When he woke up in the morning, he would find our angry mother waiting for him because he had spent all his pay.

Yet my father had a reputation for being very polite and gentle. While he beat Mother, I never heard him fight any other man. As for his children, he was very forgiving. He beat me once for every ten transgressions, usually for something minor. Often it was Mother who disciplined us for our various misdeeds—pinching sugar, stealing Father's honey, getting to the garden late, failing to draw water and so forth.

There was hardly a worker who was not a victim of colonial violence. Violence trickled down to women through their husbands. When workers were not beating their wives, they were fighting one another to prove their manhood. To prove their manhood, workers fought with their whole families for the top positions in the hierarchy of village life. Driven to the end of their wits by their husbands, women, in turn, beat their children—often without any provocation at all. When kids were not near, some women who were angry with their husbands would throw things at chickens.

Beaten daily by our teachers, fathers and mothers, to prove that we too could beat someone else, we turned to fighting one another every day. Victims of violence already, we fought as if we could never have enough. Among boys, we established a hierarchy of power. Among us, we fought duels. With boys from other villages, we had group fights. Though not allowed to fight, we cut trees and made pugilist arenas in the forest.

We fought for space and sport and knocked out each other's teeth without grudge. As often as my parents beat me, I never felt abused. They said it was for my good and I believed them. When I discovered they also beat me out of frustration, I did not hold it against them. We were all victims of a cycle of colonial violence.

Still, I remember the first day I said no to violence. In the morning, a boy called Waweru snatched my pen from my shirt pocket. I discovered it and took the pen back. In the evening, he came home with his mother to demand the pen back. Father came in and found them explaining why they had come. Father gave them money for a new pen. When they left, he started beating me. To demonstrate my innocence and anger, I refused to cry. My refusal looked like defiance and angered Father so much that he put my naked back over the fire. Still I did not scream. Surprised, he put me down. He did not apologize, but he never beat me again.

Because I was so thin, one day Father took me to Nakuru hospital to see what was wrong. From the hospital we went to a kiosk where Father bought me some cakes and tea. Without money for bus fare, we had to walk twenty miles back home. Despite the walking I was feeling very happy. Suddenly a Land Rover stopped ahead of us and Father was summoned to approach. He took his hat into his hands and approached. Why did you not take your hat off when I passed you? the white man in the car asked Father. I did not hear the car pass, *bwana mkubwa* (great sir), Father said meekly. Give me your hat, the forest officer ordered. You must collect this hat from my office before nine o'clock tonight. Yes, sir. And he drove off.

Because I could not walk to the forest office and then home, Father first walked me home, a whole twenty miles. From home, he walked another seven miles to the forest office and another seven miles back home. Finally he was home at about midnight, tired as a donkey. Fortunately the following day was Sunday.

Misfortunes do not come singly. Shortly after Father's punishment, I witnessed an even worse punishment that seemed driven purely by colonial sadism. Our donkey, Toto, had strayed into the compound of drunken forest guards to eat *machicha,* fermented lees of maize meal beer (*busaa*). Out of malice, sadism and drunken pleasure, the guards shot her dead. The following day, Mother was called to go and fetch Toto, whose stomach was now bloated like a balloon. Father was not at home so I accompanied Mother to the guards' compound. When we arrived, I remember feeling very scared of the guards who were drunk, hostile, red-eyed and sounded very threatening. When I saw our dead Toto, I was filled with emotion and cried. We were asked to take her away but we could not and Mother sent me to go and fetch my Uncle Johana. I came back with him to the guards' compound.

Toto's legs were tied up with tough sisal ropes and both Mother and Uncle pulled and dragged her out of the guards' compound one mile away to a spot where they were told to bury her. They dug a deep hole and buried her. But when we were leaving the place, the guards turned up and ordered us to exhume her, fill up her grave with soil, drag her to a new spot about eight hundred meters away, dig another grave and bury her there! As Mother and Uncle did all this, the guards were standing by laughing stupidly and maliciously, especially their leader. He had ugly scars on his face that made him look very cruel—not to mention that he liked beating workers brutally when he was drunk. To me, he looked like the one who had killed Toto and the very personification of colonial brutality and sadism. Mother and Uncle did not finish reburying Toto until six o'clock—more than ten hours since we first appeared at the guards' compound.

A Boy's Independence

Now I felt like a man and wanted my own *thingira*. I was only twelve years old and Father thought I was too small to be on my own. I insisted and after giving in, Father allowed me to take a potato store hut as my own. I liked this because I loved to eat potatoes and could roast some every night without Mother knowing it. But the main reason I wanted my own hut was to have a place where girls could visit me unbeknownst to my parents.

One very dark night, it was raining cats and dogs and I was alone in my *thingira*. Suddenly, I heard movement outside and a large stone was hurled at the door of my hut, which broke it away. Huddled in my bed, I was so scared that I could not scream. Then I heard somebody right behind the wall where my bed was, below the window. I tried to reach for a machete near my bed but my hands would not move. I was petrified. When the man outside pushed the window open I found my voice and screamed with all my strength: *"Mutheeeeeeeeeer.......... Fatherrrrrrrrrrrrr...........Mutheeeeeeeeeeer..................Fatherrrrrrrrrrrrrrrrr."*

Father heard and rushed outside. The thief ran away. Father quickly fixed the door. I packed my bedding and went back to the big hut. With the danger now over, Father could afford a laugh. Did I not tell you that you are not yet big enough to sleep in your own hut? Yes, I am not, I now admitted, feeling humbled. Two years later, I was big enough and moved back to my own hut.

My Sister Dies

Throughout the Mau Mau period, we saw many deaths. But none pained me more than my one-year-old sister's death. Wairimu was a sister whom all of us loved. She was a little angel—one of those children that everybody adores. I was very close to her.

One evening I was coming home from school when, a hundred meters from our hut, I heard a sharp scream coming from inside. I knew it was my sister's and thought something terrible must have happened for her to scream like that. I ran home as fast as I could and opened the door. What I saw shocked me. There was a cloud of ashes over the *riiko,* fireplace,. Another of my sisters had been passing Wairimu to another girl over a pot of boiling porridge on the fire. One of them had her hand burnt by the steam of boiling porridge and let Wairimu fall into the pot, which in turn toppled over and spilt its contents into the fire. I saw my sister writhing and crying in unbearable pain. Most of her dress was soaked in hot porridge that stuck to her and was everywhere near the fireplace. Our older sister was trying to wipe the porridge off from her clothes but this only burnt Wairimu more. I ran to her, tried to take off her dress but it came off with some skin and gave her horrible pain. With some presence of mind, I took a knife and cut the dress into two. I then carefully separated the dress from the burnt skin but still more skin peeled off. As I did this, my sister cried from the excruciating pain that I felt with all my heart. As we all cried with her, I asked, Ngai, Murungu, Mungu, Jehovah, Allah, God—all of them—why, why, why did you let this happen to my little sister? My heart ached with pain and anguish. Why was it not myself, who was bigger, instead of her? Nobody answered. Holding my sister where I could—she could not sit—I made her wet with my own tears, which I could not stop from flowing. Shortly afterwards, Mother and Father came and started their walking journey to Nakuru town to take Wairimu to the hospital. Fortunately, when they reached the main road five miles away, they caught a bus and reached the hospital that same night.

Father returned the following day. He told us Wairimu had been admitted into the hospital and Mother had stayed in town to be able to visit her daily. Doctors had said she was not bad and would get well soon. Mother was gone for one week and we all thought Wairimu was well on her way to recovery. I prayed for her every minute.

One evening after school, I was standing outside our house when I saw Mother coming home without my sister and carrying a bundle of something on her head. Immediately I knew my sister was dead and tears spurted out of my eyes like water from a geyser. I did not run to meet Mother but stood where I was, transfixed in extremely painful grief. I cried and cried and cried. Mother tried to console me but nothing could. My brother Mungai had refused to stay. Why could my sister not stay? I could not eat and fell asleep crying. When I went to school, I was still crying. In class, I cried so much that every page I looked at got wet. Teachers asked me to go home. For a whole week, I was out of school and cried all the time.

I still cry for my sister and ask myself: Why do gods harvest loved young souls so early and leave to last forever old, evil ones of dictators? Some say gods like to have the same souls that humans love and so take them early while giving old, evil ones enough time to repent and change. Nothing makes it acceptable.

End of the World

In our village, the birth of new political parties and freedoms was like the coming of summer after a long, cold and dark winter. People's spirits, faces and hopes blossomed. The feeling of doom that had descended upon them after the execution of Kimathi disappeared, and they sang and danced for freedom like people who were poised to win soon.

Belief that victory was near was reinforced by the support that the cause for independence got from the Soviet Union, the United States, India, Egypt, newly independent Ghana under Kwame Nkrumah and other movements for freedom worldwide. People no longer felt isolated. In our village, we felt that we were part of an unstoppable global movement for freedom. The new day of freedom was about to be born. These were exciting times.

At first, political parties were allowed to operate only along district and ethnic lines. The purpose of this was to promote racism and weaken Africans. Even as Britain was preparing to give up classic colonialism in Kenya and Africa, she was not giving up imperialist designs on Kenya after independence. Africans reacted against this by demanding and winning the right to form countrywide parties that recruited followers and campaigned for independence across ethnic lines.

Two parties that emerged from this were the Kenya African National Union (KANU) and the Kenya African Democratic Union (KADU). The big difference in these parties was that KANU wanted independence now, opposed ethnicity, wanted a multiethnic united state and was opposed by colonial settlers. On the other hand, KADU promoted ethnic hostilities, wanted *majimbo,* or the splitting of Kenya into ethnic states, and was a tool of colonial interests. Settlers used KADU to preach fear that big communities—the Gikuyu and Luo people—were conspiring to dominate small communities and begged the British government to preserve colonialism to protect threatened ethnic groups. Moi, Kenya's second president, belonged to KADU and Kenyatta would later belong to KANU.

Everybody in our village supported KANU and especially the campaign for the release of Kenyatta and the freedom fighters who were languishing in detention camps and other prisons. People looked up to Kenyatta to turn Mau Mau military defeat into a political victory that would win the country independence.

As our hopes grew, we would look at the white forest officer and say: Soon, sir, you will go back to your country and a son of the soil will take your job. We would look at white district commissioners and district officers and spit on our chests to bless our ancestors: Soon you will all pack and go and we shall have our own DCs and DOs. The sight of white police officers would provoke us even more: You may swagger as much as you wish but soon you will be no more. Our strongest reactions, however, were reserved for white settlers. When they, in their cars, passed us on foot, we would look at them and say a prayer: Everything that has a beginning has an end. The land we till for you shall soon revert to its rightful owners and the mansions we built for you shall soon be ours. But people's blood boiled most when they saw African home guards, loyalists, chiefs and *askaris.* Your days are numbered, you traitors and quislings. Soon you will pay for your treachery and chicanery. The traitors were accused of more:

> Home guards, you are thieves.
> You are robbers.
> You wait for the rounds
> So you can go to rob.

> When your child cries
> You tell him:
> Maina, stop crying,
> It is nearly patrol time
> So I can go and rob for you.

We were inspired to study hard at school because with the departure of colonial administration, there would be a lot of vacant jobs to fill up. Even before Kenyatta was released, the air smelt of hope and a sense of jubilation.

While KANU and the world campaigned very hard for Kenyatta's release, KADU and colonial settlers did their best to block his release. Sir Patrick Renson, the governor, and *Kenya Weekly News,* a newspaper for settlers, spoke for them when they said that Kenyatta was stained with the "mark of the beast" and would never be released "because he was the leader to darkness and death." Colonial settlers wanted Kenyatta to die in prison. Oginga Odinga fought back and told Parliament that Kenyan Africans had no other leader but Kenyatta, and there would be no independence without Kenyatta. These people you call leaders to darkness and death, Odinga said, before they were arrested were the political leaders of Africans. Africans respected them as their political leaders and even at this moment, in the heart of our hearts, they are still our political leaders.

Unbeknownst to all, as Odinga was fighting for Kenyatta's release in the colonial parliament, the British were working on Kenyatta in prison to turn him into an instrument of their interests before releasing him and allowing him to lead Kenya.

As the campaign for Kenyatta's release reached its peak, I remember hearing that 1960 would be the end of the world. Catholic catechists taught us that two Portuguese girls and a boy—Lucia, Jecinta and Francis—had seen the Virgin Mary while grazing sheep. The Virgin Mary had given them a letter saying the world would end in 1960. Therefore, there was little time for people to prepare themselves to go to heaven. There was no time to waste fighting useless political battles. This talk dampened our spirits and distracted us from our fight for independence. Why seek freedom when the world was ending?

When 1960 came and the world did not end, people had no choice but to continue fighting for independence. But who could have been behind this frightening propaganda? I suspect the Catholic Church propagated it on behalf of the colonial forces. They must have thought that with it they could keep the African so worried that the desire for freedom would die in him.

When Kenyatta was released from prison on August 14, 1961, there were hearty celebrations in our village. The sun of freedom had risen and that of colonialism had set. In our own home, we bought, fried and ate a pound of beef and a loaf of bread and drank a cup of tea with milk to celebrate this important landmark in our lives and history. White settlers understood what Kenyatta's release meant. For them, it was not just the end of the colonial era. It was the end of the world—a world in which, in Harold Macmillan's words, "the settlers had never had it so good."

Capitulation

When Kenyatta was in jail, the settlers were asking themselves: Whom can we groom to take over the leadership so that our influence is not broken? When he was released, he answered them, "We are determined to have independence in peace, and we shall not allow hooligans to rule Kenya... Mau Mau was a disease, which had been eradicated and must never be remembered again."[2]

Kenyans were astounded. Instead of promising Africans freedom, equality, justice and restoration of stolen lands, Kenyatta begged colonial settlers to forgive him: "I suffered a prison and detention term, but that is out of the past and I am not going to remember it... If I wronged you forgive me, if you wronged me, I forgive you... Let us forgive and forget."[3]

People could not understand Kenyatta when he called Mau Mau a disease and asked settlers to forgive him. Was he regretting his people's struggle for independence? Was fighting for freedom wrong and criminal? Nor did they understand Kenyatta's reasoning when he told colonial settlers that they were free to keep the land they had stolen from Africans. This was strange logic, maybe the logic of betrayal: "We want you to stay and farm well in this country.... I think that those who have been panicky about their property, either in land or in any kind, will rest assured that the future African government, the Kenya "government, will not deprive them of the right of owning the property which they own at present."[4]

After the declaration of an emergency in 1952, almost the whole of the Gikuyu population had been put into concentration camps or villages and over 100,000 were arrested and put into detention camps and prisons. Up to 1956, Mau Mau casualties were 11,503 killed; 1,035 captured wounded; 1,550 captured unwounded; and 26,625 arrested.[5]

Instead of promising Africans restitutional justice for all the crimes that the British police and armed forces committed against Kenyans during colonialism, Kenyatta heaped praise on the settlers: "There must be no revenge on foreigners in a free Kenya. They worked very hard for what they have achieved and when we get independence, we, too, must work hard, if we are to get the good schools and hospitals and other things that we need."[6] Africans had not heard this logic from Kenyatta before. White colonialists had land and were rich because they had worked hard and Africans were landless and poor because they were lazy!

Before he went to jail, Kenyatta told Africans that colonialists had stolen land from Africans. After release, he was telling them that colonial settlers had worked hard for what they had and would therefore keep land after independence. If Europeans kept land after *uhuru*, for what had Africans fought? What did independence mean without land? Earlier in London, Odinga had told the British that

Dedan Kimathi was a hero of Kenya. Now Kenyatta was calling Kimathi and other Mau Mau hooligans. What did this mean?

People had always believed that after independence, African collaborators would not only lose their government jobs, they would also pay for their crimes against African humanity. Instead Kenyatta now told people, "I am not for those who have been in the forests or detention camps; I am for the African people. All of them. I do not support or fight for any particular individual, race or tribe, but for all the people."[7]

Had Kenyatta crossed the floor and become a collaborator? As he had told the settlers, he now asked African collaborators to forgive people and Kenyans to forget their treachery. I remember people were very eager to see how Kenyatta would deal with his own son Peter Muigai. People said he had called his father a dog and said Kenyatta would never return after his imprisonment. After release, Kenyatta forgave him and others in the name of reconciliation. Many people called it capitulation.

Kenyatta did more than forgive African collaborators. As he had allowed British settlers to keep their land, he promised to retain colonial African police, army and loyalists in his government and keep Mau Mau out of it. Before his imprisonment, Kenyatta had asked people to root out *ithuki,* stumps that blocked people's path to freedom. Now he was offering to rule the country with these same stumps. To gain the acceptance of those who had jailed him, Kenyatta would reward service to colonialism and punish sacrifice for freedom. He would also use his government to promote and protect British interests in Kenya and East Africa.

How did Kenyans take all this? When fighting for *uhuru,* people had thirsted not just for freedom and land but for justice as well. By forgiving settlers and collaborators, letting them keep their loot and positions in government without demanding even an expression of remorse or change of heart, Kenyatta was denying people land, freedom, justice, change and independence itself. At a personal level, by legitimizing colonial civil service, land tenure, the legal system, the killing, detaining and depriving Kenyans of dignity, Kenyatta was accepting the guilt and sentence that were imposed on him at Kapenguria trial. Thereafter, everything remained as determined by the colonial order—whites rich, Africans poor, Mau Mau a prohibited organization, Kenyatta guilty of managing Mau Mau, Dedan Kimathi guilty and buried in Kamiti Maximum Security Prison!

During the bitter struggle for *uhuru,* freedom fighters had sang for many years:

> Our people, I have been wondering
> Shall I get back the lands
> Which were left to us by Iregi
> From Ndemi and Mathathi generations.

Now they knew they would not get those lands back. Again they sang from within the belly of the beast:

> Young man, when you go home
> Greet my wife.
> Tell her you left me in Manyani [prison].
> If God wills I shall come home,
> I shall not die,
> The first shall be last.

Now they knew, the first and the last under colonialism would remain the first and the last after independence. It was incomprehensible. Why had people struggled so hard, so long, only to remain in the same place? Fearing a backlash, Kenyatta allayed people's anxieties by lying: After independence, you will be free. But how could people be free without land, restitutional justice and under a government that was run by their remorseless and unchanged enemies? By taking Kenyatta as their leader and the only concession that colonialism would make to them, Kenyans lost the aims of their struggle and the very things they hoped Kenyatta's leadership would give them—land, freedom and independence.

During the Mau Mau war, freedom fighters had taunted collaborators: After independence, you will pay dearly for your betrayal and lose everything you stole from the people. Collaborators had taunted back: We will rule you now and our children will rule your children after independence. With Kenyatta on their side, collaborators had won, and the freedom fighters lost. And so had Kenya. In our pre-colonial past, no one had taken up arms to fight his own people and lived. Betrayal and treachery had always been punished with death. Now, Kenyatta had set that centuries-old logic on its head by making collaboration forgivable, profitable and fashionable. Simultaneously, Kenyatta had made patriotic sacrifice and defense of the country thankless and to be shunned. By betraying Mau Mau, Kenyatta had sterilized Kenya's womb against the birth of other heroes.

What Happened to Kenyatta?

The Kenyatta who went to jail was not the man who came out of detention. Though Kenyatta talked of securing freedom for all, he seemed more interested in securing for himself the head place at the feasting table as an African king. Was this, then, all our people had suffered, gone to prison and died for?

Bildad Kaggia, a founding member of Mau Mau, told me that Kenyatta did not change much in prison. He had never fought to create an egalitarian African society but to be king of an African, capitalist kingdom that was better served by mercenary collaborators than by principled Mau Mau, which he jettisoned. According to Kaggia, Kenyatta was always a king and dictator, never a democrat and a socialist. People always misunderstood him and expected from him what he could not deliver. Had people known Kenyatta better, they would not have asked him to give them more than an African king or accused him of betrayal.

It is true that when people sang, Kenyatta is the king of black people, *Kenyatta niwe kingi wa andu airu,* they wanted him as their king. But he had also promised people land, *ithaka,* and independence, *wiyathi.* When he turned his back on the recovery of stolen land, he betrayed the people. Still, people were wrong to seek service and kingship from the same person; kings do not serve people. The people serve them.

Whatever Kenyatta was before he was jailed, he came out of prison weaker. His hardships in the desert had won the British his capitulation. Some people say Bruce Mackenzie, an MI6 agent and Kenyatta's minister of agriculture, recruited Kenyatta to serve British interests while still in prison in exchange for power. If so, it must have been because the British realized that, as an African king and capitalist, Kenyatta was safer for their economic and Cold War interests than an African socialist like Kwame Nkrumah. On the other hand, Kenyatta must have found the capitalist West a more natural ally than the communist world. Thereafter, he did not need recruitment to the West. Ideologically, he belonged there.

Apart from Kenyatta's ideological concurrence with the West, for survival while in prison, he had learnt to fear those who were more powerful. Equally, he expected those who were weaker than him to do his bidding or perish. In prison, fear of power turned Kenyatta into both a prisoner and dictator for life.

Whenever Kenyatta had sensitive things to talk about, Ngengi Muigai, his nephew, once told me, he never did so in the presence of servants. Kenyatta always warned him, Never speak of sensitive matters within earshot of these people. They are the ones who will testify against you. Kenyatta must have lived and ruled in perpetual obedience to the British, in fear that if he went against them they might topple him and try him again. He would loot for himself and protect what the British had pillaged.

Public trust is difficult to cultivate, but when won, it is lasting. With what he said, Kenyatta disappointed many who had given him the benefit of the doubt. Kaggia told me that though he and others imprisoned with Kenyatta disagreed with him, after his release, they supported his leadership to avoid a public fight that could have delayed *uhuru.* For an early self-rule, most people overlooked Kenyatta's betrayal and marched with him to a stillborn independence. A few others did not.

The People's Party

One day, everybody in the village was summoned to assemble. Upon arrival, a youthful but stern African DO addressed us in the presence of the white forest officer, white police inspector, African area chief, village headman and teachers. For the first time, I saw an African calling the shots in the presence of whites. It was unprecedented and exciting. He was so serious, stern and authoritative that he sent chills down my adolescent spine.

He announced that in the assembly there were men and women who had licked salt, *cumbi,* and others that had tasted bicarbonate of soda, *igata.* In a threatening voice, he commanded, Those among you that have eaten bicarbonate of soda have broken the law and are enemies of our government and African independence. Reveal yourselves now, *mwiumiriei.*

Up to now I did not understand what he was talking about and I guessed everybody else was confused like me. Noticing hesitation, he ordered again: Those who have eaten salt stay where you are. Those who have eaten soda move over to that corner. There was movement and commotion in the assembly and many people moved over to the corner. As soon as they got there, their names were immediately taken down. It was a shock to see some friends reveal themselves as having eaten soda. When and where, I wondered.

As the sorting-out proceeded, I learnt that those who had taken soda were people who had taken an oath that opposed the retention of land and government in the hands of settlers and African collaborators after independence. They were members of an underground political movement called *Kiama Kia Muingi,* the People's Party. They opposed the granting of independence under conditions that negated aspirations of African people. They were prepared to return to the forests to fight against betrayal. They resisted Kenyatta's capitulation to colonial interests.

All men and women underwent screening throughout the night at the center. The following day, the innocent were allowed to go home with a warning not to resist government policies. Those who had taken the oath were loaded into lorries and taken to old and newly opened detention camps all over the country. Mutha, my friend, was one of those whose parents were detained. He and his siblings remained alone in the village until after independence. It was painful to see them trying to survive and barely managing to celebrate independence without parents. After independence, the detained were released as dogs that had tried to snatch Kenyatta's bone but danger was now over. But having opposed Kenyatta's collusion with colonial interests, they were not left alone after release. To warn others never to dare question Kenyatta, they were denied re-employment in the forest and expelled with their families. It was sad to see my friend's family pack and go where they had neither home nor work.

Kenyatta Speaks

Despite the People's Party's opposition to Kenyatta's policy of "forgive and forget," after his release Kenyatta was still the greatest political fascination in Kenya. My greatest ambition was to see and hear him speak. Lionized and demonized in the same country, Kenyatta was a living legend who I wasn't about to miss when he came to Nakuru town to address a political rally.

Everybody in the entire stadium seemed jubilant, entertained by teams of young men, young women and *nyakinyua,* old women traditional dancers, who sang praise to Kenyatta, Mau Mau, Oginga Odinga, Achieng Oneko and called for *uhuru* now. The dancers' songs also ridiculed colonial settlers and the KADU party, their local allies. I felt truly exhilarated. This was not a meeting. It was a celebration.

Soon Kenyatta and other KANU leaders—Tom Mboya, Oginga Odinga, Wasonga Sijeyo, Achieng Oneko—entered the stadium wearing traditional Luo caps, together with Bildad Kaggia, Paul Ngei and Fred Kubai and took their seats on the leaders' platform. After some more dancing and singing, the meeting started. The star of KANU, Kenyatta, spoke last. He seemed larger than life, with his big hair combed backwards, his big captivating eyes, his Kinyatta belt, brown leather jacket and Luo traditional cap. As he walked to the microphone, the entire meeting went wild with cheering, whistling, clapping and ululating. Then the African lion roared: Harambeeeeee.

Hiiiiiiiiiiiiiii, the public roared back.

Harambeeeeeeee.

Hiiiiiiiiiiiiiiiiii!

Harambeeeeeeeeeeeeeeeee:

Hiiiiiiiiiiiiiiiiiiiii, they roared back even more forcefully.

Ndugu zanguni, my fellow citizens...

Kenyatta then gave a stimulating speech in which he talked to the people about the independence that was coming soon but also engaged the unsuspecting crowd in extraordinary doublespeak. In one part of the speech, Kenyatta lambasted colonialists as enslavers of Africans, condemned imperialists for robbing African people and accused African collaborators of licking the behinds of their colonial masters. Then he begged colonial settlers to stay and farm their land for development. He urged people to forgive and forget treachery. He thanked Africans for sacrificing themselves for land and freedom, and then warned them that there would be nothing in return, *hakuna cha bure.* They would get no free land! He crowned his speech by praising the bravery of the people and downplaying that of the Mau Mau. They were cowards who had gone to the forest to hide! Despite all these contradictions, Kenyatta was cheered and cheered until voices were lost and palms hurt. People heard only what they wanted to hear.

To go home, we walked by the main road in some vain hope that someone might give us a lift some of the way home. But the only people with cars were white settlers and a few African collaborators. Fortunately, I picked up some lost coins on the way. We bought and ate some *mandazis,* local doughnuts, for energy to get home. At last, we got home at 8 P.M. I told everybody how I had heard Kenyatta speak and seen *uhuru* coming.

Uhuru

In my life, there is no day I have waited for more eagerly than the twelfth of December, 1963: the day of Kenya's independence. To usher in independence and see the first moment of it, all of us in the village gathered at the open space behind our huts on the night of the eleventh. At exactly midnight, we cheered wildly when the Union Jack was lowered and the Kenyan flag was hoisted. We felt hoisted from hell to heaven. As we were raising the Kenyan flag in our village, Munyao, another Kenyan, raised the national flag at the highest peak of Mount Kenya, Kirinyaga, to say Ngai who lived there was now home and our country was free.

After lowering the Union Jack and hoisting the Kenyan flag, we faced Mount Kenya and an old woman, Nyina wa Mukuru, thanked Ngai for our independence:

Ngai, all your children gathered here thank you for letting us witness the arrival of this moment that we have awaited for the last 70 years.

The public intoned: The Great Peace, Ngai, give us peace, *Thai thathaiya Ngai thaai.*

Ngai, we thank you for this night when we are finally able to worship you without fear of being insulted, molested, arrested or killed.

The Great Peace, Ngai, give us peace. *Thai thathaiya Ngai thaai.*

Ngai, we thank you for delivering your children from the slavery of the British, the way Jehovah delivered Israelis from the Pharaohs of Egypt.

Ngai, we thank you for delivering us from the rule of white ogres.

Ngai, bless Kimathi and others who suffered and died so that freedom may come to us today.

Ngai, now save our lands, homes, culture and minds from white ogres.

Ngai, from the rule of white ogres, do not deliver us into that of their black offspring.

Ngai, protect us from hyenas that always return where they have eaten fat.

Ngai, let the sun never set upon our new freedom.

Ngai, let us never see the night of hell again.

Ngai, forever end our 70 years of hunger and thirst.

Ngai, wipe our tears and give us laughter.

Ngai, deliver us from the hell of this forest.

Ngai, now that our country and mother of many teats is free, may she suckle us in equality, peace and harmony.

The Great Peace, Ngai, give us peace, *Thai thathaiya Ngai thaai.*

After prayers, for the first time we formally sang Kenya's national anthem. In school, we had been practicing to sing it in readiness for this moment.

> O God of creation,
> Bless our land and nation.
> Justice be our shield and defender,
> May we dwell in unity,
> Peace and liberty,
> Plenty be found within our borders.
>
> Let one and all arise…

I felt better singing our national anthem than I did singing "God Save the Queen," yet, crafted abroad by foreigners, the anthem lacked African emotions and aspirations. It aroused nothing in me. After the traditional prayer, it tasted pallid and still does today. After singing the national anthem, we dispersed to go to bed. But my friend Kamau and I did not sleep. We wanted to see the first dawn of freedom. As we talked and waited, I wondered how happy I was when I was born. I could not remember. The joy of freedom felt like my greatest feeling. I must have known that without freedom, I could have no other joy.

When the first dawn of *Uhuru* appeared, we jumped, cheered and clapped. It was bright, beautiful and promised everything. I prayed for it to last forever. Later that night, we traveled to Kabazi in the dark to see news on the only TV for miles around. We saw Kenyatta address a mammoth rally in Nairobi. He promised Kenyans that *Uhuru* would herald a new day for them. But he did not ask the British to apologize and pay reparations for the atrocities of colonialism and the war. Instead he thanked them for their conquest and its legacies: "We do not forget the assistance and guidance we have received through the years from people of British stock—administrators, businessmen, farmers, missionaries and many others. Our law, our system of government, and many other aspects of our daily lives are founded on British principles and justice."[8]

One morning, I was on my way to church when I met Wambui the storyteller. I asked her whether the Mau Maus of her story had managed to get their homes and land back from the white ogres? She answered my question with another question: Son of Wangu, are you blind? Look around and tell me. Does it look like Mau Maus got their land and homes back? My story is not over. Black ogres have come of age. Two years later, Wambui and others had a fatal motor accident in a lorry that was taking them to vote. She died on the spot. It left me asking, If Mau Maus could not beat the ogres, who would?

CHAPTER III

S E M I N A R Y   Y E A R S   1 9 6 4 – 6 8

Seeking Another Heaven

One day, I remember attending Christmas Eve Mass in the Church of the Holy Rosary in Nakuru. The singing and everything else in the church was so wonderful that I thought that it looked and sounded like a piece of heaven. If I become a priest, I thought, maybe I can get more of this heaven both here on this accursed earth and in the next world. Like Kenyatta, I might even have the key to heaven and open its doors to my parents, friends and all the people in our village.

Though Mother was a practicing Catholic, when I returned home and told her that I wanted to become a priest, she did not hit the sooty roof of our smoke-filled hut with joy. Nor did she tell me not to. She told me to see Father about it. When I told Father I wanted to join the seminary, he asked me what a seminary was. I told him. He was nonplussed.

Why don't you want to go to a secondary school like other boys instead of going to this seminary? he asked.

It is also a secondary school, I told him. But for boys who wish to become priests.

Priests like Father Dillon or Father Tui?

Like Father Dillon, I said. None of us liked Father Tui because of his participation in night searches in our village.

But you are not a white man? How can you become like Father Dillon?

Africans can become priests, too.

I have never seen one.

Gakuru wa Gideon is training to be one.

Son, do you like girls?

Yes, I do, Father.

Why then don't you get one and marry?

Am I not too young for that, Father?

I mean later on when you are big enough.

I prefer to be a priest, Father.

If I sired you, do you not want to sire me? If you do not marry, how shall we keep our family line alive?

Through my brother, Father.

Nobody chooses to be one-eyed. I have only one more son.

I agree, Father.

Then marry and carry on the family line. If we all join the priesthood and do not marry, it will be the end of us—our people, our race and all people.

I know that, Father, but being a priest is also good for people. Taking people to heaven is a great service to them. People must not live in hell forever.

Don't they say people must be in hell before they can go to heaven? Marry. Get me, your mother, your brother and sisters. After that, take us to heaven.

I cannot marry and take people to heaven. Marriage and priesthood do not mix.

If God created us, why can't his priests marry and create? If people don't marry, where will priests come from? Priesthood grows out of marriage, why should it be a negation of it? Become one of those priests that marry.

Those are Protestant and I am Catholic.

Don't you worship the same God? If you must become a priest, become one who marries. Bear and take me to heaven.

Catholic priests don't do that, Father. They save people who are born by others.

They should save themselves from extinction before they take others to heaven. If all men became priests, humankind would end. Priesthood should mean life, not the end of it. But if you are hell-bent on self-extinction, don't ask me to bless it. After all, if Protestants and Catholics worship the same God, I don't see how he allows some to marry and others not to.

Father, will you then not allow me to live the way I want to?

You may self-ruin but don't ask me to bless it. I will be abandoning my love and responsibility as a parent.

Father, my first parent is God, our collective creator. He is the one who gives us everything, including life and manhood. Can't I make a gift of myself to him?

If God gives us life, do we thank him by ending it?

But priests and nuns do a lot of good work, Pap. They teach people and treat them in hospitals.

They should teach and heal after creating. They cannot educate and instruct the life they negate.

Father, if creating is everything, priests create when they prolong and save lives in the next life.

Father kept quiet. He was not an unreasonable man. After a short while he told me: Let me tell you this. I do not understand either the white man or his God.

Before he and his God came, we had Ngai and we had our own priests. Ngai never asked his priests not to marry. Yet they served him and society well. I wish the white man had never come. First he took our freedom, our land and then our Ngai. After independence, we thought it would be the end of them. Now he is taking my son too. What will he not take from us? He was on the verge of tears. I did not press harder. Instead, I went to Mother.

Mother, Father will not let me be a priest. Please talk to him for me. You wanted to be a nun and understand what he cannot. Please, Mum!

But I am not sure that I want you to be a priest either, Mother told me. Yes, I understand how you want to be a priest, because I was once where you are. But I am also where your Father is and I understand his fear of losing you to the priesthood. Your father and I want to live through you and your children. We do not want your life to end like a dry leaf. We want you to have children and renew yourself and us through them. If you marry, you will give us life. If you join the priesthood, you will terminate our existence. I want to see you get a daughter whom you shall name after me, and a son whom you shall name after your father. Your children will renew us—in flesh and spirit. If you don't do that, what then? Only a vacuum and emptiness. I don't say you should become a Protestant priest to be able to have both your wish and ours. I say Catholic priests should be allowed to marry. Before then, don't become one.

But Mother, I want to be a priest.

Only because you have not discovered your manhood, but we shall not stop you from going to the seminary. When you discover love, I shall not be the one to ask you to leave the priesthood.

So you will ask Father to let me be priest?

Yes, I shall, on the condition that you promise to consider very carefully before you join the priesthood. It will be an embarrassment for you to join the priesthood and then quit. If you don't think you can be a priest forever, then become a father. There is priesthood in fatherhood.

Thank you, Mum.

Mother must have talked to Father because he did not again object to my going to the seminary. When I finished my primary school, I applied to join the Mother of Apostles Seminary in Matunda.

They called me for an interview. I was excited. Father bought me my first pair of shoes. Not having worn shoes before, they did not fit so well and my feet felt awkward in them. Still, it was a wonderful thing to wear them, maybe the beginning of greater things.

On the day of the interview, very early in the morning, Father took me to Nakuru. He put me into a bus going to Kitale and returned home. Alone, I was on my way to the Mother of Apostles Seminary.

I got off the bus at one o'clock in Matunda with another boy who was called to the same interview. He had better exam results and chances of admission. Still, I was optimistic. A forest of blue gum trees hid the school from us. After the woods, it suddenly came into view, exactly as I had seen it in a dream. The hill, the garden, red brick buildings, earthen paths and grass thatched houses. I blurted out, I have seen this school before.

Where? Have you come here before? the other boy asked.

No, but I saw this school in my dream, exactly as it is. I am sure I will pass the interview and be admitted.

Then I will not be taken, the other boy said.

I am not the only one they will take, I comforted him.

As we walked up the path, we saw a few boys outside the church. The whole school was in the church. We reached the other boys, stood with them and waited. Soon the Mass was over and all the boys came out in gray khaki uniforms accompanied by teachers, white priests. Father Rector came to us and asked us one by one: What is your name?

Johnson Koigi, I said.

He was surprised and exclaimed: Johnson! What kind of a name is that? Have you come for the interview? Are you a Catholic?

Yes, I said.

Why then do you not have a Catholic name?

My name is Catholic, Father, I said.

Were you baptized in a Catholic Church?

Yes, Father.

Who baptized you?

Father Dillon.

And he called you Johnson?

Yes, Father.

Do you have his recommendation letter?

Yes, Father.

I gave him the sealed envelope. He read the letter and then told me: Follow me to the office. There is a mistake here. We do not admit boys with Protestant names.

Father Rector went behind his desk while I stood before him in his office. He took a clean sheet of paper from the drawer and started writing a regret letter to Father Dillon. I felt so disappointed that I nearly fainted. Suddenly a thought crossed my mind and I spoke:

Please, Father, can you give me a Catholic name instead of sending me home? Eh?

He looked up and touched his chin with his forefinger and his thumb in deep thought and then asked, What name?

Any name, Father, I said.

Is Michael all right for you?

Yes, Father, I said with great relief.

He crumpled the letter he was writing to Father Dillon, threw it into a bin, opened the form-one register that lay on his desk and admitted me as a student for that year. I could not believe my good luck. From being chased away without an interview, I was now admitted without one. He stood up and walked me to the door. Outside, he told me: Make sure you are back on Wednesday with money for school fees and uniforms.

Yes, Father, I said, and then added with some hesitation, Father, it might be late for me to catch the bus to Nakuru, may I sleep here until tomorrow?

Yes, I was a little afraid that the bus to Nakuru may have gone, but I also wanted to feel what it was like to sleep in this school as a student. The excitement of being in a high school was simply overpowering. Father Rector turned to me and said, to my shock, Boy, leave immediately before I change my mind! I almost flew down the stairs and headed straight for the road to Nakuru.

As I walked, my mind sorted through what had just happened. I was still puzzled at how easily my one Christian name had been discarded and another one imposed. On the way to the white man's heaven, the question of name seemed to be of paramount importance. Only those with the right names could enter. To help me get into that heaven, one white man had called me Johnson. Now, another had put that aside and called me Michael. Yet their God was universal and for all people. How come he recognized only *wazungu* names? How could he be universal and so discriminating? Anyway, now I had another name and a place in the seminary. I did not know it then but one year later I would receive a third *mzungu* name and be called Michael Clement Koigi. Somebody seemed to believe that the longer a name one had, the easier it would be to get to heaven! The trick seemed to be to take so many European names that by the time one had three or four of them, the *mzungu* God would have forgotten that one was an African and let him in.

Trekking in the Wild

As I juggled all these thoughts, I caught up with a local boy who was also walking home from the seminary. He was denied admission but promised one the following year. That year, the rector wanted him to work in the seminary's store. We walked and talked along the road, trying to stop buses to Nakuru without success. We passed the bridge and a little way up the hill, my friend invited me to his home for a cup of tea and something to eat. I went in and was momentarily on the road again, munching green maize, my thirst quenched.

Like before, no bus would stop for me. When night came, I was afraid that robbers might attack me on the road. Soon I came to a railway crossing and judged that it would be safer to walk on the train track than to walk on the road. I guessed the next railway station was nearer than the next town on the road. So, in total darkness, I took to the track and started my trek to the next station. I trekked and trekked in my ill-fitting shoes, stumbling over stones that lay on the track. Sure that no robbers could see me, I felt perfectly safe in the bush and darkness. After walking for about four hours, I staggered out of the bush into a railway station like an apparition. I was very hungry and walked over to a woman fruit vendor. She had seen me emerge and looked rather afraid.

Where are you coming from and going, young man? she asked me.

I am coming from Matunda and going to Nakuru. Has the Kampala train passed? I asked her.

No, it has not. Did you walk all the way from Matunda?

Yes, I said.

And no animals attacked you?

No, I did not meet a single one.

Young man, you must have powers. That bush is full of wild animals that are always hungry—leopards, foxes, wild dogs and many others, the woman said looking rather suspicious.

Yes, I have, remembering my long-lost *hirizi.*

Suddenly fear gripped me. This woman might think I am a *mchawi,* a witch doctor, and call people to attack me, I thought. She did not. I bought and ate a few bananas from her and suddenly dozed off. I was dead tired. The next thing I heard was the same woman shaking me.

Young man, awaken. The train to Nakuru is about to leave. Hop in.

I ran to the train and got in shouting to the good woman: *Kwa heri, asante sana,* good-bye and thank you very much.

I reached home the following day. When I narrated my adventure, my parents could not believe my luck. Choked with anger, Pap asked Mother: How can a responsible priest expose one so young to such danger? How can we entrust our son to such a person? Well, Mother said, the priest could not know what would happen. It was an accident. Father looked at me as if to reassure me and said, At least you have school. Nothing good comes from a good place, *gutiri kiega kiumaga hega.* Good luck, my boy.

On Wednesday, I traveled back to the seminary with the school fees. As I left home, I felt as if I was going to begin a new life in a better world. But it had started in a strange way. Now that I no longer carried my *hirizi,* I wondered whether I would have the same luck I had had when I survived the wild.

Eating Rats

The seminary was always stingy with food. In the morning, we drank maize meal porridge, *uji*, without bread. I was always hungry in class. For lunch and supper we ate *ugali*, a heavy maize meal cake, with collard greens. Too heavy, this food. I had enormous problems keeping awake in class and had to literally hold my eyelids open to avoid dozing off. On Wednesday, our meal was improved with a tiny piece of meat. Our favorite day was Sunday, when they gave us rice and a second piece of meat.

Our best months were August and September when we ate green maize picked from the school *shamba* three days a week. I remember once bags of maize flour were contaminated with paraffin as they were transported from town. Rather than throw the flour away, it was used to cook porridge and *ugali*. It reeked of paraffin so much that it was almost impossible to eat. We begged school authorities to throw away this contaminated flour; they would not. We only got rid of it with a strike.

Another time we were eating lunch on a Monday that was not a meat day. The vegetable had a taste of meat. Was this a pleasant surprise? Would we be getting meat on Mondays as well? We were about to ask the cook when one boy pulled a rat's tail from his bowl. Before he could shout, another boy pulled out the tiny animal's head and they shouted in chorus, God, we are eating rats! Pandemonium followed.

As we were pouring our vegetables into the drum of waste food, Father Rector, whom we called Kihara for his bald head, stormed into the dining hall demanding an explanation for all the din. When we told him we had rats in our food, he slowly walked to one table, picked up a bowl and ate all the vegetables, as we watched him in utter amazement. He then asked us with an air of superiority, Am I dead now?

Burning Bibles

If you loved democracy and justice, then the seminary was not the place for you. It taught us that all life, even in heaven, is hierarchically organized, with all power at the top to be obeyed by the bottom. In the seminary, for instance, all authority came from Father Rector; teachers and prefects and students were to obey his command without question.

In heaven, they told us, all authority belonged to God, his son, Jesus, Mother Mary and angels. Everyone else was in heaven upon invitation and pledge of loyalty.

Recognizing state authorities as small gods, the Bible also demands total obedience to them: "Everyone must obey state authorities, because no authority exists without God's permission, and the existing authorities have been put there by God. Whoever opposes the existing authority opposes what God has ordered; and anyone who does so will bring judgment on himself." (Romans: 13)

Equally ordained by God, good and bad rulers were also to be obeyed unquestioningly. The Christian God does not care whether people are ruled justly or not. He gets credit for good rule and no blame for bad rule. What kind of a God would welcome democrats and dictators alike?

I now understood why the Christian church stood by colonialism and why Father Tui was priest by day and policeman by night. Serving colonialists was obeying God. Going by Romans 13, there seemed little justice in heaven. Indeed, if priests run heaven, many would be called but few would be chosen.

Every day in Mass, we prayed to God to send more young men to the priesthood. But when they came, the seminary would expel them in droves under the slightest of pretexts. We suspected the priests who taught us violated the confidentiality of confession. When so many boys were expelled from the seminary for undisclosed reasons, we feared it was for confessed sins. Our distrust was so strong that we asked for priests from outside the seminary to confess to. We were brought some, but I never confessed again. I could never dispel the fear that anything I said could be used to expel me from the seminary and maybe heaven.

No sooner had we stopped worrying about confessions, than we were plunged into the crisis of eternal damnation. We came across a biblical passage narrating what had happened when Noah was drunk. His son Ham saw him naked while his other sons, Japheth and Shem, walked backwards and covered his nakedness with a cloth. For seeing his father naked, the Bible said, God had cursed Ham and his descendants, who it was said were black, to be the slaves of the children of Japheth, white people, and the children of Shem, Asian people.

Already we knew another part of the Bible that said that whatever the church cursed on earth was also damned in heaven. We saw ourselves cursed to slavery on earth and everlasting fire in the hereafter. Greatly shocked, we confronted Father Rector:

Is it true that whatever the Bible curses on earth is also cursed in heaven?

Yes, it is true.

Is it any use then, having us Africans in the seminary?

Of course it is, what do you mean? Father Rector asked, wondering what was going on.

But, Father, we are already cursed to be slaves of white and Asian people here on earth and to burn in hell later?

Who says so?

The Bible, Father. It says that we are the children of Ham whom God cursed for seeing his father naked. If we are cursed here on earth and in heaven, it must be useless training us to be priests.

Of course not.

How can people who are cursed save themselves or fellow Africans from this curse? Is their damnation not permanent?

I don't want to hear any more of this nonsense. It is clear that you have been talking politics here. This is a seminary, not a school of politics, Father Rector said in great anger.

But, Father, what we are talking about is written here in the Bible, we insisted showing him.

Don't make me angry, he said, without caring to look.

We did not talk to him again. But why was he angry with us and not the Bible? A Gikuyu proverb says, The river escapes through the ground that is soft, *ruui runagira haria hahuthu.* Hurriedly, Father Rector gathered his books and left the class leaving our puzzle unresolved.

A day or two later, we were in the playing field when we saw a big billow of smoke near the church. We found out later that all our Bibles had been collected and burnt. It was our hope that the alleged curse had burnt with them. With the curse dead, maybe we could now go to heaven. Still I was not satisfied. Independence had come, but the seminary and the church were still hubs of racial inequality.

Manhood Discovered

If all my disappointments in the seminary weakened my calling to the priesthood, the last straw that broke the camel's back was a woman. And she did not come to me as a harbinger of divine death, as Eve had to Adam. She came as a goddess, a savior from a lifetime of unnatural denial, a rescuer of my divinity.

I still wanted to be a priest. But when I met this girl, she lit a fire in my heart and her presence gave me a happiness I had not felt in the church. She was beautiful, had a wonderful smile and a very generous character to match. The flame of priesthood died when hers shone. I caught myself going to church to meet her rather than to pray. I wrote to her with the hand of a friend but with the heart of a lover. When I received and read her letters, I trembled.

What was happening? My seminary world was falling apart. Could I become a priest when I was in love with this girl? If I could not put out the fire of this love, priesthood was not for me. It would wreak havoc later.

There was a priest who was having love affairs with some boys; they ran to our Students Advisory Council for protection. We confronted him with the allegations that had been reported to us. He owned up and quit the seminary. Why could he not have had the courage to say no to a celibacy he could not be faithful to?

Another priest asked me to show him where a brothel was in town. I did not want a life of double standards. I did not want to bear children I was not prepared to take care of women who would trust a priest as a goat might a leopard. In the Mathari area, I had seen many children fathered by white Catholic priests.

As Mother had told me, if I wanted to be a priest, I had to be faithful to the priesthood. That fidelity was now fatally challenged by the love of a woman. With the passage of each day, that love grew to the same degree that my desire for priesthood died. By the time I finished the seminary, the priest in me was no more. When I left the seminary, I was as light as somebody ready to embark on a long safari.

Circumcised

Before I quit the seminary, society had steeled me for the remaining life's journey with circumcision. In our culture, circumcision is very important, not because it prunes our manhood, but mainly because of the values of courage, endurance, maturity, sexual responsibility, respect, honesty, self-discipline, patriotism and peer cohesion it imparts into the initiates.

From when I was a small boy, I desired circumcision because it would lead me out of childhood, entitle me to have respect, sex, a home, a wife and children. Before circumcision, I could not make love, marry, be on my own or be a warrior. At seventeen, I was a man, but without circumcision, I remained a child.

The British, in their imperial arrogance, demonized circumcision as barbaric mutilation and torture perpetrated against African children against their will. To save African boys and girls from their so-called cruel and unfeeling societies, colonialism had declared circumcision primitive, cruel and criminal. So, if you practiced circumcision, you were punished. If a parent circumcised his daughters, he could not be a Christian, get work or promotion and his children could not get schooling. But colonialism did not come to Africa to save African youth from the pain or torture of circumcision, but to enslave and exploit them.

When colonialism came to Africa, many African communities had already organized their entire social, economic and political system around age groups with circumcision as the foundation from which grew *irua,* initiation, marriage, childcare, leadership and *ituika,* power-transition, the warrior system, the judicial system and priesthood. Circumcision initiated boys and girls into manhood and womanhood from which all other duties, responsibilities and privileges of society stemmed.

During initiation, boys and girls were taught how to behave like adults; how to give and gain respect; how to be sexually responsible; how to follow certain courtship customs; how to be a responsible husband and father or wife and mother; how to be a patriot and bear sacrifice—including pain and hardship for one's family and society; how not to collaborate with enemies; and how to be a brave warrior. They learnt which taboos to observe and gained an understanding of power. They were also taught how to keep the secrets of the society and how to live with and not against the community.

To colonize our community, country and minds, our entire system of defining ourselves, our government, defense, economy and maintainance of internal cohesion had to be destroyed, and ending circumcision was the first blow. Once there was no circumcision, the initiation system would collapse along with leadership, defense, culture and a society of patriots—to be replaced with a foreign culture, economy and society of collaborators. Colonialism tried to replace circumcision with baptism and confirmation.

I longed for circumcision not merely because I wanted the freedom to have sex, but because I wanted to be all the other things that only circumcision could pass on. Without circumcision, I would be nothing, a nonperson. As for girls, circumcision was not torture. It opened the door for respect, womanhood, love, marriage, motherhood and family. In our community, without circumcision a woman was and had nothing.

Contrary to Western belief, female circumcision was not performed to torture, harm or deform women. Every Gikuyu was familiar with the procedure of both female and male circumcision and knew the act was performed with care and dignity:

Early in the morning of the day of the physical operation, the girl is awakened at the first cockcrow. After all necessary arrangements have been made, the girl is escorted to an appointed place. From there, all the candidates for initiation are led to a special river to bathe. This is done before the sun rises, when the water is very cold. They go in up to their waists, dipping themselves to the breast and holding up ceremonial leaves in their hands. As they begin to shake their wrists, they drop the leaves into the river as a sign of drowning their childhood behavior.

When the bathing is completed, all the initiates are lined up. The ceremonial horn, *coro,* is blown to warn the passersby that the initiates are about to march and the road must be cleared. As the candidates approach, the *coro* is sounded rhythmically. The initiates advance slowly towards the homestead where they will be circumcised, with both hands raised upwards, elbows bent, pressed against their ribs, with the fists closed and thumbs inserted between the first and second fingers, *kuna thano.* This signifies that they are ready to stand the operation firmly and fearlessly.

Meanwhile, the elders select a place near the homestead where the operation will be performed. This place is called *itiri.* Here, a clean hide is spread on the ground. Ceremonial leaves called *mathakwa* are spread on the hide. The girls sit down on the hide, while their female relatives and friends form a circle several rows deep around the girls, silently waiting for the great moment. No male is allowed to go near. Any man caught doing so is severely punished.

Each girl sits down with her legs wide open on the hide. Her guide, *mutiiri*, sits behind her with her legs interwoven with those of the girl, so as to keep the girl's legs in a steady, open position. The girl reclines gently against her guide, who holds her slightly on the shoulders to prevent any bodily movement, the girl meanwhile staring skywards. After this, an elderly woman, attached to the ceremonial council, comes in with very cold water that has been preserved through the night with a steel axe in it. The water is thrown on the girl's sexual organ to make it numb and to arrest profuse bleeding as well as to shock the girl's nerves at the time, for she is not supposed to show any fear or make any audible sign of emotion or even blink. To do so would be considered cowardice and make her the object of ridicule among her companions. For this reason, she is expected to keep her eyes fixed upwards until the operation is completed.

At this point, a woman specialist known as a *muruithia*, who has studied this surgery from early adulthood, dashes out of the crowd, dressed in colorful hide decorated with the skin of a colobus monkey and feathers, jingling bangles and copper rings on her wrists and ankles, her face painted with white and black ochre. This elaborate costume tends to terrify, combined with the rhythmic movement of the rattles tied to her legs. She takes from her pocket the Gikuyu operating razor, *rwenji*, and in quick movements operates upon the girl. With a stroke, she cuts off the tip of the clitoris. As no other part of the girl's sexual organ is interfered with, her operation is complete. Immediately, the old woman who originally threw the water on the girls comes along with milk mixed with some herbs, *mukengeria* and *ndogomuki*, which she sprinkles on the fresh wound to reduce the pain, check the bleeding, and prevent infection. In a moment, every *mutiiri* covers her girl with a fresh white sheet. When the last operation is performed, the silence is broken and the crowd begins to sing joyously: Our children are brave, ee-ho, did anyone cry? No one cried, hurrah! *Ciana ciitu iri kuuma ee-ho, nia maririire, ee-ho!*

After this, the sponsors hold the girls by the arms and slowly walk them to a special hut that has been prepared for them. Here they are put to sleep on beds prepared on the ground with sweet-smelling leaves. The first two leaves are used for keeping flies or any other insect away, and also to purify the air, while the last leaf is purely a ceremonial herb.

When the girl wakes up, the nurse in attendance washes her with another herb. After the washing, the wound is attended with antiseptic and healing leaves called *kagutwi* or *matei*, banishers. For the first week after the operation, the girl is not allowed to go for a walk or even to touch with her bare hands anything in the way of food.

The initiates, both boys and girls, who refer to each other as sisters and brothers, eat collectively. The invalids are entertained by their guides, who sing them encouraging songs, in which they bring out vividly the experience they gained after they themselves were circumcised. The guides sing that in a few days the wound will heal and the initiates will be able to go out jumping and dancing.

For a period of three or four months, according to the rules of various clans, the initiates do not participate in any work. They devote most of their time to learning the ways of the community and their duties and responsibilities as full-fledged members of their society. They also spend much of their days moving from one district to another singing initiates' songs called *waine*.

Though I wished to be circumcised early, I was not permitted until I was a young adult. In the past, boys were ready for circumcision when they could throw a club over the highest tree and girls when they reached puberty. When my turn came, I was anxious. I was worried that I might not be brave enough, that I might flinch when I was cut. More than anything else, I wanted to be brave. As the song went, I wanted to clench my fists and be a man when I unclenched.

I also thought a lot about becoming a man. I knew manhood meant being more responsible and doing more for my parents, brothers, sisters and everybody else. I knew freedom to marry carried responsibilities that were as heavy as the privilege of making love was joyous. I knew that to be a man meant leaving my childhood freedoms and limitations and changing my life altogether. Was I really ready to shed my old skin and wear a new one?

I also understood that while the ritual of circumcision was still intact, the duties of citizenship were now different. Yes, after initiation I was to become a warrior, but of a different kind from that of the past. Before, Gikuyu boys became warriors to defend the community against cattle-stealing raids from surrounding communities like the Kamba and the Maasai. Now all Kenya's ethnic communities had become one nation and circumcision would make me a Kenyan rather than a Gikuyu warrior. As a Kenyan, my duty would be to defend Kenya not against any of its forty-three communities, but against its internal and external enemies, including dictatorship and imperialism.

As a Kenyan warrior, I knew that though I might take up gun, spear and shield, it would not be to raid other communities for my own community, the Gikuyu. It would mean developing the whole country and promoting freedom for all.

Though physical, circumcision was primarily spiritual. It was to make me a man who could bear pain and die for what I believed in. To the extent that it armed me to lead a better life, it was to be a lifetime experience, a process without end. My initiation was to put me above the cultural chauvinism of my own community. Yes, it was to give me the stamp of my own culture but also respect for other cultures—including those that did not circumcise.

In preparation, I chose Joseph Mukundi, my former teacher and friend, as my *mutiiri*, guide. Unfortunately, my circumcision lacked tradition—the night-long dancing, singing, teasing and talking of sex, pre-dawn racing to the river, plunging and coming out of its ice-cold water frozen and waiting in line with others to bravely face the knife, surrounded by guides and colorfully dressed, club-carrying men. Colonialism had deprived us (though the girls in our year were operated on traditionally). When my day came, I walked to the local clinic. I lay on a bed instead of standing, and I clenched no fists. The anesthesia robbed me of everything. When I came out of the clinic, I did not remember what I had gone through but mourned that I had not gone to the river, singing, decorated in red and white ochre, escorted by our whole clan. I walked home to be nurtured and tutored.

One week after the circumcision, just when my wound was beginning to heal, one of the most beautiful girls in the village paid me a visit. When she came in, my *mutiiri* was, by design, not in. The girl gave me a most sweet smile. She invited me to have sex with her: Did you not approach me before I was circumcised? Now I am here for you. Come and enjoy a real woman, she teased. My manhood hardened and started to bleed. I was not to have sex until I was healed. It was a cruel punishment. Should I ignore the danger and take her? That was the test. If I did, I would suffer and be despised forever as a weak man. I looked the other way and begged her to leave me alone.

Resisting sexual temptation was considered a most important ability. Like pain, it was a lifetime test. Passing it once did not constitute enduring success, but it gave one confidence. The confidence to live what my *mutiiri* called the life of a man.

Now you are a man, he told me just before my last day with him. When your country calls, you must answer. You are now a warrior for your country and people. Before, every young man fought for his country. Today, warriors are the soldiers and the police. Even if you are not in the army and you are called, you must be ready to come forward and defend your country. If ever you see *marimu*, ogres, black, white, green or yellow, in your village, town or country, you must defend your family, society and nation against them. If you cannot do battle with an ogre that has come to eat your people, you are not a man. You are now a man free to be a husband and a father, which does not merely mean having a wife and children. It also means working hard and saving what you earn to support your family.

As a man, you must be ready to look after your father and mother when they get old. Remember, too, that when you marry, you will have your *athoni*, parents-in-law, who will be your parents as well. Take care of them, too. In your children, their blood and yours will be one.

Koigi, being a man means being respectful to those who are older and younger than you. They will give you only as much as you give. Being a man means being fair and just with other people. A man is never unkind. A man is never greedy or unfair. Never pass anyone asking you for help. A true man does not eat before his wife and children. A man does not engage in sex with uncircumcised girls or women who are too old. It is taboo to have sex with women of your blood, fellow men or animals. You must never rape a woman. An initiated man has an initiated tongue that wins where force fails.

Never commit a crime, steal, fight or kill. When you go out into society, do so as its keeper. It is your second family. You cannot have family without society. It is not manly to forsake society. It is suicide.

And this I can never overemphasize: A man is his eating habits. Always eat what is yours. Anything else will choke you and eventually come out of your nostrils or those of your children. Never take food from the mouth of another. Never overeat. Drink alcohol when necessary but never too much. Never smoke bhang or take drugs. You don't need what harms you. Always remember: What and how you consume can unman and uninitiate you.

Black Europeans

Like everybody else, educated Africans had their view of independence and what to reap from it. One day, a friend invited me to have dinner with a young educated Kenyan couple with two of the best jobs then available to Africans. The wife was a secretary and the husband a salesman in a British company in Nakuru. They earned good pay and had a beautiful car and a nice house in Milimani, the European part of town from which most of us were still excluded. For behaving like Europeans, people called them black Europeans, *wazungu weusi.*

Upon arrival at their house, I felt a little intimidated. I had not been to such a nice and tidy house before. With everything so European, I felt completely out of place. When we went to eat, we had to use knives, forks, spoons and hard starched napkins. Even meat was removed from bones not with teeth and hands but with knives and forks. When I tried to do so, the bone simply flew into the air and landed on the other side of the table. I was so embarrassed! We ate in a dim light. No one spoke—except with our eyes. Indeed, the atmosphere was so grave that I felt as if I were in church rather than a dining room. Everybody else looked so relaxed that I wondered, Had these human chameleons ever been in the African world? I felt so uncomfortable that I almost couldn't eat.

After dinner, we returned to the sitting room to chat. By my side was their little son, Master John. But his other name was Kamau.

Kamau. How are you? I said to him in Gikuyu. Little Kamau smiled back but could not talk because he did not speak yet.

Holding his little hand, I talked to him again. Kamau, please tell me your name. What is your name?

The mother spoke, Please, Koigi, what language are you talking to John in?

Gikuyu, I said, sounding almost stupid to myself.

You should not.

Does he speak Swahili or English?

He does not speak English yet but I don't want him to speak either Gikuyu or Swahili before he speaks English. If you speak Gikuyu to him now, you will spoil his accent. I want him to get an English accent. So please, only speak English to him.

Very interesting, I thought. This lady meant I should not speak to her son. I have a Gikuyu accent and could not give him an English accent. But neither could she. If this African mother could, she would give her son away to an English couple for an accent!

Yes, for this woman, the Union Jack had gone down but she would not abandon colonial culture. Thanks to the colonial school, this mother hated her tongue and culture so much that if she could, she would have absolutely nothing to do with her past, parents, country or race. Along with her colonial school generation, this woman was no longer an African. She and her husband were black Europeans.

Offspring of the colonial school, educated Africans did not belong to Africa. They belonged to Europe. Most opposed independence. Those who supported it did so not in order to restore African pride, identity, dignity and beauty but to more completely wipe themselves out and complete the mission of colonization. For themselves, they desired complete alienation from everything black and African and total assimilation into everything white and European. Because they could not themselves become white, they wanted to inherit colonialism and make it black.

Black Europeans had conflicting desires. On the one hand, they wanted European privileges they could not have without Europeans leaving Africa. On the other, they wanted Europeans to stay as their guides and models of what and who they wanted to be. They resolved this conflict by aborting *uhuru* to keep white Europeans in Africa and playing second fiddle to them. Their ambition was not to restore Africa black and free but to live in a European neighborhood, take their children to a white school, work in a *mzungu* company, have a European secretary, socialize in a white club and someday marry white.

As Oginga Odinga put it in *Not Yet Uhuru,* "The educated group reckoned prestige by the closeness of the African to the white man and his ways."[1]

For black Europeans, independence had to give them a better opportunity than colonialism to become Europeans. *Uhuru* had to preserve the colonial house and keep it as white as possible by keeping as many Africans out of it as possible. They called this exclusion "maintaining the standards".

Odinga wrote that educated Africans were separated by a great gulf from the mass of the people. Notwithstanding, they were recruited to run all the institutions of independent Kenya. Because their vision of Kenya was in direct contradiction to that of the people, instead of working as servants of the people, they ran Kenya as representatives of British interests. One of them, Charles Mugane Njonjo, Kenya's first attorney general, liked to think he was more English than the English aristocracy!

But the tragedy of Kenya was not that black Europeans were willing to sacrifice the welfare, dignity, fate and future of Kenya to promote profits of Western companies. It was that Kenyans bowed their heads to them in admiration and allowed themselves to be led to the slaughter like sheep. People lacked the guts to say no to these black ogres because they were their own children and, in part, wanted to be like them. This admiration continued even when black Europeans committed cultural atrocities against their kith and kin.

I met an old mother who told me that her son who had gone to Britain to study, and married there, had returned to Kenya but refused to come home and say hello to his parents. He wanted nothing to do with them. They were no longer his family. Other parents complained that when they went to Nairobi to see their educated sons, they were kept in the servants' quarters. Before they were allowed into their sons' house—where they were not even allowed to stay or eat—they were fumigated to kill lice, fleas and bedbugs.

A black European welcomed a friend and me into his home to eat a lunch of European food—rice, meat, Irish potatoes and bread—while his own (uneducated) brother ate *ugali* and collard greens at a lower table. Embarrassment nearly choked me.

When black Europeans became leaders, Kenyans embraced collaboration as a virtue, negated independence and set the stage for a new struggle in Kenya that would capture my attention and shape my destiny for the next thirty years.

Taking a Tribal Oath

On July 5, 1969, we were in the dining hall of Nyeri High School listening to the one o'clock news when we heard a shocking report. Government Minister Joseph Thomas Mboya had been assassinated in Nairobi. The whole school fell silent. Tom Mboya was a central figure in Kenyatta's government and was seen by many as the president's probable successor. The Western press hailed him as Kenya's brightest politician.

Mboya was from the Luo community. Though he was an ideological antagonist of Oginga Odinga, the acknowledged leader of the Luo people and Kenya's first vice president, many Luo were just as proud of Mboya. While the whole Kenyan nation was appalled by the assassination, the Luo were thunderstruck and furious. They believed their son was murdered to stop him from succeeding to the highest position in the nation. When the announcement came that the assassin was a Gikuyu man, their worst fears were confirmed. In both Nairobi and Kisumu, the central Luo city, the Luo poured into the streets to demonstrate and express their anger. When Kenyatta attended the requiem Mass, people rioted and accused him of murder. There were running gun battles between police and demonstrators.

Kenyatta had unleashed the forces of ethnic hatred that had now killed Tom Mboya to retain power in the hands of the Gikuyu elite. The Luo community believed the assassination was not the murder of an individual or a crime against all Kenyans but that it signaled their own demise by every single Gikuyu.

Now, retaliatory animosity against the Gikuyu rallied the Luo and others behind Odinga and made him a real threat to Kenyatta. The young government could only survive the political repercussions of Mboya's assassination by inciting more hatred among the Gikuyu, Embu and Meru communities against the vice president and the entire Luo community, simultaneously killing democracy in the country.

In Luo land, hot rumors said Gikuyu people were being attacked and some, like my childhood friend Njogu, were thrown into Lake Victoria. Many had to flee to survive. In Gikuyu land, many said that Luo people were being assaulted, and men were being forcibly circumcised. In our school, Nyeri High School, a lone Luo student felt so insecure that he, too, had to flee.

To secure ethnic loyalty, the ruling party forced every Gikuyu to take an oath swearing allegiance to Kenyatta, his government and Gikuyu rule. At night, vehicles drove students to the administration centers to take the oath. I evaded it, not because it was more primitive than a Christian oath, but because I did not agree with its aims.

Holidays came and I visited my uncle Kariuki at Thika on the way home. It is here that I witnessed the full-scale hysteria of ethnic hatred. The oath was given, not under cover of darkness, but in broad daylight. Administration centers were crowded with long queues of people waiting. More frightening, attending the ritual was not a choice. Those who resisted were threatened, beaten up and sometimes killed. To give the ceremony value, people were forced to pay for it. To disguise its moral repugnance, they called it tea, *chai*. Yet we had not asked for it, and the danger it was perceived to counter existed only in the minds of the elite. At the end of the day, the oath worked against Gikuyu just as it worked against Luo. It took their money and peace and forced them into a state of undeserved terror.

Fearing for my life, I finally submitted. While waiting to take the oath, I struck up a conversation with a young schoolgirl.

Why do they say we must take this oath? I asked.

Because we must protect the government of black people, she replied with assurance.

Black people! I was astonished. Protect it from whom? I persisted.

Against Luo people, she said confidently.

Do you know Luo people are black?

Are they?

They are just as black as we are, I told her.

Why then are they against the government? the girl asked.

The government is against black people.

All black people?

Including us, I whispered, not wanting to be heard.

Clearly, the dread the Gikuyu harbored for the Luo was built upon ignorance and strengthened by the fear and greed of its leaders.

I went into the hut after the girl. After inspection, we were ordered to remove all our clothes except underwear. The hut was dimly lit. We were put into a line facing the oath administrator. Alongside him stood a man with a bowl full of dark, sticky animal blood, while another assistant held peeled raw bananas. All of us were then robed with a ring of freshly slaughtered animal skin around our necks and ordered to approach. We were told to repeat after the administrator: "I am loyal to the government of most honorable *Mugathe* Kenyatta. I will never let the government leave the house of *Mumbi*. May this oath devour me if I reveal it to anyone." Seven times we recited these words, took a bite of raw banana, licked the animal blood from a stick and passed beneath an arch. When the dangerous circus was over, I was asked to pay seven Kenyan shillings so that power would remain in the hands of Kenyatta and the Gikuyu elite.

Afterward, I had no doubt that I had participated in something totally immoral and wrong. When I went home, I found people being driven to the oath every night for the entire month of August. I argued against these trips with my young father, who was very busy organizing them.

Baba munyinyi, I told him, we are Kenyans and so are Luo people. It is suicidal to rally against one another.

Son, he would tell me, be careful what you say in these times. For a Mugikuyu to speak against the unity of his people is to be a traitor.

Nothing could stop the spread of this poison. To prove that he was now in full control and crown his conquest of the Luo community, Kenyatta visited Kisumu to officially open the Russian-built hospital there. During his speech, he exchanged bitter words with Odinga and people booed him. On his way out, the emotional crowd stoned his motorcade and his security guards responded with a massacre that killed more than seventy people. Subsequently, Kenyatta arrested and detained without trial many leaders from the Luo community, including Oginga Odinga, the champion of independence who had fought hardest for Kenyatta's own release from colonial detention.

At Barclay's Bank

When I left high school, I taught at Kairi High School and then became a clerk with Barclay's bank in Nakuru. Although Kenya had been independent for six years, the country was still rife with racial discrimination. In the bank where I worked, there were two toilets—one indoors for whites and Asians, another outdoors for Africans. The exterior toilet was cramped and poorly kept. For paper, it had the big post office directories. Using it on rainy days meant being drenched in tropical downpours.

Before my friend Kariuki and I joined the bank, only one African woman was allowed to use the indoor facility. All others were barred. The official explanation that use of the more convenient indoor toilet was determined by managerial position crumbled when two young Asians joined the bank in nonmanagerial jobs and were not stopped from using the indoor facility. It was then that my friend and I decided to act. An assistant manager, Goodal, saw me on my way to the toilet and asked where I was going.

To the toilet, I told him.

That toilet is not for you.

Then I must go home and use my own.

Do you have permission to go home?

If you will not give permission, I must use this. I will not use the one outside.

Mr. Wamwere, in the bank you must listen to me. I am the manager here.

I know, but I will not use the outside toilet.

Get back to work now.

No sooner had I gone, than I saw the manager leave the inside toilet. I immediately got up and went straight for it. Goodal watched as I passed, but did not stop me. Nor did he ask anything when I came out. Half an hour later, my friend Kariuki also used the same facility. We had broken a racial taboo for African bank clerks.

CHAPTER IV

CROSSROADS 1 9 6 9 – 7 3

A Dream Come True

While teaching at Kairi High School I saw scholarships to America advertised by the African-American Institute. I told my Uncle Kariuki that I would apply for one and was sure of getting it because I had traveled once before to a land of great roads that meandered through beautiful green hills, valleys and forests that stretched for miles without end. My dream had not revealed what land this was, but when I saw the advertisement, I immediately believed it was America.

A Black Ogre

I had been in America for some time when I remembered the last story I had been told at home.

Wonders never end, the storyteller began. Not so long ago, your parents hired a black ogre who was disguised as a political liberator to manage their farm. Overly trusting this worker-swindler, they gave him the keys to the main entrance of their property, the gate of their compound, the main house, and the safe. The imposter simply looked too nice and spoke too well not to trust.

One day your parents left home on a few days' safari to trade in another part of the country. When they returned, they found themselves shut out. The black ogre told them that the farm belonged to him. He had the keys to everything. He had vacated his quarters and moved into their big house.

Unable to reenter their home, your parents sat out in the rain and cold. They were hungry for many days before they surrendered to the thief, who let them back into the farm only as his employees. Servants' quarters were their new home. They could not believe their misfortune, but had no choice. Slavery is the wage of nonvigilance.

Having dispossessed your parents, the black master disinherited you. This is why you are growing up silenced and dispossessed. To legitimize his theft, the ogre occasionally organizes sham elections and he bribes farm workers to vote for him as the manager of the farm. Your parents cannot win these elections because they have no voice, money, security or influence over the electoral process. If your parents call the swindler-ogre a thief, they are whipped and locked in the farm prison for days in a dark cell without food or water. Once, when your father asked for the restoration of his stolen farm, he was shot at and nearly killed.

I hear you will soon go to America. When you get there, ask the white man to show you how you can repossess the farm, the house and the freedom that your parents lost. Ask him to show you how you can end their enslavement and redeem your inheritance. Make that the mission of your life and the purpose of your education there, not coming back to work for the ogre.

Son of Mau Mau

I never forget that it was because my father had gone to the Rift Valley that he survived the Mau Mau war. A song I heard on the radio at home had asked:

> Where did Wamwere, son of Kuria, and his people go?
> Do you know they were the survivors
> Of the Lari Massacre? [March 26, 1953 massacre by the British]

Though the war was over, when I left Kenya, the whole country was still shrouded in the sadness of colonial days. So the musicians continued to sing:

> Deep sadness covered the land
> From the beginning of the war
> As Gikuyu, Embu and Meru were targeted.
>
> Both old men and women,
> Young men and girls,
> Even babies were persecuted.
> But Ngai saved us.
>
> Many people were wiped out.
> The country was plunged into deep silence.
> Crying, screaming and gunshots
> Crippling and killing many.

Seven years after independence, people were still looking for a way out of their misery. At my farewell party, my Uncle Kariuki spoke: As you go to America, remember you are a son of Mau Mau. We are sending you to America to gain knowledge. Behind, you have left a lot of problems. While there, work hard and fast. When you get your education, come back and help us to develop this country. If you delay, we will send a village sparrow to call you back:

> Blacksmith that forges
> Cangarara i ca.
> Stop forging and hurry home
> Cangarara i ca.
> Your wife has given birth
> Cangarara i ca.
> Delivered by a black ogre
> Cangarara i ca.
> And fed by a white ogre
> Cangarara i ca...

Koigi, he continued, look at the people gathered here this afternoon. They are poor, living in collapsing grass-thatched and soot-filled shanties, wearing torn, old clothes. They are your grandparents, parents, uncles and aunts, the ones who raised you. They have been your educators. They all wish you the best. Look at these people well. They are not city people, well-dressed, clean and perfumed and living in beautiful houses. They are the ladder you climbed to reach where you are today. Never forget them. If you ask, they will tell you they are not asking you to come back and do much for them. Merely be grateful and do not look the other way. When you meet them in the street, greet them. If you can, lower your hand and lift them up from the abyss of their oppression, poverty and misery.

Do not get lost. Before you, many went and never came back. If you don't return, this happy party today will have been a funeral. In America, you may live, eat, dress and drink better, but never forget that it is always, Hail mother, with her raggedness, hail mother, *kungu maitu, na hunyu wake, kungu maitu.* Remember to come home to your own mother.

I was forewarned by another Gikuyu proverb: Whoever eats alone, dies alone, *muria wiki akuaga ari wiki.* I had come to America not to acquire an individual passport to wealth, power and privilege, but to strive for our collective salvation from poverty and oppression.

First Impressions

The first thing that struck me about America when we arrived in the summer of 1971 was how freely ordinary people could say anything about their president without fear of arrest. The longer I stayed, the more I felt like someone enjoying release from prison. Coming to America was an eye-opener.

It might sound funny, but after years of a thoroughly colonial education, it took America to instill in me a sense of black pride and beauty. Africa should have been a natural source, but it was not. Despite independence, the African mind was still shackled to the culture of colonial abuse and devaluation, and Africans came to America feeling less proud and beautiful than other people. It was, therefore, a great sense of liberation to hear African Americans say they were black and beautiful, black and proud. Soon I was also feeling and saying exactly the same thing.

I came to America with two other Kenyans, Mwakai Sio and Clement Nyamongo. Both are friends, although they traveled a different path. In the U.S., I found three other Kenyan friends—Maina wa Kinyatti, his wife, Mumbi, and Muthumu wa Ngatho. They helped me to see more clearly where Kenyatta's economic and political system went wrong and what could be done to put things right. A great admirer of the Mau Mau, Maina particularly impressed me.

It was not just black Americans and Africans who helped me to recover my humanity and sense of self. Just as it had been a white man who gave me a European name, it was a white woman who challenged me to ditch it forever.

It was my second day at Cornell University. I had gone to the laundry to wash my clothes when a beautiful white woman approached and said hi.

Hi, I said back.

Where are you from?

I am from America, I said teasingly.

No, I don't think you are, she replied confidently.

How did you know?

Your accent. Where are you from?

Kenya.

I am Karen, she said, extending her hand.

Michael, I offered, while shaking her hand.

Your real name?

Michael is my real name, I said with some irritation.

I mean your African name, not your nickname.

Michael is not a nickname. It is my real name, I insisted.

When you were born, did your mother call you Michael?

No, but my African name is quite difficult to pronounce.

Maybe for me, but we learn many difficult names, like those from Eastern Europe. So what is it?

Koigi wa Wamwere.

Kygy wa Wamere, she tried gamely.

Ko-i-gi wa Wa-mwe-re.

Well, I will learn how to pronounce it right. Ask me tomorrow.

When I left this woman, I felt terribly embarrassed. The same name, without

which the priest would not admit me into the seminary, had now been trashed as
a nickname. Yet she was right. Michael was my European nickname, not my real
name. I did not even know what it meant. I swore never to use it again. That day
I threw away all of my books that had the name Michael Koigi on them. As for books
that I could not toss away, I crossed over the name Michael and wrote my real
name, Koigi wa Wamwere. I never looked back.

Student Activities

At Cornell University, I was a member of the African Students Association. ASA
was open to all Africans and held monthly meetings featuring African fare and
discussions of different African problems. Sometimes, we screened documentary
films on Africa. Most members of the association liked to think of themselves as
apolitical. Some were civil servants that shied away from criticizing the governments
that employed them.

In the U.S., racial groups like Native Americans, African Americans and Chi-
canos are discriminated against. Still Americans are allowed freedoms of expression,
press, assembly, association, criticism and conscience to a very large measure. It was
in the U.S. that I first demonstrated against apartheid in South Africa and Portuguese colonialism in Angola, Mozambique, Sao Tome and Guinea Bissau. I was
embarrassed that I could campaign against African problems in the US and not in
my own country.

At Cornell, I joined student demonstrations against the university administration for investing funds in companies like Gulf Oil and General Motors which
did business with apartheid South Africa and drilled oil in Angola, then a Portuguese colony. One such demonstration turned sour when students stormed a
meeting of the University Senate and held its president hostage. The president was
to be held until he agreed to denounce colonialism and apartheid in Africa and
support the withdrawal of university money from companies that traded with South
Africa and Portugal. While three rows of demonstrators, I among them, blocked the
entrance into the building, the police arrived to break up the demonstration. They
ordered us to disperse, but we refused to budge. Then they were ordered to shoot.
Standing in the front row I felt pangs of terror when I saw these men leveling their
guns at us. But no sooner had they received their orders than a line of white students, stood in front of our row to act as a buffer between the police and the black
students. When the police realized that they would kill white students if they shot,
their resolve to kill vanished. They were forced to negotiate our peaceful withdrawal.
In the midst the argument with the police, the president of the University Senate
appeared. He addressed us promising to cancel the university's economic marriage
with apartheid and colonialism. We all cheered and went home happy.

On another bitterly cold and snowy winter day, we again held a demonstration to condemn colonialism, apartheid and dictatorship in Africa. As we hollered and shivered, I was very angry that only four African students attended. What logic allowed African students to sit in their warm rooms, eating, drinking, studying and mating, when non-African students froze and risked, fighting for the freedom of their mothers, fathers, sisters, brothers and children? It is a shame I will never forget.

Though American soldiers were getting beaten in Vietnam, I had no doubt that in the final analysis, the U.S. withdrew because of home opposition. American students were at the forefront of that resistance. On the campus, I saw many demonstrations against the war in Vietnam. I heard students openly urged to reject the draft as conscientious objectors. Before I came to Cornell, in May 1970, the National Guard had shot and killed four students demonstrating against the war at Kent State University. It was a wake-up call for the whole U.S. to stand up and end the war. That determined students could, unarmed, stop a war by the world's most powerful government taught me a lesson on the power of determined youth.

So impressed, I wondered: if Americans could oppose a war they were fighting abroad, didn't Kenyans have an even greater right to oppose oppression by their own government-turned-dictatorship? I began to go to Washington, D.C., on the Africa Day each year to demonstrate against old colonialism, apartheid, neo-colonialism and dictatorship in Africa. These demonstrations inspired my fight for freedom.

Here, color did not define the enemies of Africa. White Botha of apartheid South Africa was condemned. Black Idi Amin of Uganda and Emperor Haile Selassie of Ethiopia were chanted down. We shouted down Emperor Bokassa of Central African Republic, Kenyatta of Kenya and Siad Barre of Somalia with equal vehemence as we did white Caetano of Portugal. Chanting: "down with Botha," "Haile Selassie to the zoo," "Shame to Kenyatta," "Death to Bokassa," "Away with Portuguese colonialism" and "U.S. imperialism out of Africa," we jogged and walked up and down streets of Washington until we were hoarse and could walk no more.

Clearly we associated African problems with western imperialism and capitalism. Our demonstrations condemned imperialism and supported social equality and the struggle for the liberation of Africa. I could not fathom why countries that called themselves democracies like the U.S., Britain, France and West Germany, supported dictatorship and not democracy in Africa. Their fear of communism had turned democracy into an enemy and dictatorship into an ally in Africa! They were fighting socialism and democracy in the name of freedom, while socialists battled democracy because they saw it as an instrument of western imperialism. In Africa, democracy was feared and fought by all. This is how dictatorship enveloped the entire continent. To struggle for democracy in Kenya, I had to free myself from these ideological straitjackets.

Heroes

In Africa I had my heroes—Dedan Kimathi, leader of the Kenya Land and Freedom Army (Mau Mau), Patrice Lumumba, Kwame Nkrumah and others. When I came to America, I added more to the list—Amicah Cabral, Malcolm X, Martin Luther King, Jr., Robert and John Kennedy, Mahatma Gandhi, Abraham Lincoln, Che Guevara and Jesus Christ.

One day I was listening to a tape of a speech by the Kenyan political and union leader Tom Mboya in the University Library. A woman who was listening to another tape began to weep until she could not continue. She returned the tape and left. I was curious and asked the librarian for the same recording. It was my first encounter with Malcolm X, who seemed to speak for our Kenyan masses. He said, "We have been crossed, double-crossed, triple-crossed and any solution that any one of them might come up with is just another trick."

When I listened to the dream of Martin Luther King, Jr., it did not sound like one for Americans alone. Rather, it resonated like a universal dream for the oppressed of this earth that lifted my poor soul to the high skies of hope. In any case, it fired my own energies and triggered my own dream.

Dream of Freedom

I had a dream of my own one night: My friend Wamwathani (Son of God) and I walked down a street in Petu (Our City), the capital of a new democratic and egalitarian Kenya. Petu looked like Nairobi, the capital of old Kenya, but it had no slums, was much bigger, much cleaner, prosperous, and its police did not wear menacing faces and carried no weapons. It seemed that I had just walked into this city from the old Kenya.

Wamwathani was unemployed but looked happy, well-fed, well-dressed and without the anxieties and fears which accompanied unemployment in the old Kenya. Surprised that Wamwathani looked so relaxed, I asked, Why?

Why? he asked back.

I don't understand how you can be without work and have no worries. What will you eat? Where will you stay? What about money for rent, transport, clothes, medicine and school fees? How will you manage to keep your children at school? In the old Kenya, I know if one were without work, he begged, stole or sold sex. How come you don't do any of these?

Wamwathani chuckled and for a moment didn't answer my questions. Then he said, matter-of-factly: Here, everybody eats, is clothed, has a house, goes to school and gets medical attention. And we get these things, not because we work and pay taxes, but because we are human beings. The basic belief here is that all people, with or without work, have the same needs that should be satisfied whether or not they are unemployed, too old, sick or victims of any disability. Here we live and work for and not against one another.

How is that? I asked in amazement.

Our government guarantees social security for all, Wamwathani said.

Is the government here so rich?

Yes, the government of the new Kenya is much richer than that of old Kenya. Having eliminated corruption and put the economy in the hands of nationals it has more money to share than the government of old Kenya. It is also morally richer. It is a democracy. Most important, we believe as Mahatma Gandhi did: The country has enough to satisfy the needs of all but not the greed of anyone.

How did you manage to get a democracy here? I asked Wamwathani.

There is no birth without blood. We had to shed blood, sweat and tears in our fight against dictatorship, corruption, ethnic hatred and foreign manipulation. After beating the four evils, now our government is based on the principle that people have a right to fair wages, fair profits and social security at all times.

I heard myself saying more to myself than to Wamwathani, Yet our government takes taxes and denies people everything!

My friend, that is unthinkable here. We are not angels, but we are no longer slaves to Kenyatta or to Vice President Moi—M(y) O(wn) I(nterests). If the government tries to take taxes and withhold services, we rebel and overthrow it. All religions here teach one message—rebellion against tyranny is obedience to our African Gods. We are free and have a good government because we have dared to rebel.

Farther down the street, we met a man in front of a shop who was picking thrown-away food from a dustbin. I could not believe this was possible in the new Kenya. To me this man looked normal, but maybe he was mad. But whether mad or normal, why was he allowed to eat from a dustbin in the new Kenya? I was about to ask Wamwathani this question when I suddenly noticed that the scavenging man was a half-beast. The body of this strange creature was divided into two parts. The forepart was human and the hind part was that of a pig. I looked askance at Wamwathani.

How can this be? I asked.

They are many, Wamwathani said.

How did they come to be? I asked.

They came like this from the old Kenya. They were already half-human and half-pig when they came here. Their current nature is what they chose for themselves. They talk like human beings but they live and eat like pigs. These are people who forfeited their humanity in the old Kenya. They were too greedy. They were human in body and piggish in spirit. These are inhuman people who tortured and killed innocent people whose only offense was to ask for food and dream about freedom and justice. These were the corrupt and dictatorial politicians of the old Kenya. These were the corrupt and cruel judges who jailed innocent people and sold justice to the rich in the old Kenya. These were the brutal soldiers of the General Service Unit who brutalized and raped university students seeking freedom. These are the soldiers of the Kenyan Army who killed innocent citizens in the streets of Nairobi. These were the cruel prison officers of old Kenya. These were the greedy employers who paid workers starvation wages in the old Kenya.

After Wamwathani and I parted, I went into a cinema. It was showing a film about the transformation of a farm that had belonged to Honorable Angaine, a government minister in President Kenyatta's government. Angaine joined the national struggle for independence in the 1930s. He was a member of Kenya African Union (KAU) in the 1940s and organized for the Mau Mau in the early 1950s. Angaine was so committed to the struggle for independence that legend has it that when his wife discovered his involvement in Mau Mau but refused to take the Mau Mau oath, Angaine had her killed and buried below the floor of their own house. Her body was never discovered. Nevertheless, because colonial authorities suspected him of Mau Mau activities, Angaine was arrested and detained without trial for the entire duration of the war.

In Manyani prison, Angaine was physically assaulted countless times by colonial prison guards. In fact, all his teeth were knocked out in prison. Like other Mau Mau detainees, he was starved throughout his time in detention. Many times, he suffered from diseases. He served many years of hard labor.

But Angaine was of a powerful and resilient build. He survived detention and joined Kenyatta's government after independence as minister for land and settlement. He grew to be as greedy for land as a hyena is for human flesh. Forgetting his Mau Mau comrades, he grabbed big former European settler farms totaling over 112,000 acres for himself.

Angaine's farm was never used because the minister was too busy doing other work in Nairobi. He lived in Nairobi and occasionally went to the farm on weekends. However, patches of the farm were cultivated by squatters who were allowed to do so in exchange for votes during elections. Many of these squatters were Angaine's comrades in the Mau Mau war, the same people he had suffered with in prison. As they starved for lack of land, wild animals grazed freely in most of the farm.

For Angaine independence meant having superfluous land, money, power and food. For his squatters, independence meant never-ending lack of land, poverty, oppression and starvation.

In the new Kenya, Angaine's former Mau Mau comrades and squatters now owned his farm while both he and Kenyatta were pig-men. Above all, leaders here were not gods, but ordinary human beings who walked unguarded in the streets, ate and rode with people in the same hotels, buses and trains and observed traffic rules like everybody else.

New Kenya had built big industries that people owned and managed. Yes, to develop, people had to borrow capital and technology from other countries but they never lost their independence to creditors or so-called donors. In Petu, there were foreigners of all colors. But they were visitors and friends, not masters.

When I woke up, I was not in a cinema but in my room in the International Hall of Cornell University. I had been dreaming the dream of freedom, the same dream my young father Mungai and his Mau Mau comrades had fought and died for.

This dream was more than a dream. It was a vision that I wanted to fight and live for. When I told my dream to a few friends at Cornell, some laughed it off as utopian. But I asked myself: If America, once a colony like Kenya, could develop as it had, why not Kenya? I packed my clothes and books and left America to go home and fight for my dream.

CHAPTER V

H O M E C O M I N G   1 9 7 3

Arrival

In my life, I have made many decisions, but the resolve to quit university and come home to Kenya to work for democracy was the most momentous. I saw no need whatsoever to inform my parents or my brothers and sisters that I was on my way back. I was a man going to battle and consequently it was unwise to announce my arrival or allow my people to organize a welcoming party. How could I write to them and tell them that I was on my way back home to fight Kenyatta's dictatorship. They would have thought me mad, as many subsequently did when they heard of my return. How can anybody sane throw away the key to heaven to come home and fight Kenyatta?

I arrived at Nairobi Airport unmet. Immediately, I took a taxi to Nakuru town and stayed with my brother Kuria wa Murimi. From Nakuru town, I went to the village to see my parents. Later I stopped at Mung'etho, the trading center. There was a public meeting led by the DO (Divisional Officer) in charge of our village. I asked to say something at the meeting and was allowed.

Mr. DO, I said, I wish to ask why the forest workers gathered here continue to be paid the same low salaries they used to be paid before independence. May I also ask why old retired forest workers like my father have not been given their pensions after working for the Forest Department for so many years? I understand the government's argument is that these workers were casual rather than permanent employees of the Forest Department. How long does it take to be a permanent worker, if my father who labored for more than thirty years was not a permanent employee? Yet white forest officers who were here for a much shorter time are being paid their pensions in Britain by the Kenyan government. And why are forest workers not allowed to keep cattle for the milk of their children when there is so much grass rotting here?

The DO mumbled something incoherent in reply, but the people were very happy. After the meeting, I walked home together with my parents and later many more people from the village came to see me. Contrary to my fears, my parents were happy to see me home. After all, a child is never thrown away, *mwana ndateagwo.*

But they were perplexed. How could I return home before my school was over? They must have thought that something was wrong with their son. Only Mum told me that my life was mine, and I was free to live it the way I wanted.

As for the government, it was hostile. After all, it always treated the people as its exclusive herd to send to the pastures, starve or feed as it wished without debate. Though Kenyatta had fought for independence, he seemed convinced that the ultimate good was not to work for collective welfare but to look after one's own self-interests. It was in my last year in the seminary, 1968, that Kenyatta let the cat out of the bag by scolding Bildad Kaggia (the most fervent of revolutionaries) for working so hard for people and doing nothing for himself. In a public rally Kenyatta told Kaggia, "We were together with Paul Ngei in jail. If you go to Ngei's home, he has planted a lot of coffee and other crops. What have you done for yourself? If you go to Kubai's home, he has a big house and a nice *shamba*. Kaggia, what have you done for yourself? We were together with Kung'u Karumba in jail, now he is running his own buses. What have you done for yourself?"[1]

I could not expect a government that had thus admonished a freedom fighter to welcome me home to fight for the Mau Mau dream. Kenyatta could not stomach rebels, old or young.

Means of Struggle

Having chosen the fight and the battlefield, I had to choose the spear. And the spear I needed was decided by the fact that the struggle had to begin at the stage of selling the dream. With what was I to turn my own dream into the people's dream? Journalism offered itself as the spear of the moment, the voice of my dream.

Now I had a spear, but no shield. Was I to fight or wait until I had a shield? I knew going to war with a spear alone was risky, but the greater danger was to wait. Writing was my spear; human rights, the shield I needed and lacked.

Without a Shield

When the editor of the *Sunday Post* agreed to publish some feature articles by me, I was overjoyed. I could now tell the whole world how badly our people lived.

My first article was on forest workers. I showed how poorly fed and clothed the children of forest workers were due to miserable wages. They were not allowed to keep cattle though there was so much grass everywhere. I showed the cruelty of an African government worker denying my father and others a pension while it paid white forest officers living abroad pensions for the work they did during colonialism. I attacked the Civil Servants Union for taking membership fees from forest workers, but failing to protect them against the injustices of casual employment that deprived them of almost all workers' benefits. I visited our forest workers' homes and saw the terrible food they ate and the terrible squalor they lived in; I reported what I saw. And to illustrate how these abysmal working conditions were remediable, I showed that in neighboring Tanzania forest workers lived better.

The government's reaction to my article was swift. Japheth Shamalla, an official in the Ministry of Natural Resources, called my complaints "rubbish" and invited me to emigrate to Tanzania.

After independence, the extreme exploitation of women continued. It was still common for men to beat women in their homes. Education of girls was still considered less important than that of boys and employment was seen not as a right, but as a privilege that spoiled women. Though African men and women had fought together, after independence men had moved into the position of the colonizers and women had taken the place of Africans down the ladder. Worst of all, the oppression of women was considered so natural that it was thought abnormal to challenge it. So when I wrote an article in 1973 challenging this state of affairs, some young friends from the University of Nairobi called me crazy: Oh God, who do you think you are now, an American telling Africans how we should treat our own women? This is Africa and our women are happy, my friends told me.

I charged back: White settlers said the same about us in Europe when we were fighting for independence: "Our Africans are happy under colonial rule. They only need to be left alone." If your wife is happy when you beat her, my sister is not happy without an education.

That is the trouble when some of us become too educated, they told me, sneering. You think you are now better than your own people, don't you?

No, I don't. I only think that we should treat our women better than we do.

Go to hell with your know-it-all attitude.

What more could I say to my friends? But I knew they had heard.

In 1973, I wrote an article called "Tribalism is an ideology of exploitation." There was a lot of tension between the Kenyatta government, which many Gikuyu people identified as their own, and the Luo community, most of whose leaders the government had detained without charge or trial. In trying to defend their government, many Gikuyu people who had, in fact, not benefited from the government, talked very derogatorily of all Luo people. Yet in our village, I knew a Luo family that was exactly like us. In school, I had many Luo friends. Why should I hate these people who endured the same problems that I suffered, merely because President Kenyatta was at war with Oginga Odinga and other Luo leaders? While this hatred helped Kenyatta and his government to stay in power, I did not see how it benefited poor Gikuyu people, who were only made poorer by loss of love and Luo friends. This is why I wrote that Kenya could not possibly benefit from "tribalism," and that the ethnic hatred Kenyatta preached against Luo people was in essence the same hatred that white colonialists had preached against the Mau Mau and Gikuyu people. This article drove many in the Kenyatta government crazy. Immediately they called me a traitor and demanded that I be taught a lesson. I was yet to write my most provocative article.

I put my finger in the mouth of the lion when President Kenyatta declared that all armed robbers would be hanged when caught. Kenyatta wanted poor people who robbed with penknives, needles or mere sticks hanged because he believed that they made Kenyans poorer and created insecurity. I believed and wrote otherwise. The people who were robbing Kenya and creating insecurity in the country were the corrupt leaders. They used the violence of the pen and had the power to plunge millions into poverty that in turn forced destitute, powerless and illiterate people to resort to robbery for survival. If the rich who robbed from the poor with the violence of dictatorship did not deserve to die for their crime, how could poor people who robbed much less from the rich and from one another deserve to die? I wrote in my article that hanging poor people who robbed little and not rich people who robbed much was inherently unjust. For me, it was worse for an ocean of water to rob water from near-empty cups than for an empty cup to rob water from an ocean.

I had contradicted the president. And by contradicting the president and condemning the police in public lectures at the University of Nairobi, I had sinned against our political god, and the police would not rest until they had cast me into an everlasting hell. From then on, I would be hunted down like a rabid dog.

Every time an article appeared in the *Sunday Post*, the police came for me. They came for me at work, at home and in the streets. When they came for me at home, they searched everywhere for books they called subversive and took them and me to the police station. At the police station, I would be questioned about what I had written and why I had "bad" books. After interrogating me for two or three days, they would let me go or take me to court, where I would in turn be remanded to prison for some days or weeks until the charge was thrown out.

As time went on, the police increased their pressure. At about ten at night, they would come to the one-room house I shared with a friend. They would tell me they had been sent to come and stay with me in the house. I would ask them whether this was a house arrest and they would say no and take seats. They would then lean their guns against the walls and make themselves comfortable. At first I would stay awake with them late into the night, afraid they might kill me if I went to bed. Later I guessed that if they wanted to kill me it would not be my staying awake that would stop them. I would then draw the cloth curtain between them and our bed, and we would just go ahead and sleep. In the morning, we would wake up to find them dozing in their seats. We would then make tea and drink together.

It was a life of incredible terror orchestrated against us by the provincial police officer, James Mungai, and the divisional police chief, Wang'ombe. They arrested me so many times that I lost count and lost faith that I could use journalism to effectively challenge the injustices of dictatorship under Kenyatta. I guessed that to be effective, I needed to go to Parliament and challenge the system under the protection of parliamentary immunity.

Politician on Foot

In Kenya, many people join politics armed with money and the desire to acquire power to get richer and protect their stolen wealth. When I joined politics, I had nothing. I was armed only with my democratic beliefs and principles and the desire to use Parliament to acquire justice and a little of the cake of independence for the poor people of Kenya. When I decided to join politics, I went to my parents and told them that I intended to join KANU, the ruling and only party, to contest for the local parliamentary seat in the coming general elections. Amused, Mum asked a succession of questions:

Do you really think you can fight and defeat Babu Woods (the local MP) in a parliamentary election? Is *bunge,* Parliament, not for rich people? How can *maskini,* a poor man, like you go to Parliament? Who will vote for you?

Other poor people, Mum. Are poor people not a majority in Nakuru North?

They are, but they all ask for *coro mai,* keeping of the trumpet moist.

That is because there is really no one who speaks for them.

Well, try if you wish, but it will not be easy.

But you will give me your vote, Mum?

Mine is yours, but it will not be enough to take you to *bunge.*

My father, who was quiet all this time, then spoke: Son, we are a small house.

Yes, Pap.

And when a small house fights and wins a case against a big house, it moves away. Have you heard that?

No, I have not.

Yes, it does. And when it loses, it also moves away. It is hard to fight and win against these rich and powerful people. But why don't you come with me to our garden in Kiura. We must chase away animals that are eating our maize.

Yes, I will.

When we arrived in the garden it was just beginning to get dark, and a few *ngima,* monkeys, and *njege,* porcupines, had just moved into the garden to eat maize and potatoes. My father shouted "Oi Oi Oi," and the animals flew out of the garden at great speed. But some porcupines got stuck in the tiny holes through the fence that my parents had built at the edge of the forest to keep animals out of the garden. When we attacked them, they fired their sharp quills at us quickly and ferociously. We had to take cover inside *githunu,* a garden hut. We killed two porcupines and took them home.

On our way home, my father told me, Fighting rich, powerful and corrupt politicians like Babu Wood is like fighting porcupines. They eat your crops and you must chase them out of your garden. But they will fire quills and kill you if you do not take cover. I am not a politician, but in politics I believe it is no different. You must take very good care.

I will.

I began the campaign for the 1974 general elections without a car and with the help of a small group of friends. Every evening we went into villages to talk with workers in coffee and sisal plantations, forest workers and peasants. During the day, we would hop onto a mini-bus that would drop us at a trading center from which we would walk into villages and farms where we would talk, eat and live with the people for days. We always traveled light and washed and dried our clothes in young men's huts at night and wore them again the next day. Each morning we would wake up in one village, take whatever breakfast people gave us and walk to the next village talking to workers, peasants, small business owners, students and young unemployed people on the way.

As the campaign went on, I walked from one village to the other, from one trading center to another, one plantation and farm to another, one primary school to another and one forest to another. At first I thought my campaigning on foot only served to demonstrate my poverty and weakness, but people were fascinated by a politician on foot. For me, it was a real revelation to see that families in coffee and sisal plantations lived just as poorly as forest workers did and sometimes worse.

I will never forget one night when I visited a working family in the coffee farm of a government minister, Mwai Kibaki in Bahati. They lived in a tiny, round hut that was half-filled with thick smoke. A small child was eating *ugali,* a maize meal cake that is hard even for adults to eat, with *sukuma wiki,* tough green vegetables, together with her parents, brothers and sisters. They all slept on the floor and had no tables. Their bedding was faded and torn. They could not even afford a lantern. No politician had ever been into their hut, and they thought it a great privilege that I could visit them.

As it turned out, the contest was not between the sitting MP and me but between Kihika Kimani and me. Kihika Kimani was a powerful and wealthy local politician who ran Ngwataniro, a huge land-buying company that had taken millions of shillings from poor peasants and workers to buy them land; however, he had used the money to buy himself a lot of land. The company had also bought a fleet of vehicles that Kihika now used to campaign against me.

In our public rallies, Kihika depicted me as a poor man. Because I was thin, he said I had tuberculosis. He said I had no business seeking parliamentary leadership, because I had no home, no land and had not liberated my parents from the poverty of forest life. He ridiculed poor men who wore tattered clothes and went to his office every day as desperadoes who "cut grass with their testicles," wore *chapatis* (a flat bread) on their buttocks and *thigonji,* scones, on their knees. Equally, he dismissed old women who opposed him as poor, miserable beings whose faces were so sunken that they could carry water in the hollows between their eyes and ears! This contempt for the poor drove many poor people into my political camp.

As Kihika Kimani depicted me as a poor man, I depicted him as a thief and a corrupt leader. I asked him to read company account books and tell people how much of their money he had swindled and how much was still safe. I challenged him to give people the land he had bought with their money and to stop using people's money to buy his own land. I told people that Kihika was using their vehicles and money to campaign and bribe them with and that they would be roasting themselves in their own fat like a pig if they voted him in. When he accused me of immature youth, I reminded him that horns come after and grow taller than ears, *ciukaga thutha wa matu na ikaraiha kumakira.* As Haile Selassie's dictatorial monarchy collapsed in Ethiopia, I reminded Kihika that the Kenyatta government too would face the same fate if it continued to oppress the Kenyan people.

Enraged, my opponent burned down shops in Bahati that belonged to my supporters. For this, I called him a witch doctor who deserved to be burned alive. I was arrested and thrown into jail for two weeks. To stop me, Kihika, Njenga Karume and other GEMA leaders summoned old men and women from Rugongo village and offered them money to sign a statement claiming I had visited them at night to persuade them to oppose Kenya's land tenure system. When they mentioned my elimination, one old man, a distant relative of mine yet a political opponent, objected.

Yes, he said, the leadership of rebellious young men like Koigi should be rejected but Koigi should not be killed.

Why? asked one GEMA leader.

If we eliminate young men, for whom then are we developing the country? the old man countered.

The GEMA leaders gave up, but not completely. One night we were driving home after visiting a place called Subukia. On our way home, we passed a crossroads where a big lorry barely missed the back of our car as it lunged for us. We were scared stiff but not enough to give up our campaign. Nor did our political opponents give up their designs against us.

One evening, two days before I presented my nomination papers to the District Commissioner, an exercise without which I could not stand in the election, Kihika even hired renegade former Mau Mau freedom fighters to kidnap me. Mwangi wa Wakairici led the kidnappers. He was a man who always spoke in riddles that I never understood. He came to Jogoo Commercial College, our campaign headquarters, and asked if he could take me to Subukia and introduce me to more Mau Mau freedom fighters. Since it was evening, I asked him whether we could go another day, but he said that this was the best day. I collected some campaign posters, put on my jacket and asked my friend Njoroge to come with me. Wakairici said it was best if I went with them alone because their car was already full. We agreed but when we went to the car, what I saw completely unnerved me.

The car was a big three-seat Pajero packed with seven big men with faces that were tense, grave, contemptuous, hardly concealing hostility and almost sorry for me. Immediately, I felt a chill of terror run down my spine and instead of getting into the car, I turned and asked Wakairici to come back to the office with me. Back in the office, I whispered to Njoroge that I did not feel safe to go, and he offered to go in my stead. He took the campaign posters from me and got into the car with the seven men. Without their prey, Wakairici and his men did not go to Subukia to campaign for me. They ended up in a bar where they drank and bought Njoroge beer for many hours. Later, we learnt that their mission was to take me into a forest and tie me to a tree for three days to make sure that I did not present my nomination papers to the District Commission. Though I had escaped the kidnapping, I knew danger was not over. *Kuhonoka nyongo ti kuhonoka ndigana,* to escape from the foot and mouth disease is not to survive from the East Coast fever.

Wherever I went, I was followed by my opponent's well-known, violent and armed thugs who intimidated me and were looking for a chance to attack me. I was therefore forced to be permanently on guard. But without a gun, I could only protect myself with a bit of military guile. While in the United States, I had bought an oversized U.S. military camouflage jacket that I wore everywhere I went whether it was raining or the sun was very strong. This gave Kihika's thugs the false impression that I concealed a pistol or some other weapon in my big jacket.

One day we were on our way to a public rally at a place called Rongai. Just before we got there a Land Rover driven by Kihika's thugs stopped and blocked the road ahead of us. I sensed danger and my heart beat very fast. Convinced they were ready to attack us, I jumped out of our tiny vehicle, put my right hand inside the jacket as if I was about to draw out a pistol and boldly ordered them to either drive on or remove their car from the road. My bluff worked—they drove on. But my opponent had more than these brutes on his side. What hired crooks could not do for him, the police did.

It was the last day of the campaign. The Swahili paper *Taifa* had published a lie that I had stepped down. I needed to counter this lie by going to every trading center. As Kihika went around the constituency in a convoy of more than 50 cars telling voters that I had stepped down, my supporters and I followed behind them in a tiny convoy of four vehicles disclaiming the lie. When we reached Subukia center, it was a market day and there was a huge crowd that clamored for me to get on a tabletop and tell them that what they had just heard was not true. When I did, I heard police whistles and sirens and saw police running to the station from every corner of the market. The entire police force at Subukia Police Station was waiting for us. Once they were in the station, they armed themselves with truncheons, hoes, guns, big clubs and shields. With sirens blaring, they charged at and chased men, women and children in all directions. They beat up old women, kicked children, broke arms and split lips. Everywhere, all was blood, chaos, cries, shrieks, trampled food and clothes. Running men, women and children were forced to take refuge in the waters of Subukia River. In the meantime, police were inching closer and closer to our car. When we saw how menacing they were, we got into the car, wound up the windows and sat tight. When the police reached the car, they started knocking the doors and windows of the car with truncheons, but we did not open them. Finally, they lifted our car up and carried it to the station with us inside. Once we were at the station, we came out and complained of police brutality on behalf of my opponent. Instead of stopping the brutality, the police inspector had us locked up until about one in the morning.

After release, we hurried back to town only to find that at three in the morning the police had rounded up and locked up all our election agents. As a result, our agents were not present in polling stations to inspect and certify that every ballot box was brought to the station empty and not stuffed with stolen votes before the voting started. As a matter of fact, when I went to Kabatini polling station, a few minutes after voting had started, to the chagrin of the presiding officer of the station, I lifted the ballot box and found it full of votes already. Outside the polling station, my opponent's supporters carried baskets of money that they gave to the voters as they went into the polling station.

I had no doubt that the election was rigged against me. I thought of filing a petition against my opponent's election, but realized that I could get no justice under courts that were under the direction of the same government that had rigged the election for my opponent.

The rigging of my election was yet another concrete proof that our songs of democracy were a sham and Parliament was not, as I had thought, the people's voice. It was the voice of the rich and the powerful. Unable to use Parliament to advance freedom and democracy, I had no choice but to struggle for the same from outside its walls.

Struggle for Land

It all started with an auctioneer's notice: Properties of Nakuru District Ex-Freedom Fighters Organization (NDEFFO) were to be auctioned because the company had not paid bank loans for four farms. The organization's four thousand members were furious. What had happened to the money they had contributed to buy land? For years members had been working without pay on the company's farms. Where was the money that had been saved? Where were the earnings from the sale of milk, animals, wheat and building stones from the company's quarry? Here was corruption on a grand scale.

When the auctioneer arrived at the farm, members dared him to touch anything. He did not and left the farm as he had come—empty-handed. After blocking the auction, members began to call for a general meeting to discuss the critical situation. They demanded the election of new directors, accusing the old directors of corruption. But the old directors would hear none of it, and refused to call a general meeting.

Despite the fact that company law was flouted, the registrar of companies in Nairobi seemed unconcerned and did not institute legal proceedings against the directors nor demand future observance of company law.

One day in 1974, I accompanied some members of the company to the registrar of companies. We complained that the directors were not doing what the law required them to do. We urged the registrar to institute an investigation into what was happening in the company and enforce the law. In reply, the registrar asked us why we thought we could make better directors of the company than the ones who were already there. To me, he sounded like a man who was in the pockets of the corrupt directors.

Despite our difficulties, we collected members' signatures for an extraordinary general meeting to be called and convened by the members themselves. In the meantime, however, the directors were organizing gangs of thugs to terrorize people. They derisively called the NDEFFO rebels *Withare*, "run for your life." The terror gangs would roam the streets of the villages at night looking for opponents to brutalize. Victims would be lucky to escape with a severe beating; at worst, they would be marked with lacerations in the shape of a cross on the stomach. They would then be released to go and frighten others into silence. When people reported these atrocities to the police, nothing was done.

Looking at the members of NDEFFO, I felt sad, frustrated and cheated along with them. The former Mau Mau freedom fighters had won neither land nor freedom. They had shed their blood in vain. Unable to give up, they had denied themselves food and other necessities in order to raise money for land. That land was now slipping through their fingers like fine sand. Why could the organization not rise up more forcefully to say no to this continued theft of their blood, sweat, land and freedom?

Instead of taking their fate into their hands, people still begged the police to come and protect them. Soon, however, even the seemingly unending patience of the poor and the weak vanished. When the police did nothing to stop the terror or disband the terror gangs, rebel members organized their own militia to patrol the village at night and protect their own. One night I was visiting Engoshura village from town. On my way back, I was confronted by one of the militias:

Who are you and where are you going? they asked.

I am coming from the school, and I am going home. I was afraid to say my name.

We asked you who are you. What is your name? All the time they were getting closer to me.

Convinced that this was the directors' militia that was baying for my blood, I immediately took to my heels and ran as fast as I could. Unfortunately, I was running in the dark and I could hardly see where my feet fell. The militia gave chase over the wet and slippery ground. I ran into a rut, staggered, fell, rolled, got up and again ran so hard that my lungs hurt. Finally, I came to the house I had been visiting and swerved into the compound. The militia followed.

God, is it Koigi that we are chasing?! one of the militia exclaimed when they saw me. Why did you not tell us it was you? In the dark, we could have hurt you for nothing.

I know, I said, but I did not know it was you either. I thought it was the enemy militia.

No, it is we—not the enemy, they said in great relief, laughing. It was a close shave.

Another day, I was shocked when I found a few old Withare members near the offices of KANU, the ruling party, carrying a big sisal bag. I asked them what the bag was for.

We want to carry Wanyoike wa Thungu in it, they told me.

How will you get Thungu, the fully armed head of the presidential bodyguards, into that bag?

We will capture him.

Presidential bodyguards will kill you all! Don't dare.

They did not proceed, but I was shocked at how much they were willing to risk for their land and freedom.

As time went on, the temperature in the NDEFFO villages continued to rise. Once, a meeting was called by Thungu himself for the purpose of intimidating rebel members. We wanted to hear Thungu speak. As soon as he was on the platform, he said he had been sent by President Kenyatta to tell members—

Before he could finish his sentence, a member shouted: Don't tell us what Kenyatta sent you to tell us. He did not buy this farm for us.

Knowing what side the presidential bodyguard was on, the rebel members were not prepared to let him have a smooth ride. But he too was a fighting man.

What? Did somebody say something? He was surprised that anyone had dared to interrupt him. This he was not prepared for.

Yes, said the daring Mwangi wa Kibuthu. We are telling you Kenyatta did not buy this farm for us. We don't want to hear what he said. We know what side you are on. Get down and get lost.

Shut up, you old man, or I will break your bones! exploded the furious bodyguard. I am not here to be contradicted by the likes of you nonentities! But if you really are a man, contradict me again, and you will see.

Three old men now stood up, and spoke to the bodyguard: Mr. Wanyoike, said one of them, We warn you! If you do not want to die on this farm, stop talking now. You did not buy this farm for us, and we are not your children.

The whole meeting murmured, and the bodyguard seemed clearly shaken. He was not expecting this. Sensing danger, the meeting organizer got up and requested that the presidential bodyguard come down from the platform. He said he did not have men to ensure his security. The bodyguard had no choice. He turned tail and returned, thoroughly shaken up, to Nakuru town.

Defend Yourselves

A couple weeks later, elections were over. The people in power had lost but refused to vacate office. When the new directors went to take over company offices the following day, the old directors savagely fought them off with machetes, inflicting upon them serious injuries. The new directors went to the police for escort into the office but, as in the past, the police did nothing.

A little after this, Thungu organized a delegation loyal to the directors to visit President Kenyatta at the State House in Nakuru to give him a distorted view of the elections they had lost. But the winning opposition swore not to allow such a one-sided delegation. They mobilized their supporters, who were in the majority, to go along.

Once in the State House, the old directors told their version of things and the new directors told theirs. Surprisingly, when the new ones complained that the old ones had attacked them when they went to take over company offices, Kenyatta lost his temper: You are all the time complaining of being beaten. Are you children who cannot fight back and defend yourselves? He drew out the long sword that he carried in the sheath of his walking stick, put it up in the air and asked, Have you ever seen me put this sword of mine down?

It was now clear from what Kenyatta had said. Under attack again, the victorious opposition, now legitimately in power, could not go back to Kenyatta and request protection, nor could they go to his government and police. Their taking office depended not on their winning elections but on whether they could muster enough strength and courage to do so. Equally, the losing side now knew that they could ignore the fact that they lost the election and remain in office as long as they could muster enough violence to fight off the incoming directors. Kenyatta had given them his tacit approval to do so if they could. Through his refusal to face injustice and support justice, Kenyatta had now planted the seeds of war between the two groups. When we left the State House, it was with a sense of trepidation of approaching war. Some did not approve of this. Why were they paying taxes to employ the police, if the police were not there to protect them? they wondered.

Demonstration at the State House

It was to make sure that Kenyatta understood this that we decided to organize a demonstration outside the gates of the State House when Kenyatta left to go to his farm at Rongai. The day before the demonstration, we drafted and typed a memorandum to give to President Kenyatta during the demonstration. It reminded Kenyatta that the war for independence was fought over land and freedom. We made signs: "Wanyoike wa Thungu: Stop killing our women and children. We fought for land and freedom, not landlessness and hunger." The old men took the memorandum and placards with them, and I went home. We were to meet in the morning outside the gates of the State House for the demonstration.

In the middle of the night, I was awakened from sleep by a loud knocking at the door. I recognized my brother Kuria's voice and opened the door. He came in, followed by several policemen led by Wang'ombe. I could see that he was under arrest and I wondered whether they had come to arrest me too.

Why have you come to my house so late in the night? I asked them.

We have been to see your sister and your brother here. She says you are the one who wrote and typed that memorandum that the Withare women gave to President Kenyatta tonight.

I was surprised to hear this because we had agreed that the demonstration would be held in the morning. But the questioning continued:

Do you have a copy of the memorandum? We want to see it.

Yes, you can see it. Can I show it to you tomorrow morning?

No, we want to see it now. Do you have a copy of it here?

No, I don't. It is in the office.

Take us to the office right away. We must see it tonight.

Okay, let me put my shoes on.

No, you don't need to. You will be right back. Your slippers are enough.

When we reached the office, I gave them a copy of the memorandum but instead of letting us go home as they had promised, they arrested us. We were locked up there for three days. All along, however, I had been wondering how come the memorandum had been given to Kenyatta before the planned demonstration. It was Kuria who told me the whole story.

When we parted after writing the memorandum, the old men were on their way home at night when they met some Withare women heading for the State House carrying babies on their backs. The men asked them to turn back since there would be a demonstration the following morning. The women said they were going to the State House that night whether the men liked it or not. They were tired of harassment and would not go home before they had told Kenyatta so.

You men can have your own demonstration tomorrow morning. We are having ours tonight.

Under the circumstances, the men had no choice. They had to go along with the women. They could not let women carrying tiny babies demonstrate before Kenyatta alone. Since no one could publicly enter State House with placards, they had to smuggle them in beneath the babies. At eleven, when the national anthem was being played after all the evening's entertainment, women who had cleverly mixed in with the *nyakinyua,* traditional dancers, and had gone up to the front during the dancing, suddenly took out their placards and raised them up for Kenyatta to see. Kenyatta and his bodyguards were shocked. Perhaps most thunderstruck was Wanyoike wa Thungu, the head of the presidential bodyguards, who could read his name clearly printed on the placards. Such a thing had not been seen before. Seeing this, police and bodyguards went berserk and went straight for the demonstrating women and grabbed the placards from them. As they did so, State House officials were all asking, How the hell did these madwomen get these placards in here? Who searched them?

Anyhow, as police and bodyguards grappled with the demonstrating women, one named Nyambura threw the memorandum in an envelope to Kenyatta as she was hustled into a police car. The envelope fell at Kenyatta's feet. When Isaiyah Mathenge, the provincial commissioner, picked it up, Kenyatta asked for it.

After Nyambura was taken to the Central Police Station, the whole Withare membership went to the police station to demand her release. While they were all there, the police asked for my brother Kuria Murimi, one of the leaders of the opposition whose women had demonstrated. When Kuria came forward, he was arrested and asked about the memorandum, and how the police could get a copy. He explained to the police that he had spent the day in Nairobi, and he did not even have the keys to the office.

After we had been in the police station for three days, we were paraded before

Officer Mungai. He asked us many questions and threatened to have us beaten up. Pointing at some placards on the table, he asked me: Why did you help the old men to draft the memorandum to the president and write ugly slogans on these placards?

Because I can write and the old men cannot.

Have you ever seen a man beaten until he cries like a child?

Yes, my father shed tears of blood at Kwa Nyangweso colonial torture center at Bahati, and since then I have seen someone beaten and tortured to death at this police station.

Young man, do not talk to me like that and look down when talking to me. I am not from your *riika* (peer group) and can strangle you with my own hands if you make me angry. Now get out of my office. And remember I would not have released you had *Mzee* (President Kenyatta) not ordered me to let you go.

Before we left, Nyambura had a parting shot at this most brutal and frightening policeman: Can I have one of your cigarettes?

He could not refuse. He lighted one for Nyambura and we walked out of his office almost majestically.

Fire and Blood

After the demonstration, Kenyatta was said to have summoned the head of his bodyguards and called him a dog for exposing the president to embarrassment. That apart, nothing was done to solve NDEFFO problems. Emboldened by government inaction, the defeated, corrupt directors now started openly to organize a war by evicting the people who had won elections from NDEFFO farms. They wrote a declaration of war and pinned it on buildings and tree trunks all over the property. The declaration was shown to the police, yet, as before, they did nothing. The newly elected directors were compelled to write a reply to the declaration of war and post it. Its language was chilling: "In your declaration of war against us, you have promised to burn our houses and uproot our crops. In return we promise you one thing. If you burn one house belonging to us, we shall burn all your houses. If you uproot one crop belonging to us, we shall mow down your whole fields. If you chop off one of our ears, your heads will roll." Meant to scare, this language did not deter the old directors from planning their war. Instead, the reply became a prophecy that was fulfilled to the minutest detail.

The old directors prepared for war as if there were no government in Kenya. Trucks openly ferried weapons and fighters from one farm to the other. The fighting started in a farm called Karirikania (the reminder), at 3 A.M. on July 20, 1975. One new director popularly called Gentleman was attacked by an armed group of about seven men. They tried to draw him out of his house to kill him. When they attempted to get into the house, they suffered the injuries of one who follows a bee into its hive. In turn, Gentleman had machete cuts everywhere on his body—head, hands, arms and legs. But he was alive and his attackers had fled. Another old man called Mataceca (the one not to be toyed with) and his father, Githaiga, were almost untouched. Yet they had killed three of their attackers. When the new directors arrived in town after fighting from 3 A.M. till dawn, the old were as excited as the young.

On receiving them, we did not dare take the wounded to the government hospital. We feared for their freedom. Instead we took them into a laundry room that belonged to one of the new directors. The police had moved into Karirikania when the fighting was reported, but made only a few arrests.

Near Nakuru town on Engoshura farm, the old directors were preparing for another battle. They slaughtered a cow, ate, drank and said prayers. When they emerged from feasting, they formed lines of battle, hoisted a red flag on a high post and started marching toward the homes of their opponents.

A little earlier, Mungai had been at the farm to check the state of affairs. When he was told that war was nigh, his reply was shocking: Let the cowards lose.

For Withare, there could be no more illusions. To survive, all had to fight—men, women and children. Upon this realization, they too formed themselves into battle lines. All armed men hid in the dark green maize fields. Near the houses, young boys and girls sat on the roadsides waiting to see who would come. Behind the youths, women carried baskets full of stones and hid behind houses.

When the old directors' army arrived, they proceeded to the house of Karanu, one of the new directors, and set it on fire. At that, all hell broke loose. The young boys and girls screamed and women started throwing stones at the old directors' army, which panicked and started to retreat in all directions. But they were already encircled from behind and their retreat proved disastrous. As they scattered through the maize fields they found the real Withare army waiting for them. They were knocked down to the ground, hacked with machetes, beaten up with clubs and speared to death. Those who escaped screamed for help amid the unbearable shrieking and groaning of the injured and the dying. As they ran to their own home compounds, Withare men, women and youth gave chase. The Withare mowed the old directors' maize fields and set their houses and tractors ablaze. The chaos, the screams, the groaning, the blood, the burning homes and the loud bursting of burning rubber tires of lorries and tractors was a frightening scene from hell.

By five o'clock in the evening, the whole Engoshura farm was just fire and smoke. Long lines of fleeing supporters of the old directors headed for town carrying only personal belongings on their hands, backs and heads. It was impossible to go onto the farm. Only the police could go in, but hundreds of people came from the town and stood on the road that went by the farm to see what was going on. They huddled in small groups, talked in whispers, wondering where the government was.

The police came in vans and carried the wounded to Nakuru General Hospital and the dead bodies to the mortuary. At the hospital, the police had cleared whole wards of other patients to accommodate the fallen and injured fighters.

In the evening, my brother Kuria and I went to the general hospital to express our sympathy to the wounded and see what medical attention they were getting. But when we expressed sympathy to the injured of the other side, one woman sneered at us: Some have come only to find out when others will die. Unable to express our humanity to the enemy fighters, we said good-bye to our fighters and left the hospital to go home. Now we knew we had broken the backbone of those who were refusing to vacate office after losing elections.

The following day, newspapers reported the fight for land and announced that fewer than ten people had been killed. The real death toll was over twenty.

After this battle, the farms were in the hands of the new directors. They went straight into subdividing and distributing the commonly held land.

Subsequently, war leaders from both sides were arrested, charged with murder and destruction of property and taken to prison. After some time, however, charges were dropped, and they were all released, but the police were still determined to stop members from having a share of their own land.

Women Win Again

One day, a lorryload of police arrived at the Engoshura farm. They found a group of women tilling their new plots of land on a mutual support basis. They positioned themselves in front of the women and faced the women with guns aimed at them. The women were not frightened, nor did they look at the police. The police boss was furious and ordered the women to stop tilling. The women just continued working. The warning was repeated a second time. Unheeded, the police were ordered to take aim at the women and wait for orders to shoot. At that point, one of the women spoke: Friend, you seem to me to be a Mugikuyu, so I suppose you will understand me. I can speak to you only in Gikuyu. As you see us, we have only one body, right in front of you. There are no others. You may order your men to shoot. But we shall not stop working on our land, nor shall we move an inch from where we are. If colonial police did not move us from this land, neither shall you.

The order to shoot was not withdrawn, and the women did not stop working. Tension was extremely high. But as the women worked and awaited death, suddenly tears started rolling down the cheeks of one policeman. He could not stand it any more. The injustice of the order was obvious, the pain of having to shoot at innocent women intense. Maybe one of them was a sister, a wife or even a mother. Noticing his policeman in tears, the police boss ordered all the policemen back onto the truck and left the victorious women not singing songs of victory, but happily working their land, simply enjoying the rhythmic sound of their rising and falling hoes.

At His Last Best

Unfortunately the NDEFFO land drama did not end with this victory. The defeated directors organized yet another delegation to appeal their double defeat to President Kenyatta. Learning about this, the victorious directors now in power invited all members of NDEFFO to the State House.

With Kenyatta listening, the spokesman of the former directors was allowed to present their case to the president, accusing the other side of all manner of crimes including introducing foreign ideologies. After finishing his formal speech, Kenyatta wanted to continue, but the women interrupted him. He looked up and roared, Who is that? Are you booing me?

No, the women replied. But give the other side a chance to present its case also.

Kenyatta ignored the plea and started to speak again. Again there was booing.

Have you forgotten whom it is that you are booing? Kenyatta asked angrily. Do you know that if I snap my finger like this you people will be taken to eat beans up on the hill? (He meant Nakuru prison.)

Yes, *Mzee*. But give the other side a chance to speak, too. How can you decide a case like this without listening to both parties?

After a brief silence Kenyatta asked, Where are the others? Nobody told me there are two sides here. Who is their spokesperson?

My brother Kuria Murimi was the spokesperson. He could not come forward, because two policemen had pinned him to a chair. Unable to stand and speak, he put his hand up. Is it you? Kenyatta queried. Speak then.

Kuria read a memorandum explaining how the complaining directors had mismanaged and driven the company into bankruptcy through theft; how opposition to them had saved company farms from being auctioned; how they lost the election and why it was fair for them to give the directors who had won elections a chance to run the company.

After the memorandum was read, Kenyatta asked what the people wanted him to do. The people said they wanted to tell Kenyatta everything that had gone wrong in the company because they wanted to end this problem once and for all. Kenyatta agreed to listen, and for six Saturdays, Kenyatta sat at his great court the whole day listening to NDEFFO people. Kenyatta was at his most democratic, something he was never to be again. Each person spoke who had anything to say.

Their right to speak had been won by their courage to say no to the most powerful person in the land.

After the sixth day in Kenyatta's great court, he ordered fresh elections for
NDEFFO that were again resoundingly won by the new directors. It took the new
leaders more than three election wins and a victory in war to convince the government that people who wanted change could not be stopped from taking power.
For the people, it was a big lesson. For exploitation to end, the exploited must say
no to it, and power must be taken away from the exploiters.

Politician of the People

Upon returning from the United States, I immediately made contact with J.M. Kariuki, who was a great spokesman for the poor. Having read *Mau Mau Detainee,*
his story of imprisonment at the hands of the British, I was overwhelmed by the
colonial brutality he had suffered while fighting for independence. Afterward, as
Kenyatta's private secretary, he was one of the few Mau Mau detainees who were
allowed into the House of Independence, yet he fought for the hungry who were
shivering in the cold and rain outside the House. He was rich, but he fought for
the poor. He had land, but he fought for the landless.

The government and his detractors labeled him a communist. On a few occasions, my friends and I visited J.M. at his Kanyamwi home and we had long ideological discussions there. We tried to convert J.M. to scientific socialism, but he
would not be converted. His ideology was based on the Scandinavian model of social
democracy, and he defended it vigorously.

Even if J.M. fought for the poor, he did not live like a poor man. Still the poor
loved him because he shared his wealth with them by making generous contributions to *harambee,* fund-raising functions, to which he was invited all over the country. Though J.M. gave to the poor and criticized great inequality in society, he did
not believe in complete equality among people. Once, when visiting him at his
Gilgil home, we tried to share a bottle of whiskey with his watchman. He would
not touch it. When asked why, he replied that a slave does not disobey his master.
I was surprised that the employee of a social democrat should see himself as a slave
and see his social democratic employer as his master.

J.M. Kariuki was a colorful and flamboyant traditionalist who had three wives
and many girlfriends in Nairobi, Nakuru and other towns. He had a capacity to reach
out to every group in the country and particularly impressed the nation when he
was the only Gikuyu politician to attend Tom Mboya's funeral at Lusinga Island.

But Kenyan people loved J.M. Kariuki best for his sharp criticism of the Kenyatta government: "A small but powerful group of a greedy, self-seeking elite in the
form of politicians, civil servants and businessmen has steadily but very surely

monopolized the fruits of independence to the exclusion of the majority of our people. We do not want a Kenya of ten millionaires and ten million beggars."[2]

J.M. fought against the substitution of black for white land grabbers who proliferated after independence: "I believe firmly that substituting Kamau for Smith, Odongo for Jones, and Kiplagat for Keith does not solve what the gallant fighters of Uhuru considered an imposed and undesirable social injustice."[3]

J.M. also condemned giving people symbols of independence to live on instead of food, clothing, shelter and freedom: "It takes more than a national anthem, however stirring, and a National Coat of Arms, however distinctive, a National Flag, however appropriate, a National Flower, however beautiful, to make a nation."[4]

Above all, J.M. condemned the injustice of forcing Kenyans to pay money for the same land that had been taken from them, which they had fought and died for. "Do not return me to Bunge (Parliament) if you expect that I will change my convictions on the land question; on the repayment of loans on land which we fought for and that is our God-given right; and on the necessity of land-ceiling legislation."[5]

J.M. opposed payment of pensions to the British colonial officers by the government of an independent Kenya. J.M. told us the Kenyan government behaved contrary to the real interests of her people because it continued to be under foreign control " ...Dressed in a new cloak labeled 'economic adviser to such-and-such a ministry or to so-and-so'...they advise us in their interests and we follow them like sheep."[6]

Like Kenyatta, J.M. was a Mugikuyu. When he was killed, Kenyatta's leadership and the Gikuyu people were blamed for all of the country's problems. Yet the whole country from north to south and from east to west loved J.M. The mottoes of J.M.'s leadership were: An elephant's tusks are never too heavy for it, *njogu ndiremagwo ni muguongo wayo;* and there are no children of the stomach and others of the back—all people and ethnic communities are equal, *gutiri mwana wa nda na wa muguguongo.* J.M. therefore fought for the poor and was generous to all communities, and condemned and eschewed the nepotism and tribalism that divided and continued to divide the country and fuel corruption. He wrote in the *Daily Nation* of March 2, 2000, "Nepotism and tribalism have set in and are greatly assisted by the inequalities...These are evil and must be condemned in no uncertain terms. We must all join hands to eliminate them and restore credibility to public life. We must strive to ensure that the next generation will not blame us for having failed to correct the strains of public life."

I was among those who adored J.M. Instead of hiding the country's problems, he was brave enough to see and speak about them most clearly and loudly. He was the people's voice. He called KANU politicians who were close to Kenyatta greedy hyenas close to the president only for what they could get for themselves. Once he disparagingly talked of Mwai Kibaki, one of Kenya's ministers, as *kimundu,* an amorphous and useless person, and called him a coward with a good mind but a weak heart. Many people even saw J.M. as a messiah. When Nakuru politicians were very hostile to J.M. and Mburu Gichua, the mayor of Nakuru, asked him what he was doing in a hotel in Nakuru, J.M. beat him up with his *bakora,* his walking stick, just as Jesus had beaten the money changers in the temple.

Then, on March 2, 1975, J.M. disappeared. People feared he was dead. A week before he disappeared, I met J.M. and asked him about an earlier shooting incident in Nairobi. He told me, Socialist, they are playing with me, but I will show them that I am not a person to trifle with. He had a big smile on his face, and I was happy to hear him say that.

There was so much tension in the land! Before J.M. had been shot at, government agents led by Patrick Shaw (a mercenary within the Kenyatta government) had tried to kill him by blowing up a bus in which he was expected to travel to Mombasa, killing more than seventy people. When these government agents failed, they spread rumors that blamed him for the bomb blast. They claimed it was the work of a fictitious clandestine organization that J.M. led called *Maskini* Liberation Front (Poor People's Liberation Front). Clearly the government was preparing people for a great tragedy.

Two days after J.M. went missing, Ngugi Ngigi told me that J.M. was dead. Days later, J.M.'s body was found dumped in Ngong Hills. He had been lured out of the Hilton Hotel by Ben Gethi (a senior police officer who later became police commissioner) captured and brutally murdered. A champion of the new struggle for land and freedom that I had seen unfold in NDEFFO was silenced by a brutal assassination engineered by the government of Kenya. To disguise his features, J.M.'s body was doused in sulfuric acid, his fingers were cut and his penis had been severed and put in the pocket of his coat. His teeth had been knocked out and his body was riddled with twelve bullet holes. The whole country was plunged into a period of very painful mourning and blamed Kenyatta and his government for the murder. A select committee of Parliament was appointed to probe the murder and discover those who were behind it. The select committee named as prime suspects persons who were highly placed in Kenyatta's government like Mungai, Thungu, Kenyatta's minister of state Peter Mbiyu Koinange and many from the criminal underworld. That these suspects were never tried for the murder either by Kenyatta or Moi might be considered proof that men in both governments were highly implicated in J.M.'s assassination and in many others before and after.

But proof of Kenyatta's implication in the assassination of J.M. came from Kenyatta himself. He was coming from Mombasa when he stopped on the way to address a group of Kenyans. Then he posed this question to his audience and through the radio to the whole nation: If a leopard is stealing and eating your animals, what do you do to him?

Innocently the crowd roared back, Kill him.

To Kenyatta, with that answer, Kenyans had endorsed his government's murder of J.M.

In the aftermath of the assassination, Kenyan musicians cried for J.M.:

People of Kenya
Now J.M. is dead
With his teeth and eyes plucked out
Neither for stealing nor murder.
Do not shed blood for him,
Leave everything to Ngai.

Oi Oi Oiii
J.M., the beloved of the people,
The darling of both young and old.
He was murdered for his goodness
And what shall you die for?

Leaders,
Now J.M. is dead
With all his fingers cut
Had he fed his goats on someone's sweet potato plants?
Should you fail to stop this, I warn
Some of you will be murdered for much less.

Government,
Now J.M. is dead
Together let us uncover his killers
To avoid shedding blood for him.
Fire from the hut of reeds can spread to that of grass.

Oi Oi Oiii Oi Oii
You felled him like a banana plant
Neither for stealing nor murder.
The accursed did not know
Forty babies were born the day he died,
Kariuki is not dead he is still with us.

Other musicians warned that blood would beget blood:

> Should you hear tu tu tu
> It will be neither rain nor fog
> It will be the blood of J.M.
> Crying for the people of Kenya.

They warned that his killer would end the same way they had killed him:

> One who put J.M. on the path of hyenas,
> One who cut his limbs into pieces
> Will be rolled in an empty hive
> With all the masses of Kenya looking on.

Three years later, when Kenyatta himself died in 1978, and his coffin was drawn on a carriage pulled by horses, people thought the words of this song had come true.

Despite threats, working people, peasants, university students and politicians came in private cars, buses, taxis and trains from all over the country to attend J.M.'s funeral. But it was also frightening to see heavily armed police in uniforms and plainclothes lining the entire way from the road to J.M.'s home. The heavy presence of the police did not, however, stop political leaders from saying what they wanted to say at the funeral.

Somewhat tongue-in-cheek, Mwai Kibaki told people that however long it took, one day Kenyans would have to be told who it was that had killed J.M.

Waruru Kanja and J.M. had been detained together for fighting for independence, and they were so close in politics that they referred to one another as eaters of the same food, *muria imwe*. When J.M. was followed everywhere by Special Branch agents, Waruru gave him his car to travel in. At the funeral he condemned Kenyatta's government as one of thugs and killers.

Charles Rubia said he had been warned that he would be killed if he came to the funeral. Now he dared those who had sent him those warnings to kill him here.

In a poem, Tom Mboya's brother, Alfonse Okuku, said it was the people's failure to act on earlier assassinations that had led to this assassination:

> In 1965 they killed Pio Gama Pinto,
> Many said it didn't matter because
> Pinto was a mhindi. [an Asian]

> In 1969 they killed Tom Mboya,
> Again many said it didn't matter because
> Mboya was a Mjaluo.

Then they killed Ronald Ngala,
And many said it didn't matter because
Ngala is just a Mswahili.

Now they have killed J.M.
Shall we again say it does not matter?
It is just Gikuyus killing one another.

Today it is J.M.
Tomorrow it will be you.

Okuku's poem reminded me of one by Pastor Martin Niemoller, a victim of the Nazis:

First they came for the Jews
And I said nothing because
I was not a Jew.

Then they came for communists
And I said nothing because
I was not a communist....
Finally they came for me
And nobody spoke because
No one was left to protest.

The most moving tribute came from Kirori Mutoku, an old man who had been detained by British colonialists at Manyani prison in the desert. He told people how much J.M. had suffered for independence at Manyani. J.M. had nearly been killed for speaking for other detainees and for refusing to surrender to the colonial authorities. Once a prison officer practiced target shooting by firing at a piece of timber, which J.M. was ordered to hold up on his head. With tears in his eyes, the old man also told how J.M. was tortured before he was killed, how his teeth had been knocked out and how he had twelve bullet holes on each side of his body. Finally, Kirori posed the question: How was a man who fought so hard for an African government killed so brutally by the same government? Then he concluded bitterly, The independence that J.M. fought so hard for has turned into the poison that killed him.

This was a frightening commentary on our independence.

CHAPTER VI

DETAINED BY KENYATTA 1975-78

Arrest

After J.M.'s death, things took a nasty turn for me. I started being trailed by the police almost twenty-four hours a day. A vicious campaign was mounted to vilify and harass me. Those who took part in this campaign whispered, Koigi is a traitor. He opposes the politics of his own people. Koigi is bad. He opposes land-lessness and unemployment. Doesn't he know that *itihingagia mbugi*—the entire herd can't all have bells? Koigi is subversive. He criticizes the police. Koigi is dangerous. He must have given people an anti-government oath for so many to have voted for him without money. The more of this I heard, the more apprehensive I got.

After the burial of J.M., there was still a lot of political tension in Nakuru. The government was determined to throw Mark Mwithaga, its MP, out of Parliament for his role as vice-chair of J.M.'s parliamentary select committee which now implicated the Kenyatta government in the murder of J.M. On the other hand, people in town were mad. To them, jailing Mwithaga would be rubbing salt in the gaping wound of J.M.'s assassination. I was right in the center of this whirlwind of both local and national politics.

Sometime after six o'clock on the evening of August 8, 1975, Mirugi Kariuki, Kuria Murimi and I stood in a group on Kenyatta Avenue talking about what was going on. Just then Danson Mahugu crossed the street to where we were and told us that James Mungai, Kabiru Kimemia, Kihika Kimani and others had had a meeting last night. They will detain you and jail Mark Mwithaga, he warned.

The pit of my stomach hurt, and we all looked at one another in consternation.

Why should they detain me? I asked, not directing my question to anybody.

They say if they jail Mwithaga when you are free, you might run for the seat against Kabiru. So they must get rid of both you and Mwithaga, Mahugu explained.

And what offenses will they be detaining me for? I asked Mirugi, the lawyer among us.

I don't remember, he said, but we can check.

That night I went with Mirugi to his brother's home. His law books revealed that one could be detained for just about anything. To detain someone without charge or trial, only the will of the president or detaining authority was needed. With that explanation, I knew I was at the mercy of my enemies. They had access to Kenyatta. I did not.

The next day I went to my office at Jogoo Commercial College to finish typing a paper on ethnicity that I was to deliver to the a conference of churches that was to be held in Nairobi later that month. At about 9 A.M., I heard a knock at the outer door. I did not open it because there was no school that day. A little later, I felt hungry and walked across the street to visit my friend Kimani. We often went to have tea and eat *mandazi,* a popular Kenyan pancake, together.

As Kimani and I talked, across the street, sitting at the newsstand, I saw a man observing us over an open newspaper. When I pointed out the man to Kimani, he told me the two men standing right behind us were also observing us. I turned to look at them and they quickly looked into the shop windows. We gazed at one another in the glass. When they lowered their gaze, I knew they were after me.

They are everywhere. Why are they not arresting me? I asked Kimani.

Maybe they do not want to do it here, Kimani replied.

Let us go for our tea, I told Kimani. Maybe they will arrest me there.

It is strange but now I felt it was better to be arrested than to be kept in limbo. I saw my arrest both as the loss of my freedom and the first step on the road to my eventual liberty.

On our way to the Rugongo hotel for our tea, we bumped into Kabiru Kimemia—the man who was being groomed to be the next MP for Nakuru—and I angrily asked him, Why have you sent the police after me?

No, it is not me, he was beginning to explain, when a police inspector hopped out of a police car, saluted him and explained that they had come to arrest me. Suddenly, I was completely surrounded. Not wanting to be frog-marched to the car, I left Kabiru and Kimani and walked into the open door of the waiting police car. As I took those few steps towards the police car, somehow I felt that I was beginning a long journey.

I was taken to Central Police Station, put into a van with more policemen and brought back to my office for a search. On the way, a policeman whom I later came to know, Mwaega, asked me, Why have they arrested you?

You tell me, I shot back, very angry with him. I thought he was playing games.

A little later he asked the same question.

Don't be stupid, I told him and kept quiet.

The search in the office was a search for subversive ideas, so all books and every paper in the office were put in one big pile for sorting out. Safe papers were put in one heap and subversive papers in another. As the search progressed, I noticed that when Mwaega held a paper he thought was subversive, he would glance at me. If I winked, he would put the paper in the safe area. Sensing his sympathy, I told him later, Take me to the toilet. I have a bad stomach.

Ah! he teased, are we about to catch somebody? Is it why you have diarrhea?

Take me to the toilet or let me go there myself, I said.

I will take you, Mwaega said, but be quick about it.

Out of the hearing of others, I asked Mwaega to help me hide the paper that I was writing on ethnic prejudices, hatred and conflict. I felt that if they found it, they would call it subversive and use it against me. He asked me where the paper was and where he could hide it. Later, Mwaega plucked the paper out of the typewriter and put it behind a big cupboard where I found it three and a half years later.

After the search, I was taken to the Elburgon Police Station where I was interrogated for three weeks. In August, Elburgon is a very cold place and without a mattress and blankets, the police cell was extremely cold. I was kept alone and given very little food. I was never given a hot drink. Without a door of solid metal or wood, the cement floor of my cell was always cold and flooded with rain that came in through the iron bars. I was not allowed to have shoes or socks on and therefore shivered uncontrollably on rainy mornings and nights. Denied warm water, I did not dare take a single cold bath for three weeks. In the cells next to mine, other prisoners were beaten daily. The inspector in charge was particularly brutal with prisoners.

Though my detention became more and more inevitable the longer I stayed in the police cell, in contravention of both the constitution and the law that required my presence in court within five days, I was never formally told why I would be detained. But from my friend Mahugu and interrogations, I had enough to surmise.

Interrogations

Mr. Wamwere, do you know who is publishing seditious pamphlets against the government?

No, I don't.

Do you remember calling the police exclusive servants of the rich?

Where?

During a lecture by Mr. Mungai, our boss. It was on the relations between the police and the public and was organized by the University of Nairobi Extra Mural Department—Nakuru Branch. Do you remember?

Oh, yes. Is that why you have arrested me?

Not quite, but you talk the way these seditious pamphlets are written today.

I have no monopoly on any ideas.

I know, but since we have no way of finding out exactly who is writing these pamphlets, we are forced to assume that you are either their author or know something about them.

And you conclude that just because I use words that are similar?

Yes. You know, Mr. Wamwere, to be quite frank with you, it is not easy to find out who is writing and distributing these seditious leaflets. This is clandestine work by individuals whom we can only catch with the help of a public that is unfortunately not too cooperative right now. You have already incited them with rabble-rousing lies. On the other hand, what we tell people is true but dismissed as oppressive. That leaves us with only simple clues to go by in finding out who might be doing all this. What you said in that lecture is very much like what these tracts say about the government. The ruling party is a rich man's party. The government belongs to the rich. The police are an arm of oppression.

I thought that we were immunized against reprisals by the University's academic freedom? Did the police not promise that what we said there would not be used against anybody?

Yes, but we heard. And what we hear we don't forget. That is our job—not to forget lies spoken about us.

What is not true about what I said?

That the police serve the rich only. That police are hired to protect properties of the rich against the starving poor. That the law and order we keep only helps the rich to exploit the poor. That we oppress because colonialists trained us to do so and have been taught nothing different after independence.

Even if you call this false, am I not entitled to my opinion by the constitution?

Depends on how you interpret it. But you are too cold now. We will continue tomorrow.

When tomorrow came, I was put in a Land Rover and driven to the Criminal Investigation Department (CID) offices in Nakuru. In the same office, suspects were being beaten with tire whips, buffalo-skin whips, wooden sticks and fists. They were bleeding, screaming, crying, begging for mercy and saying whatever the police wanted them to say. I knew I was brought here to confess guilt, beg for mercy and promise never to oppose the government again. As others were beaten, I continued to argue, wondering when my turn would come. It was terrifying.

Mr. Wamwere, you accuse us of torture, don't you?

Yes.

Have you ever seen it?

I am seeing it.

Are you? Can you know thistles before they touch you? Let us now see whether anything can make you wiser. Do you remember criticizing Kenyan leaders by name?

Yes.

Which?

Kenyatta, Koinange, Angaine, Mathenge, Moi, Omamo, Ngei and Kibaki.

What for—what is it of yours have they eaten?

They have stolen public land.

Pray they don't ever hear you calling them thieves. They will fry you alive. Do you know such an untrue allegation against the president is treason and punishable by death? What is wrong with a leader acquiring land?

What I say is neither untrue nor treason.

Do you know the law better than me?

Land is collective property and no one should take it from others without their consent. Leaders already receive higher salaries for the jobs they do and therefore don't need any land. When they grab so much land, they are taking it from the unemployed and landless people who need it more. If leaders want to run the government, they should give up owning land. If they want to farm, they should give up leadership. And if they choose farming, they should only take what land they can use. Owning land they cannot use is, to me, theft.

As a Gikuyu, isn't it wrong to criticize your leaders? Is it not against African and Gikuyu culture for a young man like you to criticize your elders?

I don't think so. In the Gikuyu culture, if an elder does wrong, he is criticized. Traditional *barazas*, councils of elders, are democratic institutions where people are able to criticize anyone and everybody that had done wrong. Kenyatta himself says in *Facing Mount Kenya:* "In the eyes of the Gikuyu people, the submission to a despotic rule of any particular man or a group, white or black, is the greatest humiliation to mankind. It is African culture that allows Gikuyu people to see submission to tyranny as humiliation."

We say we are democratic. In criticizing my leaders, I am only trying to live up to democratic ideals. After all, what is the meaning of *uhuru* if it is not our freedom to criticize and support our leaders? Why am I being treated like a criminal for doing what democracy allows me to do?

Thank you for the lecture, but you are not here to ask but to answer questions. Do you remember that one of the people you write to abroad (Maina wa Kinyatti) called Kenyatta names?

Yes, I do.

Can you remind us what he called the president?

This was a tough one that could get me into real trouble. But they knew everything. It was no use pretending that I had not read Maina's letter. He asked if

Kenyatta had gone crazy and why did he continue to hoodwink our people after betraying the Mau Mau.

What did you tell him?

Nothing.

You are lying but do you think it was a good letter?

It was not my letter.

You subscribe to the same views, don't you?

Why?

Because you did not write back to tell him that he was wrong.

How do you know that?

Don't worry how.

I have no right to tell people what views they should or should not have. Other people are entitled to their own views.

Easy way out! Let me take you home before I think of making you cooperate.

Why don't you let me go alone?

Alone, where? I am taking you back to Elburgon Police Station. It is the home you have chosen.

Next time they came, they took me to a roadside with a thick bush and a big forest behind it. They said, Mr. Wamwere, since you will not help us, we want to help you.

Let me go home then?

You may go. That is why we brought you here.

You want me to escape?

We want you to go home.

Why don't you deliver me where you arrested me?

If you are a coward, then tell us something about NDEFFO.

I don't know much about NDEFFO. I am not an official of the company.

I know. We only want you to answer a question or two.

Okay, I said, wondering what passersbys thought we were doing here and what would have happened if I had taken their bait.

You are aware of the July 20, 1975, incident when some people were killed in NDEFFO farms?

Yes.

Which side did you fight on?

I did not fight on any side.

Which side did you support then?

The Withare group.

Why them?

They were fighting for justice against oppression and exploitation.

By whom? Is any leader ever right to you?

Yes, but old directors of NDEFFO only wrecked the company through theft and refused to vacate office when they were voted out.

Was Withare right in giving members equal pieces of land like communists without the consent of the directors?

People were hungry and could not wait forever for their own land. They took the land when directors would not give it to them.

Was that also why they killed people?

Both sides killed.

But who started the war?

The Kimunya group organized and began the war against the Withare group. The Withare group only responded in self-defense. The government is also to blame because it did not stop the war by enforcing justice.

What about the 1975 demonstration by the Withare women in the State House in Nakuru, what role did you play in it?

I drew up the memorandum to the president and wrote slogans on the placards.

Why?

Members requested me to, and I could not refuse because they had paid for my education.

What is that, I thought your parents paid for your education?

They did but the fees they paid could not build schools or pay all the teachers.

The slogans you wrote insulted Wanyoike wa Thungu, the president's bodyguard, eh? How could you dare? You are so suicidal, aren't you?

For the last interrogation, I was driven past Nakuru to Gilgil where we took the road to Ol Kalou and passed the junction to J.M's home. One of them asked, You know that road goes to J.M's home?

Yes.

Did you go to the funeral?

Yes.

All the people there said we killed J.M. If we did, why have we not killed you? Are you more powerful?

No.

After passing J.M's place, I did not know where they were taking me. We drove in silence until we reached the town of Nyahururu and then went down to the falls. Involuntarily my heart began to pound. Is this where I would end my life's journey?

Mr. Wamwere, would you deny you are a communist?

Grandmother Kagiri – Mother's mother.

Mother for all seasons.

Father and Mother.

Waiigo, Margaret Wanjiru Mukundi, and me at 15 years old, 1965.

From left: friends Kariuki Kihara and Mungai, and my cousin Kuria wa Murimi, 1970.

My brother Kuria and friends in our village, 1973.

Addressing a campaign rally in 1974.

Reading Oginga Odinga's *Not Yet Uhuru* at Cornell University, 1971.

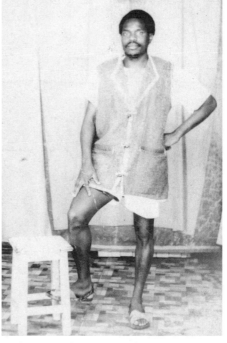

In the prison detention uniform, 1979.

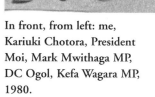

In front, from left: me, Kariuki Chotora, President Moi, Mark Mwithaga MP, DC Ogol, Kefa Wagara MP, 1980.

As a member of Kenya's Parliament, 1980.

My sister Mwihaki, Mum
with a load of firewood,
and Mrs. Baita, a neighbor,
1983.

With Nduta, 1984.

From left: Wambui, Ragui, Nduta, me, and Wamwere arriving in Copenhagen Airport, Denmark, 1987.

A cartoon in the *Kenyan Daily Nation* mocks my problems in exile, 1987.

Ripping the face of dictatorship (Moi), 1987.

Parents' house, demolished by police at the instigation of the ruling party, KANU, 1987.

KENYA

Kiambu MPs, including Mr. George Muhoho (right, striped tie) and Mr. Njenga Karume (light suit), lead local Kanu officials and others on a march through Kiambu town.

Message to Dissidents

Loyalty demonstrations take place all over the republic

It begun in October when Luo leaders publicly disassociated their community from Raila Odinga who had just been detained without trial under the Detained and Restricted Persons Regulations of 1978 for the second time in the 1980s. Then there was a lull, until three weeks ago when the jailing of Kimani wa Nyoike, a former member of parliament for Nyandarua South, for his association with exiled dissidents ignited the current wave of anti-dissident activity. What at first looked like a routine condemnation of wa Nyoike by Nyandarua leaders soon turned into a nationwide affair, with party branches throughout the country organising demonstrations to denounce the exiled and jailed dissidents. The denunciation is largely uniform, with Mr. Andrew Ngumba providing the easiest target as a mere "thief" who fled the country after siphoning funds from his Rural Urban Credit Finance Co. Ltd., which collapsed in 1984; Mr.

Koigi wa Wamwere as the disgruntled lout who went into self-exile and set himself up as a dissident leader after failing to regain the Nakuru North parliamentary seat in a 1986 by-election, and Prof. Ngugi wa Thing'o as simply a confused ideologue of suspect political leanings.

The message to the exiled dissidents and their sympathisers from the far-flung anti-dissident demonstrations and rallies orchestrated by the political establishment is loud and clear: The ordinary Kenyan has no time for their manoeuvres and the foreign media, particularly the *British Broadcasting Corporation (BBC)* as well as the self-exiles' host governments, Norway for Wamwere and Sweden for Ngumba, should take note of the mood of the Kenyan people, and accordingly cease providing publicity and succour for a handful of dissident activists of dubious credentials.

Wa Nyoike's jailing was the fuse for

the current demonstrations, and for many politicians, the fact that he was one of their own as an MP and former assistant minister spurred them on in distancing themselves from his activities, especially if they had associated with him at any one time in his long career in public life. But what next after the demonstrations? President Daniel arap Moi provided a hint on Monday this week, when he told a rally in Kapsabet Town that those who sympathised with the dissidents, either in government or in the public service, would be publicly named and relieved of their jobs. That would suggest that the government is well aware of certain well-placed individuals who may have links to the dissident movements, but also raise the question why no action has yet been taken. It was the president himself who appeared to set the stage for wa Nyoike's appearance in court when he told a series of rallies that the government would not let up in the fight

In pro-Moi demonstrations, I am called mjinga (a fool), Professor Ngugi wazimu (a mad man) and Andrew Ngumba mwizi (a thief).

Kenya

against dissidents, whom he broadly hinted had found some form of support in certain elite business and political circles. Wa Nyoike's subsequent jailing raised speculation that a number of similarly well-known figures might end up in the same predicament, but nobody of national stature has been brought to court on security-related charges since.

An even more explicit pointer came on Tuesday this week at the Mombasa demonstration, when Mr. Shariff Nassir, the MP for Mvita and assistant minister for national guidance and political affairs, threatened to name in two weeks' time those in the government who sympathise with dissidents. "Some of them are close to President Moi and pretending to be Nyayo followers," Nassir told the massive crowd, adding that he would also expose those behind the distribution of leaflets urging school strikes in Mombasa if the police did not do so. Another interesting pointer came from the MP for Changamwe, Mr. Kennedy Kiliku, who urged the president to screen cabinet ministers and top civil servants, adding that Wamwere and Ngumba had agents in the country amongst wealthy politicians. Kiliku also linked the poaching of wildlife to the dissidents, although this was refuted by the Coast provincial commissioner, Mr. Simeon Mung'ala. The massive demonstration, which again served to illustrate Nassir's organisational prowess, ended with effigies of Wamwere, Ngumba and Ngugi being thrown overboard from a ferry in the middle of the Likoni channel in a symbolic act of drowning dissidence in Kenya.

While politicians have had a field day hurling all manner of accusation against the dissidents and their sympathisers, the president has not commented at length on the matter, even coming out publicly to refute allegations by a number of leaders to the effect that dissidents are behind the current nationwide wave of student strikes. A fortnight ago, Prof. Sam Ongeri, the minister for technical training and applied technology told a demonstration in Kisii that the dissident activists were behind the school strikes. Similar claims were made by Mrs. Grace Ogot, an assistant minister for culture and social services, at a separate meeting called by Luo leaders to denounce the Wamwere, Ngumba and Ngugi trojka.

Coming out with a similar claim was a nominated MP, Mr. Ezekiel Barngetuny, who called a press conference a fortnight ago to blame dissidents for the schools' unrest as well as the extensive poaching activity in Kenyan national parks.

The widespread attacks on the Norwegian and Swedish governments have also drawn some reaction from the government, with the permanent secretary in the ministry of foreign affairs and international co-operation, Mr. Bethuel Kiplagat, being obliged to clarify late last month that the Kenya government enjoys cordial relationships with both countries. Kiplagat was reacting to a rally in Nakuru where local leaders asked the government to launch investigations into the extent to which Scandinavian envoys in Nairobi aid subversive elements. The vice-

president, Dr. Josephat Karanja, had earlier expressed concern in a meeting with the Danish ambassador to Kenya at the stance taken by Norway and Sweden in providing safe havens for self-exiled Kenyan dissidents.

Attacks against the two countries have, however, not ceased, and with President Moi having cancelled a state visit to Norway earlier this year, it is clear that the government is not at all amused by the freedom and impunity with which Wamwere and Ngumba are operating in Norway and Sweden respectively. Only a week ago, the Norwegian ambassador to Kenya, Mr. Neils Dahl, told a local daily newspaper that his mission was concerned about the various calls for Wamwere's extradition and had asked his foreign ministry in Oslo for "comments and instruc-

During the Mombasa demonstration on Tuesday, marchers tossed effigies of dissidents into the sea.

Pro-Moi demonstrators casting our effigies into the Indian Ocean, 1988.

Police leading me into court to be charged with treason, 1990.

In court with the dreadlocks I vowed not to cut
before Moi was out of office, 1991.

Mothers on hunger strike for our freedom, February 1992.

Mothers demonstrating for our freedom,
February 1992.

Striking mothers curse Moi with
their nakedness, March 1992.

From left, Professor Wangari Maathai, Margaret Kinuthia, my sister Njeri, Mum, cousin Wangu,
Wangeci, and other mothers wear chains to make ours more visible, May 1992.

Mirugi's mother and I celebrate Mirugi's and my release, January 1993.

From left: Mirugi Kariuki, Rumba Kinuthia, and I are carried shoulder-high after our release, January 1993.

Visiting my sick father in the hospital,
1993.

Koigi Is Free

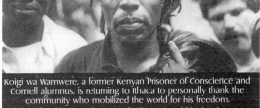

Looking ahead after my release,
from a campus publicity poster,
1993.

Koigi wa Wamwere, a former Kenyan Prisoner of Conscience and
Cornell alumnus, is returning to Ithaca to personally thank the
community who mobilized the world for his freedom.
Koigi was freed in December 1996 after four years of false imprisonment.

Celebrating my freedom with Norwegian Amnesty International group 145, 1993.

With my friend Anders Breidlid
at Fornebu Airport in Oslo after
my release, 1993.

My friend and lawyer
Mirugi Kariuki
with me after our arrest
at Burnt Forest, 1993.

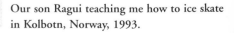

Our son Ragui teaching me how to ice skate
in Kolbotn, Norway, 1993.

Ethnic warriors on their way to attack members of other ethnic communities, 1993.

A victim of ethnic cleansing with six arrows, 1993.

Under escort to court,
flanked by prison guards
Kirima (left) and Chebon,
1994.

Lawyer Paul Muite and trial observer
Professor Micere Mugo entering court,
1995.

From left: prison guard
Tingir (standing), me,
my brother-in-law
James Maigua Ndumo,
my brother Kuria Wamwere,
and G.G. Njuguna Ngengi
sitting in court, 1994.

Mother conferring with lawyers (from left) Gibson Kamau
Kuria and Paul Muite, 1994.

With my co-accused G. G. Ngengi, greeting Mum and little Wamwere before a morning court session, 1995.

Michael Furaha of the Kenyan Embassy in Stockholm punches a Swedish journalist in the face as the journalist accompanied members of Amnesty International who had come to the embassy with petition rolls calling for my immediate release, 1995.

Christian Danbolt, Norwegian envoy and Rev. Timothy Njoya coming to court to observe the trial, 1995.

Mwandawiro Mganga, Dick Kamau, Osewe, my family, and others demonstrating for our release in Stockholm, Sweden, 1995.

Mother arguing with a prison officer for her right to see me, 1995.

Mother screaming in court after our conviction, 1995.

Secret police attack with whips members of the public attending court, 1995.

MPs and political activists were barred from seeing me in prison, 1995.

My family. From left: Nduta, Kuria, Wamwere, my sister Wambui, and Ragui, 1996.

From left: Mum, Kamau, me (wiping tear gas
from my eyes), John Kinyanjui, and others at the
mortuary Nakuru to view the body of my dead
father, 1996.

"Is this my father?" asks my son Kuria to his
Aunt Wambui when we first met at Fornebu
Airport in Oslo, Norway, December 1996.

Pen Club in Wales urges President Carter to fight for my release, 1996.

From left: me, Ragui, Mum, and Wamwere in church for my father's burial, June, 1996.

Addressing a political rally as a presidential candidate, 1997.

A hug of most happy reunion
with Nduta, 1996.

Richard Leakey, Nduta, and me in London, 1997.

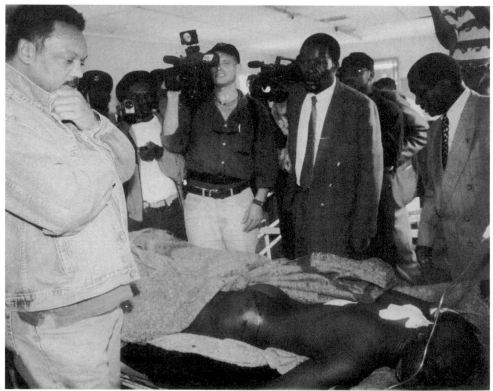

Rev. Jesse Jackson looking at a victim of ethnic cleansing in hospital, 1998.

From left: Paul Muite, me, and Muturi Kigano asking Attorney General Wako to register Safina Party.

Neil Getnick and daughter Courtney visiting us in Oslo, 1997.

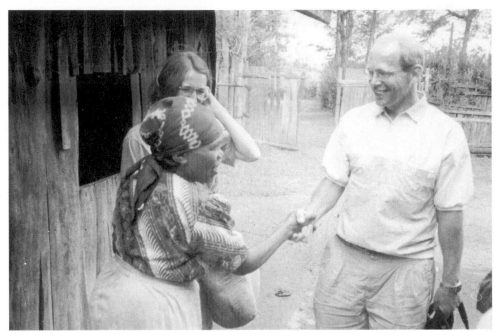

Michael Koplinka and his wife visiting my mother in Nakuru, 2001.

Meeting President Clinton and Kerry Kennedy Cuomo in Washington DC, September 2000.

I don't call myself one.

J.M. did not either but wanted to introduce communism here.

How could a man of his wealth introduce communism?

If he did not, who is trying to, you?

I am just a simple advocate of people's democratic rights.

What do you think this government is?

A dictatorship. Why else am I here?

So, you fight it? Mr. Wamwere, you are a communist. Only communists can drive people to the falls as you have. But take my warning. If you fight our freedom, we take yours. I wanted to help you but you have not given me a chance. From now on, you will be on your own. Good luck.

Conscience on Trial

I stayed at Elburgon Police Station until the first of September. On August 31, I asked a police officer who came to ask me for some information about why I was not being taken to court. We have found nothing criminal against you. But you may not go home. Powerful people want you detained because you are a communist.

The following day, I was taken to Nakuru Central Police Station where I stayed for one night. That night I met an old man. Huddled together in one corner of our cell to kill the long, cold and sleepless hours, he was the first to break the silence:

What are they keeping you here for?

They say I am against the government.

For how long have you been in?

Three weeks.

Mmmm. That is a long time. Why do they say you are against the government?

Because I say a few people are accumulating too much land and wealth at the expense of *wananchi,* the toiling masses.

What do you think they will now do to you? Take you to court?

Release or detain me. So far they have failed to fabricate against me a case that is good enough for their courts. They might detain me. I overheard something to that effect.

You must have a difficult choice to make. You are a young man and I can see you are worried. Well, if you want to speak for the poor in this country, you must realize that your detention sooner or later is inevitable. Mark you, simply being detained is the least that could happen to you. They can kill you as they killed J.M. Speaking for the poor is not like speaking in a school debate. They can harass and ruin you economically and politically. On the other hand, you can surrender, mind your own business and you will see what good friends of yours they will become.

That will not be an easy thing to do. Living against one's beliefs and convictions is a very difficult, trying and cruel thing.

Will it be more difficult than seeing your wife, if you have one, children and life driven into ruin while you are in detention?

I don't know, I said feeling hot and fearful. Despite the cold, I was beginning to sweat.

Well, an educated young man like you can't work for the poor without losing your chance to accumulate property and letting your family fall into poverty. This will be a difficult choice. Death, detention and imprisonment become unacceptable as the price of good leadership when a leader fears losing his wife, children and property. This fear will be the greatest enemy of your political beliefs. If you accept suffering and loss of your family as the cost of keeping your conscience, you will find it easier to bear death, detention and imprisonment when they come in the course of your political work.

Well, I sighed.

I know what you feel but that is the price you have to pay to become and remain a worthy leader of the people struggling against their poverty and wretchedness. It is ironical and almost contradictory. Redeeming people from misery with the ruin of your family!

I see what you mean.

And don't forget that other than your own fear and pain of seeing your wife, children, parents, brothers and sisters destroyed by poverty and misery to save themselves, they too will see your political beliefs as their enemy. They will do this in the belief that without your ideals you will do more to help them out of poverty and misery. If your parents aren't with you in your hopes, aims, dreams and ambitions, they will despise and disown you as their son. Those of your brothers and sisters who don't share your political beliefs will call you crazy. Your children will call you an irresponsible, unworthy, reckless and unloving father for allowing them to live in poverty. Your wife will revile you and threaten you with divorce unless you give up your ideals. She will ask you to mind your own business and stop being an uninvited brother's keeper. Instead of sympathizing with you when you have problems and your conscience is on trial, your wife will blame you for the family's endless turmoil. Finally, she will crown her disgust with you with a divorce. If your family prevails against your conscience, you will be broken and forced out of your role as a people's leader. You might even be forced to exploit people to end the poverty of your own family. However, if your ideals prevail, your family will help you to work for people and them and endure whatever that might entail.

I have never forgotten these words.

———————————————

On September 2, 1975, I was driven from Nakuru Central Police Station to Kilimani Police Station in Nairobi. The following morning, I was taken to the officer in charge.

Do you know why you are here?

No.

We are going to detain you.

Detain me as people were detained in the colonial days?

Sensing my fright, he tried to calm me with lies.

No, no, it will not be like that. We will only hold you for some time and then let you go home. I will read you the detention order. Please sign here.

I will not sign if doing so means consenting to my own detention.

You must sign it.

I will not. You do not need my signature to detain me.

I will force you to sign it.

I remembered the proverb that says, When a bull is knocked down, it does not refuse to be branded with a hot iron, *ikurundwo ndiregaga ruoro.*

Where are you going to detain me?

I don't know.

For how long will I be held?

I don't know.

What is my exact crime?

I don't know.

Will I now be taken to court?

No.

Why not, if I have committed a crime for which I am being detained?

I don't know.

Can I contact a lawyer before I am detained?

No. You are already detained. Please stand up and turn around.

When I turned, a police officer standing nearby tightly blindfolded me with a piece of cloth. Someone then led me outside by the hand into a waiting vehicle. I was driven around for about two hours. Finally, the car stopped somewhere and I heard some heavy gates opening. I was taken out of the car and led through another heavy gate. When I was inside, the door closed behind me. When the blindfold was taken off, I saw that I was in a quiet compound with only one low-lying building and a sandy volleyball pitch. There were many prison officers, and someone with some epaulets on his shoulders told me that he was the officer in charge. Later I learnt his name was Edward Lokopoiyet. There were three plainclothes police, including one who wore a big straw hat and red shoes and looked like a cowboy.

I was asked to follow the officer in charge to a building labeled Isolation Block. I wondered, Is this a place for the insane and lepers? This must be how the Kenyatta dictatorship viewed ideas of freedom and justice—as contagion, as insanity. I was in this cage to isolate those ideas and stop them from infecting people. The compound measured forty-two yards long and eighteen yards wide and the low building measured about twenty-four yards by ten yards. Within the building, there were smaller cages that measured eight by six feet each.

On entering Isolation Block, I was led into a cell. A prison sergeant called Jack Mutembeti asked me to strip naked in front of officers and wardens. My clothes were taken away, and I was given an ill-fitting prison uniform, *kungurus.* While stripping naked before these men humiliated me, the police and prison officers seemed to enjoy it immensely. After my clothes, my name and humanity were also stripped. From now on I was and would be called Kamiti 7/75.

I was led inside. As we walked along the corridor, I saw cells with tiny, steel-wire-barred windows called *judas* blocked with pieces of cloth. Suddenly the cloth fell off from one window and I saw someone inside. No, no, *Mzee,* old man, said the officer in charge, hurriedly putting the cloth back. I recognized the face. But who is it I quickly wondered? The face came back to me. Yes, it is Achieng Oneko who has been in detention since 1969. I was frightened. This then is detention! I had been thinking that this building was a halfway station on the way to a detention camp in the desert. So they would not be taking me to Manyani, Lodwar, Maralal or Lamu where the British detained Kenyatta, J.M. and others. Was this then the place where I would stay until God knows when? Another cell was opened and I was led inside.

From now on, Lokopoiyet told me, this will be your cell. While here, these *askaris*, prison officers, will tell you what to do and not to do. You will stay inside all the time. You will use this one *bakuli,* bowl, for your urine during the day and this other one for your stool at night. You must not talk unless you are calling or answering an *askari.*

In addition, here is a list of prison rules and regulations that you must obey and follow. If you fail to observe them, I will order you to be punished or caned. While here, do not make groundless complaints. Do not make false accusations against prison officers. Do not cause unnecessary alarm. March as ordered. Eat any food provided. Do not throw away food. Do not refuse to wear the prison uniform or exchange it with someone else. Never remove the mark on the prison uniform. Never disobey an order to cut your hair. Never tamper with locks, lamps, lights or other property. Never be a nuisance. Do not make noise—singing, coughing or talking. You must always whisper. Never malinger.

Welcome to Hell

Man, where are you from?
Nakuru.

Who are you, brother?

Koigi wa Wamwere.

Oh no, so they brought you here, too?

Yes.

Mundu son of Wamwere, how is Nakuru?

It was on fire when I left.

Don't worry. This place is for men and women. You will make it.

These words gave me courage. The place was hell. No one should have been here. Yet the words and presence of those here now meant everything to me. That I was not alone here made all the difference between sanity and insanity, life and death. I felt sorry for these detainees but for my own sake, I was happy to find them here. Their presence and denied life gave me life. My thinking seemed logical and illogical at the same time. Two and a half years later, this twisted thinking would come back to me. When Ngugi wa Thiong'o was detained in January 1978, on the one hand we were angry that the Kenyatta government was still detaining people who spoke for the people and freedom. On the other hand, we almost welcomed Ngugi's detention because, being internationally famous, his imprisonment would help focus world attention on all of the forgotten, incarcerated innocent victims in Kenya. Other times, we seemed happy to receive new detainees purely because of the news they brought from outside!

After three days' confinement, I was allowed out to meet my fellow detainees. This was when I saw that we were detained in a desert, albeit an artificial one, that the detainees did all they could to fertilize, water and plant with grass, flowers and crops.

The Tree of Survival

In confinement my head felt like a heavy ball of lead that rolled each time I moved it. When I was released from the cell to join others, I felt almost half free. Now I could meet my childhood political heroes Achieng Oneko and Wasonga Sijeyo face to face and Adam Mathenge, whose political heroics in Nakuru I had heard about. Apart from satisfying my desire to be close to Achieng Oneko and Wasonga Sijeyo, who had fought so hard for Kenya's independence, I also wanted them to teach me the art of survival in this desolate valley of death. Achieng Oneko had survived nine years of colonial detention and five years of detention under Kenyatta. So I asked him straight away, *Mzee,* old honorable man, how have you survived this place so well for so long?

Young man, here is my advice to you: This is a hard place and I have seen it break many. To survive here the first thing you have to avoid is going to war with these stone walls. If you do, they will break you. You must not fight stones, because you cannot win. Your real enemy is not these walls but those who brought you here to be broken by them. Since they are not your real enemy, avoid bashing your soft fists and head against them. If you avoid hitting these walls with your bare fists and head, you may survive to fight the tyrannical government that brought you here.

You are here to be isolated and denied news because confinement breaks people faster than anything else I know. While you are here try to reduce your isolation. Do not keep to yourself in deep thought or worry about outside problems that you cannot solve. Mix with other detainees, play volleyball, play draughts with the other detainees and *askaris*. These *askaris* are hired to oppress you but they may not hate you. If you cultivate their friendship, they will tell you what is going on outside and break the very isolation they are here to enforce. Wardens work here not because they hate us, but because they need money to keep their families alive. If we are friendlier to them than the government is, they can help us. If we are less so, they might turn against us and treat us very badly.

In prison, bottled-up emotions explode and kill. As long as you are here don't worry about your macho image. If you feel like crying, cry. If you feel like laughing, laugh. If you are angry, speak out. Never keep your emotions inside.

Lastly, remember this: Prison might look calm but it is a place of storms. Detention alone is a provocation and a storm. Prison authorities will always try to provoke you into a fight because they need an excuse to destroy you and blame you for it. Caught in a storm, you can be the hard, tough tree and the storm will easily break you into two. When a storm comes your way, you must weigh your strength against its. If you are stronger than the storm, you can resist it and survive. But detention is a storm that is stronger than you and me. That is why we are here. To survive detention, you must learn to be like the lean, soft and flexible tree that bends with the storm until it is flat on the ground. As long as the flexible tree bends, the wind will never break it. It can be on the ground, but it is not uprooted, broken, withered or dead. It will stand upright as soon as the storm passes. Remember that avoiding a hurricane is not a weakness, it is necessary for survival. Coming out of here unbroken will be your only victory against your oppressors.

We were brought here with Ochola Achola. He hated all *askaris*. He refused to play draughts. He would not laugh or play volleyball. He would come out here and stand in the sun alone from six to six. Finally, he was broken and went crazy. He would keep his food for days and then swallow it all at once like a python. Dr. Mustafa recommended his release to stop the insanity, but the government refused. They released him only after he was well into eating soap and excreta. You must not walk the Ochola path.

In detention I discovered that both Achieng Oneko and Wasonga Sijeyo harbored deep mistrust and hatred not just for Kenyatta, who had detained them, but all Gikuyu people.

They are all treacherous, said Oneko one evening.

Is my grandmother, who taught me you were a hero, also treacherous?

What have I to choose between your grandma and Kenyatta? Oneko countered.

Another time, Wasonga Sijeyo asked us, Do you know how I would kill the dreadful family planning program among the Luo today if I were free?

No, we answered.

Call it a Gikuyu conspiracy against the Luo and no one will touch it.

I was truly shocked but now understood why I had been accused of being a government spy when I landed in detention.

The bitterness of Luo, Luhya, Somali and Kamba leaders in detention against Kenyatta and his government was understandable. After all, Kenyatta had detained them, denied them democratic and human rights, used ethnic prejudices to demonize them and denied their home areas deserved development assistance as a punishment for political opposition. What I could not understand or agree with were these leaders' bitterness against Kenyatta's ethnic community, the Gikuyu. Even Gikuyu leaders whom Kenyatta had killed like J.M. Kariuki, jailed like Bildad Kaggia and detained like Ngugi wa Thiong'o and I were not spared from this ethnic bitterness and wrath. Nor were the Gikuyu Mau Mau veterans and millions of poor Gikuyu people whom Kenyatta had betrayed and impoverished allowed to claim innocence.

Just as I had the pleasure of meeting and knowing famous freedom fighters in detention, I also had the horror of meeting terrible persons there. The government used detention to isolate its political enemies and also to hide people from the underworld whom it had hired to do dirty jobs.

For instance, Mwangi Mahinda and Gicheru Njau, who called himself *Mla Chake* (one who eats his own), were in detention because they were involved in the murder of J.M. Kariuki. The government had detained them because it did not feel safe with them on the outside. They were demanding more money for their involvement in the murder of J.M. than the government was willing to pay. Gicheru Njau told me that J.M. considered them friends and gave them information that they passed on to Mbiyu Koinange as they had also taken some information from Koinange, his chief enemy, to J.M. They lived on the fears these two politicians had of each other and did everything they could to keep those fears alive. Before detention, they had been arrested as suspects and incarcerated in Kamiti prison together with J.M.'s other assassins, Pius Kibathi and Mark Twist. Njenga Karume, then a GEMA boss and a close friend of Kenyatta, intervened on their behalf and had them released into his own hands.

In detention I also met a warden, Kariuki wa Ricu, who boasted of taking part in the hunt for Mau Mau freedom fighters. When he caught Mau Mau, he said, he beheaded them and took their bleeding heads to his white bosses for money.

Njoroge wa Iregi told me he took part in the battle against Mau Mau General Kago, but wept when his secret hero was shot and killed.

Corporal Kethore had always been a keeper of detainees. One morning we were having breakfast when he asked Oneko whether he remembered being taken to or from Lamu Island Colonial Prison in 1953 in a small police plane that had nearly crashed due to strong winds. When Oneko said he did, Kethore admitted that he was a prison escort in that flight! These *askaris* were the direct link between the colonial government and the Kenyatta regime.

Fed Like Pigs

The conditions of life in detention remained unchanged until a month after Oneko's release and the imprisonment of MP's Joseph Martin Shikuku and Jean Marie Seroney. Suddenly, food became extremely bad and indoor confinement increased to twenty-three and a half hours daily. For lunch we were given raw *ugali* and boiled green leaves, *sukuma wiki,* and for supper we got raw *ugali* again and half-cooked beans sprinkled with a few drops of vegetable oil. In the beans, we got plenty of weevils and cooked egg-bearing spiders, and there were snails in our dirty vegetable soup. Twice a week we were given tiny pieces of meat that were no bigger than a piece of bait for a fishing hook. With the horrible smell and look of this so-called food, I needed a pig's mentality to force it down my throat. For lack of good food and sunshine, our skin started to lose color. I developed painful piles, and my legs started to swell. The only treatment we got was vitamin C and B tablets.

I found spending all day in the tiny cage almost unbearable. Sleep was impossible in a cell that was lit with an overhead bulb all day and night. I was allowed only one book—the Bible.

Almost every day, prison alarm sirens tormented our eardrums. A strong earthquake came and prison guards could not open the cells for us when the walls and the roofs of our cells threatened to collapse down upon us.

Occasionally, the officer in charge got us together to remind us of his power over life and death. He said he could give us strokes of the cane if we disobeyed his instructions. I can even shoot you dead, he threatened, declare you unable to survive prison, *alishindwa na jela,* and close your file. In any case, he warned us, you may not know it but soon many of you will be cripples from this food and solitary confinement. He bragged that it was a privilege for prisoners like us to shake his hand.

I would wake up from a dream and find someone watching me. When I was in my cell, they watched me. When they let me out, they watched me. When I took a bath, they watched me. When I sat on the toilet, they watched me. What kind of people are these, I always wondered. They respect neither themselves nor us. Many times, I felt like exploding into violence, but held myself back knowing that that was their trap for us.

All our letters were opened and read by a chain of unwelcome eyes. Lack of privacy reduced the extremely rare visits we had with our loved ones from moments of joy to ones of anguish and mental torture. Instead of bringing relief and happiness, watched visits were full of pain and embarrassment. I always returned to detention from visits exhausted and frustrated.

But there was one thing our jailers could never rob from us—the value of life, freedom, love, family, justice and everything else that we had taken for granted before and were now denied.

If the officer in charge was bad, the worst irritant was the prison physician, Dr. Bowry. When we went to him with complaints, he would charge that we were suffering from insanity. When we complained against his dismissive attitude, he would threaten us with the eighteen strokes of the cane that the attorney general had authorized. Dr. Bowry bragged that however badly he treated us, there was nothing we could ever do to him. After all, he asked, what are you? In the colonial detention, I gave Kenyatta water. What did he do to me when he became president? I am still here and will do to you what I want.

A Nation Detained

As political prisoners, we were treated worse than convicted criminals. Clearly, while criminals injured, robbed and destroyed the lives of people and disturbed the comfort of the Kenyan elite, they did not question the ways of the government or its legitimacy. Political detainees threatened the very survival of the dictatorship.

Though legally innocent, I was to be punished for my ideas and incarcerated for expressing opinions. Penalized so harshly that eventually I would recant, I am sorry. I will not have these ideas anymore. To demonstrate my repentance, I was expected to inform on all those I knew had similar beliefs, so they too could be punished.

To make detention serve as a lifetime nightmare for us, and to cripple us so we would serve as scarecrows to potential transgressors, the Kenyatta government made detention extremely cruel. The memory of it would terrify ex-detainees so thoroughly that many would not dare risk a free thought again, let alone express it.

When we see Kenyans today paralyzed by fear, it is because they have seen Koigi lose all hope of employment after detention. They have witnessed Ochola Achola picking up papers in the streets, or the wealthy Kenneth Matiba released from detention, debilitated by strokes. They have seen Martin Shikuku on crutches and Charles Rubia whispering because he lost his voice box in detention.

Once hailed as the savior of the country, Kenyatta used the detention of a few to terrify and imprison the whole nation.

Rhythm of Agony

For a government that had lost popularity so soon after independence, granting amnesty and releasing detainees and prisoners on political holidays like *Jamhuri* (Independence Day) and Kenyatta Day had become a way of demonstrating false magnanimity and currying favor with the public. The more unpopular Kenyatta became, the more he needed amnesties to bolster his regime. We were released on no other day. Unfortunately, those to be set free were chosen randomly and not in any order we could fathom. Political holidays became times of great anxiety and the waiting so extremely painful that for nights before the day, I got no sleep at all.

To expunge pain and anxiety from my heart and brain I discovered writing. It became a treatment for my worries and fears that I did not need Dr. Bowry to prescribe for me. At first it was my novel, *A Woman Reborn*, that saved me. Then poetry.

THE WOMAN I LOVED

Woman,
When I was thrown into the stormy sea
You wrote and encouraged me
Take heart,
We shall brave the storms together
Until we reach the shore.

No sooner had the first big wave
Covered my back
Than you panicked
Refused to face storms
Embraced those who detain me
Heedless of my beckoning voice.

A POEM TO NJERI MY SISTER

Njeri,
Your love and concern for me,
Fire my heart with gratitude;

I return your love.
Detained so that I may not give
Or receive love,
I have learnt to love more,
And to value love.

AFRICA

Africa,
I want you to be proud of me
I want you to spit upon your chest
And say of me:
I bless thee
Worthy and true son of mine
It would pain me
If you were to say to me
May the breasts that suckled thee
Curse you, unworthy son.

But your crown of honor is not free
It is conferred only upon
Those who serve their country and people
With distinction and selflessness
I must work to earn it.

Africa,
When I was born,
You fought against colonial bondage.
Today you still struggle against oppression.
To repay mother's love and service,
I commit my life to struggle,
Against enslavement
In which I was born and reared,
Liberate mum from shackles,
And ensure brothers and sisters
Are born free.

Africa,
As a child
I suffered with you

Many deprivations
Your children exist and prosper
Upon your resources.
If you are not free
We have no access to them.
Enslaved by colonialism
I was conceived, born and reared in chains.
Inside my mother's womb
I heard her brutalized and harassed
By colonial soldiers and lackeys.
All the time
They booted her
Nearly forcing her to miscarry.
Daily, they forced her
To labor without rest.
In forests and plantations
She went hungry and thirsty.
When she ate a little,
She gave me some.
In the heat of plantations,
She fainted
With exhaustion, exposure and thirst.
Denied maternity leave,
She gave birth to me
In the noonday sun
Under a canopy of coffee branches
She cradled me in muddy hands
Sticky with coffee juice.
She uncovered her hair
To wrap me in her head-kerchief.
Fainting for loss of blood,
She drank sun-hot water
From the hand of colonial oppression.

On gaining consciousness
Mother was transported home
In a roofless lorry.
In her small and smoky hovel
She tenderly sucked and brought me up.

Africa,
Because of the greed of your children,
You continue to carry the white man's burden
And to be the granary of imperialists.
On what is your own
They bloat
And leave crumbs
For your children to starve on.
Driven by self-interests they lie:
You can't develop without our capital
And multinational corporations.
Taken in
We let mosquitoes
Suck our blood
And thank us with the malaria of poverty.

Africa,
Your ruling children feel
Democracy must go.
Ignoramuses,
They have not learnt
Freedom is blood of progress.
To come forward
Humanity is carried on the wheels of liberty.
Always on the move
Mankind slide on freedom.
When lost, they grind to a halt
And redeem it with blood.

Africa,
When unworthy sons kill democracy,
They want you to bleed.
Pregnant with freedom
It must be delivered.
Peacefully, if leaders are wise.
By caesarean,
If they block its birth

Africa,
With horror we see

Introduction of ruling dynasties
And murder of our right to
Make and unmake governments,
Represent people in parliaments,
Speak and write freely,
Form political parties,
Assemble freely,
Worship and not worship,
Get food, clothing and shelter,
Fight for labor,
Live without terror,
And enjoy equality.

Africa,
Greedy children promote harmful ideologies
And turn you into a divided kingdom;
Haves eating have-nots,
Greedy capital starving labor.
With class struggle silenced,
Ethnic communities turn against one another
In civil wars, ethnic cleansing and genocide.

Africa,
Your children that don't love freedom
Claim your women are free.
We who cherish equality know
Common African women need liberation.
Like common African men,
They still lack jobs.
At home they are beaten,
And invariably disinherited.
Excluded from power and ownership,
Many marry men they don't love.
Employed by sex maniacs,
Many exchange family life for work.
For a pittance
Our mothers, wives and sisters
Grow coffee, tea and pyrethrum
To make fat imperialist and African ticks.
Worked like donkeys,

Peasant women are perpetually
Economically ruined,
Starved to the bone,
Clothed in rags,
And housed in hovels.
Young African women
Are steeped in racial inferiority.
They bleach their skins
And ruin their health
For white beauty.
Unemployed and with children to feed,
Many cannot escape prostitution,
To satisfy the lust of men
And reap the AIDS virus.

Africa,
Ruling children have made justice
A commodity for the rich only.
Unjust laws give not justice,
But oppression, cruelty and death.
We go to courts
Not for protection and redress
But persecution and imprisonment.

Africa,
Because of untrammeled greed
Money has become a God.
Yoked to capitalism
We idolize its power
That deifies its possessors,
Whom priests of other Gods
Seek, worship and fear.
That gives those with it
Children when barren,
Beauty when ugly,
Power when unpopular,
And wisdom when foolish.

With money as king,
Vice not virtue rules,

Inhumanity not humanity rules,
Folly not wisdom rules,
Corruption not honesty rules,
Falsehood not truth rules,
Poverty not prosperity rules,
Disease not health rules,
Humiliation not dignity rules,
Ignorance not knowledge rules,
Greed not sharing rules,
Competition not cooperation rules,
Enmity not friendship rules,
Injustice not justice rules,
Dictatorship not democracy rules,
Hell not heaven reigns.

Africa,
Backward and ignorant,
Riddled with mercenary greed,
Myopic with self-interest,
Hostile to democracy,
Contemptuous of human rights,
Obsequious to white people,
Shackled to dictatorship,
Lacking humanity that makes us useful,
And qualifies man to govern,
Unworthy sons must no longer rule!

Africa,
We of your new generation
Are tired of seeing your children subjected
To deprivation, humiliation and discrimination,
Deception, treachery and robbery.
We are sick of seeing you
Abused,
Oppressed,
Exploited,
And excluded from the First World
By your own children.
We are ready to die
That your children
May be home in Africa

And enjoy life like anybody else.

It is our great duty
To clean the dust of dishonor
That has long settled
On your beautiful name,
Africa.

A Jungle Nightmare

Every night before sleep came, I would please myself with the idea that I was going home. A good dream would put me in an excellent mood, which in turn would provide the psychological strength I needed to survive the drudgery of prison. Unfortunately, sometimes I had nightmares.

The last nightmare I remember, I was trapped in a forest of ominous trees, a jungle steeped in thick fog and heavy rain. The black night was split by lightning, illuminating hordes of extremely frightened men, women and children running for their lives. The lightning was striking the massive trees, sending them crashing down, and pinning and killing the people. Everywhere the trapped were screaming, but nobody seemed able to help. All the people were enveloped in the same jungle, in the same darkness and in the same danger without exit. They huddled together seeking protection at the base of the trees that still stood, only to scatter in all directions when these, too, came crushing down.

The frightened, shivering people neither talked nor recognized one another. I felt completely cornered, hungry, wet and cold, yet I sweated with fear and fright. I saw no one I knew. I was running from a falling tree when it crashed down, pinning one of my legs. Frantically I did everything to free myself and screamed from the pain, but no one heard. As I struggled and screamed, I suddenly awoke, sweating and panting. Believing I was still in the jungle, I heard laughter and startled myself out of the dream world. An *askari* was watching through the *Judas* of my cell.

Why are you screaming?

Get lost, I said. Have you no shame or work?

I am on my job, he said, laughing and walking away.

It was four in the morning. I sat on my mat thinking.

Freedom from Death

We suspected something big had happened. But the more we begged the *askaris* to tell us what it was, the less they talked. Their silence more than confirmed our suspicions and also suggested that whatever had occurred had a meaning for us. We wanted to guess, but dared not. As we searched for information, in came Pastor Ngari, a prisons chief officer. He prayed for peace and stability in the new era. Yes, a new era!

With Ngari's soothing words, my heart grew wings. Either Kenyatta was dead, his government had been overthrown, or both. Only his death could bring about a new era in Kenya and, momentarily, I felt overwhelmingly happy and free. Perhaps now I would not be held in detention for nine years like Wasonga Sijeyo.

I realized that I had been praying for Kenyatta to die. While it was logical, I was surprised at my own lack of compassion. I cast my eyes twenty years back in our history and wondered. Before independence, when Kenyatta was in detention at the hands of the British, I had prayed for his life and freedom because both meant Kenya's liberation from colonialism. Now his death meant my freedom. Clearly, human oppression distorts and reduces the humanity of all—oppressors and the oppressed.

On December 12, 1978, I heard the outer door open at 4 A.M. I had not slept the whole night, waiting for my freedom and talking with Adam Mathenge. I heard the office open. Then one cell, and another. The key then clanked in my own door. For the first time I loved the sound of keys. Almost incredibly the door of the cage then opened and the bird flew free.

That morning, we laughed and said good-bye to one another. We were put into different vehicles to be driven home. As our Land Rover drove out of prison, I looked back to see several prison gates open and close behind us; I spit upon my chest and whispered to myself, May these gates never open again to me or anybody else.

Jomo Kenyatta had ruled Kenya with the iron hand of a monarch. Ultimately he had given birth to another dictator—Daniel Arap Moi, his vice-president for twelve years. Though happy to go home, I felt cheated that release came without apologies or assurances that detention was now over permanently. Their absence implied Moi's continued demand for obedience and conformity.

CHAPTER VII

F I R S T   M O I   Y E A R S   1 9 7 9

Afterr Kenyatta, Kenyans went to President Moi and told him, You are our Joshua, save us. Moi replied like Jeroboam of the Bible, If Kenyatta's yoke was heavy, I shall add to it. If he punished you with whips, I shall chastise you with scorpions.

In Parliament: 1979–82

The same month I was set free, G.G. Kariuki, one of the Gikuyu trio who seemed to run the country together with President Moi (the others were Charles Mugane Njonjo and Mwai Kibaki), invited me to his home just outside Nyahururu town.

G.G. looked me over and wondered aloud how such a small man could have struck so much political terror into the heart of Kenyatta's dictatorship. In any case, he told me, if you are interested in reentering politics, please feel free to do so.

Moi's government had now extended an olive branch and a hand of friendship. Was I to say yes or no? Knowing that I could enter politics without government harassment and persecution was tempting, but at heart I did not feel ready to surrender my freedom of thought, belief, conscience and expression for government friendship. If the government walked in my direction, we could join hands. If it walked in the opposite direction, they would go their way and I mine.

Without Kenyatta's government to steal votes for him, beating Kihika Kimani, the MP for my home parliamentary constituency, would be easy. Without a job, I got some assistance from Mwai Kibaki and with it bought a minibus that helped me to earn a living and campaign for a seat in Parliament. Economically crippled, I called the bus *Mutirithia*, one who would help me walk again.

While some in his close circles invited me back into politics, Moi was uncomfortable with the thought of me as MP for Nakuru North where he lived at Kabarak and had three big farms. At the height of the campaign, I saw through William Lasoi, Moi's closest confidant. He wanted me to step down for either

Francis Kimosop, a Kalenjin like himself, or Ngugi Njoroge, a conformist politician who taught at Kenyatta University. During the days before the polling day, I resisted strong pressure to step down that was orchestrated by Moi himself from his Kabarak home. I managed to win the election. At a victory function at the president's home, Francis Kimosop warned me on Moi's behalf, We have elected you despite accusations that you are a communist. We have elected you to work hand in hand with President Moi and his government to improve the lives of our people. If you fail to do that, we are the same ones who will hound you out of Parliament.

First Temptation

Again I was invited to G.G.'s home. When I arrived I found a big gathering of MP-elects. They were there to discuss the distribution of ministerial jobs. G.G.'s offer to me came quickly: I invited you because we want to give you an extra platform. Many MPs on our side, and especially strong ones like you, should have an additional forum from which to fight our enemies. Would you like one?

Clearly G.G. saw Parliament and ministerial jobs as weapons with which Moi and his supporters could consolidate power against perceived Gikuyu enemies. When he asked me to take a job as minister I understood his logic perfectly. Moi had released me from detention. He had protected me against rigging. It was now payback time.

I understood people's representation differently. Both Parliament and government existed not for the defense of the president, the most powerful person in Kenya, but for the security of the weak, the poor who have no protection. It is these whom I wanted to defend in Parliament, not Moi. I had many questions to ask in Parliament. If I did not put them to the government, my election would taste like ashes.

Having correctly understood "an additional forum" to mean a ministerial job, I trembled a bit and then told G.G., Thank you very much. But if you will allow me, I prefer to wait for some time before I accept this. I have never been to Parliament and would like to start from the bottom up. There are many questions I want to ask from the back. Later I may join the government.

He was surprised that I had said no. Okay, he replied, we need strong defense at the back also. I just wanted to make the offer.

I am glad that you thought of me. Thank you very much, I said. And I left.

When I won the elections, my friends were very happy for me. Many said it was my chance to do something for my family, my friends and myself, my chance to eat and my chance to be paid for my suffering.

Marriage

There are two women whose lives have been completely intertwined with mine. The first is Mum and the second is Nduta Koigi, my best friend, partner in life and divinity, my wife and mother of our three children.

I met Nduta and her two friends in Mombasa in 1979. Mirugi, Kimani and I were having a leisurely ride in town when Nduta and her two friends hailed us down for a lift. We could not resist their beauty, so we stopped. When they hopped into the car, I was smitten as soon as I laid my eyes on Nduta. I detected a very sweet soul behind an attractive shyness. When we dropped them where they asked, I immediately declared my love. My feelings for her were so strong that just being near her made my whole being tremble. Later my greatest joy would be for her to sit on my lap and for me to hold her in my arms. (More I am not allowed to say.)

When they introduced themselves to us, Nduta said she had read my interview with Salim Lone in *Viva* magazine about detention. When she looked at me, I saw interest and sympathy in her eyes and I took this to mean acceptance of me as well. Later I was lucky to discover that Nduta did not just have a sweet soul, but also steel courage that could survive incredible difficulties.

We took Nduta and her friends out one evening and had a group tour to Lunga Lunga near the Tanzanian border before Mirugi and I returned to Nakuru. By now, however, I had made up my mind that I wanted Nduta for my wife. I knew absolutely nothing about this girl but something in me had already identified her as my match.

Twice I drove six hundred kilometers to see Nduta in Mombasa. Before she accepted me we probed each other's love and loyalty: Do you really love me? Yes, both of us said. Will you ever abandon me for someone else? Never, both of us said. Will you always carry me in your heart everywhere, in and out of sight? Yes, both of us said.

On my second visit to Mombasa, I asked Nduta to pack her things and took her to Nakuru as my wife. Our traditional marriage began with making vows to each other. In doing this, we were our own priests and our consciences were our witnesses. We took a second step into our marriage when I visited Nduta's parents at Uthiru, near Nairobi, reported to them that I had taken their daughter for my wife and asked for their blessings. With my parents' and parents-in-laws' stamps of approval, our marriage was irrevocably consummated but not completely. Ceremonies and obligations of a Gikuyu traditional marriage happen throughout one's lifetime.

We chose a traditional marriage because I disagreed with the Christian church's claim that our parents and ancestors never had valid marriages outside Christianity. I feel strongly that the denial of our traditional marriage is also a denial of our humanity. We chose the Gikuyu traditional marriage ceremony because we thought it was more strongly anchored to the family and the society. Christian marriage seems to emphasize the unity of only two individuals. A Gikuyu traditional marriage is about uniting two individuals and creating bridges between two families. For sanctification, our marriage did not need a priest. It was built upon the mutual pledges of love, trust and loyalty.

But there is an aspect of traditional marriage that we said would not be part of our marriage. When a Gikuyu man marries, he talks of *kugura mutumia,* buying a woman literally with *ruracio,* dowry. But I would never buy my wife. We married each other.

Since then our marriage has been successful, happy and blessed with three sons. But it has also been a small ship sailing in extremely stormy seas whose cold and powerful winds have battered it so hard that its survival has been almost miraculous. Strangely, our marriage has survived because of the strengths it has gained from both good and bad times.

In the first years of our marriage, I took many things for granted, including my wife and her love. I learnt how valuable they were when I was detained a second time. People know a cow had milk only after her death, says the proverb, *imenyagwo yari iria yakua.*

When I was held in prison, my wife was detained at home. If it was difficult to be a widower inside, it was many times more difficult to be a widow outside. In prison, I suffered separation from my family for nine years; outside, my wife endured separation and being a single and unemployed mother for the same period. In prison, at least I got horrible food and a cage to live in. Outside, the government gave my wife and children nothing. In prison, I worried. Outside, my wife had to worry and provide.

I am most grateful to Nduta not just for her strength in bearing all her burdens but in having the enormous strength to resist calls to be taken to President Moi for money. Many a time she was asked by Philip Kilonzo, the police officer in charge of detainees, to ask me to give up for her and our children's sake. She did not ask. Nduta has not only been a supporter: She has made me complete where I was lacking and strong when I was weak. She has joined Mum and Pap as my closest heroes.

First Battle

My first battle with the Moi dictatorship in Parliament was in April 1980. It concerned a directive that Charles Njonjo, former attorney general and minister for constitutional affairs, had given on March 25, 1980 for the police to shoot to kill all suspects of robbery with violence. Of course, I did not condone robbery with violence, but I thought this directive was too dangerous for innocent suspects. The directive was also unconstitutional. Directives and decrees, whether presidential or otherwise, are not provided for in the constitution and always run counter to the rule of law. This particular directive gave police illegal powers to arrest, prosecute, judge and execute without taking suspects to court. In addition, in a country where the president ruled with decrees, the security of Kenyans would have been in double jeopardy if ministers started giving decrees as well. So I decided to challenge this directive in Parliament through my first private member's motion.

To forestall defeat, the government postponed debate over this issue while it exerted enormous pressure upon me through its ministers. Please drop this motion, I remember Paul Ngei telling me, you will only annoy the president with it. The president protected you against rigging of your elections, others reminded me. You do not repay him with a motion like this. I was even accused of being in league with the armed robbers.

Why do you seek justice for robbers if you are not one of them? some asked.

When none of these accusations could intimidate me, I was threatened with detention. But I did not budge. I judged that this was my most important test as an MP. If I knuckled under now, I would lose all my freedom as a representative of the people. If I retreated now, my political backbone would be broken for good, and I would be in Parliament only as a puppet of the government. And this I was determined not to be.

When I refused to withdraw my motion, a KANU Parliamentary Group meeting was finally called to exert maximum pressure by the president himself against those of us who had motions that Moi did not like. Would I survive?

When we got into the meeting, the president was on the offensive and fumed against all of us who had brought motions he did not like to the House. These motions, he said, are brought to give me a bad name and undermine my government. I hear one of you has called for the formation of a parliamentary implementation committee to ensure that my government implements all the motions that are passed in Parliament. Who is this MP to accuse my government of refusing to implement motions? I want this motion withdrawn immediately.

Though the need for the implementation committee was felt by all MPs who had seen the government refuse to implement countless motions since independence, Martin Shikuku stood up and told the president that he had already withdrawn his demand for an implementation committee. Clearly, Moi, like Kenyatta, did not intend to implement private members' motions.

After Shikuku, Moi talked of another MP who he said was mischievously calling for a five-day working week. How will this country develop if an MP who should be asking people to work harder is asking people to work less? Is this not sabotage?

Immediately George Mwicigi jumped up and said, Your Excellency, I have withdrawn the motion.

Looking quite pleased with himself, Moi smiled and looked down at a paper he had to see who was next on the hit list. When he looked up and said, Then there is this other motion, my heart beat faster, drops of sweat ran down my sides and my stomach tightened up. He waited but I did not jump up to withdraw my motion. If Moi attacked my motion, I was prepared to argue my case. Now the most unexpected thing happened!

This is about the shoot to kill directive to the police. It is illegal and unconstitutional. Not even I can give an order like this to the police. He did not blame Njonjo, the minister who had given the edict. Instead, he said, I have already ordered the attorney general to withdraw this in Parliament today. We could not believe our ears.

In May of 1980, however, Moi reissued the shoot to kill directive to the police, and it remains in practice to this day.

Second Temptation

When President Moi came to Parliament in 1978, one of the few positive things he said was that land prices were too high for the poor; land should cost no more than five hundred shillings an acre. I agreed and thought it was a good time to begin my campaign for land reform since the president supported it. In April 1980, I drafted a motion asking the government to reduce the price of land to five hundred shillings an acre.

When the motion was debated in Parliament, I was not surprised when all the wealthy MPs spoke and voted against it to protect their land. I was surprised when government ministers suddenly ran in, panting and sweating, because Moi had ordered them to kill the motion. How could the president lead an attack on his own idea? It was an important lesson.

Shortly after the defeat of my motion, President Moi invited my wife and me to his Kabarak home for a 5 A.M. breakfast—my first but not my last visit. After we had eaten a rather heavy and sumptuous breakfast, Moi led us into a plain room next to his kitchen that looked like a police interrogation area, for what he called a small talk. As we were seated, he talked to my wife without addressing her by name.

I invited you here because I want to help your husband. To do so, I want to advise him in your presence. If things go wrong later, I don't want you to blame Moi.

Yes, yes, Nduta said.

I smelt trouble. Then Moi turned to me. In politics, he said, I ask you to be very careful. It is a tricky business. In Parliament, do not let other politicians use you. They will ask you to say what they do not have the courage to voice and will run away from you when trouble comes.

He did not name names, but I knew he was talking about Mwai Kibaki, his vice president. Although his ideas were nowhere near my own and we had no political association at all, the fact that both of us were Gikuyu was enough for Moi to lump us together. Then the conversation shifted to land.

This land you are talking about is a dangerous issue. Remember that when you call for reform, the people who will be first to oppose you will be your own Gikuyu, who have large tracts of it. Land in this country belongs mainly to the Gikuyu and the Kalenjins. It is they who will lose when it is redistributed. And for it, they will hate you forever.

I could see what Moi was aiming at. He was trying to set me against land reform and my wife against me.

To begin with, Your Excellency, it is not true that some politicians are using me to say things for them in Parliament. What I say is what I believe. I have held these views for a long time. It was for them that Kenyatta imprisoned me and it is for them that I am prepared to die. In Parliament, only my constituents tell me what to say. No one else.

As for land, Your Excellency, I realize that many Gikuyu and Kalenjin people who have big farms oppose me when I call for redistribution. But there are millions of Gikuyu and Kalenjin who do not. Between those who have and those who have not, those who have nothing are more. If I were you, Your Excellency, I would therefore worry more about the poor than about the landed gentry.

Your Excellency, so many people line up on the roads and cheer you when you travel around the country because they expect things from you that Kenyatta did not give them. I am sure you are aware that President Kenyatta was very unpopular in his last days. When the people alongside the roads call you "Joshua," it is because they want you to deliver them from the desert where Kenyatta left them, to the Promised Land of milk and honey. Your Excellency, you need to give land to these people or they will turn their backs on you. They might even prefer the colonial government to your own.

By the way *kichana,* young man, Moi interrupted, where do you live?

We live in town, sir.

An MP should live among his own voters.

True, Your Excellency, but in Nakuru North I have no land and I cannot live with my parents because they still squat on government land.

Let me ask DC Ogol whether he can get you a good piece of land in Nakuru North.

He took the telephone, talked to the DC and then told me, See him next week. He will have something for you.

Moi then left us in the room and walked into the kitchen. He returned shaking a big traditional gourd of fermented milk, treated with pieces of charcoal from a sweet-smelling tree.

Have you ever had Kalenjin traditional milk? he asked us.

We said no.

It is very good and I want you to have some. But this *kibuyu*, gourd, is empty now. You will have some next time.

Sitting down, Moi took out seven thousand shillings and gave it to my wife. *Mama* (Lady), this is for your tea, he told her.

He excused himself from the room, promising to come back. He never did. After staying there until about 9 o'clock, we left. On reaching home, we gave away Moi's money. It was meant to corrupt; we couldn't keep it.

The following Tuesday in a KANU Parliamentary Group meeting Moi said, There are MPs here who claim to have personal ideas that are so dear to them that they will accept no other. Let me now tell everybody assembled here this: As a KANU MP, you have no ideas of your own. Your ideas are and must be those of the party. Those who think they have ideas must quit. You cannot be in the party and have ideas of your own. As for those who continue to talk about land reform, I want all this talk to stop. Where will those who are calling for reform get land to give to all the people they are now awakening? Those of you who have no land to lose must let sleeping dogs lie or you will lie yourself.

As he uttered the last sentence, he and Charles Njonjo looked at me. What Moi could not say in his kitchen, he was telling me here.

When I returned to Nakuru after Parliament, I went straight to see the DC about the land the president had promised.

The president asked me to see you for land, I said.

Yes, he said, but now I have no land for you. You should see the man who gave it to you in the first place.

Why? I asked perplexed.

Why did you say all those things in Parliament? Can't you keep quiet?

I was not told that the land was in return for my silence, I told the DC.

Maybe not, but it was. And please do not quote me on this. Had he not already authorized the land? He had and you can always ask him to authorize again.

I did not bother. Like our people, I wanted land and liberty. But forced to choose between one or the other, I preferred liberty.

Our Turn to Eat

When Daniel arap Moi came to power in 1978, he had one primary mission— to give the Kalenjin elite a chance and an opportunity to eat like the Gikuyu before them. His motto was, It is our turn to eat. Eating meant the Kalenjin elite had a right to grab the country's wealth, civil service jobs, jobs in public companies and take as much government land as possible while others looked on because they had already eaten or it was not yet their turn to eat.

For the Kalenjin elite to eat, the Gikuyu elite had to vomit up the jobs, the land and the businesses they had already taken. Moi asked James Karugu, the best attorney general Kenya has ever had, to draft a law that would empower him to annul all sales of land since 1963. Karugu refused, and Moi forced him to resign.

Kalenjin's time to eat meant that under Moi's presidency everything would belong to the Kalenjin elite and only crumbs would go to the elite of other communities loyal to Moi. As for every Gikuyu eating under Kenyatta, millions of Gikuyu people, like other Kenyan masses, ate absolutely nothing. Equally today, despite a fellow Kalenjin being president, millions of Kalenjin people, like masses of other ethnic communities, are as poor as church mice. Instead of sharing power and wealth with every Gikuyu, Kenyatta jailed, detained and killed many Gikuyu politicians and individuals who said no to his policies of ethnic and class discrimination.

From the word go, Moi's greatest enemies were the Gikuyu people. In public, however, he claimed that they were his friends because he had inherited the presidency from them. I believed Moi's doublespeak until I heard him speak his true mind at a function at Kabarak High School.

As he took his seat, he looked around and asked Kalenjin leaders who surrounded him whether "their" Gikuyu friends had arrived. Somebody said no. Let's proceed, he said, the only good Gikuyu is a dead one. I could not believe my ears. He then noticed Ng'ang'a Kihonge, a local Gikuyu leader. Feeling embarrassed, he told the councillor, You did not hear what I said, Kihonge. You are one of us by blood. From that day on I had no doubt: Moi was a tribalist.

Since I was politically disloyal to Moi, it was my turn to vomit what I had eaten. In May 1980, Nicholas Biwott, Moi's most powerful cabinet minister, pulled me aside and asked, Mr. Wamwere, what would it take for you to leave Parliament?

What do you mean? I asked.

We want you to quit being MP for Nakuru North. What would you like in return for that?

Nothing. Why should I leave my seat?

Did you ever hear of a Kalenjin being an MP for Gatundu (President Kenyatta's) constituency?

No, but so what?

If no Kalenjin could be President Kenyatta's MP, no Gikuyu should be President Moi's MP.

I belong to Nakuru North, I said. Nakuru North elected me, and it is not a Kalenjin constituency. It belongs to the people of all the communities that live there.

Shall you then be President Moi's MP?

Why not? If he does not want me to be his MP, he should live in Baringo Central, his own constituency.

This was the beginning of ethnic conflict in the Nakuru District. Since President Moi came to power, I had heard many Kalenjin leaders and their Gikuyu quislings say that in the Rift Valley all Gikuyu people were foreigners and guests. To these people, a Mugikuyu could live, do business, own land and be elected into Parliament only as a favor from the Kalenjin leaders. When Biwott failed to persuade me to vomit my parliamentary seat, Moi hit me on the back as hard as he could with detention and out fell the Nakuru North seat into the hands of Francis Kimosop, a fellow Kalenjin.

Fighting Corruption

One main reason I had wanted to serve in Parliament was to fight corruption. Before my election, I had seen dishonesty in land-buying companies. I had seen exploitation in farmers' cooperatives abetted by government officers. There was massive corruption in land distribution directed by the president himself. Protected by the highest authority in the land, elected councilors grabbed all the plots in trading centers and then sold them back to the same people who elected them. Companies like Nakuru Blanket Industries bribed union leaders and politicians to be able to underpay workers and deny them compensation for injuries suffered on the job and these companies got away with it. They would fill the big Mercedes-Benz of Mama Ngina, the wife of President Kenyatta, with expensive blankets, befriend President Moi with donations of big money and silence the leaders of workers unions with gifts of new cars. I had seen the corruption of selling, buying and denying justice in courts by perfectly respectable judges, magistrates and police officers. Corruption begets corruption. Ours was inherited from the corruption of British colonialism that had made white and Asian people rich and African people paupers in their own countries.

To fight corruption in Parliament, I could use parliamentary freedom of speech as a spear and immunity as a shield. Bitter experience outside Parliament had taught me that fighting corruption without the defense of human rights was suicidal. As an MP, I did not think that I could be silenced, detained or killed for challenging corruption.

During elections, voters demanded money and sugar for votes and candidates bought parliamentary seats for self-aggrandizement. I knew that citizens who sold votes could not demand honesty, let alone ask leaders to whom they had sold leadership to end corruption. The country was caught in a vicious cycle in which both leaders and citizens were cooking in the stew of unending corruption. But I had to fight the fire of corruption precisely because it was all-engulfing and threatened everybody.

Before I went to Parliament, I had heard President Kenyatta rationalize corruption. Instead of ordering the arrest of his dishonest friends, Kenyatta only sang them a warning from our childhood lyric:

> My little bird, hide
> If you are caught
> You are not mine.

I had heard President Moi tell people that those who steal billions and later contribute thousands to the public in *harambee* meetings were worthy leaders. In Kenya, it felt as if corruption had only friends and no enemies.

In 1979, we won an important struggle when rebel members led by John Mbure and John Mugi defeated the corrupt leadership of the Ngwataniro land-buying company. I had actively combined my campaign for Parliament with that of saving Ngwataniro from corrupt leadership.

The following year, I was coming out of my office in Nakuru when I met Mbure and Mugi. After exchanging greetings, they thanked me for helping them win the leadership of Ngwataniro. We were about to part when they invited me into an expensive clothes shop called Shah's Outfitters.

Mheshimiwa (Honorable), they told me, why don't you take two suits?

Why? I asked. I have no money and I don't need them.

The company will pay for them. It will be our thanks to you.

How will you account for it? Have members approved of this?

No, but we shall explain. It will be a miscellaneous expense.

No, thank you. That will be miscellaneous corruption. Is this not the same thing for which we removed the old leaders?

We never spoke again.

As soon as I became an MP, I realized Parliament was not exempt from corruption. After taking rights and freedoms away from MPs, dictatorship struck terror into their hearts with the fear of detention, assassination and imprisonment through trumped-up charges and blackmail. To the outside, Kenyan MPs may have looked free. Inside, they were frightened and cowed. Most MPs could not speak or vote without looking over their shoulders. Over the years, the president's friend Charles Njonjo had perfected a system of blackmail where MPs who were caught in a crime were never prosecuted or tried. They were held hostage and forced to toe the government line. Those who defied this blackmail were jailed.

My greatest disappointment came with my nomination to the Public Accounts Committee (PAC), which oversaw how the government spent public funds. Government corruption was so obvious that it was straightforward theft. Indeed, benefiting someone in government seemed to be the only rationale for which public money was ever spent. It was obvious murder of the weakest and most vulnerable.

One day a professor at the University of Nairobi called to say he had evidence that the contraceptive drug Depo-Provera, which was being tested on Kenyan women, was very harmful. He told me the drug was banned in the West for family planning and people in the government and the Family Planning Association of Kenya only allowed its use because they had taken bribes from Upjohn, the Dutch-based multinational responsible for it. Its side effects were deadly: Women endured dangerous pregnancies after using it.

I brought a motion to Parliament asking that Depo-Provera be banned as a contraceptive. People like Dr. Koinange, permanent secretary in the ministry of health, offered me bribes and made pleas: Do not spill the food on our plates, please. We will equip and supply the dispensary at Banita in your constituency.

Go ahead and equip the dispensary, I said, but do not eat by killing others.

When others in the saga of Depo-Provera were asked whether they had taken a bribe, they admitted nothing. In the heat of the debate in Parliament, it was Zephania Anyieni who asked Dr. Ellon Wameyo, then assistant minister of health, We have just been told that millions of dollars have been given by Upjohn to doctors and government officials in Third World countries to promote imports of Depo-Provera. Are you one of those who received this money?

Dr. Wameyo said nothing, but Njonjo said, I have received none of this blood money.

Parliament passed my motion banning the use of Depo-Provera for family planning. It was never implemented, however, and our women continue to bleed and die.

As time went by, I realized that even the PAC, the last institutional safeguard against corruption, was not free from it. I had been working for one year when I was elected chairman in 1981. The state then moved against me, with President Moi threatening that if I did not resign from the chairmanship, he would dissolve it. Moi's watchman on the committee was a lawyer named Kagiri. Although he had taken part in my election, he came to me whining, Please resign as chairman. President Moi says he will never allow the committee to meet as long as you are chairman.

I told Kagiri, How will the committee work independently if we permit the president to say who will be chairman? He can block the meetings of the committee if he wants, but I will not resign.

Permanent secretaries say that you will use the committee for witch-hunting.

I do not know these permanent secretaries personally and I have nothing against them. Why would I witch-hunt? On the other hand, why are they afraid, if they are clean? The chairman of the PAC cannot be chosen by the same civil servants whose investigation he will oversee. Tell them to go to hell.

A week or so later, another Moi backer was sent.

The president will dissolve the Public Accounts Committee the way he dissolved the Foreign Relations Committee if you do not resign. Resign and save the committee.

You mean: Resign and destroy the committee. The president has no right to interfere in the running of the committee. If he doesn't want the committee to run freely, let him dissolve it, but I will not help to ruin it by resigning.

Later, members of the PAC were brought to Parliament by police helicopter for a secret election. At first, they failed to remove me. Another election was called, and I was removed and replaced by a man with whom the president and civil servants could feel safe.

House of Terror

As an MP who was a marked man, I was threatened with death openly as soon as I refused to partake in corruption. A woman called Mukuhi was Moi's messenger. At every public meeting I attended with president Moi, Mukuhi would stand and recite an ominous proverb: When a kid refuses to suckle its mother, it must die, *gekurega nyina no gukua gakuaga*. One time, I overheard the president's confidant, Charles Njonjo, say, This man needs to be castrated.

Another time, Ja'afar Nimeiri, a former president of Sudan, was visiting President Moi at Nakuru. All of us had gone to the Lanet airstrip to meet him and two of us narrowly escaped being attacked by the presidential bodyguards when Moi flew into a tantrum.

Three Nakuru MPs—Mark Mwithaga, Keffa Wagara and I—had issued a statement defending Mark Mwithaga against an attack from the provincial commissioner. Moi had taken this as a personal affront. He was greeting the assembled guests when he came upon us. Suddenly he refused to greet us and stormed, You, Wagara and Koigi, you abuse my general and expect me to shake your hands?

We have not abused your general, sir, Wagara said.

Immediately, the notorious colonial henchman, Jeremiah Kiereini, rushed forward, produced a copy of the *Weekly Review* and pointed to our statement: And what is this?

At that, a furious Moi threw the clubbed stick he always carried into the air and pulled back. When his bodyguards heard the noise, they rushed forward, but were stopped by General Mulinge, who politely asked us to leave the function.

As we left, Wagara told me, This is why we should not bring our wives and children to these events. Imagine the humiliation if our loved ones had come with us.

This was more than humiliation. It was mortal danger.

Another day I was having lunch at Parliament when an old, sick government minister called Kuguru Ngibuini invited me to his table.

Mr. Wamwere, you must stop calling us names or we are going to kill you the way we got rid of J.M. Kariuki. When he called us mean and accursed, *ngundi nyumu mugirwo ni ka,* I warned him, but he did not listen. Now I am warning you.

He was the first man ever to tell me that he was one of those who killed J.M. I did not say a word.

When I went to the Kenyan Parliament, it was under military occupation, literally. One of the first things I noticed was a company of soldiers that had its barracks inside. Ostensibly, the soldiers were there to guard the late President Kenyatta in his mausoleum. Since independence, Kenyatta and Moi had always seen the legislature as a potential source of rebellion and trouble. Being weaker, Moi took the excuse of guarding Kenyatta's mausoleum to put Parliament under a twenty-four-hour watch by the army.

In addition, I was one of those MPs whom the government put under extra watch by security forces. When an assistant clerk of the national assembly told me that he had heard two Special Branch officers report my movements and what I said to whom, I was astonished. It was chilling to realize that I was under such close surveillance inside Parliament where I should have been completely free.

To lose my pursuers, I became a nomad who could not live in any one house for two nights in Nairobi. I did not want to share my harassment with neighbors. Whenever they began to get nervous with the presence of the police Land Rover outside their door, I moved on.

It was the same thing in Nakuru. Most nights I was home, an unmarked police car parked outside our house. When I turned our security lights on, it drove away in the dark without lights. This nightly surveillance would set our dogs barking and awaken us. Soon, our dogs were poisoned and killed.

Once I was to drive home to Nakuru, but changed my mind and instead drove to Thika. The stabilizer of my car snapped. Upon inspection, it became clear that the part had been sawed almost in half in the parking lot of Parliament. I could feel the noose tightening around my neck.

In 1982, I was driving home from Nyeri, where I had gone to attend a funeral. On the way, I picked up some people who had been injured in a motor accident and dropped them at Nyahururu hospital. From a bus stop near the hospital, I picked up some four people who were going to Ol Joro Orok and

Nakuru. At Ol Joro Orok, I dropped one person and branched onto the dirt road to Nakuru. It was raining heavily and the road was very slippery. Driving slowly, I saw a car with flashing lights coming up fast from behind. It slowed down and pulled parallel to us and I could see that six men in dark suits in it were observing us. I sensed danger. The strange car then sped off and disappeared. When it appeared again, it was parked in a valley in the middle of the road, near a bridge with a steep hill overlooking it. To cross the narrow bridge, we had to almost stop and there they would intercept us. We stopped some distance from them and waited. When we saw a military Land Rover coming down the hill, I started my car and moved in good speed to meet the Land Rover near the bridge. Fortunately, the Land Rover waited for us to pass the bridge. When we did, we drove up the hill as fast as we could. We never saw the car again.

On arrival in Nakuru town, I inquired to the police about the car. The police said the car's registration numbers belonged to a Mombasa car that had been involved in a fatal accident some years back and had been written off. I felt the car had resurfaced from the dead to kill again.

Others broke into my car while it was parked outside Church House in Nairobi. They stole my box of clothes and set the car on fire. I managed to put the fire out, but when I called a nearby police station to send police to the scene of crime, they took so long to come that I left before they did.

I feared the police as much as people in power fear criminals. In fact, I feared the police more than I feared real robbers. One day my car ran out of petrol at night near Limuru. I was traveling with a friend and I asked him to go to Limuru for petrol. I was left behind to guard the car. Later some people in a small car found me and asked me to come out. I said I would not. They asked why? Because I am the one guarding it, I said.

Do you think nothing now can happen to the car?

Yes, I said.

Who are you? they asked.

I am Koigi wa Wamwere, I said.

Why did you not tell us?

Because, you did not ask, I said.

Okay, come, we will take you to Limuru to buy petrol.

But we cannot leave the car unguarded here, I said. It might get stolen.

Only we could steal it, come.

Suddenly it occurred to me that they were highway robbers. They took me to Limuru. We found my friend with petrol and came back to the car. I offered the highway robbers some money for their trouble. They would not take it.

I was surprised that I should feel much safer with highway robbers at night in the forest than with the police in Parliament during the day. Instead of making me feel safe in Parliament, the police did everything they could to scare and silence me. I was not, however, the only MP who was subjected to terror.

One time, in front of his bodyguard and Simon Nyachae, his secretary to the cabinet, President Moi sounded deranged in his rage: I thought you people have brains. But you are just empty skulls without anything inside. And turning upon Paul Ngei, a minister who had raised his hand to ask something, Moi fumed, What are you raising your hand for? To tell me something? Do you think there is anything you can tell me? What can you tell me? Do you think there is anything I don't know?

On September 13, 1984, Moi told his assistant ministers:

> I call on all ministers, assistant ministers and every other person to sing like parrots. During the *Mzee* Kenyatta period, I persistently sang the Kenyatta tune until people said, "This fellow has nothing to say, except to sing for Kenyatta." I do not have ideas of my own, I said. Why am I to have my own ideas? I am in Kenyatta's shoes and, therefore, have to sing whatever he wants. If I had sung another song, do you think Kenyatta would have left me alone? Therefore, you ought to sing the song I sing. If I put a full stop, you should put a full stop. This is how the country will move forward. The day you become a big person, you will have the liberty to sing your own song and everybody will sing it too.[1]

Unfortunately, there has never been a shortage of Kenyans who have been willing to kneel before Moi and worship him for money, power, a piece of land, a job in government, a loan to do business or protection against prosecution for a crime committed.

Let Koigi Speak

One afternoon, I was on my way to visit my grandmother at Thika, a town near Nairobi. At her house, many people came to see me. They were very worried about my safety.

Are you not afraid that Moi might do something terrible to you—detain or kill you like J.M. if you continue to challenge him in Parliament?

He can, I said.

Why then don't you keep quiet for a while? He might leave you alone.

A young lady called Lucia who had been listening in silence interjected, Why are you asking someone who is not dead not to speak? Are you not beckoning death for him? When Koigi dies, he will not speak. Now he is not dead. Let him speak. I could not agree with her more: I speak, therefore, I am.

First Son

If you are living in a hell like Kenya was in 1982, it is not unusual to lose hope. But Ngai does not mean that life should end because there are problems. Even when problems seem insurmountable, Ngai will give you a reason to live as he gave us in 1982, my most difficult year in Parliament.

On February 16, 1982, we had gone to visit Mirugi and his family. Upon our return home, my wife went into labor almost immediately and I had to take her to the Annex Ward of the War Memorial Hospital. It was built by the British colonialists to celebrate and commemorate British war efforts during the Second World War in defense of their country and colonial empire.

Ngai gave us our first son at two in the morning. The women celebrated his birth with five ululations, *ngemi ithano cia kahii.* As our first son, we named him after my father, Wamwere *wa* (son of) Koigi. In our culture, the first child does not only come as a gift to his parents and others, he or she also brings gifts to many people.

To my wife and me, Wamwere brought a status we could never achieve without him. From now on, instead of being called Koigi, I had the honor and pride of being called *ithe wa* (father of) Wamwere. Equally, instead of being called Nduta, my wife now had the honor and pride of being called *nyina wa* (mother of) Wamwere. In a culture where childlessness is frowned upon, Wamwere's birth confirmed my manhood, my fatherhood and also my divinity, just as it confirmed my wife's womanhood, motherhood and divinity.

But Wamwere did not only come with gifts for his mother and me. He also brought my father into our house in flesh and blood—a great honor to my father. But being the parents of my father now gave an additional title. While my father only called me *muthoniwa,* my father-in-law, because I was called after my mother's father, could now call me *baba,* father, and call Nduta, *maitu,* or mother. This was no small honor.

Unlike our parents, who had never had electric light in their home, we did, but when he came, Wamwere was the greatest light of our home. Our culture says that the laughter of a child is the light of the home, *ucheshi wa mtoto ni anga la nyumba.* When I came home depressed and harassed, my wife's and Wamwere's laughter were the oxygen that revitalized my soul again. Whenever I came home drenched in fear that there were people out there trying to kill me, I would look at Wamwere and say, As long as Wamwere lives to sire his own children and embrace the right values, however many times they may kill me, I will never die. However many times they may kill me, the struggle for freedom, equality and justice that they are trying to extinguish by killing me will never die.

Their Parliament

I remember not believing my ears when I heard Martin Shikuku, a man who had been a popular MP in Kenyan Parliament for many years and who dubbed himself as the people's watchman, explain his success in politics:

To succeed in politics, he said, one must know how to draw votes from the people. People are like cows. I draw milk out of them because I know how to feel and pacify them into letting their milk go.

As I thought about this, I wondered, Can one befriend a cow by feeding her well and sharing her milk with her calves instead of making her feel good just once for her milk?

Workers in Greek-owned sisal estates in Kenya were employed on a piecemeal basis euphemistically called "leftover food" or *kiporo,* where workers were paid for the amounts of work they were supposed to finish each day rather than for each day they go to work. If workers went to work, worked for some hours and then fell sick, they were not paid for the time they were sick. They would have to come back and finish their work to be paid. And to make sure that they are paid for as few days as possible in a month, workers were given so much work to finish each day that they had to draw their children from school to help them finish their daily work quotas. Without such help, most would start each new day by finishing the previous day's work.

One day I took a motion to Parliament to abolish and replace this system of work with one where workers are paid for each day they work and for all days they are out of work because they are sick. The motion was defeated when Parliament voted on it. One of the MPs whom I noticed voting against this motion was Munyua Waiyaki, a Kenyan politician with a progressive reputation. After the voting I asked him, Why the hell did you vote for these Greek sisal plantation owners to continue treating people like slaves?

Because I am not a fool, he said.

What do you mean?

Come on, he said, in my coffee farm I pay workers the same way. After abolishing this piecemeal system in sisal estates, will you not do the same in coffee plantations?

For some MPs, even the survival of loved ones could be sacrificed upon the altar of self-interest. Grace Onyango was an MP and a deputy speaker in Parliament for many years. She was also the sister of Ochola Achola, the detainee whom President Kenyatta would not release until he went completely crazy in prison. When I took a motion to Parliament condemning indefinite imprisonment, the horrible conditions under which we were kept and denial of work to us after release, Grace Onyango did not say a word about how her brother was driven into insanity by detention.

But the most infuriating was Dr. Eddah Gachukia, a professor at the University of Nairobi and a nominated MP. One day I was asking a question about people whom the police had shot when Attorney General Charles Njonjo authorized them to shoot to kill suspects of robbery with violence. Sitting beside me, she whispered, Please mention the case of my son. The police shot through his leg as he drove our Mercedes-Benz on the Nairobi-Mombasa road. They could have killed him.

But Honorable, why do you not raise the matter yourself? It will convince Parliament more that this directive is wrong.

Honorable, you know what they will do to me?

Yes, I knew.

Moi would have withdrawn her nomination as MP. But was her job more important than the life of her son?

Bearded Sisters

In Parliament there were seven of us who tried to keep the spirit of the people's interests alive. We were Abuya Abuya, Onyango Midika, Mashengu wa Mwachofi, James Orengo, Lawrence Sifuna, Dr. Chibule wa Tsuma and myself. Coming from different parts of the country, we did not know each other, nor did we know our ideological closeness before coming to Parliament. Soon, however, we were able to coalesce and fight for poor people's rights and freedoms together.

Charles Njonjo, Moi's confidant, called us the Seven Bearded Sisters to indicate that like the Seven Sisters of the oil industry, we were conspirators. To make us sound dangerous to the West, he gave us beards—like Fidel Castro.

Since we were so few and the government so hostile, we stood together, supported each other's motions, asked supplementary questions and attended rallies in each other's constituencies. Soon none of us were allowed to address meetings outside our own constituencies and we were barred from giving public lectures or visiting friends at either Kenyatta or Nairobi universities.

We scared Moi's dictatorship so much with our demands for freedom and justice that the government did everything it could to destroy us. Finally, those of us who completely refused to succumb were driven out of Parliament and scattered like ape dung, *mai ma theeru,* into prison, detention and exile.

Day of Doom

As Parliament and the country went down the abyss of terror, there was Oginga Odinga, George Anyona, Salim Lone and others who were not prepared to go down without a fight. These were people whom Moi had shut out of KANU. So far Kenya had been a one-party state de facto, but not de jure. Before, people who had tried to form opposition parties had been detained, but this had not extinguished the spirit of those people whom dictatorship had locked out of all political life in their own country.

Sometime in 1981, MP Hezekiah Ougo had resigned from his parliamentary seat in order to allow Odinga to come to Parliament. When Odinga raised the sensitive land issue in a speech in Mombasa, the doors to Parliament through KANU were shut in his face. Now Odinga wanted to form an opposition party and reach Parliament through it. I was in KANU, but felt as good as dead and sympathized with Odinga in forming another party. With all agents of terror, destruction and death let loose in and out of Parliament, one could not openly state support for the opposition party without risking life itself. I felt numb with fear.

After lecturers at the University of Nairobi supported the formation of the second party and Mukaru Ng'ang'a warned that if Parliament changed the constitution to ban an opposition party, people would go underground, an emergency KANU Parliamentary Group meeting was called. At that meeting, Moi warned that if anyone went underground, government thugs would follow him there. From my days in detention, I knew the Kenyatta government had used die-hard criminals to kill both Pio Gama Pinto and J.M. Kariuki, but at this meeting, I heard the president himself admit that the government used thugs to kill opponents. I was shocked!

I wanted to oppose the change of constitution in Parliament. To do so, I decided to ask the people of Nakuru North how they wanted me to vote. At a meeting in Subukia, I told people that when I went to Parliament I took an oath to defend the constitution and wanted to do so now. As a member of KANU, I explained that while KANU had the power to throw people out of their houses, it had no right to stop expellees from building their own houses to shelter themselves from cold and rain. I wanted to oppose the change of the constitution with the support of the people and so I asked, Those people who want me to vote for the change of constitution, let me see your hands, please.

Not a single hand went up. I was overjoyed and thought that people would be with me in opposing the change of constitution. But I wanted to make sure and so I put the same question the other way round: Those who want me to vote against the change of the constitution, please put up your hands.

Again not a single hand went up and I was left on my own. They looked so grave and sad that I almost felt as if I had been asking them whether I should vote for or against my own death and not that of the constitution.

When the meeting was over, some old men and women came to me and offered some advice: Don't die for something you can't stop. Alone you are nothing. Let them do what they want. One day people will come together to put this thing right again. Their advice left me more isolated, weaker and more vulnerable. If I wanted to oppose the change of constitution, I had to do it entirely on my own against the might of government.

But we could kill the change of constitution by keeping away from Parliament and denying the government the two-thirds majority it needed to change the constitution.

As this thought came to mind, it also came out of my mouth. I made the mistake of mentioning it to Joseck Thuo, a former mayor of Nakuru, and it was reported to Moi instantly.

Another KANU Parliamentary Group meeting was called where Moi reprimanded us as King Henry VIII of England had reprimanded Sir Thomas More for refusing to speak in support of his third marriage: Every MP must condemn the formation of another party in this country. Those who do not are worse than those who are forming it. In fact, we know those who are silent are also planning to oppose the change of constitution, some by keeping away from Parliament. Your detention orders are already signed and your names will be filled in as soon as you vote the wrong way or absent yourselves from Parliament during either the debate or the vote. Only three MPs have permission to miss the House during this time. Anyone else will face the axe of the woodcutter, *cha mtema kuni.*

When detention was opposed, an editorial in the *East African Standard* spoke for the government: "It will not do for them [detainees] to plead that they should be sent to hell for a thousand years only, and then be allowed out. They sold their bodies and souls to the devil for a leg of mutton—uncooked, signed, sealed and delivered—and now they belong, permanently, to the devil and his representatives, not to Kenya."

Under such a threat, I have never seen Parliament as grave, fearful, and submissive as on the morning of June 20, 1982, when we met to make Kenya a de jure one-party state. Only Charles Njonjo, G.G. Kariuki, Nicholas Biwott and a few others had smiles on their faces. Everyone else was sad and said we were signing a death warrant for both democracy and peace in our country. By making it impossible to form another party, members felt they were making a peaceful change of government in Kenya impossible and beckoning a military coup.

Despite this awareness, MPs were so fearful that they were willing to entomb democracy and the country just to keep out of prison. I have never hated Parliament as I did that day and I have never hated myself more for being cowardly. Unfortunately, people out of Parliament were no better. We were all perfect prisoners of fear, that terrible tyrant forcing us to do the wrong thing despite our better judgment. On the evening of June 19, 1982, I even overheard the vice president, Mwai Kibaki, who seconded the motion of changing the constitution, say as someone wishing his own execution to pass fast: Oh, the sooner this passes the better!

When the debate came, I sought the speaker's eye three times. I wanted to oppose the change of constitution. Each time I rose up, Speaker Fred Mati would look at me and then look the other way. In fifteen minutes, Parliament had changed the constitution, buried democracy and plunged the country into total darkness by putting out the last candle of hope and light. Later that evening, I asked Speaker Mati why he had refused to notice me during the debate. Without looking me in the face he said, Some people are like moths. They like to throw themselves into the fire. One death today was enough.

Third Temptation

It would be my last visit with President Moi. I was asked to be at the Nairobi State House by six o'clock in the morning. The political atmosphere in the country was extremely tense and the secret police watched my every move twenty-four hours a day. When I was at home they parked their car nearby and watched. With the police as my hunters, I could not travel to Nairobi so early in the morning alone. One who travels alone is never given the right of way, *mundu umwe ndeheragirwo njira.*

I asked my friend Gilbert Kabage to come with me. In his presence, anyone planning an ambush or an attack might just hesitate. When we arrived at the State House, my friend was left in the waiting room. I was ushered into a room where I met the president in the company of Simon Nyachae and Jeremiah Kiereini, a colonial butcher who Kenyatta and Moi had continued to employ after independence. President Moi called them Simon and Jerry.

The president encouraged me to join the big political rift (which he had orchestrated) between his supporters. He had been using his ministers Charles Njonjo, G.G. Kariuki, Nicholas Biwott and others to attack his own vice president, Mwai Kibaki.

People from Nyeri, he told me, fight Njonjo because he helped me to become president. Now I want you to work with Njonjo and G.G. in Parliament.

Your Excellency, I said, between your ministers and vice president, I prefer to be neutral and independent, rather than join one to fight the other. If you ask me to join your ministers against your vice president, the latter will crush me and vice versa. Please let me out of this war. I do not have any power to fight.

By the way, Koigi, the president cut me short, what do people say about Njonjo?

They say he is the most powerful person in this country. Many even say that he is so powerful that if he says an innocent man will sleep in prison today, that person will be in jail before the end of the day.

Do they say that? Moi asked in amazement and amusement. Then he broke into a hard, prolonged laughter—*ha ha ha ha ha ha ha ha*—that brought him down from his seat, crawling on the floor on all fours with tears rolling down his face, before coughs—*kho kho kho kho*—nearly choked him. A picture of Nebuchadnezzar on all fours crossed my mind.

I did not understand the meaning of this hysterical laughter until Njonjo fell from grace later, accused of being a traitor, *msaliti*. For now, Moi was happy that he had convinced most people that Njonjo was the devil incarnate. Moi then showed me press cuttings of my criticisms of the economy, which he understood to be criticisms of his vice president and minister of finance.

Koigi, he said, this is very good work. If I were you, I would continue doing the same. You are young, educated and confident. To succeed in politics, however, you need more. Listen to the advice of older men like me and work with Njonjo and G.G.

I did not support Kibaki, as Moi thought I did. I had seen him betray too many friends. To fight Kibaki, it would not be for Moi, and to battle Moi, it would never be for Kibaki. As these thoughts were flooding my mind, Kiereini jumped in without addressing me directly: I wonder why Koigi has never come to my office. He knows where it is, but never comes for help. Do you never need anything? He asked me.

Yes, I do, I said, unable to say more.

Another MP had earlier told me how this Kiereini worked as a screener in colonial detention camps like Manyani prison. There he brutally castrated many freedom fighters with pairs of pliers, knocked out and broke their teeth with steel-covered fists. I became nauseous whenever I saw him. Moi must have noticed my discomfort.

Did you get that land I asked Ogol to give to you? he asked.

No, Mr. Ogol said that you took it back.

Moi laughed knowingly and continued, Maybe Simon has land. They are giving out some now.

Yes, we are, said Nyachae.

Give *Mheshimiwa* Koigi a good piece.

Yes, I will, sir.

Before I left, Moi said he wanted to give me some money for petrol.

As he stood up and walked toward a briefcase, I noticed that the four walls of the room were lined with similar briefcases. He reached the first one and opened it. It was full of bundles of money. He checked the bundle and returned it, saying it was not the right one. He went to another briefcase, opened it and it too was full of money like the first one. He picked a bundle from it and said it also was not the right one. He moved to a third and a fourth briefcase doing and saying exactly the same thing. Clearly all these briefcases were full of money. I wondered whether this was not public tax money and and why it was here. Moi then reached a fifth briefcase. He opened it and took a bundle of money and said it was the right one. He took out two of these and threw them at me smiling. I took the money and left. In the waiting room I gave Kabage one bundle and kept one. They contained 20,000 shillings each.

When I reached home, I told my friend Mirugi Kariuki that Moi had shown me money like I had not seen before. He replied, Moi was not showing you money, he was beckoning you into your moral grave and I am glad that you did not plunge into it. You see, brother, there is nothing more difficult than overcoming the temptation of money. In my view, it is easy to survive prison, detention and even torture, but not so the lure of money. Many people have survived years of imprisonment, only to prostrate themselves before the god of money.

As for the land, it was a bait to bind me to Moi. I took it, without swallowing the hook. I realized that the opportunity to have this piece of land had been unfairly offered. I was not the most deserving MP, but I took it for several reasons: As a family, we had no land and I wanted my parents to have somewhere to go when they stopped living in the government forest. The land was not free, I paid for it. My job was not permanent and I would need land to live on when I was no longer an MP.

Lastly, I felt ready then and I still do, to give up that land if a national land reform called for it. An excellent friend of ours, Professor Micere Mugo of the University of Nairobi, was, however, stronger than me. When Moi offered her land, she rejected both the bait and the hook.

Planting a Bomb

As we played games with corruption and dictatorship, I knew they were creating extreme poverty among the people. Destitution and desperation were, in turn, driving many people crazy. We were sitting on a ticking time bomb.

One bright morning, I was in a downtown Arab restaurant having breakfast. As I drank my tea, a waiter approached and greeted me: *Mheshimiwa,* how are you?

I am fine.

Just wanted to say *heko,* congratulations for your work. But Parliament and government must do more quickly. The ship is sinking faster than ever.

I know.

You don't. Yesterday, a young man sat where you are sitting now. He asked for two glasses of tea and I gave them to him. He was alone and I wondered how he would drink two glasses of tea at the same time. As I served other customers, I noticed a group of terrified people rushing out. The man had fished an old man's white-haired head from a gunny sack, placed it on the table, put the tea before him and urged him to drink it: Pap, drink your tea. You always drank alone. Now I will buy you all the tea you can drink.

In seconds, this place was empty. Everyone had run out. But the man was calm. Even as I called the police, he did not flinch or care to notice. What is your name? I asked him.

Githinji, he said laughing. I guessed it was not his. It meant 'the butcher.'

Why did you come to chase away our customers?

We came to drink tea. Is not your business to sell tea and food?

It is, I said, somewhat afraid.

We shall drink and eat.

Who is that?

It is my father. I chopped his head off.

Why?

He denied me my share of family land and I charged him with robbery. He is on a long journey. I must feed him.

The police arrived and handcuffed him without any resistance whatsoever. They took him away with the head of his father. *Mheshimiwa,* poverty is driving many young people insane.

Yes, I said. I wondered whose head would be next.

1982 Coup

On the morning of August 1, 1982, we awoke to the voice of Kenya's most popular newscaster, Mambo Mbotela, announcing that the air force had overthrown President Moi and had taken over the government. Though I loved neither the army nor the prospect of a military government, I felt exhilarated. The radio announcement warned that all people should stay indoors, but my hatred for Moi's dictatorship was so intense that I felt neither fear nor bound to obey the order to stay inside. As I dressed, my wife pleaded, Please don't go out. It is dangerous. Do as they say, please.

I was undeterred. If this was freedom, I was determined to see it. The gift of freedom was the best offering we could receive. A large crowd was gathering outside our home and the itch to go out was absolutely irresistible. I asked Nduta, What do you think about this?

I am apprehensive, she said.

Do you think it will stick?

No, she said.

When I went outside, I was surprised to hear a young man whom I had never suspected of being political say with great feeling, It is good that these dogs and donkeys have been overthrown.

Later I walked to town and all was quiet there. With the exception of a lonely army tank patrolling the area, there was no fighting at all in Nakuru. In town I met

Councillor Joseph Kamweru Miano. We went to his office where I called James Orengo in Nairobi. He told me a bit about the fierce fighting that was going on in Nairobi between the rebel air force and loyalist army soldiers. At about 11 A.M., the army crushed the coup.

Our neighbor, an army major, told me, Oh, it was just the air force boys. We will crush them, he told me. A very cold chill ran down my back and my knees weakened. I had just enough strength to get out of his compound.

When I reached the crowd near our home, I told them what the major had said. A heavy silence fell upon them. Some cried. None had the strength to curse. They looked down and one by one, dispersed in different directions. The crowd melted like a block of butter with a single tiny stone in it. Only the secret policeman among them remained solid. He looked like a chicken that had been dipped in water prior to slaughter. With his killers dispersed, he walked out of the cooking pot, flapped his wings to shake off the water and energetically embarked on his new task of hunting down the air force rebels and those who had supported the coup. The whole crowd was now at the mercy of the secret policeman who had looked so cowed and so helpless among them.

In an instant, an incredibly sweet dream had turned into a most frightening nightmare. Songs on the radio best expressed our horror: "Moi, march on so that we may build our Kenya." *Moi songa na mbele tujenge Kenya yetu.* "Hi, hi. How are you? I am fine." *Jambo? Jambo bwana. Habari gani? Mzuri sana.* At a moment when the Kenyan army was killing Kenyans like flies, the radio was singing, Visitors you are welcome; our Kenya has no conflict! *Wageni mwakaribishwa, Kenya yetu, hakuna matata!*

Where is Moi? was the question on everyone's mind. It was the key to every Kenyan's hope at that particular moment. Only if he were dead, prayed people who were crying for change, will Kenya be changed. God save Moi, prayed his supporters, and we will put everything back to normal after crushing these rebels once for all.

That evening Moi appeared on television, flanked by his loyal general and police chief. He was shaking like a leaf in very strong wind.

The following week, planted rumors claimed that I had taken part in the coup. Yes, I had wished the coup success, but I knew nothing about it before it happened. To my enemies however, the crushed coup was a godsend. They said I was in it and later Mohammed Warsarma, a journalist, falsely wrote that on the morning of the coup, I was at Nanyuki Air Force Base distributing uniforms to rebels. In those times, however, the truth was irrelevant and I knew they would come for me sooner or later.

It was a sunny Thursday morning when two policemen came for me. Trying to reassure their prey, they smiled deceptively. They even took tea when I invited them in, but I was not deceived. They had come for me. After tea they called me outside and requested that I accompany them to the station for a few questions. Returning for my coat, I took a good look at my wife and our son, in fear that I might not see them again.

As I was driven to Nairobi, we stopped at an army roadblock at Gilgil. The army major in charge looked into the car and inquired whether everyone in the car was an officer of the government. Kosgei, the Special Branch man in charge of the vehicle, said yes. The major then asked, What about him, pointing at me?

We are taking him to Nairobi, Kosgei said.

Mheshimiwa, honorable one, why did you not keep your mouth shut? the major asked.

I did not say anything, I told him.

Why then have they arrested you?

I do not know.

You should have kept quiet, he said, going to consult with his colleague. Soon Kosgei grew impatient.

Please, sir, give us permission to leave, Kosgei begged the major.

Get back into the car and wait. You leave when I say so, the major barked. Clearly, he was on my side. After a while he waved us on, but leaned into the car for a last time to wish me well.

When we arrived in Nairobi, I was taken into Special Branch headquarters at Nyati House, where secret police operatives were busy. They took my identity papers before I was led back to the car. I was driven to the city morgue. Bodies of dead soldiers and civilians lay everywhere. Inside, the mortuary itself was full of blood-stained corpses.

Pointing to the cadavers, Kosgei asked me, Is this what you people wanted?

What do you mean? I asked him.

You have been calling for trouble, haven't you?

I have been calling for change, not trouble.

What is the difference? Get into the car, he ordered.

I was driven to the Karen Police Station, where I was booked under a false name and kept in a cell by myself without food. As long as nobody knew I was there, the police could kill me and get away with it. From my cell, I shouted my name to the prisoners who were in other cells.

On August 6, 1982, I was taken to Kilimani Police Station, where Philip Kilonzo, the Nairobi provincial police officer, read my second detention order. I knew from the previous incarceration that Kilonzo was also the officer in charge of detainees. His predecessor, Muhindi Munene, was a cruel, sadistic drunkard who made life hell for prisoners by dismissing all their complaints and requests. Munene was the first African police officer placed in charge of detainees in Kenya. That he turned out to be so cruel was a damn shame. The white police officer, Oswald, who Munene had succeeded as the Nairobi police chief, had resigned, partly due to pressure from students at the University of Nairobi, who had demonstrated against him. I thought he was a very bad man until I came to detention and heard that he had handled detainees in a much more civilized manner.

When Oswald went to pick up a detainee, he always gave him time to pack clothes and books, time to eat a last meal with his family and say good-bye to them. Before he came to see detainees in prison, he would first visit their families to be able to tell them how their families were. When a member of a detainee's family was sick and in the hospital, he took the detainee to hospital to visit. He never treated people as his personal enemies or went out of his way to treat them like animals. Unfortunately, when Muhindi Munene took over, he reversed the humane treatment that Oswald had put into place. Perhaps somewhat aware he was being inhuman to innocent people, he anesthetized himself against guilt by drinking heavily.

After signing my detention order, I was driven to Kamiti prison.

CHAPTER VIII

MOI DETAINS ME 1982–84

Sigh of Relief

Strange as it may sound, when I landed in the detention compound, I heaved a sigh of relief. The long nightmare of my life as a Kenyan MP had come to an end. Who would have guessed when I was released from detention in December 1978 that I would be entering a more dangerous world than the one I was departing, that in Parliament I would be less free than a detainee in prison?

Joseph Mathenge, one of the cruelest and most sadistic officers, welcomed me back to Kamiti, accompanied by the same prison wardens who had guarded me previously. Mathenge initiated me into detention life by ordering that I strip naked in front of the prison officers and wardens while he tapped my head with his officer's stick. I felt angry and provoked, but contained myself. As Mathenge humiliated me, I realized that one of the prison guards, Wacira Njuki, had tears in his eyes. He was bitter that I had been brought into detention again. And having become one of my supporters while I was in Parliament, another guard, Kihara Waweru, angrily asked me why I had come to detention again. I told him I had been brought, not come on my own. Then I changed into a *kunguru*, prison uniform, and made my bed on the bare floor without a mattress, pillow or bedsheets. I did my first exercise of two runs around the block, took a cold bath and received my supper of prison food. I was locked in the cell and settled into my second detention.

The West's Betrayal

That night I slept very little, thinking about my family and the coup. If everybody in the land were willing to stand up for freedom, would the government dare to detain us all? In the logic of the Cold War, African democrats had very few allies who would come to their rescue when trouble came. On the one hand, if socialist countries could support anything in Kenya, they would support socialism, not democracy. To achieve their goal, socialist countries did not support democratic government, but a one-party dictatorship or dictatorship of the proletariat. As they criticized African dictators for capitalism, they were their partners in creating dictatorships. For them, an ideal African society would have socialism under one-party dictatorship.

The West did not support democracy in Africa either. It promoted the rule of pro-Western dictators: Moi, Mobutu, Idi Amin, Kamuzu Banda and others. In Africa, the West and the East were partners in supporting dictatorship, the former to fight communism and the latter to fight capitalism. Of course, Western governments never stated this outright. I deduced this from experience, from what I saw. Later I would read about it in *Spy Catcher* by Peter Wright:

> The fundamental problem was how to remove the colonial power while ensuring that the local military forces [like the Mau Mau] did not fill the vacuum. How, in other words, can you create a stable local political class? The Colonial Office was well-versed in complicated, academic, democratic models—a constitution here, a parliament here—very few of which stood the remotest chance of working. After the Cyprus experience I wrote a paper and submitted it to Hollis, giving my views. I said that we ought to adopt the Bolshevik model (one party), since it was the only one to have worked successfully.[1]

How could the West, which fought against communism in the name of democracy, claim that constitutions and parliaments could not work in Africa? The West claimed to fight for democracy, but had no faith it could work in Africa. I could not help thinking that when it came to Africa and the rest of the world, the West put promotion and protection of its interests before democracy.

For Western countries, democracy seemed to mean the freedom to exploit Africa. So where the West was free to exploit, as in South Africa, Kenya, Congo and Malawi, there was "democracy," but where the West could not exploit there was "communism."

Western governments and media regarded and dismissed African democrats and social activists who opposed exploitation as communists and enemies. They associated and allied themselves with one-party dictatorships, apartheid, and detention with neither charge nor trial.

Having learnt of democracy in America, I felt betrayed by it when Pio Gama Pinto and J.M. Kariuki were assassinated and America said not a word. How could Western democracy be genuine if its only goal was to exploit and allow American companies to behave like rogue killers in Kenya?

In 1981, Kenyans were enraged when dogs of the American company Del Monte mauled a Kenyan girl to protect their pineapples from hungry Kenyans.

We do not see American Marines as global guardians of democracy. We imagined them all to resemble Frank Joseph Sundstrom and James William Tyson who in the early '80s raped and killed Monicah Njeri and Lucy Kabura. They were set free despite their admission of murder and the Kenyan attorney general's recognition that justice had not been served.

The West supported the coup against Kwame Nkrumah and the assassination of African democratic leaders like Patrice Lumumba, the first popularly elected African leader of the Congo. In a recent BBC television program called "Who Killed Lumumba," it was stated that the brutal torture and murder of Lumumba was approved by President Eisenhower, ordered by the Belgian government, and supported by the British "Security Service" MI5. His only crime was his refusal to be manipulated by western powers.

If America was the leader of the free world, why did it have one set of justice for Americans and another for other people? I knew what my father would have said to my query, The fart of the rich man has no odor, *uthuri wa gitonga ndunungaga*. But if America could not dispense equal justice to those it claimed to fight for, if it could indeed violate their human rights with impunity, was I not in detention because our leaders had copied the American example? There was no way I could see Kenya merely as Western progeny. Democracy in Africa was both a political and an economic imperative. On both counts, it had to encompass a government of the people, by the people and for the people.

Both East and West had abandoned me in my cell.

Rescue

Images of my wife and child in the rain and cold for lack of rent began to haunt my every thought. I had faith in Nduta's ability but a system that could throw an innocent people's representative into prison could also starve his wife and child to death.

After my detention, my brother Kuria was also arrested and Jogoo Commercial College, where we both worked, was closed down for a month. My brother had gone to a compulsory demonstration against the coup when John Mbure (who had tried to bribe me with suits earlier) taunted him, Kuria, you tried to overthrow the government and failed! This was a capital charge and his remark made Kuria furious. He replied in kind, Was it your mother's government we were trying to overthrow?

At that, Kuria was arrested and transported to our house in handcuffs. He and my wife and brother were made to sit together in the living room without talking. The police searched the house, shredded seat covers, stood on the bed with muddy shoes and tore the ceiling with knives. My books were thrown everywhere and their covers were torn off. After the search, Kuria was taken to prison and my family was even more isolated and vulnerable. Soon they could not pay the rent for the house.

When Kuria was released from detention, he found my wife a smaller house that she could afford with her meager resources. Father Lolar, my former teacher in the seminary, paid my wife a visit and offered her a job at a Catholic center in Nakuru. President Moi called Bishop Ndingi wa Nzeki to inquire why the church had given the wife of a subversive a job. The bishop said it was precisely because her husband was in detention, and that he would be more than willing to oblige the president as soon as I was set free. Thus my family and I survived because others fought for us.

Hilary Fischer of Amnesty International and Rona Alexander of Oxfam came from London to keep my lonely family company for nearly six months. Many members of our family and community were very generous with their support. This solidarity will not be forgotten.

You cannot imagine my relief and joy during my first visit. Expecting a barrage of problems, instead, my wife and Mum told me, Do not worry about us, we are well taken care of, we are managing all right. They could not dare say who was helping them because such persons would be descended upon and destroyed.

How sweet the words of Mother sounded when I asked her, Mum, I know I am innocent, but what do the people say?

They support you, she replied, before the police ordered her to stop. *Mama, we told you not to talk politics here.* They too knew that knowledge of people's support is sometimes all that a detainee needs to survive imprisonment. A dog does not drown when the shore is in sight, *mbwa hafi akiona ufuko.*

Just having my family out there waiting for me gave me great inspiration and the strength to survive. I wanted to live to see them again. On the other hand, I did not want my love and worry for them to kill me in prison. To survive, I made a very painful decision. I would not think and worry about my family's problems more than was necessary to keep my love for them alive. Worrying about outside problems in prison does not solve them. It creates more.

Unaware that further isolation could not possibly destroy me, authorities brought my civilian clothes and ordered me to dress after my two weeks at Kamiti prison. It was time to be transferred. Where am I being taken? We don't know, my captors lied. A detainee must never know where he is or where he is being taken. I was driven to Wilson Airport where I was put into a small police plane. Forty minutes later, we came to a sandy airstrip, where playing baboons had to scamper for us to land. I had no doubt this was Manyani prison (*manyani* means baboons), where the government hoped to destroy my body and spirit.

Baboons' Prison

As they led me from the plane to the detention block, my mind revived memories of everything I knew about this place. It was a prison in baboon country. This was the prison where Mau Mau detainees had sadly sung:

> Young man, when you arrive
> Greet my wife
> And my two children.
> I left two
> Now I hear they are four
> How could I have children from Manyani?

Other thoughts about this place quickly flooded my mind:

> This was Manyani prison
> Where white prison officers
> Had practiced shooting
> Over J.M.'s head.

> This was Manyani prison
> More cruel than Robben Island
> Where Mau Mau detainees
> Were worked and starved to death
> Breaking hard rocks.

> This was Manyani
> Where Mau Mau detainees
> Were castrated by
> African and white colonial screeners
> To kill their spirit of freedom and
> Stop them siring rebels like them.

> This was Manyani prison
> Where hundreds were released toothless
> Because colonial torturers
> Had broken their teeth and jaws.

> This was Manyani prison
> Where Mau Mau escapees

Never reached home
Because they were mauled
By the man-eaters of Tsavo.

This was Manyani prison
Guarded by lion man-eaters
That had eaten so many colonial rail builders,
Indian workers and white engineers
Threatening to stop the train of colonialism
Reaching Uganda from the Kenyan coast.

Could the lion man-eaters of Tsavo
Stop the train of freedom
By consigning and killing
Detained architects of freedom?

As I was led into my cell, I thought to myself, Yes, I have survived Kamiti, will I survive the desert hell of Manyani?

As soon as the top prison officers departed, a corporal called Mwangi tiptoed over and whispered to a scared me, Take heart. You are not alone. We support you. Later, another guard, Mwema, noticed my fear and offered comfort: "We are in this prison with you. We spend all our time here. Our houses are not better than your cell. Many of us live without our families, just like you. We bear the same desert heat and eat the same food. We have survived this detention for many years and so can you."

Here, Corporal Wambua was in charge of enforcing total solitary confinement and did so with great vigor and enthusiasm. His greatest ambition was to appear in the newspaper as a government hero. In this perverted craving, I feared Wambua might do what I had heard another prison guard ruminate over: Kill a hero, become a hero. He even seemed to pray for my escape so he could recapture me. For now, the corporal made sure that no warden talked to me. I had to write on sand to communicate with friendly guards, particularly one named Jonathan. On one occasion I was given the entire results of the 1983 elections through sand writing.

Without human company, I was forced to seek the company of baboons, cats and spiders. In the dry season when there was little food in the wild, baboons would wander into the compound and I would cultivate their company by sharing what little I had with them. They quickly learnt the exact times I was fed and would appear for both lunch and supper. When Wambua discovered this, he reduced my rations so that I had nothing left to offer. Only when I complained that I was being starved were the normal portions restored. The corporal then made sure he came to work with stones and sticks so when my animal friends appeared on the prison fences, they were bombarded and driven away.

Wambua was furious when he discovered that I still enjoyed the company of four beautiful cats who came to share my food. My portion of meat was so small that I would shred it into tiny long pieces, which I would savor slowly. Soon I realized there was a price to pay for the benefit of companionship. When I was eating the rest of the meal, the cats just sat around disinterested. They became alert when I began consuming the small piece of meat. As I chewed the first few long strings, they just looked on. Coming to the next, they would crane their heads closer, mouths watering. When I took another piece, they raised their forefeet halfway. When I reached the last morsel, their patience expired and they would pounce and grab it, sometimes cutting me with their sharp claws. By and by, they made it clear that for company and peace, we had to share. We did so until they were chased away by Corporal Wambua, but not before they reminded me of the importance of sharing in life.

To sleep and build up an appetite for the ugly and distasteful food, I woke early, rolled up the sleeping mat and ran hard, standing in my cell. When the sugarless porridge was brought, I would be dying with thirst and drink it with gusto, more to soothe my parched throat than to enjoy breakfast. In addition to building an appetite, strenuous exercise brought sleep and rest at night. Sleep was one thing Wambua could not deny me.

However, in the rainy season, Manyani had more insects than any place I knew. But prison authorities did not allow a mosquito net or wire mesh, which would keep insects out. The guards kept the cells brightly lit at night, attracting insects, which swarmed during the rainy season. The worst of them were mosquitoes. Mosquitoes gave us malaria and officials denied treatment. Whenever someone fell sick, it always took three months for the doctor to come from Nairobi. Medicine took another two months to arrive.

Then there were tiny insects that got into our ears and hippopotamus beetles that flew like missiles and dug into our sides with their horns, like attacking hippos. The most frightening were deer-shaped flying insects that we called "police" because of their dark blue color and the toxicity of their acid. There was absolutely no way I could sleep after police had flown into my cell. I had to kill them before I dared try to sleep. When they landed on a naked part of the body, as long as one remained still, they would walk and go their way without inflicting any harm. If the victim moved however slightly, they would secrete a highly corrosive acid that dug deep gouges into the skin. I was truly scared of Manyani police when I saw a prison guard who could not walk because of lesions to his thighs and groin.

I shared the big detention block with Stephen Mureithi, a former deputy director of the Criminal Investigation Department of the Kenyan police and a business partner of President Moi, who had been detained for challenging his dismissal. He suffered from high blood pressure and wardens told me that Moi had forced him to sign away his part of their joint business in the hope of getting an early release.

Despite every effort I made to psychologically escape from Manyani, it was a most depressing place. For a break I would sometimes stand on the tank of the toilet and watch cars passing on the Nairobi-Mombasa road through the window. In the evening, I would strain to catch the voices of the playing and crying children who lived in the prison with their parents. To my great surprise, the sound of crying children was music to my ears, reminding me of youth and of our child.

Manyani became almost unbearable because they allowed only one book— the Bible. After boycotting it for almost a year, I gave in. For the next two years, I read the Bible both in English and Kiswahili so many times that I understood it much more thoroughly than I had in the seminary. I even tried to use it to convey ideas to my wife that I could not otherwise communicate without being censored. I cited Biblical verses to explain the condition of my captivity: "He has shut me in a prison of misery and anguish. He has bound me in chains; I am a prisoner with no hope of escape. I cry aloud for help, but he refuses to listen." (Lamentations 3:1-15) I used it to explain that I was in prison because of bad leadership and lack of justice. "Evil men live among my people… That is why they are powerful and rich, why they are fat and well fed. There is no limit to their evil deeds. They do not give orphans their rights or show justice to the oppressed." (Jeremiah 5:26–28) And "Justice is driven away, and right cannot come near. Truth stumbles in the public square, and honesty finds no place there. There is so little honesty that anyone who stops doing evil makes himself a prey." (Isaiah 59:14–15) I cursed my jailers with the Bible. "May those who try to kill me be defeated and disgraced! May those who plot against me be turned back and confused! May they be like straw blown by the wind!" (Psalms 35:23–28) I used it to express my hope that there would be justice in Kenya some day. "Our enemies are doomed! They have robbed and betrayed, although no one has robbed them or betrayed them. But their time to rob and betray will end…" (Isaiah 33:1)

My wife did not read these quotes because my letters were never passed on. The Bible had been added to the prison's list of subversive literature.

A Massacre of Prisoners

The massacre started with grains of sand in maize flour. The first time *ugali* with sand came, I tried to eat and did not complain, thinking its presence a mere accident. The following day, the same meal was served. Now I complained and refused to eat. It continued coming and I continued to complain. Finally, I was given more potatoes instead of *ugali*. When I asked why they were not cooking with clean maize flour, I was told it was because flour with sand could not simply be thrown away. It had to be eaten because there was no money to replace it. On the other side of the fence, in the compounds of ordinary criminals, without my knowledge, complaints against *ugali* with sand had been growing and would soon culminate in the prisoners' refusal to eat, with terrible consequences.

The night of May 31, 1984 was among my worst in prison. I did not sleep from worrying about the possibility of release on the first of June, which was a public holiday. During the day, I had heard names of prisoners who might be released being called out and this had given me the hope that I too might be set free. Dawn found me awake, red eyes wide-open and terribly tired. I simply could not sleep. At about seven, I heard names of those who would be released being called out. I strained my ears for any sign of my own pardon, but there was none.

That morning they were late in opening the cell to allow me to go to the toilet. Suddenly I heard a loud gunshot, then another and another, and I began to count 4, 5, 6, 7, 8, 9, 10, 11. There was a lot of screaming, wailing and shouting, "Stop or I will shoot!" "Go there, all of you!" "Line up, *Kaba!*" "Lie down! Lie down!" "Squat in line! Squat in line! *Kabeni, Kabeni!*"

In compound 14, next to the detention block, I heard a prisoner crying in great pain. A prison officer shouted, Death is what those who bring politics to prison get! If you refuse to obey orders to eat, we cannot just sit by and watch. We do what we must. Wake up! Move there! If you are hurt, it is your own fault. Blame politics, not prisons. *Ingia,* move in. Without politics, those who have died would not have to die!

An *askari* opened my cell and I asked, What is going on?

Nothing!

I heard shooting.

Yes, of elephants that had strayed onto the prison farm.

The shooting and shouting did not come from the farm. It came from the kitchen area.

They are stupid! It is their fault!

Who is stupid?

Prisoners who refused to drink porridge.

Why did they refuse?

They said it had sand, but this is prison.

So what happened?

Each bullet shot you heard took away a life.

You mean 11 prisoners were killed?

Yes, it was their fault!

My stay in Manyani ended with the slaughter of 11 souls. It was smaller than the massacre that had taken place at Naivasha prison. A prisoner there named Kairu, driven insane by the brutality of guards, reacted to the beating of another prisoner by bashing an *askari* on the head with a hammer, chiseling out his brain and eating it. The guards at Naivasha organized a retaliatory raid, slaughtering tens of prisoners.

The Manyani massacre was not reported in the Kenyan press and there was no public or international reaction, as there had been about the Hola massacre in 1959, when colonial guards killed a similar number of prisoners.

Rights for Freedom

After the prisoners' massacre, I was taken to Shimo la Tewa (the home of the man-eating fish called *tewa*) prison to attend the Detainees Review Tribunal. By now at least two Kenyan lawyers, Gibson Kamau Kuria and Kiraitu Murungi, had enough courage to come and fight for our legal rights there. The government was totally opposed to our representation and would later detain without charge lawyers Kuria, Mirugi Kariuki and John Khaminwa.

After meeting the most impotent and dishonest members of the legal profession, men who would come to the coast for a holiday under the guise of reviewing cases of detention, I was taken back to Kamiti Maximum Security Prison. Immediately, Philip Kilonzo, the security officer for detainees, visited me and made a most silly offer: Mr. Wamwere, I am shocked that you do not want to go home.

What do you mean? Did I bring myself here? I shot back.

You are not behaving like someone who wants to be free.

What should I do to show that I am in need of going home?

You should not involve lawyers in your detention. The government jailed you and only the government can grant release. Why can't you tell us that you want your freedom back instead of hiring lawyers? Do you have so much money to waste?

I talked with the government for two years and it did not listen. If I cannot be heard, maybe they can. I have a right to legal representation in the tribunal and they are my only link with the outside world.

Leave these lawyers or you will never go home!

I will not! What kind of freedom are you offering if it means losing the last and only right I have here?

You can hire all the lawyers you wish, but the government will never be forced to release you.

Mr. Kilonzo, freedom means the enjoyment of one's rights. Let me perish here rather than dig and lower myself into my own grave.

To my surprise, on December 12, 1984, Moi released us all.

Release

At the time of my arrest, we had no home. By the time I was released, my wife Nduta had built one for us. The house was such a sight to behold!

As I came out of the car, escorted by prison guards, I could hear children shouting, Wamwere come out, come out! *Uma, uma,* Your papa has come home! (*Uma uma* were likely the same Gikuyu words that British soldiers heard and used to misname the Kenya Land and Freedom Army *Mau Mau.*)

Nduta saw us from the window and came running like a most beautiful goddess. When we embraced, my whole body, mind and soul exploded in the electricity of love. Her long accumulating dam of tears burst forth. She cried and cried until I thought she would not stop. Gradually the river was dry. In the meantime, I took Wamwere into my arms. He had grown so big within the last two and half years.

CHAPTER IX

L I M B O   1 9 8 4 – 8 5

For most detainees, release from prison did not mean freedom, but entry into a world of lost jobs and opportunities, destroyed businesses, broken families, homelessness, starvation and begging.

When I refused to show gratitude for release, those in power struck back viciously and Nduta lost her job, leaving us starving and desperate. As I looked for work, some asked for a picture of President Moi together with me, as proof that I was rehabilitated. When I looked for a license to do business no one would provide one without the photograph. Without Moi's goodwill, I was dead.

Using the little money Nduta had been paid for the termination of her job to buy some chicks, we constructed a small nursery and raised the chicks for eggs. It was a hard job that kept us awake almost as if we had a newborn child. We had to wake in turns to feed the chicks and make sure they did not sleep on one another. Finally they grew up and we started selling the eggs, but it was not much money.

I applied to be a barley farmer with Kenya Breweries. With money from my brother Kuria and Ngugi Njuguna, a friend, we raised a deposit for the lease and began farming.

On October 16, 1985, our second son was born. Things had started to improve for us. When our son was born, I was away harvesting barley. When I returned, there was a greater harvest of love. Having named our first son after my father, we called our second son George Ragui. My father-in-law had come home. With the entry of both fathers into our immediate family, our two families were now enjoined as part of the same blood.

Farming was successful and it gave us freedom from need. But Moi had not authorized this and was soon asking, How is Koigi surviving alone? Convinced that my independent survival put the power of his presidency into doubt, it did not take long for him to put an end to it.

Maasai chiefs where I leased land were instructed to stop landowners from

renting to me. One chief even held a whip when I went to inquire why he was inter-
fering with my right to lease land there.

You cannot lease here anymore, he told me with his lips trembling.

When a by-election came in 1986, Mr. Mwai, who was in charge of Kenya
Breweries' barley office in Nakuru was summoned by Moi and accused of funding
my campaign. He explained that I was a barley farmer and they only paid me for
the crops that I had delivered to them. Moi pretended to understand, but called and
confronted them with the same accusation one week later. Again Mwai explained,
but was called two weeks later and accused of the same thing. Unable to bear the
pressure, he phoned and announced to me, You cannot be a farmer with us any
longer; it is too risky. I was cast back into the detention of hunger and uncertainty.

A Stolen Election

One night in March 1986, Francis Kimosop, who became MP for Nakuru North
after my detention, drove out of President Moi's Kabarak home. He stopped at a
Caltex petrol station in Nakuru town, bought a gallon of petrol and drove to his
Solai home. Inside the compound, he doused his clothes and the car. Locking
himself inside, he set the vehicle ablaze. Workers and family rushed to extinguish
the inferno, but Kimosop was badly scalded and died after a few days.

Many of us were afraid of being framed for murder. Fortunately, the rumor was
that Kimosop had left behind letters accusing President Moi of driving him to commit suicide. He said he had burnt himself because, due to false accusations, Moi had
refused to save him from his financial problems. He bequeathed the Nakuru North
seat to Ngugi Njoroge, but President Moi's sons had other ideas.

Since he had divorced his wife Lena, Moi's relations with her family had been
strained. Moi's children wanted reconciliation and asked the president to give the
parliamentary seat to their uncle Eric Bomett.

In the meantime, the people of Nakuru North asked me to stand for my former seat: Ngai wants you to have your seat back. It is why Kimosop died. As I
prepared to take the plunge into the election, I had little suspicion that the seat had
already been given by President Moi to Eric Bomett. The first inkling I had was
during a campaign meeting at Subukia. I asked people how many were willing to
vote for Eric Bomett. Not a single hand went up. When Bomett's turn to speak
came, he fumed, Whether you vote for me or not, boxes will be filled with votes
for me. Whether you vote for me or not, I will be your MP.

How could I believe this? The president's brother in law was telling people that
the election would be rigged. How could he dare? Maybe I had heard him wrong.

In the next meeting, at the Kabazi trading center, again I asked people who

were willing to vote for him to put up their hands. As in Subukia, nobody did
Bomett burst out again, You say I don't come from here. Do you think I could come
here without someone asking me to? Whether you vote for me or not, I will be the
new MP for Nakuru North.

Angry voters thundered back: *Mwizi, mwizi!* Thief, thief! How will you be our
MP without us voting for you?

Then we knew. Moi had sent Bomett to Nakuru North and would rig the
election.

The day before the voting, I was at a hotel in Nakuru near the DC's office. As
I took my tea, the hotel owner approached.

Do you think you will retake the seat?

Yes, I told him.

Laughing uncomfortably, he said, Maybe. Maybe not. Last night people in a
government Land Rover stopped here for food. When they returned to the vehicle, marked ballots fell from inside the car onto the road.

The pit of my stomach froze. The election was already rigged. To complete the
theft, my electoral agents were shut out of the polling booths for most of the day.
They could not witness when votes were stolen from me.

At Lower Solai, I found one presiding officer sitting at a table next to a window marking ballot papers for Bomett. When I asked him what he was doing, he
replied, Why punish the messenger? *mimi ni mtumwa?*

Will you stop marking those ballot papers? I asked him.

No, I will not. I am a civil servant and obey orders.

And he continued to steal votes before my very eyes.

My friend Mirugi did not even bother coming to the counting hall. It is no
use, he told me. They have already rigged it.

In the counting hall, we found ballot boxes that were brought from government offices without seals. Government clerks had spent all day stuffing them
with stolen ballots. Counting clerks showed us whole books of ballots with their
counterfoils intact. When we complained against the inclusion of stolen votes, a
DC ordered, Count them. Whoever is not happy can go to court. He knew courts
were there to confirm, not reverse the rigging.

As counting progressed, the counting hall and its vicinity were completely
surrounded by units of regular police, the paramilitary General Service Unit and
the Stock Theft Unit. They were dressed in battle camouflage and carried riot gear.
They were armed to the teeth with guns, truncheons, bayonets, whips and hoes,
and led police dogs. Moi had stolen the election and sent armed police to kill anybody who dared resist.

Thoroughly disgusted, I went home. Only my wife Nduta and *Tata* (aunt)
Fridah sat through the entire farcical exercise.

When Eric Bomett was declared the winner, many people shouted, We will never vote again. The elections are a big lie.

Later, all my agents and main campaigners were arrested and questioned by police. In addition, President Moi lashed out at my friend Mirugi, asking him to choose between politics and his legal practice. Worse, he told Mark Mwithaga, a chief supporter, *Nyamaza kabisa*, never open your mouth again.

The postelection campaign of terror culminated with a chilling warning to me from Kariuki Chotora, President Moi's butcher: In Parliament, you refused to eat. In detention, you refused to reform. Out of detention, you have refused to keep quiet. We will now crush you like a louse.

As I pondered this very serious threat to my life, I met a man in town who asked me, What shall we do now?

I wanted to tell him, We should get up and fight for our rights and freedom, but I did not. I was too scared.

At My Funeral

It was in the village, outside our old grass thatched home, next to the forest of blue gum trees. The sky was grayish, but it was neither warm nor cold. To the right of the house, near the middle of the compound, there was a ring of people —men, women and children—standing around a freshly dug grave. They seemed sad, yet were not wailing and screaming.

I could see Pap and Mum and while I knew the crowd, I recognized no faces. At the burial site there was a coffin in which my body lay. They hammered the cover shut and tried to lower it into the ground. It would not fit. It was brought up and my body was taken out of the casket. Pap and others took fresh measurements to make it small enough to fit into the pit.

I was dead and in the air just above the crowd watching my own funeral. I was not sad. I missed no one. I was not mourning. I was not happy. I was just observing, as if I had to be there to witness my own interment.

Forced Underground

Opposition parties, free and fair elections, were no more. We had come to the end of one road and the beginning of another.

Legend has it that when moles, *fuko,* went to live underground, it was because life was so unsafe above, with human beings and animals trying to kill them.

The best-known underground movement in 1986 was *Mwakenya,* which published a pamphlet called *Pambana,* Struggle, distributed at night. The next day police would descend like vultures, picking up whoever they found with the pamphlet or suspected of having delivered it. Whenever *Pambana* was published, it was a time of great terror because the police would follow me everywhere, certain I was the culprit.

I did not disagree with *Pambana,* but I did not distribute it. *Pambana* was not the only subversive publication. Many a night, I would be reading *Newsweek* or *Time* in my bedroom when I heard a car on the road; fearing it was Special Branch, I would jump out of bed to hide the copy of whatever I was reading. If they caught me with it, I would certainly be their visitor in the police station for an interrogation and they could always use what they confiscated from me to justify a future detention without charge or trial.

As Mwakenya continued to recruit and distribute *Pambana,* a fog of terror enveloped the whole country. I never joined Mwakenya because I didn't know who the leaders of the organization were. More importantly, I thought some of us were too closely watched to go underground without exposing the movement to the government agents who were following us.

Suddenly matters came to a head. The wife of one of the Kenyans who had gone underground had been watching her husband and his friends meet secretly in their house. Maybe she thought her husband should have been thinking more about the family and not the country. She attended church regularly and soon confessed to her pastor what she knew. The priest convinced her that what her husband was doing was evil and something that President Moi needed to know. He invited the wife to tell the president what she knew.

The following Sunday the wife told President Moi, who attended the same church, everything. After the confession, the pastor delivered a strong sermon. In this infamous lecture, the clergyman condemned those who had gone underground as communists and enemies of both God and state. He declared that the president had the moral, legal and divine authority to arrest, jail, detain and kill them. Those of us who heard this could not believe that a "man of God" could be so strong in his legitimization of terror.

Afterward, Moi talked to the churchgoers and reprimanded the police and intelligence agents for being asleep as underground opposition to his government was spreading everywhere. He bragged of uncovering a huge plot against his government.

Armed with the new information, police went berserk with the arrests and torture of those who were named in the confessions of the wife and all those who were suspected of being members of underground movements. The choices before us were stark: Resist openly and be destroyed, surrender, go underground and do what one could, or flee into exile.

During the struggle for independence, British colonialists sent rebellious African leaders into both internal exile, which was called detention, and into external exile in London. Had Kenyatta not gone into exile? Those who go, come back, *mathiaga ni macokaga.*

I consoled myself with one thought. I was going to Uganda, where African revolutionaries led by Yoweri Museveni had taken up arms and successfully driven a succession of terrible dictators like Milton Obote and Idi Amin out of power. Going to revolutionary Uganda held the same hope for us that filled Africans from colonial Africa who went to independent Ghana after 1957. If I followed in their footsteps, perhaps one day I would return home to free the land.

CHAPTER X

E X I L E 1 9 8 6 – 9 0

Flight

My cousin Reuben Ndung'u and I left Nakuru for Uganda on the sunny morning of July 10, 1986. We reckoned daylight was a better cover than darkness because the authorities wanted me dead and political police agents were everywhere at the Nakuru bus station.

My wife and Aunt Fridah came to see us off. To avoid attention, we shook hands casually without any display of emotion. As soon as we were in the bus, they melted into the crowd. As I watched Nduta disappear, I hummed a song:

> I have left my love
> Alone.
> I don't know the day I will come back,
> But my love,
> Doubt not
> I shall certainly return.

I wanted to be strong, but hot tears rolled down my face. I quickly wiped them away.

We arrived at the Kenyan border town of Malaba at nearly 4 P.M. and had a snack at a small hotel owned by someone that my cousin knew. When he realized who I was, he nearly jumped out of his skin. I feared he might betray us. Outside the hotel, armed border police mixed freely with traders and travelers who were crossing the border on foot in both directions. The hotel owner hired two locals to take our luggage across the border on bicycles, so that we could avoid the border post. Two other guides led us into Uganda on a path circumventing the post. Once on the Ugandan side, I felt an incredible mixture of freedom and foreboding.

The following day we traveled to Kampala, where my cousin Ben Allan Ng'ang'a received us at his friend James Namakajo's video shop on William Street. Later we met Kariuki Wang'ondu and Kamau Ng'ang'a, who were also appying for asylum. The shop was to be our headquarters for the next two months.

At our arrival, we applied for asylum under UN protection. When Kenyan security forces learnt of my presence in Uganda, they gave chase. For security purposes, the United Nations High Commission for Refugees moved us from our hotel in the center of Kampala to Seta Travelers Lodge on the outskirts of the city. As the Kenyan security forces' hunt for us intensified, to our great disappointment, Deputy Prime Minister Elijah Kategaya told us we had to leave Uganda. Uganda could not guarantee our safety.

These were interesting times to be in Uganda. My wife and Aunt Fridah risked arrest by Kenyan police to come and visit us there. In September 1986, Colonel Muammar Qaddafi of Libya and Captain Thomas Sankara of Burkina Faso visited the country. I felt privileged to see these champions of the African revolution.

Every day from the shop on William Street, I saw the National Resistance Army soldiers, who had liberated Uganda from dictatorship drive by in open lorries, singing songs that fired my heart:

> On the sixth of February,
> Nineteen eighty-one,
> Comrade Yoweri Museveni
> Started war.
>
> There were a few people
> With twenty-seven guns.
> They attacked the enemy at Kabamba,
> And the war started.
>
> When the war started
> Citizens helped.
> They joined hands with us
> And we beat the enemy…
>
> Why did the youth
> Go into the forest?
>
> They went into the forest
> To fight for your freedom.
> They went into the forest
> To protect properties of the people.
>
> They went into the forest
> To fight for democracy…

Moto wawaka, mamaee
Moto wawaka.

Fire burnt, mother,
Fire burnt.
Fire burnt in Kampala
And is still burning,
Burning, burning, burning.

Every time these songs were sung, James Namakajo would look at us and tease,
When will Kenyans sing songs of freedom again?

To Norway

Kariuki Wang'ondu and I left Uganda for Norway on September 16, 1986, and arrived in Oslo the following afternoon. From the air, the Norwegian capital looked so beautiful. Government officials met us at the airport and promised us that as refugees, we would enjoy the same rights as Norwegians as long as we followed the law.

After spending the first night in Oslo, we were taken to a place called Gjøvik. On our journey, our escort explained what a car was because he did not think Africans had seen one before: This is called a car in English. The space at the back here is the part that carries boxes and other luggage. It is called a boot in English.

I did not know how to say that I had seen and owned cars without offending our host. Later I realized that this ignorance gave rise to the prejudice and racism that would take away the equal rights we had just been promised at the airport.

At Gjøvik we were kept in a wooden cabin for four or five days waiting for our admission into the commune, which was being debated by municipal authorities. In the end, some journalists told us with some embarrassment that the council had decided not to let us stay because we were black. Officially, we were never given a reason.

This rejection was very painful. I felt disapproved of and cast out because I was black. We feared that all other local authorities in Norway might also reject us. What about the equal rights we had just been promised?

Soon I learnt that Norwegian racism does not acknowledge equal rights for black people or respect promises. It is a dog that bites without barking. Indeed, it smiles at you and even condemns racism. Because it does not howl, many think it is not there. Untouched by racism, the majority of whites deny it, refuse to fight it and even muzzle its victims. Most publicly condemn neo-Nazism but consider inequality and discrimination against black people natural and inevitable.

Only in Norway did I hear people insist that calling me *neger,* nigger, was all right because that was the only name they had for black people. When I went to a blood bank to offer blood, they would not take it—even for my own child if he were sick—because black and communist blood was infected with undetectable germs and viruses!

I saw an attempt to introduce separate schools for black children and witnessed many black flowers snipped at the bud in numerous Norwegian schools. Deeply imbedded in government and social institutions, racism in Norway does not blink when relegating black people to manual labor or promoting images of black victims of self-hate. In Norway, schoolbooks are still racist and the media routinely bombard people with racist stereotyping, myths and humor. Black people are accorded citizenship, never equality. They remain second-class citizens.

In the land of the Nobel Peace Prize, the blacker you are, the less you deserve, except the charity, aid and pity that make the white benefactors feel superior. When a black person walks in their streets, unless he or she is a visitor, many see a criminal, a liar, a pest, a drug trafficker, an AIDS carrier—anything but a fellow human being.

This country that had given Chief Albert Luthuli of South Africa and Martin Luther King, Jr. of America the Nobel Peace Prize for fighting against racism was the last place I expected to encounter the monster. Unfortunately, the descendants of the Vikings had sailed and flown far to slay the dragon of racism, while leaving it to roam and ravage freely in their own country.

Here, though, I would meet more than racism: I would be the beneficiary of a great generosity that would allow a break in diplomatic relations with Kenya for five years to save me from gallows. Here, I would continue to have a second home despite my being a constant gadfly. But I am running ahead. Back to my story.

We desperately wanted to stay in Oslo, where we could read Kenyan and African newspapers and meet NORAD (Norwegian Agency for International Development) employees and journalists who had been to Kenya. Fortunately, a few months later, I was accepted into the Oppegård commune nearby.

Family Held Hostage

Without my wife and children, I could not rest. After settling in at Oppegård, I applied for family reunion and asked Nduta to join me. She did not wish to come. While a visit was okay, coming to settle in Norway was not in her mind. She wanted to continue living at home in the African sun. Afraid of venturing into the unknown, she used every argument against mine. We could not live separately. In the end, I prevailed.

Nduta, my sister Wambui and the children were at Jomo Kenyatta Airport one hour early to check in and to clear the passport control. Wambui's papers were the first to be checked and cleared. She passed and waited for the others on the opposite side. Nduta's turn came and she gave her passport to the immigration officer. He looked at it, then at her a first, second and third time. Is there anything wrong? she asked.

Are you Mrs. Koigi?

Yes, I am.

Wait a minute, then. He telephoned another office and shortly thereafter, five men came and asked Nduta to leave the children and follow them. When she got to their office, they asked her to wait outside. She could hear them laughing and making telephone calls. The children started to cry. They informed her that she was not allowed to travel. Only the children could go. She told them that was impossible.

Go home, then.

Can I have my passport back? she asked.

Collect it from Nyayo House tomorrow morning.

The following day she went to speak with the immigration officers. They said, Why are you leaving your country, you fool?

To join my husband, she said.

You are very stupid. Do you think this government will ever let you escape the way your husband did, to join him in attacking us from Norway? Do you think we are fools, *unafikiri sisi wajinga*? Why is a young woman like you following a crazy man like Koigi? Get another man, marry and forget that fool to die in the cold of Norway. Do you know where you are taking your children?

Yes, we are going to Norway.

Norway, do you know where Norway is on the map? Is Norway your country? You will bring your children back here frozen.

I am going to join my husband and my children are going to join their father.

A father who leaves his wife and children behind and runs away? Ha, ha, ha. Woman, you can forget it. We will never let you travel.

All she could say was, Please give me back my passport.

You will never get your passport back, one of them spat.

Then give me the money I paid for it.

Forget it. All passports and money in this country belong to the Kenyan government. You will get nothing back. Now get out and go home. Get another man, marry and forget that traitor. Let him freeze in deep snow where he is. They laughed like hyenas as Nduta walked out in shame.

Soon, with the help of friends and family, she planned their escape into Tanzania. The eight hundred–kilometer journey was arduous, if not miraculous. In Dar es Salaam, they went to the Norwegian Embassy, where they were able to arrange the final leg of their voyage.

We were now reunited. Ironically, our next dream was to be back in Kenya and free.

CHAPTER XI

THEATER OF THE ABSURD 1985–89

Reign of Terror

On March 14, 1987, the *Washington Post* wrote of Kenya, "In the past twelve months sixty-six persons have been sentenced to prison on sedition charges; all sixty-six pleaded guilty as charged. At least one political detainee has died in police custody, apparently of injuries resulting from his confinement and from severe beatings."

While some of those arrested were members of Mwakenya, many others were not. They were all tortured into making false confessions that they had taken part in unlawful meetings and oaths. The government then used these declarations as propaganda against the underground in the same manner that British colonialists had attempted to demonize the Land and Freedom movement prior to independence.

The *Washington Post* continued, "Mr. Kimunya Kamana, the party secretary in the Rift Valley town of Nakuru, who has been on trial for sedition, described Mwakenya's forest meetings and oathing ceremonies; these are reminiscent of the Gikuyus' supposedly extinct Mau Mau movement, which helped Kenya win its independence."

I did not belong to Mwakenya, but had I remained in Kenya, likely I would have been arrested and tortured as a member. Many of my friends in Nakuru and Nairobi were arrested and tortured into falsely confessing that I had recruited them and administered the Mwakenya oath.

My friend Mirugi Kariuki was arrested in December 1986. The *Washington Post* wrote:

> He was reportedly kept for four to seven days in the cell without food or water whilst being prepared for the next session of interrogation and torture.
>
> During his confinement in the water room, Kariuki stated he had no choice but to drink the water in the cell, which was mixed with his urine and excreta.

In his interrogation, Kariuki said he was savagely beaten all over his body many times by more than eleven police interrogators; one officer stepped on his testicles as he lay down.

Mirugi came out with a punctured kidney that was operated on by American doctors who traveled to Kenya disguised as tourists. Others were also arrested and badly tortured. Danson Mahugu fainted and defecated on himself and Councillor Jamlich Miano was taken to court in a wheelchair. Worse was yet to come.

On February 6, 1987, one of my nonpolitical friends, Peter Njenga Karanja, was arrested on his way to the bank. He despised politics as a source of trouble and had advised me to quit. He did not vote or attend meetings. Once Karanja found me stranded on the road and gave me a lift back to town. As we drove he told me, Koigi, you better quit politics or your car will always run out of petrol.

I like politics, I countered.

How can you like politics when it doesn't help you to make money? I will never join politics because I don't want to be stranded on the road like you.

Karanja, nobody likes to be stranded.

What you choose is what you get.

I chose politics, not poverty.

When I heard he had been arrested as a member of Mwakenya, I knew he was framed. How could a man who did not believe in voting be arrested for underground politics? Because he had nothing to do with politics and Mwakenya, police must have thought of him as a most stubborn hardcore. Again, the *Washington Post* reported:

Twenty days after his arrest on Feb. 26, police brought Karanja into Ward sixteen of Kenyatta Hospital… He was wearing handcuffs and was put in a room guarded around the clock by armed police, according to hospital sources.

But Karanja was not going anywhere. The 43-year-old businessman, who relatives say was in robust health before his arrest, appeared to have been severely beaten. He died two days later.

According to expert sources at the autopsy: The feet, lower legs, thighs and arms were covered with septic ulcers. There was evidence of severe internal bleeding before death, and the tissue that holds the upper and lower intestine in position was torn. There was blood in the fluid found in the lungs.

Frustrated with his pleas of ignorance, police interrogators heated a rod of iron until it was red-hot and then pierced his knees and thighs from one end to the other with it. The pain Karanja suffered was so great that at the moment of his death he hallucinated, calling his torturers "friends."

The same day Karanja died in Kenyatta Hospital, police arrested lawyer Gibson Kamau Kuria for filing court complaints regarding torture and detention. He was acting for lawyers Mirugi Kariuki, Wanyiri Kihoro and former university lecturer Mukaru Ng'ang'a of the University of Nairobi. In the hands of a government gone mad, Kuria suffered the same fate as his clients. In an affadavit filed later from prison, he wrote:

> I was taken to Nairobi Area Provincial Police Station. I stayed in the Land Rover. I was taken in the same Land Rover and I was blindfolded. I was taken to a cell in the basement of Special Branch H/Q. I lived in that cell from 26.2.1987 until 6.3.1987…
>
> I was not physically tortured, but I was psychologically tortured. Mental torture took the form of being threatened with death, destruction of my professional life; being mocked; being called Solicitor-General or A.G. for Mwakenya; being called *wakili*, lawyer, and being asked to defend myself before them; being called a wild beast and a fool…
>
> During interrogation, I was sometimes asked to remove all my clothes, including my underwear and asked to do exercises, which were very tiresome. I protested and said I wanted to see my advocates, but they refused. On 27.2.1987 I was told to say my last prayer. I would be killed the next day. I said the prayers. The following day I told them I was ready to die. On 1.3.1987, I was given an ultimatum. One, agree never to act for certain unpopular clients. Two, accept that I was a member of Mwakenya. They took it that since I was acting for members of Mwakenya, I was a member of Mwakenya too.
>
> During the interrogation I was told that my visit together with my wife and my daughter to Koigi wa Wamwere's family in January 1985 was my first meeting of Mwakenya. The visit by me, Mr. Ringera and my wife and children to Mr. Mirugi Kariuki was my second meeting of Mwakenya. I denied the allegation and told them that I was prepared to call both my wife and Mr. Ringera to give evidence on these alleged meetings. I told the Tribunal, that with regard to the first meeting of the first detained persons, I represented Willy Mutunga, Wachira Kamonji, Koigi wa Wamwere, Dr. Oyugi and George Anyona, who were released on 12.12.84, only Koigi remembered to thank me and my firm.
>
> I further explained that I was tempted to turn down Koigi's invitation, until it appeared as if it would be slighting Koigi. I explained that I had not been to his place and that he collected my wife and me from Midland

Hotel. At his house I met Koigi, his wife, his child, his brother and some people who were helping in slaughtering the goat. After our arrival Koigi's father and mother arrived. Sometime later, Mirugi Kariuki, who was a friend of Koigi arrived. Later a former editor of *Viva* [magazine], Salim Lone, came. I explained that no political discussion took place and we were merely eating meat and other types of food. Between 7:00 and 8:00 P.M. the visitors and those who were preparing the food left. My wife, daughter and I slept at Koigi's house and left the following morning. The Special Branch told me that they know of this visit…

I was interrogated about Koigi wa Wamwere, although his name does not appear in the detention order. I told the interrogators that I had learnt that Koigi had fled the country from the local press. I told them that one Saturday in January 1987, after his name had been mentioned in court in connection with a Mwakenya case, he attempted to talk to me on the telephone. I greeted him and told him that I was not willing to engage in any discussion with him. If the Special Branch recorded the conversation, the transcript should show that what I say is true.

I was not a member of Mwakenya. I belonged to Kenya Patriotic Front, an organization whose clarion call was taken straight from the Bible:

Remove the chains of oppression,
Break the yoke of injustice,
Let the oppressed go free.

While in Kenya I belonged to Moi's party, KANU, because there was no other. On March 26, 1987, I wrote to the national organizing secretary of KANU to announce my resignation: "After much thought and heart-searching, I have decided to write this letter and tender my resignation from the so-called life membership of KANU…My conscience demands that I resign now, because to remain a member is to aid and abet dictatorship."

Upon my resignation, I joined KPF. To the government, this meant that whoever I met was also a member of KPF, to be arrested and destroyed.

For the false allegation that they met me in Tanzania, Gibson Maina Kimani, his brother Milton Chege and my cousin Koigi wa Kariuki were jailed for seven years each. Of the three who had escorted my family to Tanzania, only Njoroge Murimi escaped this dragnet. In 1988, Kimani wa Nyoike came to see me in Oslo. Upon his return, he was jailed for twenty-four months. I never met Andrew Kibathi Muigai, a nephew of Jomo Kenyatta, but in August 1988, he was jailed for meeting me. His real crimes were that he was a Mugikuyu, a nephew of Kenyatta and

did not openly express his support for Moi. As a result of all these arrests and jail-
ings, many Kenyans traveled abroad bound up in their own prisons of fear.

We ran into a Kenyan doctor visiting Oslo at a public holiday celebration.
She ran away from us. We followed her into the crowd. As we got close, she whispered to us in Gikuyu, Let us not be seen together. Give me your telephone number. I will call you before I return.

In tandem with the arrests of people who had met us, demonstrations were
organized all over the country to denounce Kenya's leading writer, Ngugi wa
Thiong'o, the former Nairobi mayor Andrew Ngumba and me. According to the
Weekly Review of November 11, 1988:

> The denunciation is largely uniform, with Mr. Andrew Ngumba pro-
> viding the easiest target as a mere "thief" who fled his Rural Urban Credit
> Finance Co. Ltd., which collapsed in 1984; Mr. Koigi wa Wamwere as the
> disgruntled lout who went into self-exile and set himself up as a dissi-
> dent leader after failing to regain the Nakuru North parliamentary seat
> in a 1986 by-election, and Prof. Ngugi wa Thiong'o as simply a confused
> ideologue of suspect political leanings.

In these demonstrations huge placards read: NGUMBA— MWIZI (THIEF),
KOIGI — MJINGA (FOOL), NGUGI— WAZIMU (MADMAN).

By the time the *Weekly Review* of November 18 came out, screams for our
blood had gone a step further: "In Machakos District, local leaders led by the district's KANU branch chairman, Mr. Mulu Mutisya, used poisoned arrows to 'kill'
grotesque effigies of Messrs. Andrew Ngumba, Koigi Wamwere and Ngugi wa
Thiongo before dousing the 'corpses' in paraffin and setting them ablaze."

Unable to reach us, persecution was now extended to my parents: "Wamwere's
mother, Mrs. Monicah Wangu Wamwere, is facing eviction from a family plot. 'If
they have a war with Koigi, they should not victimize me,' she pleaded in an interview with the *East African Standard*'s reporters saying that the council had already
demolished her house at the Kabazi shopping center."

Mum was appealing to the same Moi government that had earlier evicted her
and her family from Rugongo forest, where, according to *The People* newspaper of
February 20–26 1994: "They were flushed out by the government in June, 1988,
as a result of her son's political activities which were constantly making local
KANU leaders, led by one of Moi's right-hand men, Councilor William Lasoi,
distressed."

The threats to evict Mum from her home were not idle. On April 6, 1989, the
Daily Nation reported that, "Maize worth more than 7,000 shillings was
destroyed when Nakuru Country Council askaris demolished a store belonging to

Mr. Koigi Wamwere's mother. Mrs. Wamwere said that early this year, her house, which had been built at a cost of eighty thousand shillings, was demolished by the same askaris on the grounds that it had been haphazardly put up."

Does all this remind you of apartheid in South Africa? Bishop Desmond Tutu, when visiting Kenya, said he knew black people in many independent African countries were subject to the same atrocities that had been suffered in South Africa.

Dreaming Treason

Our people say making war is not like drinking porridge, *mbaara ti ucuru*. I have never found pleasure in fighting for freedom and justice. It is painful but unavoidable.

Gathagu was walking on a Nakuru street when several policemen accosted him: Gathagu, you are under arrest.

Why, what have I done?

Come with us to the station. We shall tell you there.

At the police barracks, the interrogation continued: Gathagu, you had a dream. Let us hear it.

I have dreamt many dreams.

We mean the one where you became king of Kenya.

Sensing trouble, Gathagu said, It was just a dream.

We know, just tell it.

I saw a big crowd of Kenyans. They were looking for a king. They came and asked me if I wanted to be king. In the dream I did not feel free to say no. So I said yes. I was put on a chair and carried to a big stadium. Once there, some men and women of religion came, poured holy oil on my forehead, placed a golden crown on my head and made me king.

Very funny! said the police interrogator sarcastically. From what churches did the religious kingmakers come?

Their churches were not identified. They were just churches.

Do you remember the names of the high priests, the bishops and the popes who made you king?

No, I don't.

Dream king, do you know who is the real king of this country?

No, we have no king, only a president.

Say we had a king in this country, who would be him?

President Moi, I suppose.

You know then who is the king of this country, don't you? Can you tell us where he was when you became king?

I have told you. I did not see him in my dream.

Was he dead?

I don't know. I did not see him.

At that, someone gave Gathagu a hard slap on the face: Stupid, do you think you are talking to fools? Admit that you had overthrown and killed the president when you became king.

I did not see him in my dream.

Chwaa! Another hard slap and blood oozed from Gathagu's mouth.

Why are you beating me? asked Gathagu.

You are a very dangerous criminal and subversive. Did you not hear Attorney General Njonjo say that it is treason to contemplate and imagine the death of the president?

I only dreamt I was king. Nowhere did I contemplate and imagine the death of the president.

Ha, how could you have been king without killing the president? Had you asked the president for permission to be king?

No, because I did not know that I would dream the dream. How could I ask the president for permission to dream?

Don't try to be clever with us. You are subversive and we are going to charge you with treason.

The poor man thought it was a joke. But the following day he was taken to court and charged with sedition.

Your Honor, the police prosecutor addressed the magistrate, we charge Gathagu with sedition. He contemplated the overthrow of President Moi when he dreamt of being the king of Kenya. We ask the court to give him a deterrent sentence that will warn other subversives against dreaming dangerous dreams.

The court obliged and jailed Gathagu for five years.

CHAPTER XII

THE HUNT 1987 – 90

No Dinner with a Dictator

When we arrived in Norway, few seemed to know anything was wrong with Kenya, the land of safaris, the Maasai, the Leakeys and African elephants. Slowly and painstakingly, we informed them that, however hospitable Moi was to tourists, he was a terrible dictator to his own people: a bully who ruined, killed, detained without charge or trial and exiled his opponents; a corrupt totalitarian who impoverished and fleeced his country to the bone; a tyrant who sent mothers to jail and their innocent children with them; a robbing autocrat on whose farms thousands of prisoners worked on empty stomachs without compensation; an unfeeling despot whose army had massacred at least forty thousand Somalis at Wagalla.

Despite this, in September 1987, Moi was scheduled to visit Norway for whatever legitimacy he could gain from the home of the Nobel Peace Prize. I was horrified. We opposed the visit as a dictatorship-legitimizing mission. Moi fought back.

To come to Norway, Moi's permanent secretary for foreign affairs, Bethuel Kiplagat, made demands on the Norwegian government through Sammy Korir, a Kenyan living in Oslo: Tell them the Norwegian press must stop criticizing Kenya's government. Tell them the media must stop insulting the president. Tell them Kenyan fugitives must not attack the Kenyan government from Norway. Norway protested Korir's backdoor diplomacy which sidestepped Kenya's ambassador in Stockholm merely because he was not from Moi's ethnic community. Embarrassed, Moi disowned Korir, who proved that he had been speaking for the Kenyan government by playing Kiplagat's tape-recorded instructions on Norwegian national television. Kenyan exiles hit back and rallied to criticize dictatorship and celebrate our right to call for an end to tyranny in Kenya.

While all this went on, the Norwegian government replied it had no power to either tell the press what to write or to stop them from criticizing anybody. As for Kenyan exiles, the Norwegian foreign minister said, they were free to speak as long as they did not break Norwegian law. Accustomed to muzzling the press and opponents, Moi did not understand the Norwegian government's hands-off policy and accused it of attacking or at least sanctioning criticism against Moi.

September drew near. Dictator Moi should not come to our country, said Norwegians in the streets to their press. I will not grant approval to a dictator by dining with him, said politicians, one by one, until Moi's dinner table was nearly empty. Left alone with Moi, it was time for the mayor of Oslo to call off the dinner and end the state visit: Oslo will not host a dinner for Moi when he visits Norway. The last straw was when the government said, We did not invite Moi to Norway. He invited himself!

In a big huff and to our great joy and relief, Moi bowed to the inevitable. He announced he would not be coming to Norway, Denmark and Sweden. Instead, he would only go to Finland, which was more welcoming to a dictator.

Jackals at the Door

The hunt had been growing bolder by the year. Visiting Scandinavia in February 1987, Environmental Minister Jeremiah Nyaga announced in Oslo, "It is better for Koigi to sit in a Kenyan prison than for him to face an uncertain future in Norway." A few months later, another minister, Foreign Affairs Minister Elijah Mwangale, revealed what the Kenyan government thought: "Wamwere is public enemy number one."

I was tempted to dismiss this as hot air until I read the *Daily Nation:* "The MP for Embakasi, Mr. David Mwenje, said Kenyans were willing to go to Norway and bring the dissidents back." These threats scared me, especially when I remembered the Kiswahili proverb: The fearful cow is the one that is slaughtered, *ng'ombe mwenye tume ndiye achinjwaye.*

Later in 1987, I was to attend the launching of Ukenya, an organization of exiles in London. At the last minute I had to cancel because, without documents, I could not travel. Later, Sammy Korir revealed to Norwegian National Television what the Moi dictatorship had asked of him years before: They wanted me to join Koigi on the same flight and then hijack the plane to Tanzania.

They asked you to hijack the flight?

Yes.

Who gave you this instruction?

Kiptanui, the comptroller of the State House.

What is he to the president?

His personal assistant.

Is he the nearest assistant to the president?

You can't go to the president without passing through him.

What happened when Koigi did not travel?

There was a new arrangement. Two men were to come and I would take them to his home. They would kidnap and drive off with him.

Did you execute the new arrangement?

No. When I met Koigi and his family, my conscience would not let me cooperate.

———————————

One evening in September 1988, I received a call: Is that Honorable Koigi?

Yes.

We never met, but my name is Bishop Byrum Makhoha, former chairman of NCCK (National Christian Council of Kenya). I am in Oslo to seek political asylum.

You are seeking asylum?

Yes. At home things are very bad. Can we meet?

Where?

I am at the Oslo railway station. The only place I know.

Half an hour later, I was with Bishop Byrum Makhoha. He was wearing a dark suit with a red bishop's collar; a tiny gold crucifix hung from his neck.

I brought my guest home and introduced him to my family. When we had food, he blessed it. His clothing was so thin, I gave him an overcoat. For two weeks, we met almost daily. In the meantime, I tried to persuade him to give an interview to the British Broadcasting Corporation.

I am afraid, he protested.

Of what? I asked.

If I talk now, it will be risky for my friends in the army. They are planning another coup.

You will not talk about that in the interview.

I know. But maybe I should consult them first.

Soon after, the bishop informed me he was ready. We called the BBC and he gave two interviews over the telephone, one in English and the other in Kiswahili.

The following evening, a BBC executive called and complained, Do you know Bishop Byrum Makhoha well?

We met a few days ago.

This is very bad! The real Bishop Byrum Makhoha has called us from Kenya, complaining that the interview we aired on our Kiswahili service is a fraud. Luckily, we have not aired the English interview. I smelt a rat because the English of your bishop is not as good as that of the Bishop Byrum Makhoha I know. Can we speak to your Bishop?

He is not here.

Where is he?

I gave them the Tanum Red Cross Asylum Center's telephone number. The next morning, they found the so-called bishop in my home.

Did you say you are Bishop Byrum Makhoha?

Yes, I am.

The real Bishop Makhoha called from Kenya and said that you are a liar.

I am not a liar.

You are not a bishop, are you?

Yes, I am.

From which theological college did you graduate?

I went to a primary school called—

We did not ask about your primary school. What theological college did you attend?

What do you mean?

Can you name five books of the Bible?

What books?

And it only got worse. The imposter gave another interview to confess and apologize for the false interviews.

When the BBC had finished, Sammy Korir asked, If you are not a bishop, who are you?

I am an agent sent to kidnap you. I was to be paid three million Kenyan shillings if I succeeded. I traveled through London, where I worked with a white man called Tony Ward, following Kenyan dissidents who are based there.

Suppose you are lying again, how can we verify this story?

He knelt and pleaded, If you promise not to turn me over to the Norwegian police, I can prove the truth of what I am saying by revealing my contacts in the Kenyan government.

Who are they?

He removed a notebook from his pocket. In it were the home and office telephone numbers and addresses of Major Boinet, President Moi's aide-de-camp; Mr. Sembeiyo—deputy commissioner of police and head of the presidential bodyguards; and Mr. Serem, the provincial police officer in charge of the Coast Province. Others in the notebook, listed by first name only, were Njeru of the Special Branch and Kimereng, whom the false bishop had named as the man bankrolling all the agents.

After the imposter had confessed, I asked whether he was willing to tell his story to the police. He agreed, but was afraid they might torture him. Officers came and took him away.

A week later I visited London. An officer from Scotland Yard met me at the hotel and asked that I be careful while in England. We have information that you are on Moi's hit list and we don't want political blood on our streets. He gave me telephone numbers to call if I met suspicious characters and showed me how to vary my appearance. Despite all these precautions, however, when I returned to the hotel one evening I found this written message: "I came round to see you, but you were not in. Your friend, Clarence Ward." Ward, Ward, Ward! Was this man the same Tony Ward the false bishop had mentioned, I wondered.

The most serious attempt to capture me was undertaken by Kibily Tall. The plot was hatched at a meeting in Nairobi in May 1988, which was attended by Njoroge Mungai and David Mwenje, two Gikuyu supporters of President Moi. Tall met these two again to get more information about an African National Congress meeting that was to take place in Norway and which he had plans to disrupt as a decoy.

The plan was that they would travel to Norway by train and meet two Kenyan Somalis. Tall only knew that two Africans would fetch them from the station upon arrival in Oslo. It was up to him to identify these contacts. At the train station, he talked to the wrong person and was consequently arrested. He was carrying a G-3 automatic machine gun with hundreds of rounds of ammunition.

I had a chance to meet Tall and see his gun, bullets and protective vest just before Sammy Korir had the following tape-recorded conversation with him in Kiswahili at the police station: Who sent you here?

I work for the Kenyan government. I met some people in Denmark who gave me a gun and ammunition to bring to Norway.

Who gave you the gun?

A European companion who was arrested in Sweden.

What was the weapon for?

In Norway there is a Kenyan called Koigi. This is the man we were to kill.

Why?

Mr. Koigi and other dissidents are wanted by the Kenyan government.

There was a short trial in Oslo and Tall was convicted for illegal possession of arms. He was deported to France.

A Doubtful Hero

My last encounter with a Kenyan politician in Oslo was with the late Dr. Robert Ouko, then minister for foreign affairs. He stormed into town in 1989 like an angry, violent hurricane, threatening destruction and death to all those who criticized Kenya's human rights record. He vehemently defended the regime's termination of judges' constitutional security of tenure, arguing that giving the president powers to hire and fire judges would not in any way affect the cause of justice.

He argued that the only people who criticized the country were those who were jealous of what he called "Kenya's spectacular record of development." Dr. Ouko was completely unabashed while telling Norwegians that Kenya had developed twenty-five times more than it was in 1963. Why then was the foreign minister in Oslo begging for aid?

Taking advantage of a Norwegian journalist's inability to distinguish between political detainees and political prisoners, Dr. Ouko told the press that Kenya no longer had any political prisoners. In truth, Moi had not released a single political prisoner in any amnesty, up to that day. Dr. Ouko denied that torture existed in Kenyan police cells and jails.

Asked about my book *People's Representative and the Tyrants: Independence Without Freedom,* Dr. Ouko argued like Mwangale before him that I was writing untruths because I needed to justify my continued use of Norwegian taxpayers' money. Moi's supporters, in both Norway and in Kenya, were overjoyed with Dr. Ouko's press conference. It was shown three times on Kenyan television.

In January 1990, the foreign minister accompanied President Moi on a controversial visit to Washington. Shortly after their return to Kenya, Robert Ouko was found dead and burnt, his hands broken and his head shot through. It is the bitterest irony that barely four months after denying the existence of murderous forces in Kenya, Ouko himself was brutally murdered. Without permitting conclusive investigations, the government claimed Ouko committed suicide.

In the years since, Kenya's political hatred for Moi has transformed Ouko from a faithful and eloquent defender of dictatorship into a great hero, who, it is claimed, was killed because he fought corruption.

Kidnapped

To become a man and win a bride, a Maasai warrior initiate, *moran,* must approach, wrestle and kill a lion. If he fails, he must try again and again. Short of success, danger and imminent death are no deterrent. Equally, when dictatorship stands between the maiden of freedom and a freedom fighter, he too must, as often as necessary, do battle.

In September 1990, I traveled to Uganda accompanied by a friend to meet my cousin Kuria wa Kariuki at the border town of Busia. During the afternoon, we were having a drink at a table in the open when I noticed a group of men and women who looked like Kenyans throwing sly looks at me. I asked my friend who they were. He said they might be Kenyan border security agents. Immediately I left and returned to my room. That night, I was lying on my bed reading when the key in the door turned.

In an instant, the door was thrown open and five hooded men pounced. I tried to kick and push, but they were too many and overpowered me in seconds. I was pinned down on the bed and blindfolded with a thick opaque cloth. An adhesive tape laced with powerful chemicals was forced over my mouth. In seconds, I was unconscious.

When I came to, I was naked on the filthy floor of a cell. A man towered over me. Welcome home, Mr. Wamwere, he said.

My head felt heavy with sleep. The last thing I vaguely remembered was having my hands and feet bound with ropes. I was awake, but very sluggish and groggy. The man bore a triumphant smile and asked if I cared for a cup of Kenyan tea.

My captor gave me a mug and taunted, Mr. Wamwere, I am surprised that you are not dead. You will live to be a hundred.

It was not my day to die, I replied weakly.

He left with the mug, shutting the door of the cell behind him. Alone again, I wondered, Why did they not kill me?

Nyayo House

The cell was completely dark. When the door opened, a little light came in and revealed four walls painted black. Only one white button stood on the wall near the door. The cell had a thin layer of dust that smelt foul. I felt hard crusts on the floor that turned out to be dry human excreta. In one corner near the ceiling there was a glass-covered light that was never lit. Nearby, a powerful fan blew both cold and hot air alternatively. When it was blowing cold, the cell was like a deep freezer. When it blew hot air, it was like an oven.

After a time, which is difficult to measure in the dark, the first captor returned accompanied by two others, one carrying a machine gun. They handcuffed me. I protested, but the man only laughed, stepped out and slammed the steel door shut. I leaned against the wall and slowly slid down to the floor. With my hands bound, I could only sit, but never lie down on the floor. The fan began to blow cold air, my whole body shivered and my teeth chattered uncontrollably. I slid up the wall on my back, got to my feet and pressed the white button with my chin. I heard a buzzer ring in some distant room, yet no one came.

Deprived of access to a toilet, I could not resist the call of nature and was forced to relieve myself on the floor. All my life I never thought I could be reduced to this level of degradation. Like a cat, I had gone to the farthest corner of the cell and afterward used my feet to cover the waste with dust. I was very angry that these beasts had forced me to act like an animal without the most basic human rights.

Questioned

In the darkened cell there were no days—only one long night. When somebody finally came, I was too weak to talk or stand. I was forced to my feet, blindfolded and frog-marched out along the corridor into a lift that ascended many floors. I was then marched up and out onto an open roof into the wind and cold sunlight. It must have been the top floor of a very high building. From there, I was led back inside through a maze of corridors, in and out of rooms until I was finally forced onto a chair. Only then was the blindfold roughly removed. My eyes hurt in the raw light and I could not fully open them. This seemed to amuse those who were observing me.

I sat before five men, heavily built and wearing suits and ties. Behind the five stood another three men who carried heavy machine guns pointed at me like a firing squad. I was naked.

One of the men asked me whether I knew who they were.

No, I don't.

Do you know where you are?

No, I don't.

Do you know how you got here?

I was too weak to answer. They called a woman and asked her to bring me a cup of warm milk.

Have you eaten?

No, I have not.

They feigned surprise and said I should have been fed. When the milk arrived, the handcuffs were removed and I drank deeply. The inquisitors continued to ask questions about my alleged activities abroad. What I was doing in Uganda, and was I prepared to surrender, now that I was finally in their hands? Some called me a bitter man.

You were lucky to survive, but how much longer depends on you. Where are your guerillas? When did you meet President Museveni? How many men have you trained in Libya? How many guns has Museveni given you? When were you going to cross the border into Kenya and start your guerilla war? Were you planning to assassinate President Moi? Who would have been in your cabinet had you overthrown the president? Where are you hiding your AK-47s from Russia and Libya?

I told them all I had done in Europe, explained my political beliefs and why I was in Uganda when they abducted me. They did not like the answers, ordered the handcuffs and the blindfold to be slapped back on and I was roughly led back to my cage. I put my foot into the cell; it was a sea of water.

This is not my cell, I protested, pulling my foot out.

Get in! commanded the officer. Three of them shoved me into the flooded and filthy hole.

The cold water was up to my ankles and to my stomach when I sat. I was given no food. I could not sleep. The water was my bed and toilet. When I asked to be allowed out of this flooded torture chamber for clothes and food, they mocked me: We are giving you the best training for a guerilla fighter. Guerillas live in marshlands, they fight naked, they sleep in the rain, they go hungry for days and have no toilets. Here, we will turn you into a better Mau Mau than Museveni did.

I caught a cold, asked for a doctor and was given none. Living in my own sewage, and denied the ability to wash or brush my teeth, I stank like a skunk. My feet began to swell and I feared that my captors were planning to kill me before the world knew where I was. As my fear intensified, they brought my clothes. After dressing me, they handcuffed, blindfolded and led me up to the top floor where they had interrogated me previously. There I found two cameramen who snapped many pictures of me without my glasses. The photos were given to newspapers along with a fabricated story about how I was captured.

They claimed I had been traveling from Uganda in a bus, dressed like a Muslim woman with my head covered with a shawl, *buibui*. The government had cornered me at an estate in Nairobi. Two policemen said they had seen me at about 2 A.M. When they knocked at the door, I escaped through the rear into a backyard. I climbed a compound wall and tried to escape by jumping from one wall to another until I was completely surrounded. All the while, I carried a bag containing ten Russian AK-47s, ten Chinese hand grenades and several pistols on my back!

The police allegedly demanded, Come down or we will shoot.

I supposedly shouted back, How are you children of KANU? For how long will you KANU men trail me and the Kenya Patriotic Front? I am Koigi wa Wamwere. I belong to the Kenya Patriotic Front even if I am killed 100 times. KANU does not like me, but I will continue…

Finally, they claimed, I had come down meekly, put down my bag of weapons and offered my hands to be cuffed.

After another long period in the flooded cell, I was taken upstairs for interrogation. The inquisitors started by stating they had arrested my mother and would keep her for as long as I refused to confess. When I persisted, they said they would never release Mum. During the interrogation, I heard tortured women scream and they told me that the shrieks were from my mother and younger sister, Wambui. When I did not react, they continued, You think you are tough, don't you? We have also nabbed your brothers Geoffrey Kuria Kariuki and Charles Kuria Wamwere. We will destroy your family before you get us. We will not let you ruin our meal.

I could see them killing my mother the way they had tortured Peter Njenga Karanja to death. What is in a confession if it can save my dear Mum?

I continued to be interrogated and urged to surrender. The longer I stayed, the more I learnt about my interrogators. The one who always threatened me with death was Mureithi. He boasted that "they"—home guards—had castrated our fathers during the Mau Mau war and would now castrate their children and nothing would ever happen to them. Mureithi promised I would never be given a platform in court nor would I be taken to detention this time. If need be, he said, they would apply the final solution.

The one most senior interrogator was called Opiyo: I used to meet you in Parliament. You must surely know me.

At times, he would tell me that if I could afford their price they might sell my freedom back. I thought it was a bad joke. Later, I learnt that Opiyo had indeed sold release to my friend Kariuki wa Kiboi for fifteen thousand Kenyan shillings when he was at the point of death in Nyayo House.

Gideon Chelimo, a.k.a. Rono, boasted many times that the police in Nyayo House had powers to let the guilty go free and to order the courts to imprison the innocent who refused to cooperate. He was bitterly opposed to multiparty democracy in Kenya. He saw pluralism as a plot by the majority Gikuyu people to remove the Kalenjin from power, using what he called their luck of numbers, *bahati yao*. Even if the rest of the world went multiparty, Kenya would not. As for the Western demand that pluralist reforms precede economic aid, Rono was convinced that the U.S. and other powers would make noise for a while, but would shut up in the end.

During one interrogation, Mureithi stood up and challenged, Mr. Wamwere, you ran away from Kenya, but you are now here in our hands. Do you accept that we are stronger than you?

You have more force at your disposal, yet you are not politically stronger than I am.

How do you know that?

I know you are weak from your fear of opposition parties and free and fair elections.

Would you beat the ruling party in such an election?

Yes.

And in a war, would you beat us?

No, because I have neither an army nor guns.

Have you ever heard the phrase, "If you cannot beat them join them?"

Yes.

I will now give you my hand. If you shake it, it will mean you have agreed to join us and we will make peace here and now. We will drop everything against you, your family and friends. We will let you go home as a free man. Here, take my hand.

No, I will not take it, I said, after thinking for a while.

Then the war between us goes on. Handcuff him and take him to his cell. He loves it better than his home.

Hyenas Finish the Job

At home, about forty policemen stormed my parents' compound in the middle of the night of October 10. Even before my mother said a word, the commanding officer told her to take out the guns she was hiding. When she asked what guns, he charged like a wild animal and slapped her face. Other police ordered Pap and my sister to kneel down. The policemen ordered them to dig holes in the garden with their bare hands as they took photographs. They turned everything upside down. They treated my parents like animals. The brutal scene made Mum remember the colonial days.

After a long search, they found no guns. My mother was handcuffed and thrown into a car. They moved to Kuria's home to search. They had arrested him one month before and jailed him for four years. When they did not find guns in Kuria's home, they left for Kabazi center to search in the home of another brother, Njoroge. They found nothing.

Nevertheless, Mum, my brother and sister Wambui were locked up for three days. They were tortured and forced to sign papers. They tried to get Mum to admit that her son was a terrorist.

CHAPTER XIII

TREASON 1990 – 92

Charged

On the night of October 18, 1990, I was blindfolded, forced onto the floor of a Land Rover and taken to a police station where a superintendent of police read a statement to me in the presence of my chief interrogator, Rono. Beside them stood two young officers with machine guns. I was forced to sign a "statement under inquiry" and driven back to Nyayo House.

The following day, I was returned to the same office, where a chief inspector read aloud a "charge and cautionary statement." Menacingly, he demanded, Do you have anything to say? I kept quiet. My chief interrogator fabricated my reply.

In the afternoon, I was transported to Nairobi High Court in an armed convoy. From car to courtroom, two policemen lifted me by the back of my trousers, two more on the sides and one by my cuffed hands. I arrived together with Rumba Kinuthia, Mirugi Kariuki and Geoffrey Kuria Kariuki. We were all charged with treason, an offense which carried the death penalty—hanging. Later, James Gitau Mwara, Joseph Mwaura (Rumba's brother), Andrew Mureithi Ndirangu and Haron Thungu Wakaba were also charged and put together with us. We were called the Treasonous Eight.

In court I was pleasantly surprised to find Jeff Shamalla defending me; I did not expect anyone. He was retained by my family after many lawyers had declined. Also in attendance was the Norwegian ambassador to Kenya, Niels Dahl. I will never forget this gesture of support and solidarity.

Presidential Security

From the court we were driven to Kamiti prison guarded more heavily than the president. The security detail included more than twenty camouflaged GSU (General Service Unit) personnel with automatic rifles leading and following the prison vans in open Land Rovers. In the vans, each prisoner was handcuffed to a warden. Other prison vehicles were crammed with more officers carrying riot gear and heavy machine guns.

In an intimidating display of force, police motorcycles roared ahead to clear the road for the convoy. When we arrived behind the court building, our guards ran from the vehicles chanting tribal war cries—*wau wau* and *rururururururu*— competing to display the most intimidating ferocity. Their red eyes betrayed the heavy use of narcotics.

No one was allowed near the vehicle that carried us. Before our arrival the back of the High Court was cleared for a block. The entrance to the courtroom was heavily guarded and armed police in civilian clothes occupied most of the seats. Not wanting to die with us, most people kept a safe distance whenever we moved in and out of court.

The government pretended this show of force was necessary to stop us from escaping; to prevent Norway and our "guerrilla army" from snatching us and to ensure that we did not overthrow the government from within. Its real purpose was to intimidate us into surrender, to scare judges into submission, to cow the public and the Gikuyu community in particular from lending us sympathy.

We were held in block G, together with prisoners who were on death row. The implication was obvious. We were fed *ugali*, raw maize, and allowed no time out of our cells. We could not wash and were kept isolated. We could not see each other, except during mass.

At first, the government wanted us to have Mau Mau dreadlocks to convince the world that we were guerrilla fighters, and to strengthen their treason case. After several appearances in court, however, our dreadlocks became a symbol of defiance. Now the government wanted them gone. I made a public vow not to cut mine before the dictatorship was out of power.

Burn Him!

The day after we appeared in court, President Moi told Kenyans in a nationally broadcast address from Kasarani Sports Stadium, "I am surprised that Norway has protested over Koigi's arrest. Why protest when we arrest a criminal? I suppose that what he was planning was at the instigation of the Norwegian government. How can they talk about human rights when Wamwere and others were planning to kill Kenyans? Which democracy is this that involves weapons?"

As is usual in a nation of political sycophants, after the president had spoken, there was a competition to outdo him in condemning us, especially among Gikuyu politicians who feared that their silence might be misconstrued as connivance with our alleged armed rebellion. One of the worst cases was reported by the *Daily Nation*, "In Nakuru, the district Kanu women's leader, Mrs. Rahab Wanjiru Evans, called for the stoning to death or burning alive of the runaway politician [Koigi wa Wamwere] and his associates for their alleged heinous crimes against the country."

Closing the Norwegian Embassy

Days after our first appearance in court, I was taken to the toilet by two wardens who stayed outside. Once inside, I saw a piece of newspaper with the name torn off that one of the condemned prisoners had used. I read it.

> On Monday Kenya said it was breaking off diplomatic relations with Norway following an increasingly bitter dispute over the activities of Kenyan dissidents based there.
>
> A statement from the Kenyan foreign ministry accused Norway of being an accessory to illegal activities carried out by what it called fugitives.
>
> The foreign minister, Mr. Wilson Ndolo Ayah, gave the Norwegian embassy and all its workers, including 120 staff and experts and members of the aid agency NORAD seven days to close down and leave the country.
>
> The move by Kenya followed a dispute with Oslo over dissident politician Koigi wa Wamwere, who was charged with treason after mysteriously returning from exile in Norway.
>
> Norway protested to Kenya Thursday over the arrest of Wamwere, who was granted political refugee status and asked a United Nations human rights group to investigate his case.
>
> Kenya has angrily rejected accusations from exiled Kenyans in Norway that Wamwere was abducted and brought home by government agents.
>
> In the meantime Norway has urged Kenya to reverse a decision on Monday to cut diplomatic relations and denied Nairobi's allegations that it was supporting illegal anti-government activities by Kenyan exiles.
>
> "We have from our side no wish…to break relations with Kenya," Minister of Overseas Development Tom Vraalsen said.

Returning to the cell, I became very excited. By expelling Norway, the dictatorship had created a force which might help to tip the balance of international opinion in our favor. The situation was not as hopeless as it seemed. When I told the others, they shared this hope. In any case, Kenya's loss of Norwegian aid, twenty million dollars the previous year, could only weaken a corrupt government, which survives through stolen aid intended to feed the hungry.

Assumed Guilty

Having been condemned by the executive branch of government, it was now the turn of the judiciary. I have always believed that for justice to have a chance, our courts must enjoy complete independence from the executive branch. Judges must stand above politics. But this is not possible where members of the judiciary owe their positions to the president. Single-handedly he hires and fires them at will. Having appointed them, they run courts not to dispense justice, but to do his bidding.

When we appeared in court, some magistrates and judges appeared visibly scared, others hostile. I knew that none dared to be independent. Still, I respected one, unknown to me, who ruled against us, but did everything in his power to demonstrate neutrality by listening to our arguments without open negative reaction.

So when we argued or challenged the charges, it was never to win the hearts or minds of these "justices." I therefore tried to make my case with the public— the people and the world at large.

Prison Angels

One night when things got really grim and I feared we might be killed in prison, I had a chat with a friendly warden.

Without trial and conviction, they have kept us here on death row. Are they planning to kill us? Have you heard anything?

Do you feel you still have work to do in this world? he asked.

Hell yes!

Don't worry then, nobody will touch you, he offered calmly.

Maybe, I said, feeling better without believing.

It just felt like a good joke. Later I thought, maybe nobody will kill me if I refuse to die. Whenever death beckoned, I would simply say no. During Mass, Father Mbao told us to deny death's welcome: You may feel isolated here, but you are not alone. You have an ever-present companion in Jesus Christ. It must feel terrible that they have charged you with treason. But Jesus, too, was charged with treason because they believed he wanted to overthrow Caesar's government. They denied him a fair trial and tortured him to death, just as they are doing to you.

I could see the Gikuyu guards seemed slightly uncomfortable while the Kalenjin wardens became truly agitated. One even started to pace up and down the corridor. Though Father Mbao noticed their discomfort, he was not yet finished: When people ask you whether you moved this cup from here to there, think before you answer. If they want to hurt you with the truth, don't tell it to them. Share the truth only with those who wish to put it to good use. Those who wish to destroy life have no right knowing it.

By the time Father Mbao finished, the Kalenjin wardens were near rebellion. We did not see Father Mbao again for over six months. But he had given us a candle with which to light our way.

Gunfire Drama

When our lawyer Shamalla told me that the police had executed the key state witness in our case after he had killed four of the police, immediately I felt a sense of relief. Then I wept for this young man who should not have died. He, too, was a victim of tyranny and deserved life and freedom as much as we did.

Like me, Bernard Githinji Kiragu was from Engoshura. He was married, had a wife and child and was arrested in Nairobi. In October 1990, he was taken to Nyayo House, tortured, abused and threatened. When we were taken to court, he was not. Through torture and the promise of freedom he had been turned into a prosecuting witness. He signed false statements dictated by his captors saying he was a Libyan-trained guerrilla and a member of KPF who had returned to Kenya through Uganda to wage war.

The longer our trial went on, the more desperate Githinji became. By July, he had been in the torture chambers of Nyayo for nine months, longer than anyone else. On July 15, 1991, his torturers must have pushed his back to the wall, Mr. Githinji, we want you to be a witness in a robbery case that happened recently.

I am a key witness in the treason case.

We know, but that will take a while to start. We need you now.

When will I be free?

Freedom depends on your full cooperation.

We have already agreed on my cooperation in the treason case.

Here we set the rules. You must do whatever we ask or you will die here.

Perhaps realizing his true fate, Githinji's incredible endurance snapped. He leapt at his interrogator with all his fury, determined to break free. Wrestling a gun from the tormentor's hand, he shot him dead.

> Sources said the suspect had been in "protective" custody since Mr. Wamwere was charged in court with treason. At approximately 3 P.M. on Sunday he disarmed policemen guarding his cell in the basement of Nyayo House and allegedly grabbed a G-3 rifle, a Uzi sub-machine gun and three pistols.[1]

Hearing gunfire, other officers ran right into the room. A trained karate expert, Githinji knocked down two of his pursuers and blasted them, while a third escaped with serious injuries to the shoulder. A hail of bullets followed his retreat outside but missed, forcing all those who guarded his cell to flee. He concealed himself in another part of the building while searching for a way to escape captivity.

Shortly after, over two hundred officers, reinforced by General Service Unit personnel and scores of plainclothes police, besieged Nyayo House, trying to ferret him out. They kept vigil through the night as Nairobi fire brigade personnel joined in combing the twenty-six floors, one after the other. In the early hours of Monday morning, Githinji was shot dead while holding several of his interrogators and torturers hostage. The bullet that killed him also destroyed the government's case against us.

Lawyer Quits

By June 1992, we had been imprisoned for nearly two years when Lawyer Shamalla met with President Moi. Thereafter we could see that he was no longer interested in representing us. When the Koigi Support Committee and my wife asked whether my case was discussed, he became very agitated. I pursued the matter and he lied that the president had only mumbled something unintelligible.

In August, Nduta came to see me and the officer in charge of Kamiti prison allowed us a contact visit. I felt terrible in that prison uniform, but embracing my wife for the first time in two years was heaven. She came to court and was completely dissatisfied with Shamalla's representation. Paid better than the others, he did the least work. Nduta asked him to remove himself from the case and he took this escape route.

When Justice Omolo ruled that we should get a Queens' Counsel before the trial could proceed, we took this as a major legal victory. Not in the eyes of our lawyers G.B.M. Kariuki and Martha Karua, however. Upon congratulating them for their good work, their reply came as a thunderbolt: We do not want a Queens' Counsel. Why should we do all the work and surrender credit to a white lawyer when the case is nearly over?

Incredulous, we responded almost in unison: The trial has not even begun and a QC will bring more international attention and pressure the judge to do more justice than any local lawyer can. The West still thinks better of white opinion and we can use this prejudice to our advantage and save our lives.

Hen and Hawk

In our forest village, there was a hen we called *kahonokia,* the savior. Children and even grownups feared and admired it. When it had tiny chicks, no one could go near them because, to protect her chicks, the *kahonokia* would viciously attack anyone who approached.

My enduring memory of this hen was the many times when hawks would swoop down and capture one of the chicks. The hen would leap into the air, literally flying after and fighting the hawk until the predator let go. Some of the chicks would later die from injury, but most survived.

The hen was so much the darling of us children and the village that when it died of old age it was not slaughtered and eaten, it was buried. After many years, the memories of the *kahonokia* faded, until I saw another mother hen save her chicks from a human bird of prey.

My mother began a hunger strike in February 1992. She feared her sons might die in prison while there was something she could do to save them. She knew that I was innocent and had a lot of support. At the height of the demands for multi-party democracy, she saw no reason for her son to be in prison any longer, since that is what I had been fighting for.

When the Ford party was registered, Mum had a discussion with its interim leaders, pleading with them to demand my release and that of others. At first they agreed, but then they forgot about it. They were too busy sharing positions of power they had yet to win. They said if the government did not release me, it would be their first act when they came to power. What would happen if elections were rigged and they did not gain office? She could not rely on opposition leaders to rescue her children from prison.

She decided to stage a demonstration and embarked on a mission of petitioning for the release of political prisoners. In January 1992, my mother and others formed the Release Political Prisoners group (RPP). She met members of the Tent of the Living God and they agreed to support her in the fight. They were happy to hear that her group was planning to demonstrate against the oppressive government. Later, she was called to address a women's meeting in Nairobi. She asked, If I go into the wilderness and stay there without any food for as long as it would take to have my sons released, will you support me?

Yes! they shouted with one voice.

After the meeting, she met Professor Wangari Maathai and told her of her plan to stage a hunger strike at Uhuru Park. Many women were sympathetic and agreed to support the cause. They wrote a letter to Attorney General Amos Wako, demanding the release of fifty-two political prisoners and informing him of their intention to go on a hunger strike if we were not set free. He did not take them seriously.

Some other mothers of the accused accompanied Professor Maathai and Mum to the office of the attorney general. The mother of Mirugi Kariuki, Mum and Professor Maathai were allowed into the office. Inside, they gave him a letter to deliver to the president and told him their sons were not criminals, they were advocates of change. Since change had now come, they should be released. In the meantime, they informed him that they were going to Uhuru Park to stage a hunger strike, until he brought them answers.

All they took was water. After hearing the news, many people gathered there. They brought water, Bibles, hymn books and blankets to keep them warm. An Asian sympathizer donated a tent to shelter them from the scorching heat. He was later shot in the streets of Nairobi by police.

The mother of Rumba Kinuthia joined them at Uhuru Park. There was a very big poster reading FREEDOM CORNER. As days passed by, many people came with food, despite the fact that they were not eating. It was given to street children who stayed with them, but were not on the hunger strike. They sang and showed courage. They were determined to starve themselves to death if need be. My mother told me, We knew that what is right is mightier than the strongest weapon and received consolation in the fact that even if our bodies were physically brutalized, nobody, including the president, could dictate the destiny of our spirits.

Cursed with Nakedness

As they entered the fifth day of the hunger strike, the rays of the sun soothed their hungry bodies. All was calm. But the presence of armed anti-riot squads was an omen. Many people continued coming to see them, among them Augustine Njeru Gathangu, who was charged with sedition, but was out on bail. He moved the assembly to tears recounting the beastly conditions under which prisoners in Kenyan jails were kept. More riot men were brought in and tension mounted. They surrounded the area and denied access to visitors.

Reverend Njoya said afternoon prayers, and Mukaru Ng'ang'a successfully defied the police to join the mothers. When the reverend wanted to leave, officers stopped and asked him to order all the people in the tent to leave. They shouted, No way! We are ready to die here. When they dared the police commander to shoot them, he was at a loss and moved away to consult with other officers. In the meantime, the mothers asked everybody to come into the tent. Many did so and they held hands to show their solidarity in life and death.

It was now 4:00 P.M. The police commander and his three officers stood like statues at the tent entrance, studying which side to attack first. Professor Maathai seemed to be the main target. The first tear gas canister exploded against her head. The next was thrown at my mum. Pandemonium broke out. Everywhere people dove for cover, trampling the women like bags of maize. It was a scene from hell.

There was fresh blood everywhere in the tent. Quick action by sympathetic motorists saved the unconscious by rushing them to the hospital. Taxis came and helped those who were badly injured. An enraged man took a pail of water and splashed it in the face of a riot policeman who had hit him with the butt of the gun as he carried Professor Maathai to safety.

Completely desperate, the mothers resorted to their last weapon—female nakedness. They stripped naked to cast a curse upon the inhuman Moi and his policemen. The women threw their clothes at them and challenged them to a duel.

Whatever happened to the African sense of shame that a son could take a whip and beat his naked mother!

In Kenya's history, this was the second time women had damned their oppressors with their nakedness. When British colonialists detained the African leader Harry Thuku in 1922, Mary Nyanjiru, an enraged woman, took off her clothes to curse the British and challenged the Kenyan men to exchange their trousers with her skirt. The British gunned her down along with many others.

Soon the spreading battle had reached the city center. The mob pursued their attackers and the police hit back. At the Freedom Corner the tent was in ruins. Tension still reigned as most of the mothers refused to listen to any pleas to put on their clothes. The police stole their money.

But they would not leave. All their sympathizers were evicted except fourteen RPP members and Ngonya wa Gakonya, the leader of the Tent of the Living God. At 9:45 p.m., fifty policewomen in several vans came for them. They dragged and bundled them into vans. Curious journalists were beaten up and chased away from the scene to keep this forced eviction from the eyes of the nation and the world. My sister Jecintah Mwihaki, Mirugi Kariuki's mother and Mum were taken away in the same van. Ngonya was bundled into another van alone. A prison's Black Maria carried the fourteen RPP members to Embakasi Police Station; they continued their hunger strike until they were released two days later.

The next day our mothers and their supporters returned to Nairobi, dug their heels in the bunkers of All Saints Cathedral and resumed the protest. To the bitter disappointment of the government, the church grounds were crowded with supporters and journalists from all over the world. Like Jesus, the mothers had come back to life.

Mothers in Chains

In addition to being on a hunger strike, the mothers decided to yoke themselves with chains to make those of their sons more visible. To avoid being dispersed again they went to court manacled together to hear the ruling of their sons' application by Lady Justice Aluoch, Justice Gideon Mbito and Justice D.K.S. Aganyanya. The application was dismissed, and their sons were hustled into the court dungeons. The mothers shouted, We will walk the length and breadth of Kenya for our sons! Then tearfully, slowly and in chains they found their way out of court, into the streets and back to the bunkers of All Saints Cathedral, announcing to the whole world, "We will remain chained as long as our sons languish in prison. Colonialists put us in chains. Our leaders continue to put us in chains."

On April 1, they went to the State House in Nairobi but GSU men blocked their entry at the gate. The following day, police visited them at the All Saints

Cathedral. Looking in from the windows, the police pleaded with them to eat, but they said no. Only Njeri Kabeberi talked to the police. The police begged the bishops to ask the mothers to open the doors to the bunker, but they would not. The police finally gave up and left.

When their strike was not broken, people began to organize sympathy strikes in other towns. Some organized hunger walks from Nakuru to Nairobi. Some were successful, others were arrested.

Pressure was being applied on the protesters from all sides. Moi wanted them to go and kneel before him. A few did. Mum did not. She told the press that she could not go on begging and kneeling for her innocent sons. Moi was furious with her defiance.

Elections came and the government rigged them for Moi. Problems and worries began to set in. Opposition leaders could not now release us and Mum feared Moi would hang us. Still, she vowed not to go home and refused to visit the president.

One Sunday after church service, Kuria kicked on the door of the bunker and went in. Nobody believed they were seeing Kuria free after Mum had refused to see Moi. Yet it was true. He was free. The press asked her, "Are you now going home?"

"No, I will not go home before Koigi, Mirugi and Rumba are also free. The government has given me one of my precious stones. I want them all and I am ready to carry this cross till the day I get my other sons back."

After the elections Pap suffered a stroke in December. It came after learning that the government and KANU had rigged the election. He was living with grandchildren whom he loved greatly. Now, he feared he might never see his sons again. His worries worsened when the police spread word that when Kalenjin warriors perpetrating ethnic clashes attacked Engoshura, they would burn our house first. Given the bestiality of the dictatorship, there was no reason to disbelieve these rumors.

Two fires were now lit. Which one would my mother put out first? Her husband was sick at home and Koigi was still in prison. She decided to fight both. She sent Kuria home to be with his father and went on fighting.

We Too Go Home

Moi was still the bully who sits on another boy and will not get off before he is begged to do so. Our mothers wrote him another letter asking for our release. Two days later they were rushed to court. It was amusing to see prison officers competing to be the first to tell them that their sons were going to be released. The government entered a *nolle prosequi* and brought the treason case to an end. The mother hens had landed with their chicks bruised but alive.

We wanted to walk out of the prison gate and go to the cathedral to meet our mothers, but an official brought a comfortable Toyota Cruiser to drive us to Nakuru. We said no, we were free people and wanted to decide how we got home. The official was under pressure not to let us go to the cathedral in the daylight because the state feared a celebratory demonstration in Nairobi. So it was 8 P.M. when he finally opened the doors. It was dark and drizzling. As we passed through the outer gate onto the main road, we could hear singing in the distance. In the valley below, our people were waiting. Had we not been carrying luggage, we would have run, but we walked to our people and freedom.

CHAPTER XIV

REVISITING OLENGURUONE 1993

Aluta Continua (Struggle Continues)

We reached the happy souls waiting for us in the small valley—singing, dancing and laughing. They carried us upon their shoulders, hands raised up waving the V sign for victory. They whisked us to the cathedral for a long overdue reunion with our mothers. Celebrations lasted all night; we were singing and eating all the good food we had missed. That same night I spoke with Norwegian Television and thanked its government and people. I talked to my family and promised an early reunion.

Yes, from that day in June 1982 when Parliament extinguished the candle of pluralism to the morning we woke up at the cathedral, it had been a long, dark and dangerous night in which many had suffered and died. We did not awaken to the dawning of liberty but the chilly and foggy morning of pluralism without real freedom. Democracy meant more than a multiparty system. As long as dictatorship was still embedded in the government, laws and the constitution, we were not truly free. Moi had killed political parties before. He would never be the one to foster either fair elections or democracy. *Uhuru*, not yet. The struggle had to continue.

International Campaign

Immediately after my arrest, friends in Norway had started the Koigi Support Group that organized a campaign for my release. Though small in number, they were to prove the truth of the African proverb: A champion fighter is not measured by the size of one's calves, *njamba ti ikere.* They were able to ensure that the Norwegian press continued to write favorably about my case and to encourage the African correspondent for the Norwegian Broadcasting Corporation to visit me in prison.

Amnesty International called for a fair trial for us as political prisoners. And in a few countries, they fought for our immediate release. In Ireland, the campaign was relentless. The American and British governments did precious little on our behalf but before he left Kenya, American Ambassador Smith Hempstone told Mirugi Kariuki that he wished they had done more for our release.

The Slave of Waithanji

When people forget the lessons of history, nothing is too evil to be reenacted. When I was growing up in Rugongo forest village as a child of colonial slaves called forest workers, we had a slave, *Ngombo ya* Waithanji. Slave of Waithanji. He had no other name. Everybody called him Ngombo ya Waithanji. Waithanji had bought him as his property and he (and everybody else in the village) treated him not as a person, but as a piece of his property.

Because Waithanji had a slave, he seemed to live a little more comfortably than other forest workers. His slave drew water for his wife. He cut and brought firewood home and toiled in the garden every day. We worked in hard conditions, but Ngombo ya Waithanji worked even harder. Almost invariably, he was sent to draw water in the dark. He was ordered to the forest to cut and fetch firewood in heavy downpours. He labored on Sundays.

Ngombo ya Waithanji was beaten just as harshly as a donkey and sometimes worse. When he was whipped, he never fought back. He ran away screaming, but always returned when he was called. Many times he stood against a wall and took all the blows that landed on him. On the way home from the fields, if Ngombo ya Waithanji did not lash the donkey to move fast enough, he was beaten to beat the animal.

Ngombo ya Waithanji never spoke. He did not rebel against enslavement, so he appeared to accept it. He never complained. Maybe he was a slave only because he could not fend for himself in any other way.

People admired Waithanji for owning a slave, in the same way they seemed to look up to the white man for owning them. Though their admiration for the white slave master was tinged with hatred, they did not seem to mind owning slaves themselves. If only they could find a breed of human beings like Ngombo ya Waithanji, who was one degree less able than them and could endure subjugation so well without rebellion.

The way nobody ever questioned the existence of a slave amongst them made me suspect that if our people could, they too would enslave others. Despite the knowledge of how evil slavery was, they had not overcome the human duplicity that the Swahili proverb warns against: The spear is sweet for the pig. To the human being, it is painful, *mkuki kwa nguruwe mtamu, kwa mwanadamu mchungu.* We are shackled, slavery is abhorrent; we enslave, our victims are fair game.

In 1885, driven by racism and the precedent of military conquest, European colonial powers came together in Berlin to carve the African continent into colonies in a deadly process that historians call the "Scramble for Africa": to take Africa from the Africans and share it among themselves.

Since Europeans began to concede to independence and abandon formal and direct domination, the African ethnic elite have engaged in a second Scramble for Africa. Using negative ethnic stereotypes and military conquest against other communities, the aim is to balkanize Africa into ethnic states.

Initially, elite from majority ethnic communities like the Gikuyu in Kenya, or the Hutu in Rwanda, foster ethnic hatred and use democratic elections to create an ethnic dictatorship to steal from their own and other communities. When this dictatorship is challenged, they progressively employ imprisonment, terror, assassination, war and genocide to eliminate all opposition from their own and other communities.

Similarly, elite from ethnic minority communities like the Kalenjin in Kenya, or the Tutsi in Burundi, often use ethnic rivalry, military might and rigged elections to create ethnic minority dictatorship and black apartheid to steal from their own and other communities. When they are challenged, they increasingly use imprisonment, terror, war, massacres, evictions and genocide to eliminate all resistance.

When it is impossible to eliminate opposition to ethnic dictatorship, the final resort is to destroy the multiethnic united state and divide the country into ethnic states where dictators can steal unchallenged. Like Caesar, who would rather be first in a barbarian village than second in Rome, ethnic leaders would rather be first in a tiny ethnic state than second in a democratic, multiethnic state.

The process of European colonization and settlement in Africa involved massive eviction of African peoples from their ancestral lands into colonial villages where they did not own the land they lived on in order to create space and land for European settlers. When I was born, this process was still going on and being resisted all over Kenya, especially in Olenguruone.

Forty-two years later, when I was reborn from Kamiti prison, a second expulsion of Gikuyu people was going on and being resisted in places like Olenguruone, Londiani, Molo and Burnt Forest. This time, however, the uprooting was not in the service of a European, but an African, ethnic elite. Specifically, Gikuyu people were being uprooted from Olenguruone, Molo, Londiani and Burnt Forest to create space and land for the minority Kalenjin elite who had achieved power. In 1949, I was born to spend my childhood passively suffering the consequences of the first eviction of Gikuyu people from their land. In 1993, I was reborn from Kamiti prison to actively resist the second eviction.

Ethnic Cleansing

As ethnic fighting raged in the Rift Valley, President Moi announced two decrees that barred visits to areas where people were being killed or evicted and literally forbade victims of ethnic attacks from screaming. To expose this horrendous situation, I joined with fellow Kenyans to form the National Democratic Human Rights

Organization (Ndehurio), which in turn organized and sponsored musicians to visit clash areas and tell the world what they had witnessed. Their songs caused a national sensation and were banned immediately. The musicians were arrested and tortured. Anyone found listening to this music was charged with sedition:

> Oi, oi, oi
> Our people are finished
> Before our very eyes.
>
> It was on Saturday
> The eleventh of September
> The year nineteen ninety-three
> When we musicians went to Molo.
> Now pay attention and listen
> To everything that we saw there.
>
> We were shocked upon arrival
> When we saw with our eyes
> How devastated Molo was.
> We cried and went home sad
> Unknowing what more
> Awaited our people…
>
> ———————
>
> What we saw and heard
> Parents being slaughtered
> With children looking on
> Despite government lies
> That Kenyans are protected
> There is no peace in the land.
>
> Please look and see
> These tiny babies
> Left without a father
> Or a mother
> Both killed with arrows
> With the babies looking on.
> I want to tell you
> Tomorrow it will not be Molo
> It will be your place.

Go to Londiani
Or to Burnt Forest
The cry is the same
Of people being killed
Please we beseech you
Stand by Ndehurio, Koigi wa Wamwere
And other self-sacrificing leaders
Mirugi Kariuki and Rumba
That preferred prison to abandoning people.

When Kerry Kennedy came to Molo,
She collapsed in shock and sadness
On seeing somebody that was shot to death
With seven arrows like an antelope.
When she told the press what she had seen
The government of the accursed said
White people cannot tell between the living and the dead
Her story was slander and lies...

———————————

The rule we have today in Kenya
It is pure ethnic dictatorship
Of, by and for one community
Crippling and killing other people.

———————————

You the leader
You love money
More than people
You think not of the future
You do not care what we think...

When you push me to the wall
And I have nowhere to run
I must turn and face you
Even if you have to swallow me
To wither is not to die
Mau Mau may come back.

You have put people's money
In your bank accounts abroad.
I hear you are a billionaire
As rich as Mobutu
While we pay taxes
Even to fertilize a cow!

Idi Amin persecuted
The nation of Uganda
Today he is no more
There is peace in Uganda
They eat and drink normally.

———————————

I, Sammy Muraya,
When I sing
I shed tears
I remember my dear wife
We parted for her to go to Molo
To check on her parents
When there was war.

When she did not return
Ndehurio took me to Molo
When we reached Molo town
We thought it wise
Not to enter Olenguruone
First get information
From those who came from there.

The person we saw
Told us in shock
That the parents of my wife
Were dead.
They were shot with arrows
Their entire village was killed
They were now
In the big mortuary in Nakuru.

Back we turned
To the mortuary in Nakuru
When we entered
I fainted and collapsed
When I saw the body of my wife
Covered with arrows
And swollen with poison.

When out of ethnic hatred, Gikuyu people are condemned, attacked and killed as a people, it is acceptable for them to defend themselves. Negative ethnicity does not condemn people for individual guilt but for collective identity. In the minds of "tribalists," all other people and especially men are born guilty. This is why the wombs of pregnant Gikuyu mothers were split and unborn fetuses taken out, checked for their sex and killed if found to be male. Only little Gikuyu boys dressed as girls escaped from Molo, Londiani and Burnt Forest.

In defending themselves, however, Gikuyu people must also reject the idea that the child of a snake is a snake, *mtoto wa nyoka ni nyoka.* They must stop the violence against innocent children, men and women. In fact, the Gikuyu people have a good chance of ending ethnic conflict in Kenya by putting out the fire of ethnic hatred instead of using it to defend themselves.

Ironically, Gikuyu people were dying at the hands of a man their elite had put in power. In their misguided arrogance, the Gikuyu elite had always seen Daniel arap Moi as a watchman-president who would, for a salary and the title of president, guard their homes and properties while they slept. They never imagined that the watchman would ever want to sleep in their homes or own the businesses and the lands he guarded., or avenge himself against their contempt for him. They even ignored what Michael Blundell, one of Moi's white colonial mentors, had written in *So Rough A Wind:* "His mission was to advance his Kalenjin people."[1] They were now reaping the wisdom of the Swahili proverb: He who plants cunning, harvests ruin, *mpanda hila huvuna ufukara.* Moi was now taking from the Gikuyu to give to the Kalenjin—power, jobs, land, businesses, homes.

To take from the Gikuyu, Moi had to demonize and silence them as "tribalists" and "criminals." Musicians had already fallen. It was now my turn.

Burnt Forest

I would pay the highest price for my continuing opposition to dictatorship and ethnic cleansing when I was arrested on September 18, 1993.

When I accompanied Mirugi, his wife and brother to Burnt Forest, Mirugi and I knew we were violating a presidential decree. We were stopped on our way out of Burnt Forest and a police inspector asked us where we had been. He searched our vehicle and found nothing. But we were Gikuyu and he feared what his superiors might do to him if he let us go. So he took us to the local police station and searched us again before the whole station. He asked his superiors in Nakuru whether he could let us go. After meeting the president, they said no. Officials were on their way to Burnt Forest.

David Kipkemboi arap Korir was the CID (Criminal Investigation Department) boss who led the team from Nakuru. He came into the office fuming:

Mr. Wamwere, you want trouble, don't you? Now tell Sweden to save you.

I don't know what you mean.

What are you doing in Burnt Forest?

I was on my way to Eldoret.

You are such trouble! How did you ever come out of Kamiti prison alive?

I was released because I was innocent.

If you want to be president so much, why didn't you run in 1992?

I was in prison when elections were held.

His lips trembling with barely controlled rage, Korir stammered, I wish I could get the authority. I would love to kill you with my own hands.

Indeed, I feared he had come to murder us. When he ordered Mirugi Kariuki to be taken out into the night, I feared a firing squad was waiting in the darkness. Then I saw Mirugi's wife sitting in the corner. Maybe Korir would not be so cowardly as to kill a woman and she might live to tell where and how we had died. Korir interrupted my train of thought:

You say we are waging war against your people? Big coward you are! If you are man enough, bring your wife and children here instead of leaving them in Sweden.

I would rather have them where they are.

No, he said. Bring them here, then we can face each other like men. Don't you people say, the earlier the better, *tene ni tene thutha ni mugiano*? Tie him up, he ordered.

Now I had no doubt. It was Moi and Kalenjin security officers who were behind this war. Two policemen came with a long, thick sisal rope. When they started tying my hands I felt humiliation and sudden fear.

You are violating my human rights, I complained.

Korir laughed and addressed another senior police officer, Do you know that animal called human rights?

No, sir.

We were arrested and taken to the CID offices for interrogation. I did not know Korir and was surprised to see golf equipment in his red carpeted office. To play golf, I thought, he must be a very sophisticated police officer. I was told later that Korir was one of the cruelest officials in the country and had risen from a driver to the provincial head of the Criminal Investigation Department. When he wanted to kill a suspect, he would force the poor soul to kneel down on the soft, beautiful red carpet in his office facing the door. Unseen, he would grab a golf club, assume a position behind the victim and hit the back of his head with all his strength. Brain matter and blood would scatter on the carpet. The monster would then ring downstairs and order police to take the dead man to the morgue and clean the carpet. This is how he earned promotion.

We were charged with entering a restricted area, an unconstitutional charge, and possessing a gun, which was not true. Later they added another false charge of administering an illegal oath to the Gikuyu people in Engoshura to fight the Kalenjin. To ensure that we ended up in prison, new security rules and regulations were drafted, backdated and signed by President Moi to make our presence at Burnt Forest "illegal."

One evening while we were still in the cells, I was called out to meet a visitor, Ishmael Chelang'a, the District Commissioner and one of President Moi's men. He led the ethnic clashes and cleansing in the Nakuru District until he died in a helicopter that crashed because it was too heavily laden with weapons for ethnic fighting. When I was led in, he was seated and dressed in a Muslim *kanzu*, long gown, and *kofia*, cap, to disguise himself. He quickly stood up and greeted me:

Mheshimiwa, how are you?

Not so fine, as you can see, *Bwana* DC, I said.

I am sorry, but this will end, he said.

When? I asked.

As soon as you say so, he said with a smile I did not like.

What do you mean? I shot back.

This is what we should talk about. I don't think a man of your abilities should be in a police cell instead of home with his family and outside doing useful work.

Moi does not think as you do.

I don't think it is *Mzee*. He is too big for this. You see, I, like you, want to change many things that I don't like. At the university, I was a radical. When Africans were fighting Ian Smith in Zimbabwe, I went down there, trained as a guerrilla and fought with the Zimbabwe People's Revolutionary Army (ZIPRA) forces against the white settler government. When it fell, I came back and *Mzee* gave me a chance to change things here from within. He gave me a job that now allows me to bring about social transformation that I desire. In your circumstances, my advice is to do as I did. See *Mzee* and ask him to offer you a job that will support you, and at the same time, permit you to promote the same improvements in our society that you are now pushing for from outside. I have talked to him and he is willing.

To do what?

Let you in.

Why can't he end this police and judicial harassment and persecution first, before offering me a job to change society from within?

I don't know, but he may be trying to reach you.

By putting me in prison? It is a most costly way of being reached.

You never allowed him another way.

I don't want to reach him. I want my freedom back.

For what? He has to know you will use it well.

Opposing Moi is not misusing my freedom. Freedom is a right, as long as I don't break just law.

Mzee does not object to your freedom, even for opposition. He is only asking you to do it from within.

I don't want to join KANU and his government, even for my freedom.

My brother, it is easier to fight the system from within with freedom than from without and in prison. At the very least, it is safer and more comfortable.

I don't believe it is possible to fight the lion from within its belly.

Then you have to wrestle with it from outside.

Yes, unless it stops wanting to eat me.

Mr. Wamwere, I am sorry but you are throwing away a great opportunity. It is not a very wise decision you are making. Should I tell *Mzee* you have said no?

Tell him to end this harassment. I want my freedom and am tired of being told: Support me or die in prison.

Kwa heri ya kuonana (good-bye and see you) in court.

Kwa heri.

After a month in police custody, the state let us out on bail, while pondering a more permanent solution to the problem. In the meantime they would not let me travel to Norway to be with my wife, who would soon be in the hospital to give birth.

I was staying with Gibson Kamau Kuria in Nairobi when we heard of a raid on Bahati Police Station on the BBC. At breakfast, Gibson told me, Koigi, it is good you are here. Had you been in Nakuru, they would have put this on you.

They still can, said Njui, a friend then.

Gibson gave him such a bad look. He thought he was exaggerating.

Two days later I sensed trouble. Moi was at the airport on his way to Ethiopia when he asked publicly why the police had not arrested members of the opposition for attacking police stations.

Afraid they would not allow me to travel, I spent the week trying to secure my sister Wambui's passport, which was accomplished in the nick of time. Had I failed to get the passport that day or taken it to Nakuru the following morning, she would never have made it to Norway on November 6, 1993. Our sons, Wamwere and Ragui, would have been alone when their mother went to the hospital to deliver Kuria, our third son.

CHAPTER XV

SECOND TRIAL FOR MY LIFE 1993–95

Last Arrest

It was on Friday the fifth of November when Njui, Maina Kamami and I left Nairobi on our way to Nakuru court for the mention of my case. As we drove, Njui was so apprehensive of my arrest that he wondered whether we should have been going at all. I have a habit of feeling danger less when it is most imminent, so I did not harbor the same fears. In any case, I told Njui, We must go to court and then report to the police. If we don't, I will be inviting another arrest. Have you heard of Catch-22? Whatever you do, you lose. I am tired of running and living in exile.

We reached Nakuru at 7:30 A.M. and had our breakfast at the Green View Hotel. I saw Mirugi briefly in his office before going to meet lawyer John Kagucia. As we climbed the stairs, we passed a young woman sitting on them.

Mr. Kagucia and I discussed whether the court would grant permission for travel to Norway. We agreed that they seemed split into two factions over the issue. One group wanted me to go Norway and never return, while the other pressed for my arrest and elimination. As we talked, a large gang of men stormed into the office along with the young woman whom we had passed on the stairs.

Furious, Kagucia demanded, Who are you?

We are police!

What do you want in my office?

We want to arrest him, they said, pointing to me.

Do you have a warrant? Why are you arresting him? Kagucia pursued.

He knows!

I don't, I said.

Can I have more men, sir? One of them asked into his walkie-talkie.

Get out! Kagucia shouted. You don't arrest people here without warrants! My chambers are not for arresting people. Get out! Don't come into my office uninvited.

Mr. Kagucia, it is okay, I tried to reassure him. I will go with them.

Arrested without reason or warrant, I saw little point in arguing with lawless and primitive police officials who were looking for an excuse to unleash violence. I did not want anyone else hurt. In any case, I had no power to resist. I was put into a Land Rover to be driven to the provincial CID offices. As I was being abducted, Njui and Maina tried to follow in my car, but they were chased away: Go back if you do not want trouble!

I found my brother John Njoroge and cousin Kuria Kariuki at the CID offices already in custody. We were forced into a police vehicle and driven home for a search in a convoy of four vehicles. Once there, we found my mother, sister Wambui and brother Kiarie. Before the search commenced, I asked the officer in charge, Mr. Dinda, do you have a warrant?

No, I don't, he scowled.

What exactly are you looking for in my house?

Nothing!

They were on a fishing expedition. They combed through all the houses, the stores, the toilet and the entire garden. I was surprised that they did not separate what belonged to me from what belonged to Mum, my sister, brother or father. Everybody related to me or found at home was guilty by association and had to be searched. Even my sick father was probed on his deathbed!

When they finished scrutinizing the houses, they wanted to examine my car, but Mum did not have the keys. Not wanting them to return, I told her, Mum, if you get a knife, we can open the car for them.

Suddenly a policeman fished a key from his pocket and said, Sir, I can open the car.

Wait a minute, I said, how do you have a key for my car?

He ignored my question and opened the driver's door and the boot of the car. Later he used the same key to start and drive the car to the CID offices in town.

Blinded

When we were driven away, my sister Wambui followed. She wanted to know where they were taking us. She stood outside the CID offices, watching, when Korir passed by and greeted her:

Dear, you are here. How are you?

Fine.

We are so busy. Let us go to the office.

My sister followed, rather confused.

I thought you would come home, not here, the man mumbled as they climbed the stairs to his office.

Wambui kept quiet but she now knew. He thought she was his girlfriend. As they entered his office, she wondered, How shall I extricate myself. As if in reply, he said, I will give you the keys, go home and wait for me there. Before he reached his pocket, he said, But wait. Let me tell the boss we have arrested this thug, *mkoru.*

Sir, we got him. He is here. We have already searched his home and his brothers' homes. Should we proceed and charge him? Something was said on the other end to which Korir said, Yes, sir.

He put that phone down and took another into which he barked an order: Inspector, take them all to the Bondeni Police Station and book them there. Don't let anyone see or know where you are taking them. When you finish, report to me immediately.

Terrible Torture

We were driven back to the CID offices and later to Bondeni Police Station, where we were held in the same cell with young men who had been so badly beaten that they were sweating and bleeding all over. They could only sit down a little, try to lie down and then stand for short periods. Their backs and buttocks were bruised and swollen and the soles of their feet were ruptured and bleeding. Talking was an effort.

Who beat you like this? I asked rhetorically.

One of them said, They arrested and took us to Lake Nakuru National Park yesterday. Once there, they drove to a secluded bush, inaccessible to tourists, which they called their office. Out of sight, they hoisted us, stretched our hands apart, tied them to distant trees and suspended us from strong branches. They forced our mouths open and poured water down our throats. Taking turns, they beat us up with hoes, rhino whips, wire whips and truncheons. Hoping somebody would hear and rescue us, we screamed as hard as we could but the louder, we yelled, the more viciously they whipped us. Only buffaloes heard and came to watch this incredible spectacle of man's inhumanity to man. They looked at us with their eyes wide open with wonder and flapped their ears each time a whip lashed one of us. Sometimes they grunted and stamped their feet, asking questions I don't know.

I was pounded and battered, a man named Rastaman Kirio told us. When I was unconscious, they cut me down and poured gallons of cold water to revive me. When I came to, they questioned me. While I was being interrogated, Daniel Kigochi was strung up and being beaten. They asked me to admit that I had gone to raid Bahati Police Station with you on the night of November 2, 1993. I could not. They said if I did not want to die, I had to admit that I wore jeans, white shoes and dreadlocks, because that is the uniform of your army and the same things you wear. They said your army is called URA—United Resistance Army and that is why we always said *ura kana umarwo* (flee or be caught) at the bus station. But these Gikuyu words mean flee or be caught. When I denied these allegations, they put me up again and beat me some more, until I passed out. We screamed in pain and terror, but no one heard us.

He was suddenly interrupted when the door opened. My brother, cousin and I were called out. We were taken to three different locations. As we were led away, I saw my sister Wambui and sister-in-law *Mama* Eunice standing outside the police station. Nobody knew where I was, nor was I meant to know. I pleaded with the officer in charge to let me reach my lawyers or my family on the telephone, but he refused completely. I was given one dirty meal a day and put alone into a dusty cell without a mat to sleep on or a blanket. The nights were chilly and I had only a jacket. When it got bitter cold, I had problems choosing what part of my body to cover. My palms were not big enough to serve both as pillow and cover for my head. Fighting the cold, I couldn't sleep and hunger gnawed.

While I thought about my own problems and the torture of Rastaman Kirio and Kigochi, I would soon confront the incredible torture of Muciri. He, too, was arrested and badly beaten in connection with the "Bahati raid." The police even broke his leg. Not satisfied, they pushed matchsticks into his penis and forced them all the way into his bladder with a piece of wood. Muciri bled and screamed in excruciating pain while his torturers laughed. The matchsticks remained in his bladder until the court ordered their removal in a hospital.

From a sympathetic policeman, I learnt that Korir had told a press conference that the state was going to charge me with the capital offense of raiding and robbing the Bahati Police Station with violence. With the taste of death in my mouth, I wondered how I could escape—but I was too closely guarded to make a run for freedom.

The following day I told Superintendent Wagada, the investigating officer, that the state could not possibly charge me with the crime. On the night in question, I was asleep in the house of Gibson Kamau Kuria, my lawyer. I had enough witnesses to confirm my alibi. I told him the charge was fabricated and politically motivated. Even as I spoke, I realized there was nothing he could do about it. The charge was unrelated to the "raid." It was merely a means of getting rid of me and would have nothing to do with alibis, evidence or the lack thereof.

Trial by Hyena

On the morning of November 9, the police transported me to Court No.1, Nakuru, Chief Magistrate William Tuiyot presiding. There, I was charged with the crime of robbery with violence, punishable by death, together with my brother John Njoroge, cousin Geoffrey Kuria Kariuki, Kinuthia Ngengi and the two young men who told of torture at Bondeni Police Station—Daniel Kigochi and Rastaman Kirio. Later, my brother Kuria Wamwere, brother in law James Maigua and G.G. Njuguna Ngengi were charged with us.

Weakened by a heart stroke and years of forced labor, the arrest and capital charges against five of his sons proved too difficult for Pap to shoulder. On January 31, 1994, our dear father was killed by a second heart attack. Pap's death left us all shattered and feeling both guilty and powerless. I hadn't even been able to visit him.

Three other persons, Muciri, Mwangi and a government informer, J.J. Waigwa, were later charged for the same offense. Eventually, all were released and only Kuria Wamwere, James Maigua, G.G. Njuguna Ngengi and myself were held. When we first appeared before Judge Tuiyot, he was asked to transfer our trial to another court since he was already handling two other cases against me. The magistrate beamed gleefully, rubbed his hands together as one preparing to eat a great meal and said with a salivating mouth, This case is the real thing. The others are nothing, *bure*. This file is before me and only I will handle it.

Tuiyot's behavior reminded me of an old story. One day a hyena and the kid of a goat were quenching their thirst in a river. The kid was drinking in the lower part, below the hyena. Suddenly the hyena called out, Hey you!

Yes, sir, the kid answered timidly.

Stop soiling the water for me.

Sir, I am drinking water below you. I cannot possibly soil the water for you. The water is not coming up your way. It is flowing downstream. The water I am drinking is the one that is soiled.

Stop insulting me, the hyena shot back angrily. Then he demanded, Are you not the one who abused me one week ago?

No sir. One week ago, I was not born. I am only four days old.

If it was not you, it was your mother and you must pay for it.

Days later, the hyena made a feast of the unfortunate kid. In the court of the hyena, the kid could not win a case brought against him by the hyena, *fisi akiwa hakimu kondoo hawezi kushinda kesi.*

From that day on, whenever I sat in the dock, I felt like the kid and saw a hyena in the magistrate's chair.

Tricks Galore

As Tuiyot's bias against us became more obvious, we fought harder for his removal.

Tuiyot belonged to a cabal of Kalenjin tribalists and President Moi's advisers that planned and supervised ethnic killing of over two thousand and cleansing of over half a million of the Agikuyu from the Rift Valley after taking their land and torching their homes, stores and crops and robbing their animals. It was executed to punish the Agikuyu for denying Moi votes in the 1992 presidential elections and to ensure that no Gikuyu presidential candidate got 25 percent of the presidential vote in the Rift Valley province. Such support in five provinces is constitutionally necessary to win a presidential election.

Ethnic cleansing was executed mainly with war that was waged against unarmed Gikuyu people by Kalenjin security personnel masquerading as traditional warriors. When Gikuyu youth failed to leave town and urban centers in the Rift Valley, they were rounded up, charged with non-bailable, capital allegations and locked up while their businesses were destroyed to convince them that the only place where they could be safe was in the Central Province, the traditional home of the Gikuyu.

When arrested, these young men were taken to Tuiyot's court only. Only he could guarantee they would remain in prison though innocent. Gikuyu youth were rounded up in several sweeps and ours was only one of them. We sat in prison with many other groups accused of capital robbery with violence, and others, like Kimani, Kariuki, Muthee and Zaki, who had narrowly escaped ethnic killing from Londiani were accused of perpetrating murder against their dead attackers. It was a truly bitter moment to witness these innocent young people being convicted of murder.

Our bitterest foretaste of injustice was, however, when, a group of 30 Kalenjin warriors was arrested for killing and maiming Gikuyu people and animals and burning their houses and properties. They confessed their crime and were taken before a judge in Nakuru court for trial. They were all released on a technicality to go and continue killing Gikuyu people. In releasing these tribal warriors, a signal was sent to us who opposed them: We would take their place in prison. Feeling impregnable and beyond reach, in cruel jest, Tuiyot had even dared tell another Kalenjin who had killed as he set him free, I know you have murdered. I will release you to go and murder again.

In the war of ethnic cleansing, it was Tuiyot's job to use the courts to scare Gikuyu leadership into silence, retreat and defection—in return for non-prosecution and security—and terrorize Gikuyu people and especially their young men out of the Rift Valley.

Given this backdrop to the trial, we asked to be tried by a magistrate who was from neither the Gikuyu nor the Kalenjin communities and whose fairness and neutrality we could trust. We wanted to be tried by an independent and fair-minded magistrate. And that was certainly not Tuiyot. Instead of removing himself, he stayed and buttressed his bias with as many tricks as his warped mind could muster.

Throughout the trial, Tuiyot was a referee who wore fighting gloves, jumped into the ring on the side of the prosecutor and remained there kickboxing our counsel and our witnesses as hard as he could. One time when the going was rough for the prosecution, he unashamedly told the state counsel, Mr. Onyango, watch out. These people might sweep our feet off.

Tuiyot did not just harbor ethnic hostility. He was also full of political animosity and made little effort to conceal it from the political opponents he was now trying. Once, when our lawyer Paul Muite asked him to look into a dispute between officials of an opposition party, Tuiyot called them rogues, *mikoras*. Throughout the trial, the judge displayed a fanatical zeal to protect President Moi from exposure as the real instigator. How could we expect justice from a magistrate who considered himself KANU by blood, *damu?*

The British jurist Lord Denning wrote about a judge who talked too much. It was Tuiyot. When Mum went to court, he told her, *Mama,* even if I convict your sons, they will be free to appeal to other courts.

When he saw Joseph Ngugi, the court reporter for the *Daily Nation,* across the street in town, he called him over and told him, I am convinced Koigi was seen at Bahati Police Station on the night of the raid. He was involved.

When Kibutha Kibwana, an outstanding human rights activist, paid Tuiyot a courtesy call on a trip to observe the trial, Tuiyot boasted, I will dismiss alibi evidence from Dr. Gibson Kamau Kuria. He is lying for Koigi.

Finally, when David Sullivan, an observer from the U.S. visited him, Tuiyot left him in no doubt that we were dead meat: In the U.S., how does the government control riots after a major conviction?

It took a lot of effort to sit before Tuiyot and pretend that we were going through a fair trial. Often I felt punishment or even execution without trial was fairer than a long, useless trial just to justify a predetermined sentence. Throughout the ordeal, Tuiyot behaved like a special magistrate with special powers. No higher court dared to reverse his outrageous decisions.

I have always thought that where there is truth, there is justice. In our case, truth was acceptable to the court only if it was used against us. When it was in our favor, it was jettisoned. The court encouraged obvious lies from witnesses whenever they assisted the prosecution case. When lying proved too embarrassing, Tuiyot encouraged prosecution witnesses to feign confusion. In a situation of war, he said, it is easy to get confused.

As in the court of Mr. Fang in *Oliver Twist,* in this court enough fantastic tricks were played daily as to drive angels blind with weeping. Whenever there was an unwanted observer, like Jacob Seabrook QC in court, the prosecutor would provide an excuse to postpone the trial and Tuiyot would grant these requests. On the occasions when we petitioned for an opportunity to address the court, the judge would rise and leave. When we asked to have testimony read back for correction, it was never done. It is said that every accused person must have his day in court. In Tuiyot's court no freedom of speech was tolerated. He acted as if there was always a person whispering to him, If thou let this man go, thou art not Caesar's friend. The court is a court of record. In our trial the judge recorded what evidence he liked and left out that which he did not like.

To convict us and protect perpetrators of ethnic clashes in court, Tuiyot was promoted to chief magistrate and given over a thousand acres of prime land in Molo.

Muzzling a Witness

A well-known lawyer, Mathias Akhaabi, traveling to Nairobi from home was forced to put up at the exclusive Rift Valley Sports Club rather than journey at night. While at the club, he came upon a meeting between Tuiyot, the prosecutor and a hostile defense witness in the restaurant. That night Akhaabi telephoned our lawyer Mirugi Kariuki to inform him of the illegal and clandestine meeting and volunteered to come to court as a witness in defense of legal professional ethics. When we first complained about the meeting, both the court and the prosecution vigorously denied their involvement. The defense then offered to produce a signed affidavit, but the court hastily ruled against its production. They never imagined that Akhaabi would have the courage to come to court and refute their denials.

When we called him as our last witness, the reaction of the court was one of utter shock. It made Tuiyot visibly wet the collar of his white shirt with sweat. The magistrate tried to block Akhaabi as a witness, saying the defense had already closed its case. Unable to stop him from stepping into the witness box, Tuiyot and the prosecutor changed their tactics in panic. Muite had asked Akhaabi to narrate how he had found the presiding magistrate, the prosecutor and a defense witness in a meeting, and as a lawyer explain why this was irregular. The prosecutor never gave him a chance: Your Honor, I still object to allowing this defense witness to tell lies about the court and about me. Your Honor, this man is a liar and an idiot. He is a fool and I will never sit here and let him tarnish the name of the court and mine. He never saw me.

Akhaabi tried to defend himself: Your Honor, what Mr. Onyango is saying about me is not true. Your Honor—

Tuiyot now saw his chance: Shut your dirty mouth! You are a madman, a stupid man and a fool! I will not allow you to come here and abuse the court. You have been paid money to lie. Get out of that witness box or I will have you thrown out!

Tuiyot foamed at the mouth. As his frenzy reached its peak, the prosecutor would not be outdone. He left his seat and moved toward Akhaabi gesturing, hurling more insults and pointing his finger as if he were going to hit him: Shut up, you fool! You are a liar! Get out of there, madman!

With nothing to lose we jumped into the fray: Mr. Akhaabi is telling the truth! You, Tuiyot and Onyango, are the liars! You are the real mad people who want to hang us! There was a meeting between the three of you and your denials are the only lies being told in this court. Let Mr. Akhaabi tell the truth!

Tuiyot left Akhaabi, faced us and thundered to the prison guards, Take them out and never bring them back to my court again!

Cowed Witnesses

Lawyer Akhaabi was not the only defense witness who came under fire from Tuiyot. Some others were treated worse. Anthony Njui was threatened with death; he was later charged with a capital offense. Isaak Njoroge lost his job while still in the witness box. Police arrested Hassan Macharia and broke his leg. Dr. Samuel Gitau lost his commission with the army. A teacher, Kiongo, was threatened with the loss of his job. John Ngwenyi, Jeffrey Michuki and Gibson Kamau Kuria were threatened with incrimination in our alleged crime. Dominic Kamanga, a prosecution witness, was charged with perjury for giving truthful evidence that was helpful to the defense. Punishment meted out to defense witnesses was a very serious detriment to our case.

On the night of the "Bahati raid," I was with a good friend, Karin Stephensen, an employee of the Danish Embassy, in the house of Gibson Kamau Kuria. Had she come to testify, she would most likely have risked deportation from Kenya, but she would have assisted the diplomatic and international community to see how false the charges were, especially given the West's unfortunate tendency to believe a white person more readily than black people. But she did not come. A human rights lawyer and friend, Kibutha Kibwana, had advised her not to come, not because he wanted me hanged, but because he did not want Karin deported from Kenya.

Initially, Karin was very enthusiastic about signing an affidavit in support of my alibi. Later, her resolve was weakened following instructions from the Danish minister of foreign affairs warning her that if she came to court to give evidence, she would be risking the closure of the Danish embassy and would be on her own.

In 1997, I visited Copenhagen and asked the minister why a government so supportive of human rights in Kenya would not give Karin, their own citizen, encouragement and protection in pursuit of justice, a fair trial and the rule of law in Kenya?

The minister told me I was being cruel when I asked Karin to come to court and give evidence. He said they could not allow her to testify because Danes were not in Kenya to be my "foot soldiers." Most shockingly, he revealed that the reason they called for a fair trial and at the same time forbade Karin from going to court was because they never believed I would come out of the case alive! When I protested against this hypocrisy, the minister furiously shouted, Get out of our streets!

Before I went to Gibson's house on the night of the alleged raid, I had visited my cousin Njeri. When Lawyer Mirugi asked her to come and support my alibi, she would not, for fear of losing her job. Whoever said blood is thicker than water?

Bishop Joseph Kimani was my Member of Parliament. At the Bahati Police Station, he saw men who had been shot and killed, but their gun wounds had not shed a drop of blood! When he queried this mystery, he was imprisoned. Out of prison, he was too scared to come to court as our witness.

Kafka's Court

In Tuiyot's court, the most incredible things were admitted as good evidence. According to the prosecution, the police killed three persons during the raid on the Bahati Police Station. Two persons were killed on the spot while a third died later. When doctors testified, they said one of the so-called raiders had died a day before, another had died a whole month before and the third body was thoroughly decomposed by November 2, 1993. When this was revealed in court the defense asked the prosecution, Do you still want to go on? A cold silence was the only response.

The police said our weapon was a homemade gun. They presented a piece of bent bicycle metal pipe that had no trigger and could not accommodate a bullet or fire one. Yet they were believed.

During cross-examination, policeman Moses Ndung'u said he had identified James Maigua, my brother-in-law, by a gap in his upper teeth. During cross-examination, our lawyers asked him,

Are you sure his gap is in the upper teeth?

Yes.

Please go close to the dock, look into Maigua's mouth and tell the court, in which teeth is his gap?

It is in the lower teeth, Your Honor, he told the court, seeming perplexed.

You lied to the court when you said you identified Maigua by a gap in his upper teeth, did you not? our lawyer pressed.

I didn't, Ndung'u insisted.

How then is Maigua's gap in the lower and not in the upper teeth?

It shifted, Your Honor. The whole court burst into laughter.

From the second to the fifth of November, I was daily in Nyayo House where police had some of their headquarters and torture chambers and I even visited the office of a police officer there. In court, the police claimed that, at this same time, they had looked for me all over Kenya, but had failed to spot me!

In court the police alleged that on November 2, 1993, we broke a globe of electric light in the Bahati Police Station. When the court visited the scene over a year and a half later and saw electric wires being laid in the ceiling, it asked, What are the wires for?

We are installing electricity, sir, a police lady told us.

Your Honor, the police witness claimed they had electricity here on the second of November, I pointed out to Tuiyot.

We came to see, not to collect evidence!

Were my ears wrong? Was the law a complete ass or was I going crazy?

Blows in Court

My friend Waruru Kanja once said, One who is muzzled must fart, *ndungituma andu kanua na umagirie guthuria.*

One day we wanted to make a statement in court. Suspecting the judge might not allow us to speak aloud, we brought a written version. When we asked to make the statement, Tuiyot refused to listen. Frustrated, I leaned over the rails of the dock and tried to pass the statement to the press. A prison officer grabbed it from me. As I argued with him, my codefendant G.G. Ngengi grabbed the officer by the shirt and took the statement back from him. Angry, the officer struck G.G., Kuria then boxed him in the face and an exchange of blows ensued as they tried to drag us out of court.

Women in court screamed, Uuuu, Uuuuu! Help, help! They will kill them! They will kill them! There was total pandemonium. Angry young men jumped into the dock and joined the fight. Plainclothes police officers whipped out their pistols, but did not shoot. A sense of real danger must have enforced a sense of restraint on all of us. The boxing, pulling, pushing, screaming and yelling died down. The young men jumped out of the dock back into the court. Calm returned and the prison officer agreed to let us give our statement to the press. We did so and were peacefully led back to the dungeons down below.

The following day, G.G. and I were falsely charged with attempting to escape. G.G's wife, *Mama* Grace, and *Mama* Njoroge were charged with assisting our escape attempt.

Toward the close of our case we had another near-physical confrontation in court. After the state counsel had finished making his oral submissions, Tuiyot had demanded written submissions from our lawyers instead of letting them make them orally. They refused to do so and withdrew from the case. Left on our own, we asked the court to let us make oral submissions. Again the judge refused and demanded written submissions. We refused and tried to explain why. Incensed by our stubbornness, Tuiyot ordered, Throw them out of my court!

The prison officer we had fought with before hesitated. Angered by their refusal to throw us out, Tuiyot yelled, I said throw them out! Did you not hear me? What sort of *askaris* are you?

I shouted from the dock, They are guards with a better sense of justice than you!

What did you say? he demanded.

These guards have a better sense of justice than you have. You deny us the right to speak and instead of being ashamed, you are now asking guards to attack us. What kind of a judge are you?

Terribly hurt, he limped out of court like an injured and defeated bear. As he left the room, we, too, were dragged out, but we managed to shout after him, You are an executioner, not a judge! You are trying to conceal our innocence from the world! We would rather die than give you written submissions!

Lawyers Harassed

From the beginning, Tuiyot never liked our lawyers. They were too good for him. As David Sullivan, the American observer from Yale University put it, a defense team composed of the Honorable Paul Muite, Dr. Gibson Kamau Kuria, Mirugi Kariuki, Kathurima M'tu Innoti and Olary Cheche was definitely a first-class and formidable team anywhere. Always in the court to assist the defence were lawyers Juma Kiplenge and George Orina.

Apart from their legal skills, our lawyers fought for our lives and liberty because they were absolutely committed to the cause of human rights and the political liberation of Kenyans. Knowing we had no means of paying, they represented us pro bono. Although the court tried to wear them out by protracting the trial, they remained steadfast.

Trying to stop the state from using the courts to eliminate their political enemies was a very dangerous enterprise. Previously, Mirugi Kariuki and Gibson Kamau Kuria had been detained without trial by the KANU government for daring to act for political dissidents who had been detained. Gibson Kamau Kuria testified in court that when the state found him undeterred, it resorted to tapping his telephones, shadowing his every movement and finally threatening him with death. This is what forced him to go into exile in the United States. After his return to Kenya, state agents tried to burn his home down.

Tuiyot always accused our lawyers of politicizing the case. In fact, it was President Moi who made the case political when he decided that I should be charged with an offense that I had not committed. To put a political enemy who had refused to participate in the corruption that feeds dictatorship behind bars, evidence was fabricated against me. To intimidate and silence lawyers, the government accused them of being political; they arrested and interrogated them with the same police officers they were cross-examining. Fortunately, none of these tactics worked.

Scaring Off Observers

On April 22, 1994, a courageous woman, Gro Hillested Thune, sat in court taking notes as a neutral observer from Norway. Suddenly Tuiyot thundered, You, what are you doing?

Everyone looked at one another before they realized that Tuiyot's eyes were riveted upon the white woman. The magistrate continued to play God: What are you writing?

I am taking notes on the proceedings. I am an observer, Thune said, her voice trembling.

Who gave you permission to take notes in my court? Let me see them.

For a while Tuiyot studied the writing, but most of it was in Norwegian.

You must surrender this to the police, he said.

For once the prosecutor was wiser than the court when he immediately advised, Your Honor, it is better for the court to keep the notes.

Tuiyot returned Thune's notebook with a stern warning, Do not write again, or you will be removed!

Sometime after the prosecution had started making their final submissions, two journalists, Jan Gunnar Furuly and Finn Eirik Strømberg, arrived from Norway to report on the trial. At the same time, an observer arrived from the Geneva-based ICJ (International Commission for Jurists). After sitting in court for some time, the three men decided to visit Bahati Police Station. After all, observation of a trial should include visiting the scene of crime. Consequently, the whole legal team joined them and drove to Bahati Police Station together. When they arrived, they introduced themselves to the officer in charge and asked to look around. Permission was granted and they made an informal tour of the station.

At the end, the Norwegian photographer asked to be allowed to take some pictures. The officer asked for time to contact his superiors in Nakuru. When he returned he refused to allow pictures to be taken and grabbed the photographer's camera. The journalists and lawyers got into their vehicles and left for Nakuru, giving the address of a place where they could be reached for the return of the camera. On the way to Nakuru, they were stopped and placed under arrest.

We are arresting you for taking photographs of Bahati, Bondeni and Central police stations, all of which are restricted security areas.

One of the arresting officers grabbed Kampekete, the African observer, and gave him a very hard slap on the face before pushing him into the police vehicle: What do you think you are doing, joining hands with these white people to criticize an African government? Traitors like you should be taught a lesson.

They were taken to different police stations and questioned. Several ridiculous allegations were made, including one that they had smuggled guns for a nonexistent guerrilla army, the February Eighteenth Resistance Army, through Uganda. Subsequently, they were released and told to report the following morning.

In court Kampekete and the journalists were charged with taking photographs of Bahati Police Station. They were then bonded, released and later allowed to travel home. When Gunnar returned to Oslo, he wrote that what he had seen in Kenya was classic Kafka. They came to observe how full the cup of injustice was— and were themselves made to drink from the same cup.

Kangaroo Court

From the outset, Tuiyot never wanted an open court. Given his mission of subverting justice, he feared that the public could see through his intention. He preferred to conduct a kangaroo court in darkness. At the beginning all the seats in court were occupied by plainclothes police. When we complained against this, members of our immediate family were allowed in. As more people demanded admittance, Tuiyot tried intimidation. Police would stand at the door and search everyone entering. Searches, too, failed to discourage the public and our judge had to resort to harsher tactics. Once he glared at two women in court and demanded menacingly, Do you have rain in your place?

Yes, we do.

So people are digging and planting now?

Yes.

When will you dig and plant if you are all the time in court?

We have finished our work.

And you have nothing else to do at home?

To supplement threats and add intimidation, police would follow the public and warn them against coming to court:

Were you with these people when they raided the police station? the police would ask a member of the public.

No, the person would respond.

If we see you tomorrow, you will come to the police station and tell us that there. Do you hear?

The poor man or woman would not show up in court again.

On September 27, 1994, twelve members of the Release Political Prisoners group came to court. When Tuiyot arrived, he looked at them and asked, Who are these people and what are they doing here?

They are members of the public, Your Honor, our lawyer answered.

I don't want to see people who are dressed queerly in my court and will not proceed until they have been removed.

Immediately police arrested them. They put them in custody for one week merely for wearing T-shirts that said, Release political prisoners.

On September 30, 1994, a man came into court carrying a bag containing a chicken head and skin for making fishing bait. He was arrested and that afternoon, Tuiyot announced, Today police searched and arrested a man who was trying to bring the head of a bird into this court to frighten me with his witchcraft, *urogi*. But I will not fear because I am a Christian.

Blood and Tears

On August 11, 1995, Kenyan newspapers reported that the government's efforts to exclude people from Tuiyot's court had turned catastrophic in an orgy of official violence. The *Daily Nation* wrote:

> A trip to Nakuru ended in blood and tears for Safina leaders and members of the press when Kanu youth-wingers set upon them with whips, bolt-studded clubs and other weapons outside the law courts.
>
> The violent reception was to dissuade leaders from visiting a fellow Safina member and violent robbery case suspect, Koigi wa Wamwere, who is held in the town.

Dr. Richard Leakey, a man with no legs, was cornered by the abuse-hurling mob and severely whipped in the frenzied attack. His attackers, also armed with axe-handles, pelted him with stones and rotten eggs. He made frantic efforts to escape as the mob surged forward and managed to reach his car, parked some ten meters away. He struggled to open the door as a barrage of lashes tore into his back. He looked like he could collapse under the attack, but an aide pushed him inside the car. The vehicle drove off as some plainclothes police officers fired into the air. Dr. Leakey's description in the *Daily Nation* was chilling:

> I was just about to go into the courthouse when we saw three or four people walking with placards written in Kiswahili: "We don't want to be divided by a mzungu [white man]." Suddenly a missile hit me. I think it was an egg. I was whipped solidly as I made my way back to my car. Because getting into the car was quite difficult, I was thoroughly thrashed whilst trying to do so. The windscreen was then smashed with a pick-axe.
>
> Afterward lawyers and several others visited Mr. Koigi wa Wamwere's

mother at Engoshura. Policemen manning a roadblock about five kilometers from Nakuru Town did not stop them.

From Koigi's home, there was trouble when the team headed toward
the Nakuru GK Prison to see him. There were groups of Kanu youth-
wingers lining the earth road that leads to the prison. About a kilometer
away, prison officers stopped the four-car convoy of lawyers and journalists. They said that they had instructions to stop them from seeing
Mr. Wamwere.

"You cannot see Koigi today," said prison officer George Okumu.

"We are lawyers. We have a right to see them," asserted Muite.

"You cannot see him today as Safina members. We have instructions
not to let you through."

As lawyers argued with prison officers, the number of Kanu youth-
wingers continued to swell. By now Safina team, the press and Koigi's
mother were in a trap. They could not drive toward the prison or back to
town.

After about an hour, a senior prisons officer arrived and ordered his men to withdraw.
As they moved away, the wingers descended on the lawyers and journalists. The *Daily
Nation* car was showered with stones and journalists were knocked down and beaten
with truncheons, rungus and whips and left writhing on the ground. Car windows
were shattered. A prison alarm sounded and scores of officers in anti-riot gear with guns
cocked arrived. The wingers retreated temporarily. Suddenly, the prison wardens
themselves set upon the press and some of the lawyers.

Muite's Mercedes-Benz was seen driving through a hail of rocks...

Furious wingers were heard shouting, Beat him thoroughly. These are
the people who sell us to whites, *piga yeye kabisa, hawa ndio wanauza sisi
kwa wazungu.*

As the BBC correspondent Louise Turnbridge was whipped and she
screamed in pain, others shouted: Beat this BBC slut, *piga huyu malaya.*

When Mirugi went to her defense, he was viciously attacked with whips and truncheons. He fell, got up and tried to escape through the maize field. He was hit on
the head again and collapsed in the field, where he was found unconscious a few
hours later and taken to the War Memorial Hospital together with four journalists.

In prison, we had heard that Safina officials were coming to see us. In response,
KANU officials asked the government to stop the visit. Then Moi announced

through the Kenya Broadcasting Corporation that if Safina officials were planning to cause trouble, the government was ready to deal with them.

That morning, no prisoners were taken to work outside. From very early, all prison wardens were put on alert. As prisoners were taken to court, wardens armed in riot gear with automatic weapons took positions around the prison. All prisoners were locked in their wards and cells. No one, however sick, was taken to the hospital in town.

At noon, security sirens blared. All wardens, except one, left our block for battle. When they returned, one of them, Robert Loriew, had blood splattered on his trousers and all told gruesome stories of how they had brutally beaten our visitors. One narrated how he was ready to kill Mirugi Kariuki and face murder charges if his orders had been defied.

I felt real pain in my stomach when I heard a warden who claimed to be a born-again Christian brag: I taught that BBC slut a real lesson. She is one of these stupid journalists who have given this country a bad name. I grabbed her blouse and tore it into shreds. If only I had my penknife, I would have cut her trousers into pieces and tossed her to the vultures of KANU. She was lucky. It was fun grabbing and raising her by the hair and then letting her drop like a stone. When she screamed, I remembered this woman, Lady Chalker, who is giving *Mzee* [Moi] hell with their money. You would never think that a white woman could scream.

He sounded as if he had beaten Lady Linda Chalker, who was in Nairobi to announce that the British government would withdraw aid to Kenya if the KANU government continued to violate human rights and renege on economic reforms.

Even the provincial prison chaplain had taken part in the melee and tripped a TV reporter to the ground. As wardens sang of their bravado, officer George Okumu was complaining that he had missed his chance to get his hands on my mother, "that troublesome woman." He had been arguing with her and Muite. When he looked for her again, she had disappeared. As the prison wardens came back, he asked, "Who helped Koigi's mother to escape?"

I did, said Sergeant Chebon.

Why did you do that?

She asked me for help. In our (Kalenjin) tradition, I could not refuse assistance to an unarmed woman. In war, it is cowardly and useless to kill women and children. When they asked me for help, I showed them a way out.

Sergeant Chebon's Kalenjin traditional chivalry had not appealed to Kalenjin warriors during the tribal clashes, nor did it gain favor with the officer in charge this time. The sergeant lost his recent promotion and was transferred to another prison.

When the American television program *60 Minutes* covered this story, they reported exclusively about Dr. Richard Leakey's beating.

Poison in Prison

Before Sergeant Chebon saved Mum, we had a frightening encounter with him. Though four of us were on trial in the same case, G.G. Ngengi and I were kept in a separate block from my brother and brother-in-law. Being on medical diets, they had their own cook just as we had ours. When we were put in the same block, their cook, himself a prisoner, came over to prepare meals for us all. He was a young Kalenjin man called Chepkok. Months after he had joined us, Sergeant Chebon unceremoniously took him away. We protested, and he was allowed to stay.

Suddenly, he was removed again. We asked Chepkok what had happened and he was frank: *Afande* does not like me. Three times he asked me to put poison in your food. When I said no, he threatened me: Why are you cooperating with our enemies?

Sergeant Chebon thought Chepkok was under some ethnic obligation to help kill Gikuyu prisoners. Chepkok believed otherwise. For this, he had to be replaced with another who would cooperate.

We requested a meeting with the officer in charge and told him the whole story. In the presence of Sergeant Chebon, the officer questioned Chepkok. For telling the truth, Chepkok was put into a waterlogged cell without clothes and blankets for seven days. We had no choice but to take our complaint higher.

The court ordered an inquiry. We stayed in our cells on the day the investigator came to the prison.

In the morning, the officer in charge summoned his deputy and senior officers, Sergeant Chebon and the entire special security team to a meeting with us. Chepkok was brought from his waterlogged cell and questioned: Was it I who asked you to put poison into these prisoners' food?

No, *Afande*. It was *Afande* Chebon.

Chebon said nothing in self-defense.

We asked that our cook be restored and that Sergeant Chebon be removed from our section. Later we gave statements to the investigator, but realized it was a coverup. When he came to court, he dismissed our claims and fears as baseless. Afterward, Chepkok was transferred to a worse place, Naivasha Maximum Security Prison, as punishment for his honesty.

A Missed Assassination

One Saturday in early March 1994, I was transferred from Nakuru to Kamiti prison in Nairobi. The following Monday I was needed in the Nairobi High Court for a constitutional reference. Mirugi Kariuki and I were challenging the constitutional validity of the presidential decrees that forbade travel to Molo, Londiani and Burnt Forest. I was reluctant to go to Kamiti. Instead, I preferred to travel, under armed escort, to Tuiyot's court in Nakuru in order to apply for permission to bury my father.

The following day—Sunday at 2:30 P.M.—a General Service Unit Land Rover arrived at Nakuru prison from the State House, packed with heavily armed men. In the vehicle, there was room for only one more person. They said they had come to make sure that I was in Nairobi for the constitutional reference case the following Monday and had a letter from the State House authorizing them to take me to Kamiti prison, supposedly to ensure maximum security.

The GSU commander asked to see the officer in charge, who looked at the letter and said he could not surrender me for two reasons. First, prison officers had already taken me to Kamiti prison the day before. Second, GSU had no authority to transfer prisoners from one facility to another. The former insisted that his letter from State House could not be countermanded and demanded evidence that I was not in Nakuru prison. He was taken to my cell and saw it was empty. Satisfied, he requested that a prison barber give all his men haircuts!

Had GSU taken me, I would not have reached Kamiti prison. There would have been a report that I had been shot in the back trying to escape from lawful custody.

A Godsend

On the last Saturday in November 1994, I woke and did my usual morning running on the spot for about forty minutes. After exercising, I felt an urge to urinate and went to the toilet, where, to my horror, I passed blood. Scared stiff, I knew I must be seriously sick. I thought of bilharzia, but had not dipped my feet in any snail-infested water. Nor had I had sex to contract syphilis or gonorrhea. I called for the prison medical orderly and explained to him what had happened. He had no idea what the problem was and gave me Panadol. When I asked him to send me to hospital, he said he would tell the officer in charge to organize it. He left and did not return until the following day.

In the meantime, I continued to pass blood. And though the officer in charge did not take me to the hospital, he peered into my cell every two hours the whole night.

Back in court on Monday, Dr. Mwangi came to see me there, took a blood sample and put me on some antibiotics. Two days later he admitted me into the Nakuru Nursing Home for more tests. The prison demanded and received a court order to transport me to the hospital. I was taken in a Black Maria with ten wardens armed with automatic G-3 rifles and pistols. Two police cars and an unmarked vehicle escorted us.

On arrival, we found the nursing home completely surrounded. The gate to the hospital was manned by gun-toting police. Officers with dogs guarded the front entrance. Two military Land Rovers full of armed soldiers were parked 20 meters away to keep a watchful eye. Other policemen stood across the road to keep at bay a large crowd of *wananchi*, citizens who were eagerly waving the victory sign in the rain. It seemed I had come to the hospital more to escape than be treated. I was tested and ordered back for admission.

Drs. Malick and Mwangi met me at the operating room on Friday, where they performed a two-hour procedure. When I came to, my head heavy with sleep, hardly able to lift my limbs, police and prison officers converged and completely encircled me like human vultures wanting to devour me. They cuffed my hands and ordered me to dress. When I could not, they roughly dressed me and demanded my immediate discharge. A furious Dr. Malick told them, You are not taking him out of here. He is in my care and will not leave before treatment is completed. He was admitted here by court order.

Doctor, we are the court order and demand you discharge him now. But discharged or not, we are taking him out now.

By now the hospital looked like a military barracks with uniforms, dogs and guns everywhere. As I was unable to walk, guards took me out of bed and frogmarched me through a corridor of amazed patients and hospital staff. Seeing how weak I was, a sympathetic nurse asked the wardens, Can I come into the vehicle and support him?

You may.

The kind nurse came into the Black Maria to support me, but on the way back, it was driven so fast and roughly that she could hardly support herself as all of us were tossed up and down like tennis balls. As we parted inside the prison, she bade me a soothing farewell: We love you, and then added, The rough ride reminded me of Biko's trip.

Biko had not survived his. Would I survive mine? I wondered.

That afternoon, I returned to court to fight for my right to treatment and admission into the hospital. Drs. Malick and Mwangi were called for a meeting with Tuiyot, our lawyers, police bosses, prison authorities and the state counsel. The argument against my admission into the Nakuru Nursing Home was that it was a private hospital. It was agreed that I be admitted to the government hospital that same day.

I was taken to War Memorial Hospital that evening at six-thirty. The delay was deliberate. When we arrived, we found senior police officers wearing dark sunglasses everywhere. The hospital was completely ringed by armed men in camouflage. A police superintendent entered first and then escorted me into the admission office where we encountered scared nurses who explained in trembling voices why they could not admit me: Sir, we are not able to admit you because there is no doctor on duty. Only a doctor is authorized to admit. Secondly, we don't admit on weekends and we have no empty beds. Please try again on Monday.

The nurses had obviously been intimidated. I was driven back to prison.

CHAPTER XVI

DARKNESS BEFORE DAWN 1995–96

Sentence

We were convicted and sentenced on October 2, 1995. After we endured almost two years of imprisonment, Tuiyot drew the curtain down upon the scene of judicial tyranny. In keeping with the character of our trial, we were not taken to court for judgment and mitigation. That whole morning, we were locked up in our cells, an ominous sign that the judgment was against us.

In the gray and rainy afternoon wardens hurriedly unlocked our cells and marched us to the officer in charge. We found him seated behind his desk from which he gravely pronounced, Today, your judgment was read in court and I have been authorized to deliver it to you. You, Koigi wa Wamwere, G.G. Njuguna Ngengi and Kuria wa Wamwere have been found guilty and sentenced to four years and six strokes of the cane each.

My heart missed a beat. Caning was brought to Kenya by the British government, though outlawed against its own citizens. After independence, both Presidents Kenyatta and Moi retained it. It was strictly for African men, but recently I have heard a female magistrate call for its application against women. It was the Sword of Damocles throughout my days in prison.

You, James Maigua Ndumo were found not guilty and set free. From here all of you will be escorted back to your cells to pack your things. When you are done, Maigua will go home and the three of you will start serving your sentences.

That same night, the three of us were put into a Black Maria and driven out of Nakuru prison in a convoy of ten vehicles. Because it was raining and chilly, we shivered in our thin prison uniforms. From Nakuru it got colder and colder as we climbed the road to Nairobi. I feared they were taking us to the notorious Naivasha Maximum Security Prison. As we passed Naivasha town, it got so unbearably frigid that I wished we were going to a prison on the warm coast. Instead, they took us to Kamiti Maximum Security Prison.

I did not see how we could survive under the officer in charge, a Mr. Tiren. At reception, he bellowed with glee, Trash like you who are always causing trouble for the government deserve to die!

Is it your intention to kill us here? we asked.

If you want to live, don't give me any trouble.

With the exception of David Kipkemboi arap Korir (the golfer), I had never before met a man as crude as Tiren, who would so openly threaten my life. I was terrified when I thought of spending four years and receiving six strokes of the cane under this monster. Would he be the one who would decide what I would eat, what I would drink, where I would sleep and who would administer the canes to me? Every encounter with him made my heart pound, my hair stand on end and sweat pour down my sides. Unable to stand his sight, I avoided contact as much as possible.

Forced to think of torture and caning, I remembered prison warden Tingir. He was the strong young man always chosen to administer strokes to prisoners. Each time he committed this barbarity, he would return to our section boasting of aching arms and shoulders: Where these people are, they are living corpses. I strike them so hard that they ejaculate, vomit and spurt blood from their buttocks at the same time. I make sure that they will never ejaculate again.

Why don't they run? How do they take such pain and not die?

Before we cane, we pillory them firmly with ropes on a wooden cross and blindfold them. The doctor will have certified they are fit to receive their punishment. The day before, we make a brine of salt and soak a piece of cotton cloth overnight, which we tie to the buttocks while the cloth is still wet. A doctor and a prison officer inspect the arrangement and give the final go-ahead if they are satisfied. I stand behind the prisoner with my long cane. I have practiced often how to deliver unbearable blows. I swing the cane from the left, hit the buttock and go up into the air before crashing it down hard on both buttocks from the right. If the cane lands properly, it lacerates both the wet cloth and the skin. The brine then sinks into the fresh wound evoking a sharp, long and piercing scream of pain from the prisoner.

Few can receive more than one stroke at a time and walk themselves back to the cells. They sleep on their stomachs for weeks before they can sit. This is how you teach these bastards how to keep away from crime.

Little did I know that my turn to be emasculated and paralyzed in this manner was so close. Visualizing the horror, I could hear Tuiyot and Moi saying, Caning must stop political rebels from giving birth to more rebels. When we are finished with him, at least there will be no more of his seeds to worry about.

Bloodletting

Having sentenced us to four years and six strokes of the cane rather than death, Moi and Tuiyot expected the world to hail their magnanimity. The people of Kenya were wiser. They knew that with six strokes we did not need a death sentence to succumb in Kenyan death camps, where prisoners die every day from abuse and neglect. Immediately after judgment, our supporters intensified the campaign.

Release! release! they sang everywhere, release, release wa Wamwere!

> If you go
> Down
> To Kamiti Maximum Prison
> And meet
> Koigi wa Wamwere
> Tell him
> That his country, motherland Kenya
> Will soon
> Be free.
> All of Motherland Kenya
> Will demand
> Freedom and justice.

Outside Kenya, the demand for our release also gained momentum. In London, Amnesty International led the struggle. In America, that great daughter of Kenya, Professor Micere Mugo, gave free lectures on university campuses. Another friend, Jonathan Cuneo of the Cuneo Law Group in Washington, D.C., lobbied many senators and congressmen. Don Edwards and Joseph Kennedy II, Senators Harris Wofford, Paul Simon, Paul Sarbanes and Vice President Albert Gore ultimately wrote letters of "safe passage" for American trial observers and sent a stern message to the Kenyan dictator on behalf of the American government. Michael Koplinka Loehr led the effort from the Kenyan Human Rights Initiative at Cornell University, where I had started this journey.

Incensed by all this pressure, it was not long before the patience of the Kenyan government snapped. On October 17, 1995, my wife and members of Amnesty International in Norway went to the Kenyan Embassy in Sweden to present a petition with thousands of signatures. Before they left Oslo, they rang Kenya's ambassador in Stockholm, Dr. Idha Salim, who agreed to receive the delegation and accept the petitions.

Arriving in Stockholm, the Oslo contingent teamed up with the Swedish branch of Amnesty and local journalists. Together they proceeded to the embassy. My wife later told us the story:

While we waited outside for our time to enter the embassy, Dr. Salim came out twice, without greeting us or saying anything. This was a bad sign, but we were determined to present our petition. When the time came, we entered together. Instead of being properly received as we had been promised, two men sneaked out of rooms behind us, grabbed our cameras and with vicious blows opened a wide and deep gash above the eye of one of the journalists.

As we were assaulted, Dr. Salim looked on from the door of his office, making no effort to restrain his men. Obviously, this was planned. Someone asked me to go outside. As I left, the attackers were dismantling the cameras to destroy the film. The journalist followed me outside with blood streaming from the open wound onto his face and clothes. I had seen Kenyan police shed the blood of Kenyans many times. I never imagined they would dare attack foreign citizens in their own countries.

When the international press reported this barbarity, President Moi claimed Nduta, Amnesty International and the journalists had raided the embassy in Stockholm and threatened retaliation. When the Swedish government stood its ground, Michael Furaha, the thug who led the assault, was recalled.

Moi's effort to silence the campaign for our release did not work. On November 15, 1995, my old friend from Cornell, Neil Getnick, testified before the Congressional Human Rights Caucus of the U.S. Congress and spoke powerfully on my behalf:

> Koigi wa Wamwere is to Kenya what Robert F. Kennedy was to America —a person who embodies the experience and hopes of his generation. In Koigi's story is the tale of Kenya's political development over the last quarter century culminating in the current regime of President Daniel arap Moi. As we speak, Koigi sits in solitary confinement in a Kenyan jail cell following a conviction after a twenty-three month trial, which has been discredited by numerous international legal observer missions.
>
> I know Koigi. We were friends and classmates twenty-four years ago at Cornell University. We spent much of our freshman year speaking of the future and how we might make a difference in the world.
>
> Regarding the ethnic differences that Congresswoman Lee talked about, let me point out something about Koigi.
>
> Koigi is from the Gikuyu community. At the time he came to the U.S., a fellow Gikuyu, Kenyatta was in power. So Koigi came to Cornell as one of 3 young men who were selected to study at the Hotel School for four years, return and obtain powerful positions in the business community. He had no tribal, but human rights differences with Kenyatta. And so, at the end of that year, he announced that he had chosen to give up an assured life of riches and return to Kenya to act on his concerns.
>
> That was the last time I saw Koigi. But such was the measure of the man that I remain profoundly affected by him. He went on to play a pivotal role in the quest for human rights in Kenya. I followed the story of his

detentions, his emergence as the leader of the opposition in the Kenyan Parliament, and his exile to Norway under United Nations protection.

In 1994, I co-founded the American Lawyers Koigi Committee, a group of American attorneys seeking justice for Koigi in the face of his unjust trial. Earlier this year, I founded the Kenya Human Rights Initiative, a program of the Center for Religion, Ethics and Social Policy at Cornell University, to focus on Koigi's case in supporting human rights and an open democracy in Kenya. I appear today, having been designated by Koigi's legal defense team as his legal counselor in the United States.

Koigi is recognized as a determined opponent of tribalism, brutality and corruption in Kenya. So much is written about the injustice of Koigi's imprisonment that no one can overlook the reason Moi government has targeted him. His treason trial started in October 1990 and did not end until January 1993, thereby insuring that he would be excluded from the allegedly open multiparty 1992 elections. Once free, Koigi continued his human rights efforts. He founded the National Democratic Human Rights Organization and led the group in investigating government sponsored ethnic–based violence in the Rift Valley and other parts of Western Kenya, which has claimed over fifteen thousand lives and displaced more than three hundred thousand people since it started in May 1991.

The Kenyan government responded by imprisoning Koigi again and putting him on trial for his life...

Fearing that the Kenyan government would ultimately attempt to silence him, last year Koigi surreptitiously delivered a letter from prison to a visiting trial observer. A copy of that letter was then passed on to me. This is what he said.

"We are one hundred percent innocent of the charges for which we are being tried in this court. This trial has been most unfair and we expect no justice at the end of it.

The real problem is President Moi. He is afraid that I might contest the Presidency in 1997, so we must be destroyed now. Moi also wants to use this trial and the judiciary in general to effect his diabolical policy of ethnic cleansing against the Gikuyu people who live in the Rift Valley.

If Moi could, he would have detained us without charge or trial. But today, Western donors disapprove of this.

Moi wants to find out from this trial whether he can, in the future, abuse law and criminal justice to dispose of political opponents and still count on western donors to finance his dictatorship!

Western donors must impose diplomatic and economic sanctions against Moi's dictatorship. Only that can earn innocent people freedom and end the long lasting suffering of Kenyans. Convey our best regards to the American people. One day, we shall also overcome."

As symbolized by these words adapted from our own civil rights movement, Koigi had come to embody what Martin Luther King, Jr. described as "a committed life." Let us, in turn hear Koigi's plea for Kenya, for Africa and the world and fulfill his hope for humankind.

Prison in Hospital

After being unwell in prison for a long time, in November of 1996, I was finally referred to Nairobi Hospital by Drs. Ling Merete Kituyi and Njoroge to be tested and treated for stomach ulcers and other health problems. Prison authorities saw my admission into hospital as a defeat for their principle that a prisoner must always be in and be treated in prison. They were determined not to lose on the other fronts.

When the doctors came to examine me, prison wardens listened and witnessed everything. Soon they were telling doctors where to sit in my hospital room. Room fifteen was no longer a hospital room, but my prison cell. Indeed Lady McMillan ward had been converted into an extension of the sickbay of Kamiti Maximum Security Prison.

Doctors complained against turning a section of Nairobi hospital into a prison and the obvious breach of medical ethics and confidentiality between doctor and patient but administrator Michael Sheldon was too weak and easily ignored by Tiren. Encouraged by the loss of control over the hospital ward, soon prison guards were saying which nurses would come into my room and which would not. In matters of the health of inmates and the running of hospitals with imprisoned patients, prison officers were no longer deferring to doctors and hospital administrators.

As I observed this, I was reminded of one Dr. Mustafa. He is the only doctor whom I saw truly and firmly able to establish the authority of medical services over prison services, not in Nairobi Hospital but in Kamiti prison. He had come to treat Martin Shikuku when we were in detention together. When Shikuku was in the office where Dr. Mustafa was to examine him, Dr. Mustafa firmly but politely asked the officer in charge to leave:

I now want to be with Mr. Shikuku alone. Will you excuse us please?

I need to be here, sir.

Get out please, insisted Dr. Mustafa. I don't see patients in the presence of other people.

Darkest Hour

As time went by, I felt less safe in Nairobi Hospital than in Kamiti prison. One morning I had just finished my breakfast when a white doctor, whom I had not seen before, entered the room.

I am Dr. Silverstein, the doctor began.

I am Koigi. I don't think we have met.

No, we have not. Can I take your temperature and pressure?

Sure, Doctor.

As he began his examination, I searched my memory. Where had I heard his name? It shot into my consciousness like an arrow. This was President Moi's personal physician. He had been mentioned in unflattering circumstances. Just then Dr. Silverstein finished his examination and ordered the nurse, Prepare to take Mr. Wamwere to the operating room.

A sharp sensation electrified me. I said, Please, Dr. Gikonyo is treating me and I would prefer that he take me to the operating room.

I know Dr. Gikonyo has been seeing you, but it is quite okay.

I would like Dr. Gikonyo to take me to the operating room.

Okay, Mr. Wamwere, Dr. Silverstein gave up. I was only trying to be useful.

Why did you say no to him? a jailer asked me. He is a top doctor.

Do you know who he is? I replied, still shaken.

No, I don't, he admitted.

He is Moi's doctor.

Ooph—he is that big!

Big, not safe. Say you are a sheep who is caught by a lion. The lion wants to eat you, but is unable because everyone is shouting, No, don't, don't, don't! You fall ill in captivity and the lion takes you for treatment. A fellow sheep is attending you. The fox that is the lion's doctor comes along and offers to take you to an operating table. Will you go?

No, I will not, he reasoned.

Why? I shot back.

The fox-doctor does not keep the lion alive by keeping the sheep alive.

Dr. Gikonyo soon found I had a heart problem that required special treatment abroad.

Doctor, I will need bail to travel abroad, I told him.

And you will get it.

No court will give me bail. Even coming here was incredible luck.

Don't worry. Leave that to me.

Dr. Gikonyo was also Kenneth Matiba's doctor when he was released from detention for specialized treatment abroad, after being crippled by strokes in

Kamiti. He knew what he was talking about. Still, I was afraid. Especially when I was told that as Dr. Gikonyo was trying to arrange bail, another physician was telling the *Daily Nation* that I might be discharged back to prison that same day.

When Tiren heard of the possibility of bail, he reacted with panic, fearing that the prey whose demise would earn him promotion might slip through his fingers. He demanded my immediate discharge in a tug of war that Dr. Gikonyo ultimately won.

Mum Does It Again

When Mum came to see me during my hospitalization, the wardens would plead, *Mama,* if we allow you in without permission, our jobs will be no more!

Soon she tired of having her rights sacrificed on the altar of other people's jobs. Enough was enough. She pitched camp at the ward's entrance.

I will stay here until I see my son, whether in the corridors as they move him back to Kamiti prison, or wheeling his body to the mortuary.

Asked by the *Daily Nation* why she camped at the hospital instead of going home, Mum replied, "I can go home, yes, but to whom? My sons are in jail and my husband is at the mortuary. What is the point of going there? I will stay here until we can go home together."

In time, Mum staged a hunger strike and vowed to continue until she was allowed to see me, "I have lost my appetite completely," she told the *Daily Nation*, "and I suffer from insomnia. The fact that I have been denied access to my own son is affecting me psychologically. I will continue to suffer with him."

Thinking of my mother sleeping outside caused me unbearable pain. I felt guilty sleeping in a warm room while she was cold and hungry because of her love for me. I should have been caring for her, not the other way around. I didn't think Mum could succeed this time, and did not like the idea of her pushing so hard. I preferred to serve time in prison, rather than have her sleeping in the hospital corridor for my freedom.

Once, when she was allowed to see me in the presence of Dr. Gikonyo, Mum asked whether I knew that she had pitched camp in the corridor. I was going to ask her to go home when she gave me such a stern look that I stopped dead in my tracks.

Soon members of Parliament started to issue public statements in support of Mother's cause. On November 8, 1996, guards closed my room suddenly and took positions that suggested someone was coming to take me out of the hospital. For twenty minutes, I heard commotion and movement outside my room. I was unchained and asked to come to the door. There were fourteen members of Parliament accompanied by a crowd of people. I was asked to wave, to prove that I was alive and well. Only my lawyer and Mum were allowed to enter the room and see me. This visit gave me hope for freedom.

Mum camped at the hospital for twenty-one days, saying, I don't mind being on this bench at all. Don't you know that when Jesus was removed from the cross, his body was handed over to the mother who was keeping vigil at the scene? If she had been away, who would have been there to receive the body? I will sit here until Koigi is discharged. If he dies, I will be here to take his body.

CHAPTER XVII

FREEDOM 1997

Released on Bond

Finally, Mother's courage, patience, determination and prayers were rewarded. On December 13, 1996, Lawyer Muite, armed with recommendations for specialized treatment abroad, went to court to request bail. Others present were the Norwegian charge d'affaires Ove Christian Danbolt, Second Secretary in the American Embassy James L. Huskey and the Release Political Prisoners activists. After hearing the application, Bernard Chunga, the deputy director of public prosecutions, told the court on behalf of the Kenyan government, "The attorney general has given due consideration to the reports and recommendations by the doctor treating Mr. Wamwere at Nairobi Hospital. In view of these recommendations, it is the A.G.'s considered opinion that this is a deserving case."

Presiding judge A.M. Cockar concurred: "Now that the attorney general is not opposed purely on medical and humanitarian considerations, I order that Mr. Koigi wa Wamwere be released on his own bond of shillings, two hundred thousand. It is my hope that Koigi will return to Kenya one day, after undergoing treatment, to face the appeal he has lodged in the High Court. He cannot stay abroad forever."

Mum jumped up in joy and shook hands with Justice Cockar before hugging Paul Muite: At last, God has answered my prayers. He has unchained my son.

Back in the hospital, I was watching the 7 o'clock news when it was reported that I had been granted bail to go to Britain for treatment. In short order, Muite arrived to confirm the news of my bail and freedom. Tiren, my tormentor who had wished to kill me in prison, also came in to sign my release papers begrudgingly, in compliance with the court order.

Prison guards were withdrawn and Mum immediately stormed the room, accompanied by relatives, the press, Members of Parliament and friends who completely filled the tiny space. How different freedom is from captivity! After an imprisonment of thirty-nine months, it tasted, felt and smelt so sweet.

Exactly one month later, my brother Kuria and our friend G.G. Ngengi were also at long last freed.

In an ironic twist of fate, Tiren fell ill subsequent to our release. Seeing the humanity in everyone, Mum visited him in the hospital. On his deathbed, this monster begged her, *Mama*, ask your sons to forgive me. I never meant them harm!

Visiting the Morgue

On December 19, 1996, I was discharged from the hospital and immediately left Nairobi for Nakuru tailed by two white undercover police vehicles. My friend Mirugi Kariuki welcomed us into the town in a convoy of ten vehicles. It was a truly triumphant entry into my hometown from which Moi and other perpetrators of ethnic cleansing wanted to evict us.

As we entered Nakuru, business came to a standstill. For close to an hour, our convoy caused a heavy traffic jam as it proceeded slowly through the marketplace and onto Kenyatta Avenue, all of us flashing the V sign and shaking hands with everyone.

On our way to the mortuary to see my father, police vehicles joined our convoy just outside the offices of the KANU party, where we found riot police and GSU personnel stationed strategically. As we came out of the roundabout, we saw smoke ahead and realized that the police vehicle in front had dropped a smoking tear gas canister.

Soon I heard gunshots, screams and saw choking tear gas clouds. People were running everywhere I looked. My eyes began to sting and tear terribly, I was choking, but we did not stop until we reached the mortuary. We finally arrived and washed our faces from a water tap outside. Mum, a few friends and I went inside and for the first time, I saw my father in death. Forced to confront the cruelty of the Moi government even more painfully and keenly, I was overcome with loneliness and felt exposed and defenseless. I was furious that my father had been kept lying in the cold for three years.

We went to Christ the King Cathedral for a thanksgiving service. As we said Mass and I thanked all the Kenyans and foreign supporters, the police stood outside the church in full riot gear. They escorted me from the church to my home, where I spent the night. The following day I went to Nairobi and on to Norway the same night.

Meeting Our Son

When we arrived, journalists, officials of the Norwegian foreign ministry and friends waited at Oslo airport. At the front were Nduta, Wambui and our sons Wamwere, Ragui and little Kuria, whom I was seeing for the first time. At that very instance, the sadness of losing my father transformed itself into the joy of receiving our son into my hands. Still, one life could not quite replace the other.

Meeting Kuria was the greatest moment of our family reunion. As we looked at each other, I felt pain that my son had grown this big without my seeing him. Kuria himself could not believe that his *baba*, father, had finally come home. In a beautiful picture, the *Aften Posten* newspaper captured Kuria pointing a finger at me and asking his aunt, in Norwegian: *Er han pappa min?* Is he my father?

Kuria had every reason to be disappointed with me. I brought him into this world, but was not there to be with him. As he grew, his Mum showed him pictures of his *baba* wearing dreadlocks. But when he saw black men on the street with dreadlocks and pointed, his mother said they were not his *baba*. Each time, the little boy felt disappointed and remained so for the first three years of his young life. In fact, Kuria missed his father so much that one day he asked,

Mum, can you please buy me a Pap? I want to have a Pap like Eirin.

Kuria, where shall I buy you a Pap?

From the shop, Mum.

Kuria, you must wait. Your Pap will come home one day soon.

I can't say how Kuria felt going home with his pap, but I felt wonderful with this son whom I feared I might never see. At home, I could not wait for my wife to give me the hug that I had dreamt of for thirty-nine months.

In the first days of our reunion, it pained and amused me to hear Kuria ask his mother, Why is he sleeping here? Why is he asking me to do things?

It was a great pleasure to be together, but nothing could bring back the life we lost in three years of forced separation. I left a child in the womb of his mother and came home to find a big boy playing football. I left our two older sons as young boys and returned to find them already initiated into manhood by my great friend Thomas Ngari Wanjohi. It is a service impossible to forget.

With our family reunited, it was time to return to Kenya and properly honor our father.

Burying Pap

Pap died from heart failure on January 31, 1994, a victim of years of forced labor under the British and a corrupt government after independence. We were finally able to come together to bury him three years and five months after his death.

Keeping Pap in the mortuary for over three years had accumulated a huge bill, over two hundred thousand shillings. With the help of our Norwegian friends, we had to settle this debt before we would be allowed to take him. The Moi government had not only been cruel in hastening my father's death, sadistic in denying us the right to bury him, but callous and mercenary in making a huge profit out of our grief. But that is the way of maggots. They feed on dead flesh.

Though we chose to bury our father on May 1, Labour Day in Kenya, residents of Nakuru did not attend the official holiday celebrations. To all of us, it was time to finally lay Wamwere Kuria to rest.

Commenting on the burial the following day, *The People* newspaper reported, "Like a scene from the movie *Cry Freedom,* burial of Koigi Wamwere's father had all the ingredients of South Africa's apartheid era burial parades. It was as if the whole of Nakuru was waiting for the occasion."

Traffic police controlled the mass of humanity waiting to bid farewell to the man who had given his family to the struggle for a truly free nation. As we mourned, there was also a sense of joy. People jostled for the best viewing positions, whistling and waving, ignoring rumors that General Service Unit thugs would attack them. They had been sighted that morning marching through Nakuru. There was fear they would disrupt the burial procession. The paper continued, "On roads leading to the church, women could be seen with babies strapped on their backs, old men and women soldiering on with walking sticks and young men waving the V-salute. Small boys and girls, some aware and others unaware of the unfolding events, ran helter-skelter along these routes."

At the church compound there was a temporary parking bay and two large tents. Men with *huduma*, service badges, directed vehicles to the parking and ushered guests to the church. As people arrived, few knew that in the wee hours of that day, the house of the priest in charge of the church, Father Mirango, had been broken into and the loudspeakers to be used during the requiem Mass stolen. Father Mirango told me they were raided at about 3 A.M. while asleep and nobody heard anything. When they woke up the message was clear: We can kill you if we want. Keep away from the burial. They were not intimidated and ten priests officiated at the ceremony.

My mother, brothers, sisters, our sons Wamwere and Ragui, relatives and friends were at the mortuary at 9:30 A.M. The cars carrying and escorting Pap's body started from the mortuary at about 10 A.M. Walking behind the vehicle that our friends Kanyingi and Macharia had provided for this final journey, hundreds of us formed a long procession walking for eight kilometers from the morgue to the church, dancing, singing and branch-waving, led by a mesmerized police that cleared vehicles ahead of us on the Nakuru-Nairobi highway.

We entered the church shouldering the casket, wrapped in the green, white and black flag of the Ford Asili party, which Pap favored. Through the aisles, I could hear people chanting, "Koigi, Koigi"and others saying "I have not seen him, *mimi sija-muona,* and they are with Raila Odinga, Paul Muite and Rumba Kinuthia."

The ceremony started with the song "Receive My Soul," *Pokea Moyo Wangu,* with a well-choreographed children's choir dancing in the main aisle. It was Father Wanyoike who set the mood.

Mine is a word of hope, he said as he began the sermon. We are living at a time when fear is becoming the worst enemy of man. Why? he asked rhetorically. He recounted the suffering of our family and asked, What has this family done to warrant all this? For three and a half years, this body (pointing at the coffin) has been lying at the mortuary due to politics, *siasa. Mzee* Wamwere died after knowing that many of his sons were in jail. The government refused the sons to come and bury their father. Let those concerned know that whatever has a beginning has an end...Maybe there is no single day that Mobutu thought he would face a challenger.

This one is fearless, *gaaka gatimakaga,* a woman interjected. And indeed the father continued with his moving sermon: I am not here by accident...and I will say what I want without fear. Today, some people broke into the church...They came to instill fear. What have we done to deserve all this? Lowering his voice, he turned to the front rows where opposition leaders and legislators Mwai Kibaki, Wamalwa Kijana and Raila Odinga sat and said challengingly, A seed has to die to germinate. These people are pegging their hopes on you. Don't let them down...Don't eat fat and keep quiet, *usipate vinono unyamaze.*

Reverend Timothy Njoya took the podium to read the eulogy. He recounted the sad demolition of my parents' house in 1988 and how they were forced to come and live with me at Engoshura. As he read his personal condolence, I was surprised to hear him say, He married a heroine and bore heroes. Others have born thugs, *wengine wamezaa majambazi.* Today we are here because Wamwere is more powerful in death than in life.

As politicians were called to the dais, all had something to say. Jomo Kenyatta's nephew Ngengi Muigai said, The Wamwere family may be poor property-wise, but they are tycoons in the fight for justice, liberty and equality. I hope they shall always remain so.

I was called to speak on behalf of my brothers and sisters. I thanked our father for bringing us to this earth and for what he taught us:

> Never worship power,
> Black, white or yellow
> Whatever it promises you,
> However it threatens you.
> Never worship money.

I ended by making a promise:

> To our dying day,
> We will always try to do right
> And fight against evil.

To our dying day,
We will always struggle for democracy
And fight against dictatorship.

Rest in peace
Our beloved father
We will meet again.

When I finished speaking, Mum was called to say a few words: For many years I agonized over whether my sons would come home, they did. These three and a half years, I wondered if I would ever bury my husband, today I will. They failed to break me. If today we have been able to bury Koigi's father, with determination, we can also win our freedom.

A full three quarters of us ran the four kilometers to the grave and laid Pap to rest as heavy rain pounded us. In the downpour that many believed to be a blessing from our father, boys could be seen hanging recklessly from tree branches; nobody left until the ceremony was over. The following day, it pleased me to read in the *Daily Nation*, "Wamwere Kuria was buried a hero."

When we retired, I was completely drenched and exhausted, but satisfied. We had repaid a heavy debt to my father that I hope Kenyans will share with all those other simple, ordinary working Kenyans who toiled, fought, sacrificed, suffered and died for Kenya, but were never given a decent burial.

Child Heroes

In the struggle for freedom and justice, we suffer with our children, but their contributions are rarely acknowledged. When our youngest son Kuria told his mother to buy him a father, he spoke of a suffering that is difficult for anyone who has not been fatherless to fathom.

The mark of missing a father in the first ten years of a child's life is indelible. Where is Papa? he asks when he sees other children fetched from school by their dads. Why can't I be like other children? he asks when other children talk about what their fathers bought them or where they were taken for holidays.

Invariably, children suffer hardships, lack of guidance, poverty and destitution, but are hardly mentioned when their parents are honored. My wife and children are heroic. They fought for my release and gave me reason to survive. On April 17, 1995, our sons wrote to President Moi:

Your Excellency,
    We, the children of Mr. Koigi wa Wamwere, would like to send our

greeting to you in the name of Jesus Christ, who died and was resurrected during this holy week.

Your Excellency, we are writing this letter to you as children without their dear father. Although we have been living in exile since 1987, we are still Kenyans and we believe that Your Excellency will understand our feelings. We appeal to you as the president of our nation, as a father and a grandfather. We are small children aged thirteen years, ten years and fifteen months who would very much like to be with our dear father.

Last time, we were very happy when Your Excellency released our father after two and a half years in remand prison. We are now appealing to you to release him again because even our late grandfather appealed to you before he died.

It is sixteen months now since our father and uncles were arrested. We are very much worried that we might not see them again in our lives. Our dear grandfather passed away thirteen months ago and he is still awaiting burial by his sons. We feel strongly that our entire family has gone through a lot of suffering starting from the old ones to the young ones like us.

As African boys, we are preparing ourselves to be circumcised in June and it is very important for our dear father to be with us during that very important day in our lives. Please let our father come, join us and bury our grandfather to allow his soul to finally rest in peace.

Please listen to us. We are small children who are powerless...

Yours faithfully,

Wamwere Koigi

Ragui Koigi

Kuria Koigi.

Nduta says that when our children were not writing letters, they were asking her questions that brought tears to her eyes. Why is our father in prison? When will he be back? When he comes out, will he be as old as Nelson Mandela? When eating, little Ragui would ask in a tiny voice, Does Daddy get enough food to eat, Mummy?

All over the world other children wrote letters to President Moi to ask for my release. One of them was the daughter of my friend Neil Getnick:

Dear President Moi,

You may be the governor, but the land is not yours. Please take my advice and let Koigi be free. Courtney—aged eight years.

In 1997, my two sons visited and confronted William Tuiyot, the judge who convicted and sentenced me.

Why did you jail our father? they asked

My hands were tied, he blurted out.

Our children do not only suffer. They inspire. One morning in Oslo, our youngest son Kuria looked up at me and challenged, Papa, you should be in Africa fighting lions!

I Refused to Die

You were in the mouth of lions, many people ask, how did you get out?

One of Kenya's greatest legends of survival is of Lwanda Magere, from the folklore of the Luo people. Lwanda Magere was a great warrior who defied death in countless battles with neighboring communities like the Kalenjin. In epic clashes, he left thousands dead without getting hurt. Spears thrown at him twisted and broke when they hit his body. Knives rebounded like bird feathers. His armies were never defeated, no matter how many warriors he lost, because no one could kill him or survive his spear. Nobody knew the secret of his strength.

In a Kalenjin village, he met and married a beautiful girl. Then he got sick, but his body would not heal when she treated him. He asked her to treat his shadow instead and he got well. There lay the secret of his life, strength and survival.

The next time he went into battle against Kalenjin warriors, they speared his shadow and he died. Upon death, he turned into a big stone that his people revered. From all over Luo country, they came to sharpen their spears and knives against the stone of Lwanda Magere, believing it made them sharp and successful. He had defied death even in the hereafter and continued to give life to his people.

Lwanda Magere was a legend. The reasons for my survival are less certain.

We do not survive solely because of what we do, but because of what others, including our enemies, do or fail to.

A long time ago, a hyena was looking for food when it found a donkey that was tied to a tree with a long strip of cowhide. The hyena looked around and seeing no human being nearby, concluded that his prey was secure. He taunted God, You always claim to give and take away. Take this away if you can.

With his mouth watering, he looked at his fat meal and wondered where he should start eating. To prolong the enjoyment, he told himself, Begin with the strip of cowhide, then the hind legs and finish with the heart, the best part. Chewing the tough and dry cowhide was tedious, but he mustered enough restraint. Be patient, Mr. Hyena, he told himself, you will soon be eating the sweet fat.

Suddenly he bit through the strip of binding and the donkey started running.

The hyena gave chase, but his meal disappeared. Many times I was one such meal to my captors.

In prison, there is no better medicine than physical exercise and sleep. They provided fitness, rest, peace and emotional freedom. But they are only a part of the story.

The mystery of the General Service Unit toughs sent from the State House to fetch me from Nakuru prison for certain elimination, only to find their bird had flown, has led me to another question. In my life's journey has some power, destiny or spirit, some God, nature, process of evolution or fluke intervened? The many times I was denied medical treatment, yet recovered, made me wonder anew.

Many a time, I was small prey caught under the paws of a lion, waiting to be eaten. A lion knows no justice, rights or morality. One reason I was not killed was because people from all over the world banged pots and made all kinds of noises to frighten the lion into letting me go, just as Pap had scared leopards away in my childhood.

Though dictators prefer to eliminate their enemies, sometimes those they entrust with killing, undiscovered good people, spare their targets. I am sure this played a part in my survival.

An assistant commissioner of prisons once told us, One must always be very careful with a politician. One moment, he is your prisoner, the next you are saluting him as your president. Colonials ordered us to do this and that to Kenyatta. No one thought he would ever be free again. A few years later, we saw the same British masters hugging, laughing and giving him the power they had nearly killed him for earlier.

Before the radio was confiscated during my first detention, we were listening to an event broadcast from President Kenyatta's home at Gatundu. A delegation of Luo people was singing and dancing for him. Suddenly, their spokesman asked Kenyatta for the freedom of Oneko, a man who was imprisoned with us.

Oneko does not care to go home, Kenyatta thundered.

He does, *Mzee,* the Luo spokesman insisted.

Are you sure?

Yes, *Mzee,* he confirmed, amid cheering ululations.

Where is the head *askari?* Kenyatta demanded.

I am here, sir.

Bring me Oneko. Now!

Yes, sir.

Minutes later there was frantic banging at the iron door of our isolation block. Quickly, we were herded together and locked in. Oneko was ordered to pack and say *kwa heri,* farewell, to us before he was whisked out.

When we were finally let out, we turned on the radio program again and were stunned to hear Oneko and his jailers, Kenyatta and Koinange, laughing and calling one another *mrefu,* the tall one, and *kafupi,* the short one, in complete harmony.

Early in prison, I learnt to be that small, thin and pliable tree which is able to lie flat on the ground when the storm comes. Many a time, I lay low to let the hurricane pass. When life is good, I let go and enjoy it, but I never abandon the capacity to endure adversity if it strikes.

In prison it helped me to have known poverty. When they subjected me to brutal conditions, I survived like a poor man. When they fed me raw, dirty food, or forced me to bathe and drink water with my own urine and excreta, I survived like an animal. I preserved my humanity under an exterior of bestiality.

I know if you are drowning and your child is on shore crying, Papa! Papa! you fight harder to survive than if no one is beckoning. Yes, at first, having a family made my captivity more painful to endure. Later, their love provided the motivation to go on. I fought to live and to see them again.

Indeed, I survived the horrors of imprisonment not only because of what I did, but also because of what I refused to do. When I returned to Kamiti prison for my second detention, I was shocked to hear that Senior Private Ochuka had sold his life for food. He asked for a "presidential" diet of fried meat, *chepechepe,* for confessing to treason. In prison, dictatorship was one enemy too many. Addiction to cigarettes, good food and sex was a very easy path to perdition.

Ultimately, I refused to die. Do you still remember the question I asked my warden friend?

Will they kill us or shall I live?

Do you still have work to do?

Yes, I have.

Don't worry then. You shall survive.

How do you know?

You do not die when you have work to do.

We still have the Mau Mau revolution to see through.

CHALLENGING DICTATORSHIP: 1997

Today, whenever one reads about Africa, it is about problems—hunger, war, ethnic conflict, disease, AIDS, poverty, corruption, human rights violations, dictatorship, torture, coups and even slavery.

In December 1997, I ran for the presidency of Kenya. I wanted to start a real war against all those problems; against the deprivations of my childhood, youth and adulthood; against the hardships that still plague and kill people all over Africa; and against enemies I have seen my people wrestle with since I was a toddler and which I hope to overcome someday.

Despite the introduction of multiparty politics in 1992, President Daniel arap Moi has retained the powers of a dictator. The second multiparty election in 1997 was a farce, as was the one in 1992. Though only Moi could win, people sought no alternative to rigged elections. I took part in the campaign to ask for a chance to stop Moi from stealing elections. People had no stomach for the price of freedom.

For thirteen years, I walked through the fire of detention camps, prisons and exile looking for freedom. I never met anyone who said to me, Here, take it for free. All I heard was: More toil, more sweat, more tears and more blood. Many Kenyans, however, thought I had it all wrong. They lined up behind negative ethnicity and corrupt money and voted for the status quo. Some have called Kenyans "happy slaves." The people who fought the Mau Mau war of national independence are still capable of ending the rule of human predators. But when?

During the campaign, my community, the Gikuyu, told me: We want only one of you to stand against presidential candidates from other ethnic communities. I countered, There is no them and us. We are all Kenyans. Subsequent damnation was swift: No votes for you. When the Gikuyu elite said, All we want is a return of the late president Jomo Kenyatta's good old days, I responded, Then you ate honey and we endured the stings. Remember our songs of agony:

Even now water is bitter
Both at home and at work
To the young and to the old
It is bitter, what shall we drink?

When you go into an office
Looking for help
You meet an angry person
When you try to enter
The person says: I am busy
Water is bitter, what shall we drink?

Let us move forward, I urged, not backward to Kenyatta days. I was rebuffed. When I went to other ethnic communities, they said, In Kenyatta's time, you ate. It is now our turn. I continued to plead: Let us vote for the best Kenyan, not our ethnic candidates. Kenyans are only two tribes, the rich and the poor. No one should starve. We must all eat together.

A Gikuyu politician had predicted the response among the Gikuyu in Finance magazine: "While Koigi might have good intentions and national backing as a leader, his Achilles heel is that he hails from a community that worships money and is likely not to give him strong support.... Knowing as they do that he is not a bourgeois, even a petty one, they will not give him the support they would to a multi-millionaire."[1]

When I went to other communities, the question of money did not even arise. They said, A Gikuyu has ruled. It is our turn to rule and eat, precisely because we are poor. Do not even bother running.

Where are my human and democratic rights? I asked. I nearly gave up, but I have many reasons why I did not.

Having come out of prison on bond in December, 1996, I wanted my candidacy to force the courts to hear my appeal. They did and both my conviction and sentence were set aside. For this, some called me selfish, but it was nice to put Kamiti prison finally behind me.

Though Kenyans had won the right to challenge a president in an election, I wanted to taste it to know it was real. For many years, I had been tortured and imprisoned without charge or trial for criticizing both presidents Kenyatta and Moi. It was immensely liberating to be able to say openly, I want to be president of Kenya without being imprisoned, tortured or assassinated.

For so long, I had fought for the freedom and equality that I did not see envisioned by the leading presidential candidates: President Daniel arap Moi, Mwai Kibaki of the Democratic Party, Wamalwa Kijana of Ford Kenya, Raila Odinga of the National Development Party or Charity Ngilu of the Social Democratic Party.

Now was the time to ask voters to provide the means for building such an alternative and I could not have lived with myself had I not tried.

When I was in prison, lawyer Paul Muite, who defended me with valor, and anthropologist Richard Leakey and others founded an opposition party for which I proposed the name *Safina,* Noah's Ark. It was to save every Kenyan from the flood of our unending problems. When elections came, however, I did not vie for presidency on its ticket. Leakey, Safina's secretary general told me he did not believe that I, a Mugikuyu, had a right to be president of Kenya. In President Kenyatta, we had served our turn. I wondered, Were the children of British settlers still fighting those of the Mau Mau? As for Muite, *Safina's* leader, he believed presidency was for him, not a poor fellow like me. But I was not heartbroken. I picked another party, KENDA, and fought on.

During the campaign I went back to the village where I grew up only to find it was no more. It had been razed in 1988 by the government of President Moi. When I looked at the ground where our hut had stood, my stomach hurt, I felt sad and tears came to my eyes. I feared my past had been erased along with the abode that my dreams always associate with my childhood. As if to negate my fears, a powerful flood of memories overwhelmed me. The people's heroic history of survival shall not be sullied with the oppressors' history of shame. I will tell it here in a language of African culture and oral tradition.

THE MOTHER OF FATE

To know a tree is to know its stem, branches, flowers and roots. The story of the stem, without that of the roots, branches and flowers is an incomplete story of the tree. My story, therefore, starts below with that of my taproot and secondary roots, then comes to me, the stem, my branches and flowers. Every Kenyan and indeed, every human being, has a taproot. I tell you about mine only as an example.

In my life, I have many mothers. Best-known is the woman who bore me. The woman she was named after and the daughter I name after her are also my mothers. Indeed, the honor of motherhood goes to more than one woman. It is shared between Mum, Great-Grandma, the woman before and after, nature, God, truth, history, Earth, Kenya and Africa.

But roots and mothers have enemies. You cannot talk of one without the other.

BURYING THE PLACENTA OF MY ANCESTORS IN AFRICA:
THREE MILLION YEARS AGO

In the place we call Africa, the history of my ancestors is as old as Mount Kirinyaga (Mount Kenya) and Mount Kilimanjaro. It is the history of the three hominids whose footprints were found by Mary Leakey at Laetoli in 1978. It stretches more than 3.6 million years back. It is the history of *Kenyanthropus platyops* who lived in East Africa 3.5 million years ago. It is infinite. As our history gained in years, our mountains grew higher and our societies bigger.

THE LAND WAS ALWAYS OURS—FROM TIME IMMEMORIAL

In the fight of our people with white colonialists, we used to intone, The land is ours and nobody can rob it from us. Why? Kenyatta told the tale in *Facing Mount Kenya*:

> In the beginning, when mankind started to populate the earth, the man Gikuyu, the founder of the Agikuyu people was called by the Mugai (the Divider of the Universe) and given as his share, the land with ravines, rivers, forests, game and all the gifts that the Lord of Nature (Mugai) bestowed on mankind. At the same time Mugai made a big mountain that he called Kirinyaga (Mount Kenya) as his resting place when he was inspecting the world. He then took the man Gikuyu to the top of the mountain of mystery, and showed him the beauty of the country that he had given him. While still on top of the mountain, he pointed out to Gikuyu, a spot full of fig trees (*mikuyu*), right in the center of the country called Mukurwe wa Nyagathanga where he commanded him to descend and establish his homestead. Before they parted, the Great Divider told Gikuyu that, whenever he was in need, he should make a sacrifice to him by raising his hands towards Kirinyaga and he would come to his assistance.
>
> Gikuyu did as was commanded. When he reached the spot, he found a beautiful wife whom he named Muumbi (creator). Both lived happily, and had nine daughters—Waceera, Wanjiku, Wairimu, Wambui, Wangari, Wanjiru, Wangui, Mwithaga (Warigia) and Waithira—no sons. The nine daughters became the founders of nine clans—Aceera, Agaciku, Airimu, Ambui, Angari, Anjiru, Angui, Ethaga and Aithirandu—that were together called children of Muumbi, or Muumbi's tribe. Women continued to be the heads of their clans for generations.
>
> When this matriarchal system became patriarchal, men decided to change the original name of the community from children of Muumbi to Gikuyu nation. When they attempted to change clan names, the women were furious and threatened not to bear any more children and to kill all male children. The men gave up and retained clan names as they were.[2]

WE RULED OURSELVES DEMOCRATICALLY

When the white ogres came to Africa, they said it was not to eat us, but to civilize us because we didn't know how to rule ourselves. They lied. The concept and essence of democracy as "rule of the people, by the people and for the people" was in Africa long before white people came. By the time they came, our people knew about both democracy and dictatorship. This is why they could see that colonialism—the rule of white ogres—was dictatorship coated in sweet lies. Kenyatta tells us how democracy in the Gikuyu community evolved from an earlier dictatorship:

> Gikuyu government prior to the advent of the Europeans was based on true democratic principles (not called so because Agikuyu did not speak English).
>
> According to legend, once upon a time, there was a king in Gikuyu land, named Gikuyu, a grandchild of the elder daughter of the founder of the tribe. He ruled tyrannically for many moons. People could not cultivate the land, as he commanded all able-bodied men to join his army and move with their families at any time and wherever he chose. Thus the people lived a nomadic life and suffered from lack of food. At last, they grew tired of wandering and decided to settle down. They implored the king to let them cultivate the land and establish permanent homes, but owing to his autocratic power, he refused to hear or consider their plea. The people were very angry with him for turning a deaf ear to them, and in desperation revolted against him. The generation that revolted was called *Iregi* (Rebels), and the next that cut down forests and cultivated the land was named *Ndemi* (Cutters).
>
> After King Gikuyu, the government was changed from despotism to democracy that was in keeping with the wishes of the majority of the people. This revolution was known as *ituika,* derived from the word *tuika,* which means to break away from and signified the breaking away from autocracy to democracy. This achievement was celebrated all over the country with feasting, dancing and singing for six moons which preceded the new era of government by the people and for the people. In order to run the new government successfully, a revolutionary council, *njama ya ituika,* was formed to draft a new constitution that entrenched democracy in Gikuyu government.[3]

Under generational democracy, one-man, lifetime dictatorship was impossible since government power was vested in a generation and handed over to another generation, never an individual, to last no more than thirty years. Moreover, as a young generation held executive power, a younger one made up the army, an older one the judiciary and an even older one, religious authority. Generational dictatorship could not be because no generation held absolute power.

MOTHER AFRICA LOST MILLIONS OF HER CHILDREN: 700–1900

Whether it was before or after black Mother was called Africa, between 700 and 1900, she lost about 14 million children to Arab slave hunters, about 40 million to European human captors, misnamed slave traders, and about 280 million to resultant loss of population growth. Contact with foreigners brought Africa plenty of tragedies and no gains. Human thievery would not be the last. At the coast, our people were badly affected by this holocaust. Today, many carry the names of those who branded them like cattle.

THE ORGY OF RAPING MOTHER AFRICA: 1884–1885

On November 14, 1884, fourteen white powers, Germany, Great Britain, France, Portugal, Austria-Hungary, Belgium, Denmark, Italy, the Netherlands, Russia, Spain, Sweden-Norway, Turkey and the United States of America met in a conference in Berlin that was nothing but an orgy of raping Mother Africa. From this rape, Mother Africa conceived a pregnancy from which fifty black European colonies would later be born.

A PROPHET FORETELLS COLONIAL DOOM: 1800

Once upon a time, there lived in Gikuyu land a great medicine man known as Mugo wa Kibiru. His national duty was to foretell future events and to prepare the nation on what was to come. One early morning, the prophet woke up trembling and unable to speak. Here is how Kenyatta describes the story:

> When Mugo spoke, he told elders that during his sleep, *Ngai* (God) had taken him away to an unknown land. There, he had revealed to him what would happen to the Gikuyu people in the near future. On hearing the warning, he was horrified, and in his endeavor to persuade *Ngai* to avert the evil events coming, he was badly bruised and exhausted and could not do anything but obey *Ngai's* command to come back and tell the people what would happen.
>
> After a little pause, the prophet continued his sad narrative. In a low voice he said that strangers would come to Gikuyu land from out of the big water. The color of their body would resemble that of a small, light-

colored frog (*kiengere*) that lives in water. Their dress would be like the wings of butterflies and they would carry magical sticks that produced fire. In killing, these sticks would be worse than poisoned arrows. The strangers, he said, would later bring an iron snake with as many legs as a *munyongoro* (centipede). This iron snake would also spit fire and would stretch from the big water in the east to another big water in the west of the Gikuyu country. Further, he said, when a big famine came, it would be the sign to show that the strangers with their iron snake were near at hand. When this came to pass, he said, the Gikuyu, as well as their neighbors, would suffer greatly. The nations would mingle with a merciless attitude towards each other, and the result would seem as though they were eating one another. He also said that sons and daughters would abuse their parents in a way unknown hitherto by the Gikuyu.

Notwithstanding, the seer urged people not to take up arms against the coming strangers, because such actions could lead to the annihilation of the tribe. Attacked, strangers would be able to kill from a far distance with their magical sticks. When the warriors heard this, they were very angry and said that they would take up arms and kill the iron snake and the strangers. The great seer, *murathi,* calmed the warriors and told them the best thing would be to establish friendly relations with the coming strangers, because the spears and arrows would not be able to penetrate the iron snake, and therefore the warriors' attempt to fight the strangers and their snake would be futile.

The great medicine man advised the people that when these strangers arrived, the best policy would be to treat them with courtesy mingled with suspicion. Above all, to be careful not to bring the strangers too close to their homesteads, for they were full of evil deeds and would not hesitate to covet the Gikuyu homeland and in the end would want to take everything away from the Gikuyu.[4]

FORETOLD STRANGERS KNOCK AT THE DOOR: 1880–90

When the people heard what Mugo wa Kibiru had said, they were very worried and did not know what to do except wait and face the coming danger. Many moons afterwards, about 1890 or thereabout, the predicted danger began to appear. The strangers dressed in clothes resembling the wings of butterflies started to arrive in small groups. This was expected, for prior to their arrival, a terrible disease called *ndigana* or *nyoongo* (gall fever), had broken out and destroyed a great number of Gikuyu cattle as well as those of the neighboring tribes, the Maasai and the Kamba. The incident was followed by a great famine, which also devastated thousands of people.

The first few Europeans who passed near the Gikuyu country were more or less harmless, for they passed through along the border of the country between the Gikuyu and the Maasai or between the Wakamba and the Gikuyu. They were thus directed according to the prediction of the great medicine man. The white people with their caravans kept coming and going the same way from the coast to Lake Victoria and Uganda. In their upward and downward journeys, they traded with the Gikuyu with little or no conflict. When they arrived at points of trade, their men, whom we called *mikuna ruku* (woodpeckers), would knock trees several times and Agikuyu men and women would appear with food to exchange for beads, cloth, copper rings and other items of trade.

At last, misled by European cant, the Gikuyu thought that the white people with their caravans did not mean any harm and befriended them. Forgetting the words of Mugo wa Kibiru to treat *athungu*, or white people, with "courtesy mingled with suspicion and not to bring them near their homesteads," the Gikuyu began to welcome the Europeans in close proximity to their homesteads.

LETTING IN OGRES: 1890

In this year, Waiyaki wa Hinga, the leader of the Agikuyu who lived around Dagoretti (part of Nairobi today), signed a treaty with Fredrick Lugard of the Imperial East Africa Company. According to Kenyatta:

> These early Empire builders, knowing what they were after, played on the ignorance and sincere hospitable nature of the people. They agreed to the terms of a tenant, *muhoi,* or a traveler, *muthami,* and soon started to build small forts or camps, saying that "the object of a station is to form a center for the purchase of food for caravans proceeding to Uganda," etc. For "Gikuyu was reportedly a country where food was extraordinarily abundant and cheap."
>
> The Gikuyu gave Europeans building rights in places like Dagoretti, Fort Smith, and others, with no idea of the motives which were behind the caravans, for they thought that it was only a matter of trading and nothing else. Unfortunately, they did not realize that these places were used for the preliminary preparations for taking away their land from them.[5]

After these treaties, Lugard and his men harassed the Gikuyu people by stealing their food and raping their women. In retaliation, Gikuyu men burnt down Lugard's fortress at Dagoretti. Lugard admitted:

> The Gikuyu promised to be the most progressive station between the coast and the lake. The natives were very friendly, and even enlisted as porters to

go to the coast, but these good relations received a disastrous check. Owing
largely to the want of discipline in the passing caravans, whose men robbed
the crops and otherwise made themselves troublesome, the people became
estranged, and presently murdered several porters.[6]

Despite the British being at fault, Lugard tells us that it is the Gikuyu that were
"taught a lesson," and compelled to make "the payment of fifty goats daily, and free
work of three hundred men to build the fort they had destroyed."

This was the beginning of the suffering and the use of the sticks that produced
killing fire, as Mugo wa Kibiru had predicted in his prophecy of the coming of white
people. At this point the Gikuyu had no doubt. It was not butterflies that had
floated on to their land. They had let white ogres into their huts with dire consequences.

By the time Europeans reached Gikuyu country, our society was egalitarian.
However, it seemed to have had a lost past of corrupt civilization from which it had
inherited a metaphor of exploitation called *irimu,* an ogre. They were beings that
looked exactly like people, males and females, short and tall, healthy and sickly, beautiful and ugly, just like people. Sometimes ogres appeared in the disguise of great
dancers that wooed Gikuyu girls to marry them. However, ogres were cannibals
with one or more extra mouths they concealed in the back of their heads with
hair. People who were taken in by their beauty, smooth talk, superior dancing,
need for help or any other guile always ended up in their forest caves where they
were eaten. Other times, ogres invaded, took over entire villages and ate everybody in them. In Gikuyu folklore, the struggle between society and ogres was
ongoing and unending.

PEOPLE'S FIRST DECAPITATION: 1892

To break resistance to colonial penetration, the administration of white ogres kidnapped Waiyaki wa Hinga, the leader of Agikuyu, took him to the coast and buried
him alive at Kibwezi.

BLACK MOTHER IS BORN IN SHACKLES: 1895

Out of the 1884 European rape of Africa, a black daughter was born called the
British East African Protectorate. She was born a mother of forty-two black children with different languages and cultures. She was born to feed and work for her
white father and his white children. Though the white ogres despised the black
Mother, they raped and begot black ogres with her. To weaken her, the British
enslaved, starved and even killed her black children. To date, the British have never

stopped raping, milking and despising their former colonial daughter and begetting black ogres with her.

A TOWN GROWS OUT OF COOL WATERS: 1896

A town sprang up in the place of cool waters and was named after it—Nairobi. Later, instead of cool waters, only endless poison of poverty and corruption came out of the shantytown.

SKIRMISHES WITH PORCUPINES: 1896–97

After invading the land, white porcupines were eating crops of the people. When the Gikuyu and the Kamba tried to drive them out, the porcupines shot back and killed them with their fire-spitting quills. British military expeditions were predatory, punitive and, at other times, merely reckless. Farther to the west of Kenya, Koitalel arap Samoei, a Nandi leader and an *orkoiyot,* a diviner, was leading his people against the colonial builders of the railway line for ten years. Eventually the British tricked him into a meeting for an agreement, where they shot and killed him.

TIME TO START MILKING: 1902

Boxed into a milking pen, the British fixed sucking pumps—Hut Tax and Village Head Ordinance—to black Mother's teats and started milking and bleeding her, always to the point of collapse. Niggardly fed, she suckled Europeans in the colony and white ogres in England. Black children could not, however, touch her milk.

THE IRON SNAKE SWALLOWS THE LAND: 1905

More of Mugo wa Kibiru's prophecy was fulfilled when the Kenya-Uganda railway (the iron snake) was completed. With their feet firm on the soil, the Europeans now began to claim the absolute right to rule the country and to have the ownership of the lands under the title of "Crown Lands," where the Gikuyu and other Africans now lived as "tenants at will of the [British] Crown." The impregnable iron snake was gobbling down all the land.

BLACK MOTHER LOSES HER LEFT ARM: 1905

When Samoei was killed, the Nandi resistance to colonialism collapsed and black Mother lost her left arm.

NGIRIMITI (SLAVES) ARE BORN: 1906

The Masters and Servants Ordinance of 1906 categorized all white people as masters and all black people as their servants. After decades of enforcement of this law that was the foundation of colonial racism by police, army, government, politics, schools, churches, private employers, radio, newspapers and courts, to this day in Kenya, even black people identify white with master and black with servant.

BLACK MOTHER BECOMES A MERE HAND: 1908

With the Orders in Council of 1908, the British government grabbed "half of all the land worth cultivating in the country, including most of Gikuyu country," called it white highlands, gave it to European settlers and legislated that Africans could work on the land only as laborers and squatters, not as tenant farmers. Free people were now mere hands of white farmers.

THE WHITE MASTER TAKES THE WHIP: 1908

A Gikuyu proverb says, What is defecated on is also urinated on, *Ikumirwo ni thugumirwo*. Without the whip, black children and their black mother could not be enslaved and white people could not be masters. After conquering the country of the Abagusii, the settlers had their largest meeting so far. They advocated the Whip and Pass Laws to control the natives; they declared that the amount of land held by natives should be limited and that the natives should be forced to work for them.

A GOD IS BORN: 1911

My father, Wamwere wa Kuria, was born a colonial slave but also as the god that brought me from the infinite past and would give me life and power that would project me into the unfathomable future.

A HEROINE PROTECTS AFRICAN CULTURE: 1914

Mekatilili wa Menza led the Giriama people in a rebellion against colonial invasion of the British and their effort to stamp out people's culture through the destruction of *kaya,* secret forest shrines and places of worship. She was captured and exiled to Mumias for five years.

A WHITE DRAGON SWALLOWS THOUSANDS: 1914–18

Oginga Odinga tells us in *Not Yet Uhuru:* "During the First World War, Nyanza (and the whole country) was milked dry for carriers, many thousands of whom never returned to their homes but died of disease in service, though they wore no soldiers' uniforms (and therefore got no credit for the victory of the war). It was during the war, too, that land leases were extended for the white settlers from 99 to 999 years. After the war, the African harvest of the war victory was anything but a reward. Hut tax was doubled from five rupees to ten and though it was cut to eight rupees in 1921, the settlers, affected by a fall in world prices, enforced a one third cut in wages of all Africans. The law for the compulsory carrying of *kipande* (every African over the age of sixteen had to carry a fingerprinted card) was passed in 1915 and was rigorously enforced in 1921."[7] This is what "democratic Britain" did in recognition of the services African people rendered during the war.

BLACK MOTHER IS CALLED KENYA: 1920

Born earlier and called the British East African Protectorate, the black Mother was now called Kenya. The new name was a European mispronunciation of the Kamba name for Mount Kenya: Kii-nyaa.

MOTHER KENYA SPEAKS: 1921

In Nyanza, small meetings were being called at night, for the people were hiding their first sallies into organization. The people were agitated at the East African Protectorate becoming Kenya Colony, annexed to the British Crown. A group went to a District Commissioner to say that they did not like what the Europeans were doing, and they rejected the Colony.

Who asked you to say that? the spokesmen were asked. Who is behind you? To this question came the reply, *Piny Owacho* (The Country Says).

The government interpreter told the District Commissioner that two chiefs were behind the movement. The people insisted on, "The Country Says."[8]

CHURCHILL CLAIMS MOTHER KENYA FOR WHITE OGRES: 1922

As soon as Mother Kenya expressed displeasure at her forced marriage with a white ogre, Winston Churchill came down to shoot hippos, bless the colonial project, drink whisky in the sun and claim her for the white man. Kenya is "a white man's country," he said.

A BRAVE DAUGHTER CHALLENGES MEN TO FIGHT
FOR MOTHER KENYA: 1922

When Harry Thuku, the first labor hero, organized the first strike in Kenya and one of the earliest recorded in Africa and held mass rallies to challenge Churchill's vision of Kenya. He was exiled in the semi-arid Kismayu (in present-day Somalia) in the typical colonial belief that decapitating independence movements would kill freedom. When Thuku was arrested and held in the Kingsway Police Station, Nairobi, a woman called Mary Nyanjiru expressed the highest form of protest by pulling up her dress, right up to her shoulders, challenging men to be brave in demanding the release of their leader: "You take my dress and give me your trousers. You damn cowardly men! What are you waiting for? Our leader is in there. Let us get him." The British colonial police were quick to kill Nyanjiru and the other protesters in cold blood.

THE BRITISH COOL THEIR BITE: 1923

Kenyatta and others knew the British were cooling the bite of the rat when a Kenya White Paper declared, "It is the mission of Great Britain to work continuously for the training and education of the Africans towards a higher intellectual, moral, and economic level than that which they had reached when the Crown assumed the responsibility for the administration of this territory."[9]

It is beyond our comprehension, Kenyatta argued, to see how a people can reach a so-called "higher level" while they are denied the most elementary human rights of self-expression, freedom of speech, the right to form social organizations to improve their condition and, above all, the right to move freely in their own country. These are the rights that the Gikuyu people had enjoyed from time immemorial until the arrival of the "mission of Great Britain." Instead of advancing "toward a higher intellectual, moral, and economic level," the African has been reduced to the state of serfdom; his initiative in social, economic and political structure has been denied, his spirit of manhood has been killed and he has been subjected to the most inferior position in human society.[10]

TAKING FATE INTO THEIR HANDS: 1924

When Africans woke up from talking, they formed the Kikuyu Central Association (KCA) to champion the fight for the recovery of their territory, government, independence, freedom and dignity.

AFRICAN (ITUIKA) DEMOCRACY IS SUBSTITUTED
WITH COLONIAL DICTATORSHIP: 1925

As the juggernaut of British colonialism rolled over Kenya, gobbling land and people, it also crushed traditional democracy, which most people never associate with Africa, and plastered a colonial, fascist dictatorship over it. About this Kenyatta had no doubt when he wrote:

> From *ndemi* generation onwards, the principles of democratic government, as laid down by the first *ituika,* continued to function favorably until it was smashed by the British government, who introduced a system of government very similar to the autocratic government that the Gikuyu people had discarded many centuries ago. The present system of rule by the government officials supported by appointed chiefs, and even what is called "indirect rule," are incompatible with the democratic spirit of the Gikuyu people...
>
> The spirit of *ituika,* namely, changing of government in [generational] rotation through a peaceful and constitutional revolution, is still ingrained in the minds of the Gikuyu people. About 1925–28 was the time when the *ituika* ceremony was to take place corresponding to the last great *ituika* ceremony that was celebrated about 1890–98.
>
> It was the turn of the *Irungu* or *Maina* generation to take over the government from the *Mwangi* generation. But after a short time, the *ituika* ceremonial dances and songs were declared illegal by the British government. In this way, the present generation, *Irungu,* has been denied the birthright of perpetuating the national pride and enjoyment in the peaceful institution that afforded their forebears the most harmonious participation in the social, political, economic, and religious organizations of the tribe.[11]

KENYATTA DEFENDS FEMALE CIRCUMCISION: 1928

As the General Secretary of Kikuyu Central Association, Kenyatta disagreed with colonialists and Christian missionaries that Africans practiced female circumcision, a custom greatly misunderstood in the west, because they were barbarians; that the practice was barbaric and contrived to torture and deprive women of sexual pleasure; that the practice in particular and African culture in general were criminal and needed to be uprooted with the force of colonial law and guns. With a hint of irony and sarcasm, Kenyatta suggested that between the African and the European, it was the Christian and colonial culture that was barbaric because it turned both white and black into ogres.

Without supporting circumcision's unqualified perpetuation, Kenyatta explained the physical operation at length in order to illustrate the care that was taken to make it safe and argued that the physical operation of girls and boys was the very heart of an institution of initiation that had enormous educational, social, moral and religious implications, far apart from the operation itself. The Gikuyu could not imagine initiation without the operation and saw efforts to abolish the operation as intended to abolish the bigger institution itself. Kenyatta asked Europeans to understand that the initiation of both sexes is the most important custom among the Gikuyu.

As to the argument that female circumcision was a male conspiracy to deny women sexual pleasure, Kenyatta argued that female circumcision was there when Gikuyu society was matriarchal and women ruled and it was the uncircumcised girl, not the circumcised woman, who was denied sex. Without circumcision, Gikuyu girls and boys were denied sex because they were considered minors who could not cope with the responsibilities of sex and its consequences: "No proper Gikuyu would dream of marrying a girl who has not been circumcised, and vice versa. It is taboo for a Gikuyu man or woman to have sexual relations with someone who has not undergone this operation." After circumcision, all things became possible. Initiation was a deciding factor in giving a boy or a girl the status of manhood or womanhood without which there was no sex, no marriage, no motherhood. Kenyatta also noted that Europeans wildly exaggerated the dangers of circumcision to strengthen their attacks on this custom:

> These "well-wishers" have gone so far as to state that almost every first child dies as a result of this operation at the time of initiation. . . . Irresponsible statements of this kind are not to be taken too seriously, for it must not be forgotten that very few of the normal cases of childbirth ever come to the notice of European doctors. The theory that "every first child dies as a result of the operation" has no foundation at all. There are hundreds of first-born children among the Gikuyu who are still living, and the writer is one of them.[12]

Kenyatta suggested that to end female circumcision, the African needed education and freedom to choose what customs to keep and discard. Otherwise, he and many Africans of his time were convinced that Europeans who had imposed the barbarity of slavery and colonialism on the African had no right to tell the African that his culture was barbaric. What sincerity was in the European who had shackled the African woman, pretending to save her from her culture but not from his chains? Whatever was wrong with female circumcision, it was not as barbaric as colonial servitude or the European belief that he was the master and the one to tell the African what was best for him. After all, the knife of circumcision did not deform and mutilate the African woman and man more than colonial guns, bayonets, axes, dogs and whips. Indeed, the barbarity of European arrogance hurt more than the pain of circumcision:

> The missionaries who attack the *irua* [initiation] of girls are more to be pitied than condemned...With such limited knowledge as they are able to acquire from their converts or from others who invariably distort the reality of the *irua*, in order to please them, the missionaries pose as authorities on African customs. How often have we heard people saying: "We have lived in Africa for a number of years and we know the African mind very well."[13]

In the African mind, there was absolutely no doubt that the white man attacked female circumcision and spared the male one because he practiced male circumcision. Had he practiced female circumcision, he would have judged it civilized. Primarily, the white man attacked female circumcision as part of a greater colonial plan to end the ceremony of Gikuyu initiation where it looked most vulnerable, not to save the African woman, whom he had already enslaved and brutalized, but to destroy initiation as the foundation upon which the African house stood. The Gikuyu organized their educational system, religious rituals, family life, military structures, government and transfer of power around age groups that started with initiation. Age groups were the pillars which held up the Gikuyu house and initiation was the foundation upon which they stood. Without initiation, the white man knew the Gikuyu house would necessarily collapse.

Age groups were also the wheels upon which the African vehicle moved and it was initiation that put those wheels to the vehicle. The white man knew the best way of defeating the African was to stop the vehicle of his society and transfer him into the colonial one where he had no control over who drove it, where he or his family sat, where it stopped or went. The colonialist also knew that the best way of stopping the Gikuyu vehicle was to demonize and stop initiation. Without wheels, the vehicle would of course stop, as it did, despite great resistance.

HOLDING ON TO DEAR CULTURE: 1929–52

Realizing that they could not free themselves from colonialism without their culture; that adopting a self-enslaving Christian culture only turned them into black ogres that ate their own, Gikuyu made desperate efforts to grab the bait of white man's education without swallowing the hook of his cultural conquest. For this, they set up their own Kikuyu Independent and Gikuyu Karing'a churches and schools that taught both Christianity and education while preserving culture and preaching resistance to colonialism. These schools and churches were banned in 1952.

A GODDESS IS BORN: 1929

Wangu wa Mung'ura and Wangu wa Wamwere-to-be, my mother, is born, the second part of a divinity that would later give me life.

LAWS SWEEP AWAY AFRICAN LIVESTOCK: 1930s

Throughout these years, African animals were confiscated and our people were forced to live on less land and work on white settler farms. Kamba Members Association, Kikuyu Central Association, Taita Hills Association and Kavirondo Taxpayers Welfare Association protested vigorously against these measures to impoverish Africans.

A WHITE WHALE SWALLOWS AFRICAN LEADERS: 1940

KCA was banned and its twelve leaders together with two of Taita Hills Association and eight of Akamba Members' Association were arrested and detained at Kapenguria for the duration of Second World War to pave the way for easy recruitment of Kenyan Africans to go and fight in the war. They were falsely accused of contacting Italian and German agents but people had faith they would come back.

A WHITE MAN'S WAR OPENS AFRICAN EYES: 1940–45

During the Second World War, thousands of African men were recruited to fight one white man for the freedom of the other. In the process they learnt that the white man who had been playing God to them could die when shot; colonial fascism of the British was no better than that of Germans and Italians; and Africans had to fight for their freedom the same way their colonizers and their allies had fought for their own.

YOUNG WARRIORS OF AANAKE A BOTI PICK UP THE GAUNTLET: 1946

This Gikuyu youth group, the warriors of 1940s, states that the lost lands could be regained only through war. Between 1947 and 1951, a network of freedom fighters extending throughout the Central Province and the Rift Valley grew. Their central demand was the return of alienated land and the formation of an independent African government.

A CRY OF ANGUISH IS HEARD: 1948–49

When 11,000 Gikuyu squatters were evicted from Olenguruone, they took an oath that was a community pledge—a commitment to a kind of verbal constitution—to resist removal and agricultural restrictions and finally fight for the independence of Kenya.

THE BLACK SPECTER OF MAU MAU: 1948

Hearing of people organizing themselves to fight for the land and freedom that Kenyatta could not win constitutionally, colonial authorities called them *Mau Mau*. Initially, this became a term of abuse against every Gikuyu who did not volunteer for the colonial government's security forces and give proof of his loyalty to the government. Later the term gained legitimacy when people flocked into the movement despite the name.

A BOY IS BORN IN CHAINS: 1949

I was born in chains but with a natural urge to be free. Ever since, my nature and chains have been in a life or death struggle.

MAU MAU IS BANNED: 1950

Though technically nonexistent, Mau Mau was banned to give the colonial authorities a pretext to arrest anybody who resisted colonial rule.

FOR THE LAST TIME, PEOPLE BEG FOR FREEDOM: 1951

Achieng Oneko and Mbiyu Koinange were sent to London as a last delegation on the land question. The British Colonial Secretary dismissed them in London as "irresponsible black monkeys," but in Paris, the United Nations was in session and lobbying was highly successful. Africans were now convinced that they had to fight for their freedom.

MOTHER KENYA IS DOUSED AND TORCHED: 1952

When black Mother Kenya refused to surrender her fight for liberation, the British colonial governor arrested Kenyatta and other African leaders, declared a state of emergency in the country and sent to prison more than 100,000 Gikuyu men and women, triggering the Kenyan war of national liberation. After putting her on fire and cutting off her moderate head, the British were convinced the black lady would surrender and prostrate herself to white men. Instead she grew a more defiant, Mau Mau head, took up a sword and fought on.

KENYA SHEDS TORRENTS OF TEARS: 1953

After a bogus trial at Kapenguria, by a magistrate whom the British had bribed to convict the freedom fighters, Kenyatta and his colleagues were given seven-year jail terms and an indefinite detention thereafter in the desert, for the "terrorism" of fighting for freedom and the "insolence" of challenging the European colonial project of enslaving African people in order to "civilize" them.

FIGHTING FOR MOTHER KENYA: 1952–63

As black ogres and children of rape help their white father to set Mother Kenya aflame, black youths Dedan Kimathi, Stanley Mathenge and others emerge and lead thousands of young men and women to Aberdare and the forests of Mount Kenya to wage a guerrilla war against colonial authorities. From there they told the whole world: "We are fighting for all land stolen from us by the Crown through its Orders in Council of 1915, according to which Africans have been evicted from the Kenya Highlands…The British Government must grant Kenya full independence under African leadership, and hand over all land previously alienated for distribution to the landless. We will fight until we achieve freedom or until the last of our warriors has shed his last drop of blood."[14]

SNUFFING OUT THE CANDLE OF HOPE: 1956

Dedan Kimathi, the leading Mau Mau general, was arrested in October 1956 and executed by the British in February 1957. Africans see the last ray of hope extinguished and settlers celebrate. But having hit the rock bottom, for Africans, things could only go up.

SHARPENING HORNS: 1957

I joined the colonial school to sharpen my horns that settlers thought were for goring fellow Africans but really were for completing the job Mau Mau guns had began.

THE CANDLE IS LIT AGAIN: 1959

The state of emergency was lifted to set into motion the release of the thousands who had survived brutalities and torture in colonial prisons, detention and concentration camps. Africans saw this as significant defeat for the colonial government. People could not help but hope that this tiny victory was the first of more and bigger victories to come.

RISING OF A BLACK OGRE: 1961

When Kenyatta was released, Africans celebrated like they had never before because they saw him as the Moses who would take them out of colonial bondage. Little did they know that the heat of the desert prison had turned him into a black ogre; he was no longer a "communist" and "an extremist African" who was intent on killing all white ogres; the British released him not to liberate Kenyans but to continue milking Mother Kenya for them.

BLACK OGRES HIJACK INDEPENDENCE: 1963

All expected the black children who had fought so hard for independence to take over the government and liberate Mother Kenya from bondage. Instead, Kenyatta, a harvester-ogre *(irimu ria nyakondo),* and other black ogres carried Mother Kenya off into an immoral marriage, not to liberate but continue raping and milking her. Mother Kenya and her black children had escaped from the jungle of white ogres into that of black ones. To enhance so-called peace and reconciliation between the people, the white ogres and the black ones now in power declared Mother Kenya free without taking the chains from her legs, hands and mind that bound and enslaved her to the ogres. This constitutional arrangement would be reproduced later in Southern Africa and other countries, with minor changes—colonial thieves would keep all their loot, colonial perpetrators of crimes against humanity would go scot-free and people who had fought and had been tortured for land and freedom would get neither land nor justice after *Uhuru* (independence). When people questioned the rationale of black ogres in government, Kenyatta told them: A government of black ogres is better than that of white ones. Few realized that changing from the cannibalism of white ogres to a combined one of white and black ones was neither independence nor freedom.

QUITTING THE GOVERNMENT OF OGRES: 1966

Oginga Odinga, Achieng Oneko, J.D. Kali, Bildad Kaggia and others left the government of President Kenyatta which had decided to join British colonial settlers and their African collaborators to exploit and rape Mother Kenya rather than liberate her.

NOT YET UHURU: 1967

When Oginga Odinga wrote his book *Not Yet Uhuru,* he reminded people that independence from ogres had never come.

THE GENIE OF ETHNICITY: 1969

When Gikuyu ogres assassinated Tom Mboya—an ogre from the Luo community—to stop him from succeeding President Kenyatta, who detained Odinga after a protest, they ended the great unity between Luo and Gikuyu peoples and let out of the bottle the genie of ethnicity that still urges ethnic communities to slit each other's throats in the wars of their ogres who fight for the exclusive right to eat their people and more.

SMOTHERING A BEAUTIFUL FLOWER: 1975

When black ogres killed J.M. Kariuki, probably the most courageous Kenyan leader since Dedan Kimathi, poor people lost a champion and a savior from ogres.

A ONE-EYED OGRE BECOMES PRESIDENT: 1978

When the old harvester-ogre, Kenyatta, died he bequeathed Mother Kenya to Moi, the one-eyed ogre, *Karithoongo,* who would blackmail her into giving him limb by limb until she was all eaten up and the old ogre Kenyatta was rescued from equal infamy.

> Woman, let me sleep with you or I will kill you.
> Okay.
> Woman, give me you little finger or I will kill this child.
> Okay.
> Woman, give me your left hand or I will eat all your children.
> Okay.
> Woman, give me your leg or I will eat you all.
> Okay.

GIVE ME YOUR TONGUE OR
I WILL EAT YOU UP: 1982

So said Moi to Mother Kenya. Okay, said a captive and emasculated Parliament to silence her cries and give Moi absolute power to rape, eat and kill her and her children at will. An angry air force answered this repression with a coup that failed. Moi killed the coup plotters and detained many, including myself.

THE LONG NIGHT OF HYENAS: 1982–91

Provoked by the coup and people's resistance, Moi and other black ogres replaced secret ballots with queuing in one-party elections, and terrorized, arrested, tortured, imprisoned, exiled and killed thousands in a period Kenyans will remember as the darkest hour in their history.

THE DARKEST HOUR BEFORE DAWN: 1990

I was kidnapped from Uganda and charged with treason with seven others, including lawyers Mirugi Kariuki and Rumba Kinuthia; Kenya broke diplomatic relations with Norway. That same year, Kenneth Matiba, Raila Odinga, Charles Rubia, Imanyara, Gathangu, Anyona and Oyugi were all thrown into detention and prison in a vain attempt to stem the tide of opposition.

RESCUING MOTHER KENYA FROM DEATH ROW: 1991

After a long struggle by Kenyans and immense international pressure, Mother Kenya was rescued from the grave of torture, death and silence through the repeal of Section 2A of the constitution to allow for the formation of opposition parties. Unfortunately, it was ogre Moi who was charged with nurturing Mother Kenya and her speech back to health. Other black ogres formed opposition parties and stood in queue waiting to carry off Mother Kenya when Karithoongo quit.

OUTWITTING RIVALS: 1992

Like a lion fighting off wild dogs that are chasing and biting him from every side, ogre Moi covered his back by killing as many people who opposed him as he could in ethnic clashes that were so brutal that they certainly constitute crimes against humanity. Subsequently, he tied the hands of fellow ogres who challenged him for the presidency and took them into the boxing ring with his hands free. He won the trophy with his hands down.

SHOWING HIS TRUE COLORS: 1997

By contesting and rigging himself into the presidency for the umpteenth time, ogre Moi revealed to Kenyans and the world that, as long as the West financially and diplomatically supported him, he would not surrender Mother Kenya to another ogre or any of her black children for nurture and care. To ensure this, after elections, he unleashed a second wave of ethnic fighting and cleansing in the Rift

Valley to punish the Gikuyu and anybody else who demanded the liberation of Mother Kenya from the rule of ogres. When armed Kalenjin ogres got too close to home, I left Kenya for Norway.

N O T E S

CHAPTER I: CHILDHOOD 1949–58
1. John Spencer, *Kanga African Union, 1944–1953,* (London: Routledge), 12.
2. Frantz Fanon, *The Fact of Blackness in the Anatomy of Racism,* 118–119.
3. Basil Davidson, *Black Mother: Africa: The Years of Trial* (London: Victor Gollancz Ltd., 1961), 32.
4. Ibid., 63.

CHAPTER II: MAU MAU YEARS 1952–59
1. Guy Arnold, *Kenyatta and the Politics of Kenya* (Nairobi: Kenya TransAfrica Publishers, 1974), 126.
2. Ibid., 132.
3. Ibid., 65.
4. Ibid., 156.
5. Ibid., 126.
6. Ibid., 157.
7. Ibid., 156.
8. Ibid., 155.

CHAPTER V: HOMECOMING 1973
1. *The Times,* April 11, 1966.
2. Odinga, *Uhuru,* 63.
3. Ibid.
4. Ibid.
5. Ibid.
6. Ibid.

CHAPTER VII: FIRST MOI YEARS 1979
1. *Daily Nation,* September 14, 1984.

CHAPTER VIII: MOI DETAINS ME 1982–84
1. Peter Wright, *Spy Catcher* (Australia: Heinemann Publishers, 1987).

CHAPTER XIII: TREASON 1990-92
1. *Daily Nation.*

CHAPTER XIV: REVISITING OLENGURUONE 1993
1. Michael Blundell, *So Rough A Wind* (London: Weidenfeld and Nicolson, 1964).

TIMELINE
1. *Finance Magazine*, July 1997.
2. Jomo Kenyatta. *Facing Mount Kenya* (London: Martin Secker & Warburg Ltd., 1938), 1–5.
3. Ibid., 187.
4. Ibid., 42–44.
5. Ibid., 45.
6. *The Rise of Our East African Empire,* vol. 1 of *The British Empire Builder* (London: W. Blackwood and Sons, 1893), 329.
7. Oginga Odinga. *Not Yet Uhuru* (London: Heinemann Educational Books Ltd., 1967), 23.
8. Odinga, *Uhuru,* 25.
9. Kenyatta, *Facing Mount Kenya,* 197.
10. Ibid., 197.
11. Ibid., 196.
12. Ibid., 130–133.
13. Ibid., 130–133
14. Odinga, *Uhuru,* 119–20.

About the Authors

KOIGI WA WAMWERE is a political activist and writer. Born in Kenya in 1949, he has been fighting for social change in his home country for nearly three decades. He was imprisoned in Kenya five times between 1975 and 1996; his execution was averted only by the combined efforts of the Norwegian government and human rights activists around the world. In December of 2002, Koigi wa Wamwere was elected for the second time to serve in the Kenyan parliament.

KERRY KENNEDY CUOMO is the founder of the Robert F. Kennedy Center for Human Rights. Since 1981 she has been working on issues such as child labor, indigenous land rights, ethnic violence, and women's rights. She featured Koigi wa Wamwere in her 2000 book, *Speak Truth to Power*.

NAN RICHARDSON has worked as an editor, a writer, and a curator with various publishers and museums in the United States and Europe through her company, Umbrage Editions.